A POET'S ALPHABET

BOOKS BY LOUISE BOGAN

Body of This Death
Dark Summer
The Sleeping Fury
Poems and New Poems
Collected Poems 1923–1953
The Blue Estuaries

Achievement in American Poetry, 1900–1950
Selected Criticism
A Poet's Alphabet

A POET'S
ALPHABET

REFLECTIONS ON THE LITERARY

ART AND VOCATION. BY

Louise Bogan

*Edited by Robert Phelps
and Ruth Limmer*

[c1970]

McGRAW-HILL BOOK COMPANY

*New York   St. Louis   San Francisco
Düsseldorf   Mexico   Panama   Toronto*

Nearly all the material in this collection appeared originally in *The New Yorker*; copyright © 1948, 1954, 1955, 1956, 1957, 1958, 1959, 1960, 1961, 1962, 1963, 1964, 1965, 1966, and 1967 by The New Yorker Magazine, Inc.

The Introduction appeared originally as an obituary in *The New Yorker*; © 1970 The New Yorker Magazine, Inc.

The essay "A Lifework," on Robert Frost, is reprinted by permission of Harcourt, Brace and World, Inc., from *Major Writers of America*, Volume II, edited by Perry Miller, © 1962, by Harcourt, Brace and World, Inc.

The essay on Dorothy Richardson © 1967 by The New York Times Company. Reprinted by permission.

The essay "A Mystical Poet," on Emily Dickinson, is reprinted by permission of the Amherst College Press from *Emily Dickinson: Three Views*, by the Amherst College Press.

"The Pleasures of Formal Poetry" is reprinted by permission of the *Quarterly Review of Literature*.

A POET'S ALPHABET

Designed by Christine Aulicino

Library of Congress Catalog Card Number: 71–121655

First Edition   06370

A NOTE ON THE CONTENTS

A Poet's Alphabet includes the entire contents of Louise Bogan's *Selected Criticism,* published in 1955; most of her articles, reviews, and miscellaneous critical pieces published since that date; and a few earlier pieces not previously reprinted. The text was reviewed and approved by Miss Bogan before her death on February 4, 1970.

LOUISE BOGAN
(1897-1970)

The first poetry review that Louise Bogan did for *The New Yorker* appeared in the issue of March 21, 1931, and the last in the issue of December 28, 1968. In this magazine, between those two dates—that is to say, for thirty-eight years—poets good, bad, and indifferent came under a perceptive and just scrutiny. Out of what they did or didn't do with language she often constructed a kind of portrait of them of lasting value. Their work was also, when this was relevant, placed in a line of descent or a tradition. Aesthetic experiments were viewed with an open mind, inflation was punctured, and entrepreneurism was put in its place. At times, the exactness and lucidity of her criticism suggested that she was attempting to create a new kind of lyric poetry out of statements *about* poetry.

Louise Bogan was born in Livermore Falls, Maine. Both her parents were of Irish descent. Her father's father was a sea captain who sailed out of Portland. Though she returned to New England periodically, when she was tired and wanted to refresh her spirit, her home for most of her adult life was New York City. She lived quietly, almost anonymously, in Washington Heights, in an apartment full of books, with a photograph of Mozart's birthplace on one wall and, from a living-room window, a narrow view, between apartment buildings, of the Hudson River. She published six volumes of poetry and two volumes of literary criticism. A third is now in the process of being printed. She also did a number of distinguished collaborative translations, which include Goethe's "Elective Affinities" and a selection from the "Journal" of Jules Renard.

All literary honors that *are* an honor to receive she received. To say that she was one of the finest lyric poets of our time is hardly to do her justice; her best poems have an emotional depth and force and a perfection of form that owe very little to the age she lived in and are not likely to go out of style, being a matter of nobody's style but her own. She was a handsome, direct, impressive, vulnerable woman. In whatever she wrote, the line of truth was exactly superimposed on the line of feeling. One look at her work—or sometimes one look at her—made any number of disheartened artists take heart and go on being the kind of dedicated creature they were intended to be. In defense of the true artist, she wrote:

> Come, drunks and drug-takers; come,
>   perverts unnerved!
> Receive the laurel, given, though late,
>   on merit; to whom
>   and wherever deserved.
>
> Parochial punks, trimmers, nice people,
>   joiners true blue,
> Get the hell out of the way of the
>   laurel. It is deathless
>   And it isn't for you.

(Reprinted from *The New Yorker,*
February 14, 1970)

CONTENTS

A POET'S ALPHABET

"Ferry me across the water,
    Do, boatman, do."
"If you've a penny in your purse
    I'll ferry you."

"I have a penny in my purse,
    And my eyes are blue;
So ferry me across the water,
    Do, boatman, do!"

"Step into my ferry-boat,
    Be they black or blue,
And for the penny in your purse
    I'll ferry you."

— Christina Rossetti

AMERICAN

LITERATURE

AT MID-CENTURY (1950)

Contemporary sensibilities, if suddenly transported into the physical world of 1900, would experience a sense of oppression and a queer kind of emptiness and freedom. To transport the reader into the full atmosphere of this world was a major concern of Joyce. The action of *Ulysses* takes place during a single day in 1904, in what, in all practical senses, was then a provincial city in a dependency of the British Empire. We receive from the pages of *Ulysses*—from its special combination of naturalism and impressionism—a distilled sense of actuality: a sense of untoward squalor and specialized glitter; a sad and ugly pathos and an outmoded and naïve gaiety; a sense of the hidden massiveness of institutions opposed to an extreme particularization of individuals. Newspapers, advertisements, and popular entertainment are at an awkward professional level; a surface gentility coats the basic density of peasant character. Basic decoration and design, from clothes to the façades of buildings and the vehicles in the street, are heavy and pretentious, when not silly and flaccid. Colors are dark or muddied: mustard brown and magenta. There is a pervasive smell of beer, horses, and human sweat. It is a period without outlet; a time when sensitive characters are forced to dream or drink their way out of reality; or indulge in impossible plans of personal ambition and social "rise."

I

It is a period from which one returns oppressed and exhausted, as though released from a trap, to even the contemporary scene and its dangerous machines.

The sense of psychic bafflement and of aesthetic barrenness, at the beginning of the twentieth century, varied in terms of place. It would be felt less definitely in what were once known as "European capitals"; in Paris perhaps least of all; heavily in the British Isles; and heaviest in America. But in the European area, in Britain, and in the United States—three areas which we must keep distinctly separated from the beginning of this discussion—we are faced with the same impression of a provisional, scattered, and shallow culture, as opposed to a culture centered, enlightened, and profound.

In literature "life" has not yet been thoroughly examined on the realistic level; "both sides" have not been clearly seen or dramatically juxtaposed (in spite of the punctual appearance —and prompt suppression—of *Sister Carrie* in 1900). And although the vision of certain poets has already penetrated to the submerged recesses of human consciousness, these findings for the most part have gone unnoticed, or have been only partially understood, when perceived. Hopkins still remains encysted in his generation, as Emily Dickinson in hers. The English aesthetic movement, after the Wilde trial, has been driven underground. Fragmentary insights, broken examples of self-knowledge, are about to surface and to merge; and the time is almost at hand when the true operations of the imagination and of the despised instinctual life of man will be laid bare. The arts' progressive exploration and dissolution of binding reality have already found —in the nineteenth century's latest years—altogether unforeseen support in philosophy (Bergson), in the science of medical psychology (Charcot and Freud), and in ethnology (James Frazer, Frobenius, and others). Meanwhile in England, in America, and even in the more enlightened centers of Europe, the weaker members of an entire creative generation have perished from what we now can only consider as a kind of psychic polar cold.

The *fin de siècle* generation of artists was the last forced to live in an almost total psychic darkness, completely deprived of those secular insights which were soon to reinforce the insights of religion at its most spiritual and "mystic" level. The Catholic church had given succor to sensitive natures oppressed by the sense of human imperfectibility, through its doctrine of redemption, from Baudelaire on. And the late nineteenth century was crowded with various reformist techniques, all, however, directed toward institutions and not toward the individual. The sensitive individual was baffled by what seemed to be a complete outer block of thought and opinion, composed of harsh determinist doctrines, bourgeois "optimism" and complacency, as well as by a complete ignorance of the inner reasons for his often compulsive conduct. Instinctively, to ease the burden of talent superimposed upon a base of active suffering, poets and artists shifted their talents over into their lives, thus exteriorizing the symptoms which pointed not only to their own spiritual ills but to the hypocrisy of the society in which they found themselves.

It is now quite evident that this generation—so misunderstood and so generally maligned during and after its lifetime—actually discovered and put into operation the methods by which their successors, with more exact knowledge at their command, made a final and successful breakthrough from minor to major art. These methods were then few, and they remain practically unaugmented after a half-century of "experiment" and "decompression." They are classically oblique methods which have always proved effective when art's frontal attacks have failed. They are the methods of wit—irony, satire, parody, outright ridicule, and caricature; the methods of sensitive naturalism, of "feeling out" the way toward centers of crude but refreshing natural vitality, and of subsequently appreciating them; the methods of assimilation, usually of the features of a foreign culture more aware and "advanced" than one's own; and the methods of dissolution of reality through imaginative means, in the small but usable frames of fantasy and the lyric approach. As we contemplate these methods our understanding of many puzzling conjunctions of talent becomes clear: the side-by-side existence and simultaneous functioning of Max Beerbohm and Thomas Hardy; of E. M. Forster and A. E. Housman; of Samuel Butler and the "late" Henry James; of Ernest Dowson and William Butler Yeats; of Synge and Dreiser; of Francis Thompson and Oscar Wilde.

Thus we see in England, as the twentieth century begins, the minor arts taking up not only the tasks proper to them, but the tasks which the major arts, bloated with the Victorian ethos, had refused. Music comes back to England in the form of the satiric *opéra bouffe* (Gilbert and Sullivan). Caricature tells the truth in posters and book illustration, where the art of the official *salons* is silent. Light (and even nonsense) verse can afford to deal with contemporary matters at a time when the "official" poets are still concerned with their poetic "charades" (Hopkins' word, applied to Browning). And when after a century of "ruling taste" a raft of objects threatened to smother the very public for which they were designed, and when the expression of open eroticism is banned on all sides, Beardsley, with his sinister rococo line, shows up every detail of that taste—basic textures as well as superimposed pattern, plush and ormolu as well as quilting, puff, tassel, and gilded distortion—and fills this surrounding *décor* with creatures openly embodying a fantastic, perverse, and deliquescent eroticism, whose disabused eyes look out on a sort of dressmakers' and upholsterers' hell. This is the terror of the end-of-the-century vision at its highest point; and this sort of vision could not be driven underground, we now realize, entirely, or for long.

Beyond that movement's debacle it is now possible to distinguish its influence on those "modern masters" who were either directly concerned in it or were able to derive from its existence both nutriment and direction: Yeats, co-founder with Lionel Johnson and Arthur Symons of the Rhymers' Club; Joyce, provincial imitator and student of aesthetic attitudes and means not only in England but in Europe as a whole; Rilke, who directly modeled himself on *fin de siècle* lines; Proust, translator of Ruskin; Gide, friend of Wilde before his downfall and his benefactor thereafter; Eliot, who discovered Laforgue through Arthur Symons' *The Symbolist Movement in Literature* (1899); and Ezra Pound.*

Because literature since 1900 is, in fact, only a fantasia on a few themes that nineteenth-century France stated early and, in

---

* "[Influences of the nineties] linger in some of Pound's later works more as an emotional attitude than in the technique of versification; the shades of Dowson, Lionel Johnson and Fiona flit about." T. S. Eliot, Introduction to *Selected Poems of Ezra Pound* (London: Faber and Gwyer, 1928), p. ix.

many instances, actually pushed at once to aesthetic and moral conclusions, it is not entirely paradoxical to linger in the former century while ostensibly dealing with the literature of the latter. Flaubert and Baudelaire, at the nineteenth century's midpoint (1856 and 1857), have already, with *Madame Bovary* and *Les Fleurs du mal*, charted the direction of modern prose and poetry: toward "innerness," poetic naturalism, the direct examination of the contemporary scene; toward the breaking of frames, "mobility, plasticity, inventiveness."*

The whole tempo and coloring of even the earliest decades of that extraordinary hundred years signals the human and aesthetic drives which we now feel to be our own with such purity and simplicity that it is a pleasure—if we take care to avoid any sentimental nostalgia—to trace our way backward toward certain clearly marked beginnings. Here is our passion for speed, early announcing itself in madcap scherzos, galops, waltzes, and polkas. And here are mankind's ultimate pre-machine record-making and record-breaking means of locomotion: the clipper ship and the thoroughbred horse. Here is our rage for uncanny and tremendous technical virtuosity, showing up in musical performance (Chopin, Liszt, Paganini); our still unassuaged Romantic passion for the ultimate in human feeling—melancholy and rapture (culminating in *Tristan*, finished in 1859). And here is a passion for the all-embracing art structure (the *Gesamtkunstwerk*), the impulse behind which we can recognize; and finally, here is the yearning for the all-embracing Infinite ("l'Azur!").

"*Il me semblait que cette musique était la mienne, et je la reconnaissais comme tout homme reconnaît les choses qu'il est destiné à aimer.*" †

It is in these words that Baudelaire expresses his emotion on hearing the first presentation of a complete Wagner opera. And it is at this point that we find the key to Symbolism in the leitmotiv; at this moment when the arts begin to wash over their

* Terms applied to the modern novel by Albert Thibaudet, *Histoire de la littérature française* (Paris: Stock, 1936), p. 534.
† Quoted from Baudelaire's "Richard Wagner et Tannhäuser à Paris" (1861) in Margaret Gilman, *Baudelaire the Critic* (New York: Columbia University Press, 1943), p. 182.

set boundaries, and to dissolve, even as they begin to mingle. For it is not, as things turn out, to be the logical, the philosophical side of Wagner and his all-embracing musical drama which is to survive as a permanent influence into our day, but the purely musical shimmer and whisper of the Rhine and of the forest which exist at this music's heart. Baudelaire's sensitive instinct at once recognized the importance of both the new sounds and the myth around which they were disposed; the crucially important myth which, in the following century, was to become indeed "cosmopolitan."

This merging of music, poetry, and mythical material took place in the period when French thought, in reaction to the excesses of Romanticism, and in competition with the "successes" of science, was beginning to rigidify into the historical determinism of Taine and Renan. This French determinism was more firmly based historically, more highly organized intellectually, and more emotionally disabused than the amalgam of hope, speculation, despair, and aspiration—replete with sentimental compromises and imperfect logical syntheses—which characterized the intellectual climate of Victorian England. Moreover, its sheer weight of authority was paralyzing, since its dissemination throughout the educated levels of French society was assured by the central and unquestioned authority of the *lycée* and the Sorbonne. The defeat of 1870 intensified determinism's latent pessimism; and it is this gloomy fixity of form and idea against which Rimbaud, Corbière, and Lautréamont reacted with violence; which Laforgue mocked with his irony; to which the Parnassians—in part—succumbed; and which Mallarmé finally resisted with centered calm.

Baudelaire brushes against the living Wagner (the exchanged letters express mutual esteem); Mallarmé touches Wagner through Villiers de l'Isle-Adam, who had known him. The example of Wagnerian music aids Mallarmé to break out from "the cold logic of the page"; and Mallarmé transferred at least the intensity of Wagner's claims for the hegemony of music to his own theory of poetry's transcendent power. The Symbolist revolt brought into French literature, which up to that time had operated more or less *en bloc,* and into modern literature at large from that time on, a permanent avant-gardism.

The Romantic and Parnassian revolutions had as their objectives conquest and organization, and a stable condition of poetry—liberty, but liberty within limits. But Symbolism habituated literature to the idea of an indefinite revolution—to an artistic *blanquisme*, to youth's right and duty to jostle the preceding generation while rushing toward an absolute. . . . Literature divided itself into normal literature and literature of the advance guard. . . . The Symbolist revolution—the last up to now—is perhaps the absolute last, because it incorporated the motif of chronic revolution into literature's normal state.*

The tenets of this "permanent revolution" have profoundly affected all "new writing," in prose and verse, in our time.

Symbolism ran concurrently in France with the development of Impressionist painting—another breakthrough from formal means to a new refreshment of color and light. The nineteenth century ends with all the arts turned toward the extreme nuance; the actual world is progressively "etherialized" by the arts so that it approaches ever more closely to the outcast world of the ideal and the dream. Poetry has already felt the vitality of the music hall and the popular song through Laforgue, Rimbaud, and Verlaine; the pitch is lowered and becomes more casual and ironic; the neck of rhetoric has been wrung. And now the European nationalist schools of music, themselves strongly infiltrated with folk song, begin to draw together into what will become an "international style." French music itself, under Debussy's mastership, becomes Symbolist and even pre-Raphaelite; Debussy, Mallarmé's close friend, writes a cantata based on "The Blessed Damozel," and a prelude based on "L'Après-midi d'un faune." He will go on to Symbolist opera; and *Pelléas et Mélisande* will entrance Parisian audiences in 1902.

Debussy's music and Symbolist poetry were to widen and deepen immeasurably both form and sensibility. "Causal relationship" in music (the sonata form, harmonic progression) was breaking down, to give way to a music

made up of chords of the 9th, the 11th and 13th—which, incapable of merging, create instead a vibrating, oscillating, glimmering sound complex, trembling, and nervous. It was no longer the full chords, the massed sonorities of the full orchestra that interested the impressionist composer, but the soft muted sonorities produced by handling

* Thibaudet, *op. cit.*, p. 485.

[the enormous post-Wagnerian orchestra] with the utmost delicacy. The mighty trombones and stentorian trumpets are muted, the shrill wood-winds . . . used in their lower registers; the strings are divided into many parts . . . the ear-shattering trumpets are lightly touched on edge, kettle-drums and snare-drums . . . discreetly muffled, and the whole is drenched with a silvery confetti of harp, celesta and Glockenspiel, with the tam-tam faintly rumbling in the distance . . . and this orchestration . . . now takes the place of thematic construction. We stand here at the frontiers of logical consciousness.*

This spectacle of the arts breaking through into a kind of dissolving beauty, at very nearly the same moment, and *in accordance with the same principles*, is striking enough. The fact that they should soon have their reinforcing philosophy, history (through anthropology), and psychology, in spite of every determinist pressure, seems to adumbrate a kind of poetic justice. Modern twentieth-century literature is so closely allied to its contingent and sister arts that it can no longer be detached from them, for separate examination. And not only is this interpenetration to continue, but it is to be accented by every new force which enters the situation: the discovery of African primitives (1905); Fauvism in painting (1905); the Russian ballet under Diaghilev's direction (Paris and London, 1909); Stravinsky's music; Post-Impressionism, and so on. These later influences, it will be noted, are either of a true primitive or a true "expressionist" nature, either in a pure form or theatricalized. After 1918, both in Europe and America, nineteenth-century Impressionism can collide and be strengthened by savage and anarchic, violent and intransigent crosscurrents. For the air has been cleared; truth has been told and insight gained, and by the arts themselves, on their own ground and according to their own means, not because of the 1914 war, but well in advance of, and in spite of, it.

It is impossible, here, to indicate in any but the briefest way the change-over in America from a largely provincial and repressive climate—social, aesthetic, intellectual, and moral—to a situation of far more buoyancy, enlightenment, and openness. American culture, in 1900, in the words of Frank Lloyd Wright, was "a life by imitation . . . spread wide and thin over the vast

* Paul H. Lang, *Music in Western Civilization* (New York: Norton, 1941), p. 1019.

surface of a continent." For American writers of the time, it was not at all a question of dissolving reality, but one of actually seeing and apprehending; of finding means directly to grasp and express contemporary life. The population at large, after the Cuban war, was openly and naïvely infatuated with power. New "publics" were forming. In the suburbs of the cities and in city "flats" a new skittishness was beginning to be added to the country's rural and Puritan core. A taste for diversion, for "news," for scandal, was fed by the "yellow press"; and entertainers were already replacing crowned heads as idols and objects of interest. The coarser strains of American humor were dying out, to be replaced by sentiment in fiction and in "magazine verse."

It was during this gimcrack era (with its undercurrents of violence) of gilt wicker furniture, hand-painted china, lace curtains, and "sofa cushions" that American realism, after a long series of false and partial starts, finally broke through. Three brutal titles announce its appearance in the novel: *Maggie: A Girl of the Streets* (1892), *McTeague* (1899), and *Sister Carrie* (1900). And we must at once add to these fiction titles the title of a book of poems in which the truth concerning American outcasts and misfits—tragic victims of personal and social ignorance and frustration—was told in purely poetic terms: *The Children of the Night*, by E. A. Robinson (1897).

Robinson wrote his early poems in a decaying New England backwater. He was to leave his native scene, in which he had experienced American spiritual forlornness to the full, to become for many years, in New York, a member of one of the "Bohemias" that had begun to form on the shadier fringes of many American cities. These Bohemias, at their beginning, absorbed the defeated and the peculiar, the sensitive and the vicious alike. The reporter and the journalist—"the newspaperman"—were a part of this nexus, along with the socialist, the anarchist, the criminal, the poet, and the painter. Here in the back rooms of saloons, in cheap cafés, in shabby lodgings, a kind of urban hedge-schoolmastering went on: an exchange of ideas, enthusiasms, scattered and fragmentary experience of European arts and ways of life, between old and young. Already, as though in response to a hidden American hunger for information concerning as many European de-

velopments as possible, journalists who were themselves amateurs
of several arts began to explode into printed enthusiasm for
European painting, drama, music, and literature. Huneker was
the chief example of this type, and he was to be followed, after
1908, by the young Mencken and Nathan, and Willard Huntington Wright, at first contributors to and later editors of the *Smart
Set*.

This pulp magazine, which began by catering to the period's
taste for "sordid elegance," soon developed into the principal
American purveyor of "modern" ideas and "new writing." Without any pretensions toward either depth of thought or liberality
of opinion, with crude and hilarious impudence, its editors attacked American provincialism from the right, as it was already
being attacked, by Veblen and others, from the left. They provided, moreover, a constant running picture of contemporary
European culture, on all levels, from the *Burgtheaters* of Central
Europe to Parisian *cafés chantants*. And along with the unknown
and talented writers constantly turning up in its pages, the *Smart
Set* provided first-rate factual and fictional reports of untouchable
subjects; for a time it specialized in vignettes of American
bordellos.

 "Truth is so rare, it's delightful to tell it." This Dickinsonian
sentence underlies the spirit of the "little American renaissance."
Truths long suppressed began to be written and to be published;
not only the social truths of the muckraker but the truths of
individual lives. Confessions and disguised autobiographies
flooded out in prose and in "free verse." And if it is now impossible to read many of these productions without a wry smile,
it must be remembered how extreme was the cultural simplicity
of the period to which they belong. This simplicity was soon
to be altered by young men from the universities who began to
apply trained critical analysis to the American scene. A series of
rather Jamesian female patronesses also appeared and became
active in the company of (in the words of one of them) these
young "movers and shakers": Mrs. Jack Gardner in Boston;
Mabel Dodge in Florence and New York; Harriet Monroe, along
with the somewhat less "genteel" Margaret Anderson and Jane
Heap, in Chicago; Gertrude Stein in Paris. And, in the unexpected
locus of Philadelphia, about 1907, a school of American painters

took hold of realism—"The Eight," John Sloan, Luks, Glackens, and the rest.

Post-Impressionism hit the United States in 1913, with the New York Armory Show; and from this influence American painting never really recovered until the depression of the thirties set in. Both American painting and American music, struck by styles and manners for which they were not totally prepared, became inundated with a wash of eclecticism. American poetry and fiction (more firmly based and more vigorously manned) were able to connect with the Post-Impressionist school directly, without being in any way deflected from their true course. Post-Impressionism in painting is based on an analysis down to basic structure, combined with new and individual (according to each artist) combinations of plastic elements and linear motifs. This anatomization of nature begins with Cézanne; and painting, after him, works toward the discovery, arrangement, or invention of "significant form."

Modern music shows curiosity concerning the hard, inviolable, and unemotional elements of rhythm, tonality, and atonality. Modern poetry, with the Imagists, endeavored to get at the pure definite subject, untarnished by thought, emotion, or moral idea. It was Imagism—invented and directed, throughout its brief life in English, by Americans—which finally turned against the outworn and exhausted forms into which the Georgian poets were able to infuse only a temporary and tepid energy. And it was not the Imagists alone, or chiefly, who developed intense simplicity, both of feeling and of means. Yeats, after 1912, and Pound, working with Yeats and the Fenollosa manuscripts, began to discover a poetic method which combined accuracy with conversational ease and was also capable of applying form to everyday material. Poetry in English no longer fled away into medieval settings; it was being made hard yet flexible, more edged yet more translucent; more "ordinary" yet more inclusive. It was this modern tone and these modern means to which Eliot, in "Prufrock" (about 1916), allied himself, having already discovered his personal point of departure in Elizabethan drama and the irony of Jules Laforgue. Yeats and Pound achieved modernity; Eliot was modern from the start.

In the face of post-1918 confusions, as well as in the confrontation of adverse "conservative" criticism, it is important to realize and to state that the large and true poetic talents, in Europe, England, and America, since before 1914, have either worked in form or toward the discovery of form. Moreover, since these poets reinforced their findings with methods passed over or discarded by nineteenth-century taste, they engaged in a task of restoration as well as of originality. The line of modern poetry is a persistent —though sometimes devious and diverted—line toward new structure, new largeness, and new power; directed by an undeviating search, not for an absolute and all-embracing aesthetic "machine," but for a commodious and flexible carrier of complicated thought and sensibility. And at the same time that it searches for form, it has an added implicit task: to heal the split between thought and feeling inherited from a century of "progress." "It is on the tragic side of the nineteenth century that thinking and feeling go separate ways, or, as T. S. Eliot expresses it, 'the substantial unity of the soul is destroyed.' " *

In these later and central years of the twentieth century, it is becoming evident that the experimental side of literature must adjust itself to "reality" and to the changes in the human situation. Without abolishing a continued "openness" toward experiment, writers must not insist upon a stubborn avant-gardism when no real need for a further restless forward movement any longer exists. To move forward is not always a crucial need. The moment comes for a consolidation of resources and for a canvassing of the ground already gained; for a recognition of the point reached. In addition, since one of the less authentic features of modern art has been the *rational* exploitation of the irrational (as in the case of Surrealism), a constant need for the examination of all experiment on the grounds of its authenticity exists. The fact that charlatans, power-lovers, and *blagueurs* function within the experimental side of the contemporary arts does not, however, invalidate these arts' tremendous accomplishment of clarification, discovery, and restitution. "O the inexhaustibility of the *motifs!*" writes the aged Cézanne in a letter. Modern art and literature, without any help from a constricting environment,

* Sigfried Giedion, *Mechanization Takes Command* (Cambridge: Harvard University Press, 1948), p. 328.

have proved that the *motifs*, of both inner and outer nature, are indeed inexhaustible.

Interpretation, rather than exploration, is the task of the moment and of any imaginable future. Interpreters early in the field have been struck by the fact that man has surrounded himself with objects which are to him emotionally opaque: which he cannot love.* Natural "things" are penetrable by the imagination, and certain modern poets have spent lifetimes in rendering the essence not only of "the fruits of the earth" but of those human artifacts into which some spiritual life has been poured by means of the sensitive touch of the human hand. Is it possible to treat, if not with considerate affection (as distinguished from "Futurist" idolatry), at least with intelligent placement, these machines that are products of machines, these tools that are the product of tools? Surely our fear of the destructive machine is linked with our emotional blankness toward non-destructive ones. It is significant that the modern poet to whom the French, since 1945, have given almost complete enthusiasm is Guillaume Apollinaire. Apollinaire, in his mature years, expressed a true joy in (if not a perfect acceptance of) the details of his environment, both mechanical and non-mechanical. "Zone" bathes airplanes, advertisements, the Paris street and its traffic in a light which had not been seen formerly and has not been seen since.

The novel was the last literary form to be struck by Impressionism; and once penetrated by this force, it ballooned out into incredible proportions, becoming, as some observers have noted, a kind of Luciferian universe in the hands of Joyce. The novel remains "the most plastic of *genres*—the most *mobile*, industrious and inventive." † Its future possibilities are obvious, and enormous. Poetry, on the other hand, has come to the end, and perhaps exceeded, its explorative and experimental side. Eliot has recently remarked that although he values "the exploration of certain poetic possibilities for its own sake . . . for the future it is a tenable hypothesis that this advance of self-consciousness—the extreme awareness of and concern for language which we find

* Sigfried Giedion, in *Space, Time and Architecture* (Cambridge: Harvard University Press, 1941), explores this dilemma at length.
† Thibaudet, *op. cit.*, p. 534.

in Valéry—is something which must ultimately break down owing to an increasing strain against which the human mind and nerves will rebel." *

All objects await human sympathy. It is only the human that can humanize. It is now equally as difficult to flood outer reality with emotion as it once was to discover the inner springs of feeling and conduct. The world, already imaginatively dissolved, anatomized, and reconstituted, must now be *felt* through experience, and experienced through feeling. *Four Quartets*, the *Duino Elegies*, and Apollinaire's songs and contemplations have already opened the way.

PRO-TEM (*1967*)

The verbal arts, which forty years or so ago were supposed to be spiralling upward toward an ultimately expressive richness and freedom, at present, according to one gloomy set of prophets, are gyrating downward toward silence. It must be remarked, however, that they are being excessively noisy on their downward way. The number of volumes of verse now to achieve some sort of print is astonishing. Where once a typewriter existed, a font of type or a multigraphing device has sprung up and a "little press" (often with its attendant little magazine) has come into being. At the same time, the often academically based critical "industries" keep pouring out close readings, explications, glosses, and commentary of all kinds, some of it of an intricacy and density that make the nerves quiver and the brain reel. Joyce, Yeats, and Eliot have furnished material for these scholarly preoccupations for many years. Frost, Stevens, and a sprinkling of younger figures now begin to claim the thesis writers' attention. Posthumously published material of recently vanished figures— letters, and various hitherto overlooked miscellanea—has now been released into eager hands, and we are beginning to see the departed modern masters shouldering up, as it were, from unexplored, or misunderstood, depths—like mythic sea creatures—

* T. S. Eliot, *From Poe to Valéry* (Washington: Library of Congress, 1949), p. 16.

their obscure reasons and their psychic scars clearly visible in what is often a harsh contemporary light.

That an immense tedium has settled down over the writings of the populous avant-garde is at the moment all too apparent. And the emotional field is narrowing; one emotional response after another has been sealed away, by some strange tacit consent, from the poet's insight and attention. The general run of verse thought to be experimental is in actuality as tightly tied to its own set of conventions as "formal" poetry ever was. After the emotional excesses (and the sham freedoms) of very nearly all Victorian poetry, techniques of intensification and of elimination had to be applied; to this we all agree. But when, as at present, it would seem that anguish, bitterness, and fright have become the most available sources of poetic expression, it is rather difficult to remember that poetry was once able to exhort, stimulate, open up, discover, deepen, interpret (and *console*). Motions are being made, from recent accounts, away from Existential "pessimism and loneliness, boredom, passivity" toward (yes!) "imaginative energy and a renewed search for some positive meaning" in man's situation and fate. Yet it was an eminent doctor of medicine, and not a poet, who recently stated the importance of "the wonder and awe in which we hold processes of great complexity and natural beauty which we do not fully understand."

Extended complaint or blame directed toward the procedures of any art in transition is misdirected and a waste of energy. The times manifest themselves with increasing speed, and we are part of the times. In the case of literature, however, one danger can be recognized: the possibility that in seeking complexity and various freedoms we may cheat ourselves of all pleasure in those formalities that language has built up over recorded (and unrecorded) time, as well as an acquaintance with virtuoso performances that are unassailably modern, though unfashionably so.

ANTHOLOGIES

ANTHOLOGY FOR THE ENJOYMENT OF POETRY, edited by Max Eastman (1939)

Max Eastman's *The Enjoyment of Poetry* first appeared in the days when young rebels (in America) had recently dared to cast religion and "morals" aside, shake off science, and step forth as hearty embodiments of "awareness." Mr. Eastman, with the passing of time, has toned down his original picture of the poet as inspired vagabond and of poetry as sheer vitalism. And, although he has built his theories on Marxist science, he has not fallen into the open trap of poetry as propaganda. But he has never gone back on his original belief in the cleavage between science and art, and he will have nothing to do with poetry which is not "general" and not clear. This insistence on clarity certainly seems to be utilitarianism working in a disguised form. And it is an insistence charged with a kind of moral feeling; because modern poets cannot be easily understood, they are to be distrusted.

The poems selected for Mr. Eastman's new *Anthology for the Enjoyment of Poetry* are sorted into sections "according as their prevailing values are of sensuous perception, emotion, action or idea" and one "devoted to purely imaginary values." Their division into categories immediately imparts an old-fashioned flavor to the book. We are reminded of a nineteenth-century habit: poems put under the heads of "Life," "Love," "Eternity," etc. And

the selections themselves remind us that the romantic-socialist rebellion against the mechanist-economic nineteenth-century world, though it seemed to leave behind "elevating" standards of art, actually dragged them along in its wake. Mr. Eastman is, of course, completely against "taste" as a criterion. "Taste" is a luxury product; it comes out of the drawing room and the "ivory tower" and leads back into these refuges. The poet—and especially the great poet—is out on the open road of life, thrilling to his own heartbeat, to "the vigorous abandon" of his mind: a minstrel. The historic process has shut him off from science and religion, but nothing can stop his search for "intensified experience."

Substituting the word "sensibility" for the outlawed word "taste" and applying this faculty to Mr. Eastman's selections, the reader recognizes good, bad, and indifferent work. At times these poems creak with sentiment, are stiff with rhetoric, or fall flat from their very fullness of "life." Mr. Eastman has not entirely rejected the moderns; here are Hopkins, T. S. Eliot, Yeats, Spender, H. D., Edith Sitwell, and James Joyce (in their clearer moments). But Mr. Eastman tends to reject the truly dramatic poem in favor of the melodramatic, the metaphysical in favor of the "fanciful," the "mystical" in favor of the ghostly, the satirical poem altogether. He chooses descriptive and emotional verse with some authority, since poetry of this kind falls in best with his general theories.

Mr. Eastman's inability to understand what modern poets are up to rises from his insistence that science is still rigid and is becoming more so. The psychological and social sciences, he says, may seem to be less fixed, but this is a delusion. Give them time and they will drive poetry out of the books entirely. He ignores the fact that during the last twenty-five years scientific simplifications have been enlarged. The universe has been extended into pure realms of the imagination, and the subconscious has become a scientifically recognized guide to the world of "practical" affairs. The cogwheels of the mechanistic universe have stopped turning; science has become humble before the intuitive thinker. All this makes Mr. Eastman rather cross. He seems to want a rigid universe against which the poet may surge and rebel. When poetry expresses complicated emotions, when the poet concerns himself with borderline subliminal states (all of great interest to modern science), Mr. Eastman disapproves. That "unintelligible" poetry can extend consciousness he will not admit. Granted that modern poetry has among its practitioners counterfeit talents, the ability to sense the difference between the real and the imitation requires more sensitive instruments than Mr. Eastman has to hand. Certainly, compared with some of the poems here included, modern poetry has advanced into regions far beyond those in which Mr. Eastman's "life-forcing" values hold.

MODERN AMERICAN POETRY: A CRITICAL ANTHOLOGY and *MODERN BRITISH POETRY: A CRITICAL ANTHOLOGY*, edited by Louis Untermeyer (*1942*)

Modern American Poetry: A Critical Anthology, edited by Louis Untermeyer, reaches its sixth revised form in its 1919 edition. The first edition came out unpretentiously in 1919. Every few years since, a new edition has appeared. The paper has broadened, the pages have multiplied until they now number 712 over all. Mr. Untermeyer has chosen poems, clipped criticism, and "researched" biographical facts about his poets until we have all the interesting and feasible information pertaining to poem and poet. We know not only what Mr. Untermeyer thinks of poem and poet but what a vast mass of other people have thought. Since 1936 this anthology, which for years began with Emily Dickinson, has harked back to Walt Whitman. The format is charming if rather unwieldy, and the volume is brought right up to the sharpest point of contemporaneity with its closing names, Delmore Schwartz and Muriel Rukeyser, both born in 1913.

Modern British Poetry: A Critical Anthology, edited by the same hand, goes back to 1920 and is now in its fifth revised edition. Pruning and care have made it shrink a little since it last appeared; it is 506 pages at present. Thirty-four poets, in Mr. Untermeyer's phrase, "have been dropped"; twenty-nine, ranging from G. M. Hopkins to Sacheverell Sitwell, Auden,

Spender, and MacNeice, now are "more fully represented." The
volume begins with Thomas Hardy (1840–1928) and closes with
Dylan Thomas (born 1914).

It is important to examine these anthologies from time to
time because they stand right at the heart of "poetry appreciation" in America. The earlier editions have sold 275,000 copies
all told. They appear in schools, libraries, and every center of
learning and "culture." Mr. Untermeyer is the chief liaison officer
between the modern corpus of British and American verse and
that numerous group of American readers who wish to find
out what's what in poetry but haven't the taste, enthusiasm, or
time to go about digging up the material themselves or make
their own choices. To such people, and to the young, fired with
their first enthusiasm for the Muse but often cut off from wide
sources of information, the Untermeyer anthologies give the tone
and temper of their basic information. So far as American poetry
is concerned, the field of anthologists is rather bare. Once there
were Griswold and Stedman; now there is Untermeyer. The
present editions are undoubtedly superior in every way to their
predecessors. The smoke has now blown away from many poetic
battles, or, to change the figure, time has now settled the poetic
sediment, and Mr. Untermeyer has always been an expert at
sensing in what direction the surface current of poetic fashion
is moving. But as for the deeper tides, he has usually been wise
after the event. He completely missed the importance of Eliot
early in Eliot's career. He now is able to present a complete
critical Eliot *dossier,* but he has needed help. He makes Robert
Frost the central figure of American poetry and tends to over-
estimate in every instance those poets whose glibness and conformity have today swept them to the top. I am willful enough
to prefer, in some ways, the good old days between 1925 and
1936, when Mr. Untermeyer let his taste run more freely. Then
no one could predict from edition to edition what poets would
stay in or what be tossed out. In they came for one edition; out
they went the next. It was a delightfully capricious spectacle to
watch, and many watchers appreciated it to the full. Now much
has changed. Mr. Untermeyer has read all the books and collated
all the reviews, and he doesn't make many howlers. He sticks
to some old favorites through thick and thin (there will, for

instance, always be Nathalia Crane), but he is, on the whole, a chastened editor. No harm will come to the taste of a nation through these extremely popular anthologies. Mr. Untermeyer, be it remembered in spite of his faults, has a basic love and appreciation of poetry, particularly the lyric. If he mistakenly likes pomposity and verbalism, he remains true to the lyric cry and simple-heartedness, which is so dangerously near, often, to simple-mindedness. But he is still capable of reprinting poems which aren't English, let alone poetry, and I, for one, would not bet on many of his favorites for the long pull. And to sandwich poems between great slabs of information, quotation, appreciation, and adulation is wearing to anyone who believes that practically nothing, as Gerald Bullett has said, "should be interposed between the reader and the poem." It is fine to be a liaison officer, though combining preacher, teacher, and special pleader with liaison officer can become rather tiresome to all concerned.

It is also fine to be an anthologist whose opinions cannot be flexed by either prejudice or false modesty. Mr. Untermeyer has accordingly included large selections from his own works. "What a pity," a poet once remarked, "that I cannot make an anthology! For then I should have to leave myself out." Such a saturnine reflection has never troubled the gentleman dealt with above.

THE NEW BRITISH POETS:
AN ANTHOLOGY, edited by Kenneth Rexroth
(1949)

A fair sampling of British poetry written just before, during, and since the war has been printed in the United States. What has been kept, by various editorial oversights, from these shores is a detailed survey of the currents of British thought and feeling that might indicate in what direction the newest generation of British poets is headed. Kenneth Rexroth, in his informative introduction to *The New British Poets: An Anthology*, now supplies this detail in quantity. He not only discourses upon the work of a variety of poets but traces the links between these men and women and their British and, when such links exist, European backgrounds. We find that a real shift has been made from the prewar school of wit and semi-realism, led by Auden, toward a new "Romanticism"; that certain "little mags" now promulgate "a new and dynamic variety of religious anarchism"; and that the most vigorous poetic talents are either Welsh, Scotch, Northern Irish, or sequestered in remote districts of England—Norman Nicholson, in Cumberland, for example. Rexroth describes the decentralization from London as one that "seems to be true always of decaying capitals; generation by generation, the major Roman poets come farther and farther away from Rome."

Rexroth admits that the tenets of this Romanticism are hard to define. A non-Marxian revolt against "a depersonalized and collapsing society" is deeply involved. The recent "Apocalyptic" movement, headed by Henry Treece, was, he says, brief and uninteresting, but because of it Welsh literary influence became more pronounced. Dylan Thomas, according to Rexroth, exhibits in his poetry an intensity that derives from the ancient "savage Welsh Nonconformity." Thomas has, as a matter of fact, supplied to modern English verse—rather belatedly, it is true—the sort of visionary violence that Rimbaud brought to Franch poetry and that Hart Crane, in a lesser degree, introduced to American verse. He is certainly an eloquent outsider. Whether or not his poetry points toward "a cultural *coup d'état*," or is just highly enough charged to be overrated by his contemporaries, remains to be seen.

The "Romantics" are busily engaged in constructing a moral-philosophic system to back up their works. The accent is on "religious personalism and political anarchism," and the ancestors of the movement are many, unexpected, and oddly matched. The names of Eric Gill, Herbert Read, and D. H. Lawrence are arrayed side by side with those of the Orthodox Russian Berdyaev, the Alsatian Albert Schweitzer, and the Jewish philosopher Martin Buber. Henry Miller and Carl Jung also share in what is described as not merely an aesthetic but a world view—"the rejection of mechanistic civilization, sterile scientism, and top-heavy rationalism, the quest for a true integrality of the person." Lorca and Rilke inject other un-British strains.

After Rexroth's enthusiastic build-up, the poets in the collection, arranged in undramatic alphabetical order, seem fairly washed-out and feeble. The outstanding talents we already know: W. R. Rodgers, Dylan Thomas, Norman Nicholson, Laurie Lee, Henry Reed, Hugh MacDiarmid, and Lawrence Durrell, as well as the ex-Surrealists George Barker and David Gascoyne, and the older and reoriented Stephen Spender. A group of women poets, rather warmly normal in tone and subject, are highly derivative in style. But it is a pleasure to come upon the rough sincerity of Sorley Maclean, one of Rexroth's young Scots. Maclean's brief poem "Knightsbridge of Libya," translated from his own Gaelic, carries on the firm masculinity of the Synge tradition:

> Though I am today against the breast of battle,
> not here my burden and extremity; not Rommel's
> guns and tanks, but that my darling should be
> crooked and a liar.

NEW POETS OF ENGLAND AND AMERICA, edited by Donald Hall, Robert Pack, and Louis Simpson (1958)

The groves of Academe were once thought to lie in the vicinity of the Muses' laurel wood, and poets could move between these two secluded areas freely and with ease. Nowadays there is a widespread belief that close contact with academic life is dangerous for the creative artist; he is warned, on all sides, that any realtionship with institutions of learning will cause his gifts to dwindle, if not totally to disappear. In spite of such warnings, poets of the younger generation have taken to the teaching profession in numbers, and some of the results of this association are coming to light. A recent anthology, *New Poets of England and America*, is edited by three young men (Donald Hall, Robert Pack, and Louis Simpson) who have themselves received fellowships, grants, and other honors, and who now teach. The volume, which has a delightfully shrewd introduction by the non-academic

Robert Frost, contains the work of forty-six young men (two of them appear posthumously) and six young women, British and American, whose ages range from twenty-two to forty. (Their nationalities and dates are listed.) Although their work seems to have escaped excessive conventional pressures, academic or otherwise, they all—with one or two borderline exceptions—write in form.

Freedom of technique has, in the last forty years, been equated in most people's minds with true poetic originality. But as we look back over the list of major modern talents, writing in English, from Pound and Eliot through Auden, we find that form, although loosened and revised, has never been wholly abandoned. Metre, rhyme, and the stanza have withstood many blows and have been transformed, but they have survived. We can even trace pattern and design of one kind or another in Marianne Moore's syllabic verse and in the rhythms, based on the truest of ears, of Pound and William Carlos Williams. The poets of the youngest generation have come to realize, it seems, that form must be experienced and understood before it can be eliminated or tampered with; that the range of poetic effects is too valuable and varied to be treated with carelessness or inattention; that the virtuosity of an Eliot or an Auden is based on both knowledge and practice; that power and nuance partially depend upon the poet's knowledgeable approach to language. These poets, moreover, have moved away from many of the more chilling dicta of modern criticism. If some of them are imitative of their elders, it is at least an imitation of other poets, and not this or that critic's say-so, that they are pursuing.

Very nearly all of the poems in *New Poets* are lyrics, but of the renovated, enlarged, and dramatic kind that has risen, phoenixlike, from the ashes of exhausted nineteenth-century "song." And the intractable subject seems to have disappeared, or, rather, been absorbed; machines, for example, are treated with casual directness. The love song written in the first person singular shows up only once or twice, but there are many disguised love poems, written in every sort of tone and manner. And the idea of death is presented from both the secular and the religious points of view, sometimes in elegies (often addressed to the young). Myth seems to be going out, while actual history

is coming in—another good sign, since it is much more difficult
to be fancy about history. Nature comes through in all aspects,
together with the night side of things—dreams, nightmares, and
the fantasies in between. The percentage of ballads is high. One,
W. S. Graham's "Baldy Bane," is as close to the shocking subject
matter of folk as the "coarse" ballads of the later Yeats. The
collection is notably free of the coldly elaborate, the foolishly
excited, and the gloomily bardic, and there is little word-spinning
or verbalism for its own sake. And if few rebellious notes are
openly struck, many of these young men and women are capable
of satiric poems that indicate the working of a sharp and critical
eye. We can only guess at the futures of these writers, and all
are not on a high level of talent, but to see so much liveliness
and accomplishment should stir our imagination and our hope.
And the notion that any involvement with the academic automatically results in the drying up of talent should be reexamined,
since some, at least, of these contributors seem not only to
have survived exposure to learned institutions but actually to
have drawn nourishment from them.

THE NEW AMERICAN POETRY 1945–1960, edited by Donald M. Allen (1960)

History seems to have fallen in a heap upon the minds and
sensibilities of many members of the latest American "school"
of poetry, and their general reaction has been to burrow out
from beneath, bearing news of a fearful underside. This group
(or series of groups), more numerous than one might suppose,
and more widely spread over the land—from Massachusetts to
Oregon and California, plus a detour into the South by way of
North Carolina—now appears in an anthology, edited in a most
neat and orderly fashion, with a preface, by Donald M. Allen.
Mr. Allen has chosen forty-four poets (ranging in age from
twenty-three to fifty), divided them according to "geographical
definition" and age, and given them space in which to describe
their thories and purpose ("Statements on Poetics") and their

careers ("Biographical Notes"). He himself adds a bibliography and discography, as well as the preface, in which he states that these poets "are our avant-garde, the true continuers of the modern movement in American poetry. Through their work many are closely allied to modern jazz and Abstract Expressionist painting, today recognized throughout the world to be America's greatest achievement in contemporary culture. This anthology makes the same claim for the new American poetry."

Here they then are—talented and untalented, false and genuine, dull and interesting, Beat and semi-Beat. We must be serious about them, since they, on the whole, are serious about themselves. The main point to be resolved at the outset should be: Is this a true avant-garde manifestation—does it, that is, arise from a fresh, creative impulse centrally related to the present growing and changing needs of art in general and poetry in particular—or is it something else? Is it, for example, a late and peculiarly American development of the post-Symbolist revolt, which brought in, very nearly fifty years ago, Dada and Surrealism? Or is it the kind of revolt that has little to do with literature, ancient or modern? We do not get much help from the contributors, although they are vocal indeed about their aims. They are against metre (their hatred of iambic pentameter is intense), they dislike symbols and comparisons, they abjure lyricism and all tender emotions, and they consider any formal living poet who has reached any eminence (Auden included) "a baleful influence." Charles Olson, the oldest member of the assemblage, allows himself to say, "The poem itself must, at all points, be a high energy-construct and, at all points, an energy-discharge"—something we knew all along.

The questions multiply. Does this new poetry arise from sources largely amateur, exhibitionistic, or otherwise out of hand? Is it a revival of an oral tradition? (Many of the youngest group have read to audiences more frequently than they have published.) Are these wild talents outcroppings of an underground idealism; does their violence stem from a deliberate attempt to extend consciousness, or are many of them actually out of control? There are one or two "naturals," who express themselves with uninhibited childish glee, but the proportion of intelligence and of regular academic training in all these groups is large, and a feeling for language, plain and fancy, appears more often than not. In the midst of the hitting, smashing, struggle, hallucination, and disorder, certain effects that show normal insight and restraint are visible, such as sardonic wit and coldly contrived shock. The collection brings up, finally, the perhaps unanswerable query: What degree of anarchy can be projected in poetry? For when its principal tenets and accepted formal procedures are assaulted with utter vigor, this art of language does not merely change, it totally disappears.

AMERICAN POETRY,
edited by Professors G. W. Allen, W. B. Rideout, and J. K. Robinson (1966)

We have learned not to hate, fear, or deride the art and literature of our day, and we have developed new (or at least newly sharpened) sets of critical tools to deal wth those uses of the imagination we like to consider "modern." No infallible method has been found, however, for the tracking down of the moment when the transitional becomes the fixed, when experiment begins to harden into orthodoxy. After a half-century during which poetry in English has been encouraged toward a free drift and flux, on the one hand, while it has been given the stiff, formal admonitions of "the new criticism," on the other, it is interesting to come upon an anthology that seems to announce, as far as American poetry is concerned, the emergence of a recognizable although still fairly fluid pattern of contemporary conventions, of a cluster of accepted attitudes, of what is proving itself to be a highly accessible style.

That this anthology should have been openly designed as a textbook ("to meet the needs of a variety of classroom situations") may or may not arouse and hold the attention of the ordinary reader. Short biographies, check lists of a poet's major writings and of things written about him, expository (but not critical) notes on individual poems—this sort of scholarly apparatus has its own kind of charm as well as its undoubted usefulness. And, although academics are supposed to be slightly behind the times, the three learned editors of *American Poetry,* having advanced briskly through the Colonial period, the entire nineteenth century, and the first forty years of the twentieth, conclude with a group of "eight of the best poets who began to publish in the 1950s and 1960s." It is a relief to be presented with the solid and broad labors of Professors G. W. Allen, W. B. Rideout, and J. K. Robinson in a period when the latest manifestations of the poetic "modern" seem, as a British critic recently remarked, to be running toward parody or chaos. The British, by the way, have lately examined this impressive volume (nearly seven hundred poems, more than a thousand pages) with meticulous care, and a good deal of sympathy, in a full-page review in the *Times Literary Supplement.* The interest and appeal of *American Poetry* are, naturally, centered differently for the American, as opposed to the British, reader. The *Times* review ends by gracefully quoting a remark by T. S. Eliot— that Emerson escaped "a certain vulgarity which marks all the great Victorians"—and by crediting the entire body of American verse with a touching "wistfulness of radical innocence." The volume's centers of usefulness are perhaps three. In the first place, the editors (after giving Edward Taylor, writing metaphysical poems in a howling wilderness, his just due) go on to settle the nineteenth century's business with all the thoroughness that Browning assigned to his grammarian. Secondly, we find ourselves, in the first part of the twentieth century, at a meeting point of several by now conventional and "received" attitudes toward its extraordinary productions. Here it is often the omissions that count. Finally, we get a good sample, with those eight youngest poets, of the poetic style that evolved just yesterday, is widely prevalent today, and, one might expect, will penetrate a largish section of tomorrow.

Let us look briefly at what has happened to the nineteenth century, under these editors' informed scrutiny. Restitution has been made to two neglected figures: to Jones Very (1813–1880), admired by Emerson, whose mysticism burned with a supra-Unitarian intensity, and to Frederick Tuckerman (1821–1873), a minor master of the sonnet form. But it is the largeness and completeness of the selections that are truly impressive. All has been sown with a full and generous hand, so the variety and the striking originality of the period's poetry (once considered so tightly tied to Victorian contemporaries) are brilliantly displayed —the neglected (and remarkable) longer poems of Poe, Longfellow's delicate best, Melville's awkward profundities, Emerson's valid transcendent moments, Whitman from youth to age, Emily Dickinson in force, and dated according to the latest and best research. The poets of true originality and idiosyncratic power having come into their own, quarrels with many of the assumptions and with the forms and the diction of the period as a whole dwindle, while an all-over impression of the time's imaginative energy is inescapable.

We now come to the editors' summing up and showing forth of what they have agreed to be the heart of those works, written just before and directly after the 1914–1918 war, that announced, in England and America, a long-overdue revolt. Delayed French influences, once they were released, hit hard, and Americans, history tells us, were everywhere in the vanguard of the fray. *American Poetry* gives a splendid view of many major engagements, including "Cantos I and II" and a comprehensive Eliot, through "Ash Wednesday." Here scholarly care outdoes itself: every scrap of foreign quotation is translated, and knotty passages yield to a clearheaded frontal attack. But the scope begins to narrow. The lyric poets *pur-sang* (with some notable exceptions, such as Frost) disappear, having been relegated to that "great mass of versifiers" who would, evidently, disturb the editors' plan to study their poets "in depth." Neither Edgar Lee Masters nor Vachel Lindsay is present, nor do we come upon Edna Millay or Elinor Wylie. Too simple, too vulgar, too Romantic? Carl Sandburg squeaks through, along with Robinson Jeffers, but W. H. Auden's long standing (not in the twenties, it is true) as an American citizen is overlooked. Wallace Stevens, that darling of professors, is well represented indeed.

In the case of close contemporaries, no bursts of vituperation or exhortation occur. The only connection with Beat rhetoric or attitude shows up in the selections from Robert Creeley, and these are frequently so slowed down that they seem to stutter a little. Although what has been called "the pathos and narcissism of existentialism" has to a certain extent worn itself out, secularized fear and trembling and an earthbound sickness unto death have become orthodox. The poets produce little anecdotes of anxiety, and these often resemble each other so closely that they can be interchanged from poet to poet. Discontinuity, fragmentation, and extreme illogicality have been around for a long time, but a kind of maundering logic, taken over from the later (and worser) Stevens, hinders intensity; many younger writers seem gloomy and dispirited rather than profound, and the original cold ferocity has disappeared from Surrealism. We are continually reminded that the subconscious, when dredged up without skill or imagination, can be every bit as tiresome as the conscious. But we are given examples of Robert Lowell, early and late, of Alan Dugan's real bitterness, of Theodore Roethke's varied insights into a long perspective of experience, of Richard Wilbur's authentic lyricism. Otherwise: a heartless immobility, post-Surreal deadpan and throwaway, flicks of wit, flattened-out moods of nostalgia, in a poetry that dissembles more than it projects. But as we have seen, as we have applied ourselves to the rich material gathered between the covers of *American Poetry*, nothing lasts forever, and it is the unexpected that always happens.

W. H. AUDEN

THE DOG BENEATH THE SKIN (1935)

W. H. Auden has emerged rapidly from the soliloquy darkened by private associations, a form that might have hampered him for a longer time. His first dramatic efforts, "Paid on Both Sides" and "The Dance of Death," were founded on the feeblest possible dramatic framework: the charade. He has written, in *The Dog Beneath the Skin, or, Where Is Francis?*, with the competent aid of Christopher Isherwood, a long, highly amusing revue, whose satire is so deft that it may stand, without cutting a sorry figure, beside the early Gilbert. Along with the satirist's wit, the imagination of a poet and the broad humor of a sane young man are also involved.

Auden's play is closer to the original music-hall entertainment so admired, in the nineties, as a refuge from the torpid, affected art and literature current at that time, than Eliot's "Sweeney Agonistes" or Cocteau's "Orphée," derived from the same source. It is less dependent on pure oddity than Cocteau's play, and it is not heavily symbolic, like Eliot's. It is a light-hearted yet fundamentally grave parable of the noble youth who descends from his class to give humanity in general a hard and unprejudiced stare.

The hero, Alan, accompanied by a comic dog called, after its quarry, Francis, sets out from the ideal English village in search of the lost noble heir. The two make their progress through the symptomatic institutions of a debased and lunatic society in the leisurely but erratic manner of all innocent pilgrims steered by an author's moral indignation, from Christian and Gulliver on. They are accompanied on certain stages of their journey by the press in the person of two journalists who comment, aid, abet, prod, rescue, sympathize, and interpret. They take boat and train journeys; they invade a tottering monarchy, a night-town, a Fascist insane asylum, a rest-cure for self-poisoned egotists, an operating theatre, and a de luxe hotel. The Dog, in spite of a lamentable taste for double whiskies, served in a bowl, shows remarkable cleverness and devotion throughout. He proves his true valor when the simple-hearted Alan falls into the clutches of a night-club entertainer; he casts his skin and stands up from it revealed as Sir Francis Crewe, the object of Alan's search. The two, in their roles of the seeker and the found, return to the village as comrades. Alan sees all in a new light and the one-time Dog sums up, in public, his general feelings about the world seen from below:

As a dog, I learnt with what a mixture of fear, bullying and condescending kindness you treat those whom you consider your inferiors, but on whom you depend for your pleasures. It's an awful shock to start seeing people from underneath. . . . You are units in an immense army: most of you will die without ever knowing what your leaders are fighting for or even that you are fighting at all. Well, I am going to be a unit in the army of the other side.

Auden and Isherwood are by no means the first young members of the English upper class who have pilloried their caste. Even the rather unsettled Sitwells have put down, in terms far from uncertain, the grotesque antics of members of the three estates. The most noticeable ingredient in Auden's attitude is his lack of hatred; he has much pity and strong anger, but he is not blood-thirsty and he does not blame. He surveys the scene from above and below; he gives it elevation, section and plan, but he does not rant against it. The hysterical, the gloomy, the portentously righteous and solemn note is missing, yet the power of his indictment is not diminished because of its absence. And there is a hint given from time to time that it is man's present (and perhaps

future) partial capacity for sense and for good, his defective
and divided nature, that helps to distort the scene.

To men of action, pity is sentimental and insight into the
human heart unnecessary. To a poet, pity and insight may also
kindle the fire of action and sharpen the pen in the hand. Auden
fearlessly incites to action, after he has shown that what must be
fought are not only the outer horrors but also the flesh on the
bones and the stupidity in the veins:

> You have wonderful hospitals and a few good schools:
> Repent.
> The precision of your instruments and the skill of your
>   designers is unparalleled:
> Unite.
> Your knowledge and your power are capable of infinite
>   extension:
> Act.

LETTERS FROM ICELAND (1937)

Those people who wish young poets to be deadly serious and all
of a piece will be annoyed and baffled by Auden's travel book,
Letters from Iceland, written with Louis MacNeice, a new collaborator. These letters, rhymed and unrhymed, are consistently
amusing and frequently brilliant, but they do not repeat the tone
of books written by emotional travelers, philosophical travelers,
trippers, or escapists. Both Auden and MacNeice are on to the
kinds of attitude which can be struck by the English, whether
poets or not, in strange landscapes. They have chosen to stick to
an amateur and detached standing; as travelers they have kept
outside the ranks of explorers, old Etonians of the Peter Fleming
tradition, and Wordsworthian nature lovers. When, in the northern wilds, they came upon a real professional English traveler,
"handsome, sunburnt, reserved, speaking fluent Icelandic," they
were more amused than abashed. Auden, having contracted to do
a travel book on Iceland (he was drawn to that country because
of his Icelandic name and a childhood interest in the sagas),

spent the summer of 1936 on the island, at first alone and later in the company of MacNeice and other friends. Rejecting from the first the idea of the necessity to brood and moon over *ultima Thule,* or to indulge in romantic *poésie des départs,* he was rather at a loss how to begin. Iceland had been visited by other men of letters and had produced some great native prose. It offered to the view glaciers, waterfalls, geysers, a volcano, and many rocks coated with sphagnum moss. One traveled through it by bus (in which conveyance Icelanders are always sick, Englishmen never) or on horseback. Auden learned to ride, stayed at inns and farm-houses, and struggled to be offhand about the scenery. ("One waterfall is very much like another.") He soon succumbed to a certain "effect of travel, which is to make one reflect on one's past and one's culture from the outside." He had brought along a volume of Byron, and he began to cast into a variation of the *Don Juan* stanza, with light-verse freedom, the thoughts and part of the life-history of an English poet of twenty-nine, then isolated at the top of Europe, where modern roars and squawks penetrated but faintly. The "Letter to Lord Byron," which makes up five chapters of the book, is always a remarkable technical *tour de force,* and in spite of its tendency to slip into rather self-preening triviality, has its moments of insight. Through this disused Byronic stanza form, Auden once more helps to break up the limiting measures which have hardened around modern poetic expression, and which force poets into stock attitudes, usually of pomposity or gloom. This stanza can accommodate the casual mention of everyday experience, as an example written after Auden's return to England shows:

> Autumn is here. The beech leaves strew the lawn:
> The power stations take up heavier loads;
> The massive lorries shake from dusk till dawn
> The houses on the residential roads;
> The shops are full of coming winter modes.
> Dances have started at the Baths next door
> Stray scraps of MS strew my bedroom floor.

Louis MacNeice, a poet of Auden's time at Oxford, who has brought a special kind of North-of-Ireland talent into the younger

English group, joined the amateur expedition. Things went on much the same. The friends played rummy in the evening and traveled through the severe and ungrateful countryside by day. MacNeice's serious contributions to the book—three poems—do not suffer by comparison with Auden's fine introductory poem, "Journey to Iceland." His lighter contributions are extravagantly funny. The two noticed different things. The spectacle of a whale being torn to pieces by winches gave Auden "an extraordinary vision of the cold controlled ferocity of the human species." MacNeice was impressed by children singing "The Music Goes Round and Round" in their native tongue.

The authors have not shirked the factual side of their job. The book has maps, charts, and guidebook information on food, transportation, money, etc., as well as quoted accounts of historic events, a bibliography of books on Iceland, and a set of Icelandic proverbs. Nor have Icelandic arts and letters, or the character and habits of modern Icelanders, been neglected. The photographic illustrations are excellent.

A good many readers must still exist who hope that bleak landscapes have an elevating influence on the human spirit, who believe that the uplift element in glaciers must be considerable. To them this book will be a disappointment. It will also disappoint those who, in their secret heart of hearts, expect portentous statements from serious and gifted young poets. Auden and MacNeice often sound, it is true, a tiresome schoolboy note. Their continual determination not to be taken in by cant makes them sheer away from emotion. The "Last Will and Testament" at the end of the book, for example, spirals up through sheer brilliance into a region where only *Coterie-sprache* can breathe. On the other hand, it is a sign of health that both young men are capable not only of humor but of hilarity. And they never project individual fear and frustration out into current blanket hatreds. Their will and testament ends:

> We leave our age the quite considerable spark
> Of private love and goodness which never leaves
> An age, however awful, in the utter dark . . .
> And to the good who know how wide the gulf, how deep
> Between Ideal and Real, who being good have felt
> The final temptation to withdraw, sit down and weep,

We pray the power to take upon themselves the guilt
Of human action, though still as ready to confess
The imperfection of what can and must be built,
The wish and power to act, forgive and bless.

THE OXFORD BOOK OF
LIGHT VERSE (*1938*)

Some years ago, W. H. Auden, with a collaborator, produced an anthology designed to lure English schoolboys toward the forbidding subject of "poetry." Now, in the preface to *The Oxford Book of Light Verse*, which he has edited, he has set himself the task of proving why poetry has lost, in great measure, its power to express ordinary life and delight the general ear. The fault, he says, lies with the results of the Industrial Revolution, which broke up an agricultural society, moved people from their bases, made the division between classes sharper, and drove the poet into gloomy romanticism and into specialized groups of his own kind: "introspective, obscure, and highbrow." A good society, Auden concludes, is the only society which can survive, and a poet in such a society will be able to "write poetry which is simple, clear and gay; light and adult."

Long ago, from an entirely different point of view—that of the "pure artist"—Yeats gave much the same reasons for poetry's muddle and decline. Poetry, he said, flourished in "the hut and the castle." It is the middle classes, bred in strength by the Industrial Revolution, that have no appreciation of poetry's impact. From simple working people come folk songs, gay snatches of all sorts, chanteys, proverbs, and nursery rhymes. From levels of society where leisure allows a cultivated taste to flourish comes verse written with high skill: epigrams and various forms of verbal play. The middle classes, with skimpy standards and frightened, insecure taste, produce nothing but a great dislike for "vulgarity" and a passion for verse reeking of sentiment or sounding, in some vague way, uplifting and "noble."

Auden takes light verse to include verse "which is neither emotional nor obscure, but . . . casual in content, popular and

unpretentious in form, and easily understood." Light verse, he
adds, can be serious. (Eliot proves this with his early *Poems*,
although Auden does not mention the fact.) But light verse,
primarily, is to be enjoyed. To quote Yeats again: "Only that
which does not teach, does not cry out, does not persuade, does
not condescend, does not explain, is irresistible."

There is no doubt whatever that the poems in Auden's collections are irresistible. From Chaucer through Skelton and the
anonymous writers of lovely little carols, ballads, and rhymes
(how nice to see "Hey, diddle, diddle" appreciated!); from Shakespeare's and Ben Jonson's songs to Herrick and "Hudibras"; from
Marvell to Dryden ("London Bridge" comes in around here); from
Swift's verses on his death, that masterful combination of cultivated form and ordinary speech, to Gay, Pope, Burns, and Blake;
from a fine collection of rough Irish ballads on to Lamb, Landor,
Tom Moore, Byron, Barham, Hood, and Praed (who is said to
have influenced Pushkin), the lightness, the fancy, and the realism flow. Then, after an anonymous alphabetical song on the
Corn Laws, we are treated to the full nonsensical talents of Lear,
Carroll, and W. S. Gilbert. Auden has long been enthusiastic
about American folk songs; he includes unhackneyed Negro spirituals along with "Casey Jones," "The Man on the Flying Trapeze,"
and "Frankie and Johnny" ("orally collected"). We get light verse
from unexpected people: Hardy, Lawrence, Housman, V. Lindsay
are printed near Yeats. The more professional modern writers of
gay rhyme have been omitted. The whole anthology is so completely clear of the musty, the pompous, the would-be, and the
hateful sides of mankind that it makes confidence in the human
breed mount. It would be fine to have a New Society to match it.

THE DOUBLE MAN (1941)

New life can come into an art only when that art becomes more
casual in tone. A shift in emphasis or a change in subject matter
does no good. A stuffy state of mind and a bigwig style will stifle
a poem about sharecroppers as quickly as a poem about peacocks
in the twilight. Once rigidity or efflorescence has set in, it is use-

less to try to escape the effects. Something else, completely different, must be done. Change must be sharp; the whole encumbered ground must be cleared, and this clearing can only be the direct result of an examination of conscience which brings humility.

Obscured as modern poetry has been by every kind of rhetorical curlicue, intellectual pretension, and spiritual gloom, the reaction had to be fundamental. W. H. Auden, in his new book, *The Double Man,* has cleared a lot away, including much of his former self. He returns to the nice, crisp, open beat of four-stress iambic lines and to the couplets of the letter in rhyme, and he has reduced modern wisdom (of which there is some) to the simple proposition that man is not perfect, or perhaps even perfectible; he must, however, keep going and try to do the best he can. Expecting the impossible of himself, and failing to achieve it, leads to dangerous self-contempt, panic, and despair.

In a rhymed letter to a trusted friend one can tell the truth, bring in many things not accessible otherwise to poetry, make a running comment upon the world and one's own soul without becoming pompous, examine the surroundings without pedantry. Auden does all these things in the "New Year Letter (1940)," of some seventeen hundred lines, addressed to Elizabeth Mayer. The poem is followed by a series of notes taking up more pages than the poem itself. These notes will undoubtedly irritate readers eager for a smooth flow of poetry as such, especially since some of the notes are irreverent. Believers in man's sublimity and the social optimists alike are in for a few jolts here. Auden ranges over embryology, psychiatry, anthropology, history, metaphysics, sociology, and modern views on the nature of the universe. He quotes Chekhov, Henry James, Margaret Mead, the authors of *Middletown,* Sören Kierkegaard, Kafka, Rilke, Wolfgang Köhler, Thucydides, and Carl Jung, among others. That it is a real enjoyment to read these notes and relate them to Auden's text will not count, perhaps, to outraged specialists in the various fields. Other people will not care for the thought of the poet as student, notebook in hand, and not wrapped in a prophetic garment.

Quite apart from its sources and philosophy, "New Year Letter" is a pleasure to read. It is full of the aphorisms proper to, and charming in, the rhymed couplet. It runs to straight, unadorned nouns and verbs, so that the occasional epithet comes as an accent and surprise. The poem has two climaxes of real power. One of these is a lyric burst, an actual emotional passage of a kind Auden has not up to now been given to.

A group, chiefly of sonnets, "The Quest," follows. It is in Auden's former manner and sounds a little composed. A short epilogue and prologue to the volume continue the cool, reticent sincerity into which Auden seems steadily to be working.

FOR THE TIME BEING (1944)

Even before *The Double Man*, Auden had changed from a closed dogmatic materialist belief toward an open moral faith. The general effect of the two long poems in his new book—"The Sea and the Mirror: A Commentary on Shakespeare's *The Tempest*," and the title poem, written in the form of a Christmas oratorio—is one of restlessness under control, of talent steadied and enlarged. The two poems, taken together, constitute the most minute dissection of the spiritual illness of our day that any modern poet, not excluding Eliot, has given us.

We are unfortunately used to writers who repeat their pattern, from youth to age, without deviation. They begin as young sheep or young goats and end up as old sheep or old goats. Americans are suspicious of "conversions." In a country where the strongest religious coloring is that of romantic Evangelicalism, we associate conversion with revivalism and expect a spiritual change to be an emotional reaction, slightly hysterical in character. Auden's change occurred on a non-Romantic level, in a region where the beliefs of Christianity and the proofs of modern psychological knowledge meet. Auden has taken less time than Eliot, indulged in fewer gestures, put less emphasis on ritual, in his search for a religious attitude. A streak of Yorkshire common sense, underneath his complexity, has kept the younger man on the side of simple feeling and away from elaborate orthodoxy.

"The Sea and the Mirror" deals with Shakespeare's *Tempest* characters after the ending of their play. Each character finds himself, but only according to his original capacity. Nothing whatever happens to the truly evil or silly people. As it turns out, the thoughts of the reformed intriguer, Alonso, King of Naples, are more interesting and more poignantly expressed than the thoughts of the reformed magician, Prospero. Alonso's letter to Ferdinand, on the delights and dangers of power, is one of the high points in Auden. The speeches are a little museum of form: one in *terza rima* is followed by a sestina, a sonnet, and a ballade. The long concluding speech of Caliban to the audience, written in a prose which combines certain characteristics of the later Henry James with baroque periods comparable to the prose of Donne and Bossuet, has an eloquence that one would have supposed a modern poet incapable of producing; and the analysis, in this speech, of the modern spiritual *malaise* restores to literature a subject long neglected under the present-day pressure of "rational" thought. The lengthy, exact, intricate, and many times terrifying recital is a perfect answer to those advocates of "useful" poetry who would reduce all expression to a mechanical base. There appear to be qualities in the human spirit, even now, that require a full rhetorical diapason for complete expression.

The oratorio, "For the Time Being," deals in a different way with the problem of modern spiritual estrangement and offers a way out through faith and suffering. Auden here has undertaken a technical problem of large proportions. He is trying to get formal poetry working on a larger than usual scale and to link it to music and the human voice, from both of which it has been long alienated. He has gone back to the one big musical form where English poetry has been successfully employed. The oratorio, under Handel, succeeded in enlarging the English song into choral magnificence. Auden gets much variety and dramatic contrast into his own work. Its lyric passages are moving, its satire (as in the Herod speech) sharp, its philosophic passages (the Simeon meditation) articulate, its humor sometimes lively and sometimes appropriately horrifying. We again realize how limited and barren the field of modern poetry has become when we are presented with such a number of human thoughts and emotions, boldly designed and arranged to set one another off. This elaborate work has an interest, an intellectual validity, an emotional range so rare that it should be read with the seriousness and

attention it deserves. That it has been seriously composed, as
opposed to being thrown together for effect, is as evident after a
tenth reading as after a first.

THE COLLECTED POETRY OF
W. H. AUDEN (1945)

A moment occurs (or should occur) when the growing artist is
able to bequeath his tricks to his imitators. The mature writer
rejects the treasured "originality" and the darling virtuosities of
his apprenticeship in art, as well as the showy sorrows and joys
of his apprenticeship to life, often just in time. "How they live at
home in their cozy poems and make long stays in narrow comparisons!" Rilke once said, speaking of the run of versifiers who
never change or grow. Once youth's embroidered coat is cast
aside, what is left? Only imagination, ripened insight, experience, and the trained sense of language, which are usually
enough.

The Collected Poetry of W. H. Auden is a sizable volume for a
poet born in 1907 to have credited to him in 1945. Auden, it has
for some time been apparent, has succeeded Eliot as the strongest
influence in American and British poetry. And he has managed,
in this collection, by skillful arrangement and deletion, to present
himself to the reader as he exists at this moment. He does not
draw attention to his growing pains or take us step by step
through stage after stage of his development. He begins the book
with one of those poems ("Musée des Beaux Arts") which announced, a few years ago, the beginnings of his maturity—a
poem that seems as simply composed as a passage in conversation. It is not filled with Anglo-Saxon compression, or clogged
with modern apparatuses and machines, or trimmed with off-
rhymes. Earlier poems on his favorite subjects and in the special
manner of his youth are included in the book. But they never leap
out at us. The general tone is one of composure and simplicity, of
that ease wherein, for a time, a young master can rest.

The collection gathers up, fortunately, poems that have so far
been scattered in plays or books of prose. The sonnet to E. M.

Forster once served as the dedication for *Journey to a War,* written in collaboration with Christopher Isherwood. Other sonnets and a verse commentary come from the same volume. The fine "Journey to Iceland" is out of *Letters from Iceland,* written in collaboration with Louis MacNeice. Some choruses from plays turn up as separate poems, now with titles. The volume also contains two prose passages—the early "Letter to a Wound" and a "sermon" (from *The Dog Beneath the Skin*) entitled "Depravity." *For the Time Being* is reprinted complete, and there are several new poems.

What is the particular thread that runs through this collection, the clue to Auden's importance and power? In what way is his great gift different from Eliot's, and in what way is it of importance to Auden's contemporaries? Auden shares with Eliot a sense of his time. He is, however, much more exuberant, restless, sanguine, and unself-conscious than the older poet. And he is a natural dramatist in a degree surpassing Eliot. Eliot can dramatize his lyrics but rarely projects dramatic action with force. Auden dramatizes everything he touches. He is wonderfully effective with that most dramatic of lyric forms, the ballad. At the same time, his purely lyrical endowment is so deep and so natural that many of his songs sound as though they had been worked up at a moment's notice as improvisations. He can sing about as many things as the Elizabethans, and with the same disregard for the demands of the high literary line and the "refined" literary tone.

Eliot's importance is based on the fact that he had the sensitiveness and the melancholy foreboding to sense the general tragedy of his period when that tragedy had not yet impressed other observers. Auden, nearly twenty years Eliot's junior, stands farther from the shadow of the nineteenth and early twentieth centuries; he is more able, therefore, to deal with particulars. He is conscious of his physical surroundings down to the last contraption of "light alloys and glass"; conscious of his spiritual scene down to the last sob of modern self-pity, down to modern brutality's last threat. He has smashed the "taboo against tenderness," as someone has said; he is not afraid or ashamed either to laugh or weep. (How gloomy everyone was, after Eliot!) He knows what Rilke felt and foresaw, what Kierkegaard rebelled

against, what modern psychiatry has plumbed. He is not ignorant
of facts or clumsy in dealing with them. He is able to absorb and
speak of any item in the extraordinary crowd of objects and techniques he finds on all sides. He is able to define and present a
range of ideas, passions, compulsions, manias, anxieties, fears,
and intuitions that at present float about, only half-perceived by
many people and most poets, in our intellectual and emotional
climate. He is at once able to act and to imagine, to formulate and
interpret.

Behind him stand exemplars he acknowledges—Rilke and
Henry James, Freud, the Symbolists and post-Symbolists, and
Surrealism at its most effective. Part of the excitement in reading
the volume through derives from the fact that we are dealing with
a poet one of whose inner urges will always be to transcend himself, that we are reading the work of one who is still a young man,
so that there will be more to come.

THE AGE OF ANXIETY (1947)

A healthy and civilized poetry should be able to express anything.
It should be varied, comprehensive, and flexible. Experiments in
the larger poetic forms have in our period lagged far behind
experiments in poetic texture—experiments, that is, in language
as such. Modern poets have been haunted by the now completely
outdated formal poetic play. Shakespearean drama has cast a
particularly strong spell over poets writing in English. The nag-
ging belief that somehow the poetic drama could be restored to
its former immense prestige has hampered the most gifted of
contemporaries. Even Eliot and Auden have succumbed to the
temptation to tinker with decrepit dramatic machines. Recently,
however, Auden has given up these attempts and has applied
himself, singlehanded, to the task of creating new semi-dramatic
structures. He has already written an oratorio. His new work, *The
Age of Anxiety,* bears the subtitle "A Baroque Eclogue." In this
long poem, a series of conversations, dramatic monologues, and
occasional songs, he tries to crystallize to some degree the fluidity
and complexity of modern character, and at the same time, as a

dramatic poet should, to stylize the commonplace, everyday scene and event.

The dilemmas of the romantic hero, fighting it out against Fate, are no longer fully satisfying or evocative to a modern audience. In a period when values are uneven, when motives are warped and masked, when the citizenry does not know exactly who it is or where it is, a poetic form is called for that combines short surveys of the situation at large with detailed inquiries into individual human types. An eclogue, as any professor will tell you, is a pastoral poem in the form of a conversation—pastoral and primitive in the time of Theocritus, and highly sophisticated during the eighteenth century. Auden's adjective "baroque" suggests the fanciful. His eclogue, far from being pastoral, starts with a conversation in a city bar, goes off into a dream sequence, proceeds (with dialogue, monologue, and song) to the apartment of the single female character, and finally frays out in the subway and the city streets. Practically nothing happens, yet a good many matters are analyzed by means of that poetic "reason" in which the happy guesses of the imagination, as well as the oddest suggestions of fancy, play a part. While his characters occupy themselves in giving various answers to their own questions (Why do I feel so queer? Is it the general situation or is it I? Who are all these other people, and are they baffled in the same way that I am baffled?), Auden takes on a subsidiary task—to point up and freshen the language with which they communicate with one another. Avoiding the more threadbare English metres, he works in a closely stressed line reminiscent of Anglo-Saxon prosody. He also uses alliteration with great vigor and freedom, exploring its more elegant as well as its massive and powerful possibilities. Again, he makes use, when the occasion requires, of archaic and obsolete words, not as a casual affectation but in order to weight, diversify, and amuse, and he deals easily with the American vernacular: witness his superb stylization of the radio commercial. Here experimental language, rescued from the useless doldrums into which the Surrealists have forced it, is restored as a useful tool in the serious poet's equipment.

This modern eclogue is clearly transitional, but by intention, not by chance. And the characters never lapse into the dullness of allegory. They are symbols, but with enough admixture of human

reality to make them interesting and plausible. The general tone
of the poem is that of high comedy. Auden is not attempting to
plumb the deepest labyrinths of the heart and mind. He is making
a survey of contemporary manners and morals on the basis of
what he considers the highest sort of ideal—the Christian. But he
allows crosslights from other ideals to fall upon his scene: see
Rosetta's speech on Israel, for example.

Auden has now reached a middle period, in which it is difficult
for any poet not to indulge in self-repetition or self-parody. He
has largely managed to dodge both these traps. His inventive
powers, both in language and form, are still enormous, and it is
delightful to watch him go about the task of revivifying old rules.
Assonance, consonance, alliteration, an ancient, closely stressed
rhythm—all these poetic procedures he frees from the books of
rhetoric, so that they again function in living poetry.

POETS OF THE ENGLISH LANGUAGE (1951)

The study of English literature as a respectable branch of learning
is comparatively new. It came into being in a faltering fashion,
making its appearance at Oxford as late as 1893, after having
been put into practice at the new University of London and in
Scotland. Once accepted, the new subject had to fight free from
one hampering method after another. First it had to escape from
the dry procedures of German philology, then from an equally
arid habit among English professors of erecting barriers between
"literary periods" and of implacably tracking down influences and
sources. This methodology was abandoned, under Professors
Saintsbury and Raleigh, only to be succeeded by teaching habits
that substituted charm for insight, so that the central qualities of
English poetry and prose were more or less obscured by masses of
anecdotes and chitchat about the lives, domestic problems, wives,
friends, and dogs and cats of this author and that. During the
twenties of this century, the emphasis shifted to the texts themselves—a shift all to the good, except that such direct analysis
soon became extreme. In the case of verse, the poem was removed
so far from any contact or contamination (even from the poet

who had written it) that it became a sort of laboratory specimen, and its dissection, in some scholarly quarters at least, was pursued with the relentless fervor usually allotted to a delicate, purely manual operation, like the boning of a shad.

The critical and scholarly need that has gradually become pressing and obvious, as psychology, anthropology, and a freshly ventilated sense of history have begun to crowd in upon the study of literature from every side, is one of relation and comparison. Although the subject of comparative literature has grown in importance, the relationship between literatures of different cultures and languages, between literature and the changes of history and opinion, of morals and manners, and between literature and its sister arts does not show up in many commentaries or textbooks. *Poets of the English Language* in five volumes, edited by W. H. Auden and Norman Holmes Pearson, is a pioneer effort to place poetry in the midst of history and life, and to connect it to other arts with which it shares a common creative source. The two editors, both scholars and teachers and one of them a major poet, are uniquely fitted for a task that involves revaluation as well as valuation. The selections range from the Middle Ages through modern times, but the editors have wisely sidestepped controversy by not touching upon the work of living contemporaries. The first volume, "Langland to Spenser," brings English poetry through Middle English (which, as the editors remark, was close to being the language of a tribe) to the beginning of the "Shakespearean poetic temper," when English became the language of a nation. Volume II, "Marlowe to Marvell," deals with the poetic situation throughout the English Renaissance into the Baroque era; Volume III traces the story through a century of tremendous upheaval and change, from Milton to Goldsmith; Volume IV, "Blake to Poe," covers the early and great Romantics; and Volume V, "Tennyson to Yeats," copes with the Victorians and their successors, down to the year 1914. The introductions to the volumes describe, often with great originality, not only the central emotional, intellectual, and power drives of succeeding eras but take into account the more subtle climates of opinion, feeling, and taste that pervaded this or that period. These prefaces, moreover, emphasize the fact that while literature is produced by human beings, it is also touched by the mystery of the

Muse—frequently breaking into new life and form just as history has, as it were, stopped happening; or at a moment when a culture seems so exhausted that nothing in the circumstances hints at the possibility of a renewal of imaginative life.

The editors' important achievement of relating poetry in English to European, British, and American history at large, over six centuries, has been accomplished with a minimum of machinery. Each volume opens with a calendar, one side of which lists poetry, work by work, while a neighboring column establishes the general background, event by event. This calendar, although it often bears out certain Spenglerian hypotheses, lacks any Spenglerian concealed pressures. To study its exposition of coincidences, time lags, and unexpected linkages is a delightful occupation. Here is French Impressionist painting showing up in the same year (1863) as Taine's "determinist" history of English literature and a year after Meredith's *Modern Love*. Here is Frazer's *The Golden Bough,* published in 1890, along with the first series of Emily Dickinson's *Poems*. Nobel invents dynamite in 1867, the year of *Peer Gynt* and Mark Twain's *The Jumping Frog;* and Freud's *Die Traumdeutung* announces a new century, in 1900, contemporaneously with *Sister Carrie* and Stedman's *An American Anthology*. The tragic year 1914 has Joyce's *Dubliners,* Stein's *Tender Buttons* and Frost's *North of Boston* to its credit.

As many long works as possible are given in their entirety— *Antony and Cleopatra* and *Samson Agonistes,* for example. And the editors have not turned away from poems bristling with difficulty, such as Hopkins' "The Wreck of the Deutschland." The unexpected and the neglected (for instance, the hymns of the Methodist Revival, and the light and nonsense verse with which the Victorians worked off some of their unconscious conflicts) appear beside the "standard" pieces of the English poetic repertoire, while the poetry of two great "mad" poets, John Clare and Christopher Smart, brilliantly set off the works of their more reasonable contemporaries. Neglected Americans—Thoreau, Melville, and Longfellow as a translator—are given their just due. E. Talbot Donaldson has been called in to write a note on Middle English, and Auden contributes a short survey of English prosody that is certainly as valuable to the lover of poetry in English as a knowledge of musical form is to an amateur of music. *Poets of the English Language* is a peculiarly modern achievement. It could have been produced only in our time, and it is a work for which we should be grateful and of which we should be proud.

THE SHIELD OF ACHILLES (1955)

In the fall of 1935, Auden and Spender, along with C. Day Lewis, formed (in spite of basic differences) a triad in the minds of British and American readers, because of a shared Oxford background and an awareness of poetry's "social" obligation. In troubled times, they had taken to heart Wilfred Owen's dictum that the duty of a poet is to "warn." The refreshment brought into the poetry of the thirties by these gifted and serious young men was strongly apparent from the beginning; this new "poetry of conviction" immediately began to influence contemporaries young and old. And at the very start it was evident that Auden was the versatile satirist and Spender the "romantic" of the group. These two were, in fact, so much each other's opposite that they acted as mutual foils, and their roles have not altered with the years.

Auden, in his latest volume, *The Shield of Achilles*, continues to treat his material with the incisive wit that is capable of serving the most serious ends. He is ceaselessly restless and inquisitive, inexhaustibly inventive, full of curious ancient and modern erudition, filled with strong likes and dislikes, and still profoundly involved with modern dilemmas, although his emphasis has shifted from political to moral and spiritual areas. He has a sense of evil as well as a sense of history, and has developed what could be called a sort of modern "occasional" poem that becomes a commodious carrier not only for his general ideas, predilections, and frankly expressed prejudices but for some genuine, though often wryly revealed, feeling. His "Bucolics," included in the volume, are examples of this delightful form, which should become valuable to poets at large as a great change and relief from the rather hampering dramatic monologue and the verbal showpiece composed on the subject of nothing. Always a master of the vernacular, Auden, an American citizen since 1946, has recently

managed to shift his diction and conceits close to the main stream
of American humor—a supremely difficult feat for a native
Briton. It is as though he had been able to tap some common
source of wild and irrepressible comedy. Purists bothered by
Auden's "unserious" side should be impressed by the sense of
measure and the religious intuitions (humane and without a
trace of gloom) in the sequence "Horae Canonicae." Auden, at
forty-eight, not only has fulfilled promises but keeps on renewing
them.

THE CRITERION BOOK OF MODERN AMERICAN VERSE (1957)

Auden, as editor, wisely casts a wide net into American poetry of
the last fifty years—a net, moreover, in which the meshes arc not
too coarse and not too fine. He does not draw back from talents
that are small but pure, and the inclusion of such talents gives the
book a density that is interesting and valuable. For Auden, it is a
poet's sincerity and intensity that count. The poets are arranged
chronologically, and the list, because it begins with Edwin Arlington Robinson (1869–1935), to whom fame came late, can include two pre-moderns, Stephen Crane and Trumbull Stickney,
who died young. From Gertrude Stein, happily considered as the
poet she was, through Anthony Hecht (b. 1922), Auden marshals
material that in one way or another deserves mention, but there is
nothing routine or formal about his choice. The experimentalists
appear along with poets working in conventional form; the
writers of light verse complement their more serious kin; many
neglected figures are given their due, while a few inflated reputations are gently cut down to size. Auden leaves out Eliot and himself, and while we understand the underlying tact involved (since,
in the broader sense, both men can be considered American),
both omissions constitute a major loss.

In his introduction, Auden points out several differences that,
he has found, distinguish American poets from their European
counterparts. In the first place, Americans tend to think of themselves as unique individuals and not as members of a professional
class or brotherhood; secondly, since Americans are more loosely

related to tradition, they can more easily break free from it. As a result, American poets differ greatly from one another even within a single generation or "school." The danger of this sense of individuality, Auden goes on to say, shows up occasionally in strain and overearnestness; the danger is not of writing like everybody else but of crankiness and a final parody of one's own manner. In a footnote Auden speaks of "the undeniable appearance in the States during the last fifteen years or so of a certain literary conformity, of a proper and authorized way to write poetry," but he refuses to link this tendency to any one cause, such as the role of patron to poet, which American colleges and universities began to take on during those years. He realizes that several factors have joined to produce poetic conformity at mid-century. "The modern" has now reached the officially accepted stage in every art, and with official acceptance a noticeable slowing down of impetus and stiffening of method is sure to take place. Poetry, in America as elsewhere, has not escaped this process.

HOMAGE TO CLIO (1960)

W. H. Auden's latest collection of poems proves his continuing power as an international poetic force. Auden assumed the position of leader of a poetic movement early in the thirties, while he was still a student at Oxford, and in 1939 he finally chose America as his permanent base of operation, where he became, at thirty-nine, an American citizen. The *chef d'école*, a usual phenomenon on the Continent, is rare in England and even rarer here. Our literary community has been, and continues to be, so loosely organized that a poetic forerunner or innovator may either fall into sudden neglect (Whitman) or take to such eccentric ways that he sacrifices prestige (Pound). The poet as leader must have convictions as well as originality, and he must have the ability to pass on a fair proportion of what he knows or has invented. And so his audience narrows, for his students and disciples will for the most part be workers in his own field. Nowadays he does not have to be physically accessible, as Mallarmé made himself during his evenings in the Rue de Rome, but he must be

fluent and industrious enough to display his ideas regularly in
print, in prose as well as verse, so that any alteration in his
method or change in his point of view can be freely indicated.
It is a position that can be extremely wearing. At present, in a
free, literate society, a teaching poet's followers, by the weight of
their numbers and the intensity of their attention, can exhaust
the very powers they admire. Their poet is in constant peril of
being battered, psychically and spiritually, into unrecognizable
shape or of being egged on to performances that are not natural
to his gifts.

Auden, now fifty-three, has withstood these pressures for many
years. His new book shows no corruption of subject, distortion of
aim, or souring of emotion. The bravura of his early work has to
a great extent disappeared, but the technical dexterity remains
unfailing, and his new poems, often written in the simplest and
most seemingly artless of forms, continue to advance from point
to point with satisfying skill. Auden has not suffered, moreover,
from that constriction of interest that often afflicts poets, like
other human beings, as they move from youth to age. He has kept
in touch with what is going on, and he has remained cool, sensible, and good-tempered without losing hold of his talent for
diagnosis and interpretation. He credits Clio, the Muse of History, with secrecy and silence, but he is more aware than many of
his contemporaries of what she has already said and what she is
at the moment preparing to say. He has always been conscious
that he is living in the midst of a historical and cultural situation
quite unlike any other, and he has kept on as a student of the
facts from which this situation stems. He is not afraid of being
light (it would be an unnaturally severe reader who could bring
a charge of frivolity against the series of clerihews at the end of
this volume) or official (he can write occasional verse that ex-
ceeds, in weight and meaning, its ostensible function). But it is
in his mastery of the dark and difficult theme that he continues to
show his full authority. The poems "Dame Kind," "An Island
Cemetery," and "Goodbye to the Mezzogiorno," and the prose
notes on personal love—shocking, profound, complex, and
warmly satiric, in turn—are new works from which the general
reader, as well as the student, can derive nourishment now and
for a long time to come.

CHARLES BAUDELAIRE
(1947)

A new translation, by Geoffrey Wagner, of a selection of Baudelaire's poetry, called *Flowers of Evil*, has recently appeared. Enid
Starkie, the English Baudelaire scholar, contributes an excellent
short introduction to the volume. But the disparity in quality
between Miss Starkie's prose and Mr. Wagner's verse is so great
that it is a puzzle how the two came together into book form.
Granted that certain insuperable obstacles to a feasible translation of Baudelaire into any language exist, it is still a disappointment to find Mr. Wagner making the most elementary blunders
in choice, in tone, and in detail. The volume is, moreover,
oddly lacking in the ordinary aids to the reader; it has no
pagination, no table of contents, no notes, and no index.

Baudelaire's vocabulary and atmosphere constitute, without
question, problems for translators. The vocabulary is filled with
those splendid French abstract nouns and substantives that
tend to come through into English sounding rather silly, and the
atmosphere, particularly that of his early work, is rather repellent
to Anglo-Saxon taste. It is the atmosphere of French Second-
Empire luxury, morbidity, and eroticism. Baudelaire was a master
of a whole rhetorical apparatus for evoking effects of horror
and lubricity. The workings of this stylistic machine are now
outmoded. And nothing is more tiresome than the reiterated
subject—so usual in the early Baudelaire—of woman as puppet,
as sinister idol of the alcove, or as erotic mannequin. Translators

are attracted, however, to Baudelaire's more overheated and
dated productions, and Mr. Wagner, no less than Arthur Symons
and other searchers in the field, has chosen proportionately more
poems from this side of Baudelaire's work than from any other.
Yet, as Miss Starkie points out, the figure of Baudelaire as dandy
and decadent has steadily diminished in this present century,
to be replaced by the concept of a man whose insights were
profound and valuable for a complex set of reasons. We now
recognize Baudelaire as the first poet who saw through the overweening pretensions of his time. He stripped man's nature
to its essentials, and he discovered, in an era when his contemporaries were still occupied with "rationalism" or with "romance,"
urban mankind's bitter loneliness and spiritual isolation. Baudelaire, as T. S. Eliot has said, learned everything for himself.
He went from the confines of his early physical excesses into
the streets of Paris; he drew portraits of the poor, the debauched,
the senile, the obsessed, and the mad in a manner as uncompromising as Daumier's. He depicted the houses, the rooms, the
roofs, the shuttered windows, and the chimney pots, and beyond
this he re-created the look and the feeling of those times of day
and of those turns of the seasons when the city's sadness is, as
it were, distilled and the full, cold mystery of existence leaks
through into our consciousness. These poems have the power to
hit us like a blow. They are scattered through his work, and
the beginner in Baudelaire needs guides to them. Mr. Wagner,
in making his choices, has merely gone through the collected
work and picked out a poem here and there, seemingly at
random. The thirty-eight selections in this volume represent
less than a quarter of Baudelaire's poetic output. To appropriate
the title *Flowers of Evil* for it seems odd to anyone who remembers
Baudelaire's careful sense of arrangement—"the inner architecture"—in his *Fleurs du mal*, in both its editions published during
his lifetime. Miss Starkie's biographical summary and her short
but penetrating analysis of the poet's present place in French
letters, combined with the French texts (here included) of the
poems, give this compilation a certain value, but the day when
Baudelaire's translators match his critics in sensitiveness and
understanding is yet to come.

JOHN BERRYMAN
(1964)

❦❦❦

John Berryman, in his new volume, 77 *Dream Songs* has discovered a method of escaping any touch or taint of the sublime
—a method compared to which Karl Shapiro's recent dislocations
and disguises are almost elementary. Berryman is out to get
language itself—to distort and maim it, not in the direction of
wit, as in Carroll and Joyce, but in the direction of funny
grammar and burnt-cork comedy. This reduction downward of
the one faculty that, we have been assured, marks us as human
(all other creatures being able to communicate only by a set
of signals) *does* bring the reader close to vertigo. Sometimes
Berryman seems to be giving us dialogue wherein amiable
animals (say, dogs or cats) are pulling human speech their
way—toward some totally disjunct and invertebrate set of noises.
These noises are not allowed to go very far, it is true; Berryman
quickly snaps back, after a line or two of pure jargon, into
various degraded styles of English (and "American"). Through
all this he uses a set stanza, a fluctuating but perfectly detectable
metre, and all manner of rhymes (some of these last very clever
indeed). These formalities, followed through in the midst of
linguistic chaos, alternately amuse and irritate. A more exasperat-
ing collection of verse has probably never been written; one
wishes somehow to intervene—to protect humble (and noble)

human speech from this heartless ingenuity, this desperate artificiality. Berryman's opinions are more conventional than one might at first suppose, his taste is Philistine, and he is hardly rebellious at all. He and his whole group of alter egos, as a matter of fact, sound sort of tired and resigned.

JOHN BETJEMAN

SLICK BUT NOT STREAMLINED,
edited by W. H. Auden (1947)

John Betjeman's *Slick But Not Streamlined* brings the reader up against some unexpectedly weighty considerations. Modern poetry, although filled with nostalgia of various kinds and degrees, is notably lacking in pathos. Pathos, it might be said, is an emotion derived from contemporary objects or contemporary experiences; it is not a yearning for the past. Modern poets have so firmly eliminated pathos from their work that the suspicion sometimes arises that they are incapable of experiencing it, that the modern sensibility has become so hardened and abstract that entire areas of emotional response are outside its range. We would not wish, certainly, for a return to the sentimental repining of early and middle Romanticism. Yet this lack of true pathos deprives modern verse of a whole set of emotional effects and reverberations. Betjeman has nevertheless made a serious and emotional contribution to the modern lyric, all the more surprising since every effort has been made by his American publishers to emphasize his lighter side. Even W. H. Auden, who has written an introduction to Betjeman's book, dwells lengthily on the poet's skill as a satirist and on his "theatrical" manner of presenting things. Satirist and wit Betjeman surely is, but a special kind of gravity underlies a good deal of his work.

Nothing is further from pathos than parody, which is Betjeman's manner of projection, and it is an unexpected experience to find him now and again pushing parody over into the region of pure feeling. (Gide observes somewhere in his *Journal* that aesthetic problems that will not yield to a frontal attack may sometimes be solved by oblique or outflanking methods.) Betjeman brings off his effects with the greatest deftness. He is capable of writing in the most glittering way about British middle-class mores; he is capable, too, of abruptly stepping into another dimension, where sensibility is all. Suddenly, we are in the midst of pathos before we realize what response is being demanded of us. Because Betjeman's interests are basically topographical and architectural, he goes directly toward visible and concrete symbols of middle-class pretensions and yearnings: churches and chapels, parsonages, suburbs, provincial gaslit towns and seaside lodgings, railways, viaducts, factories, tearooms, and hotels. He involves these various locales and structures in perfect replicas of nineteenth-century verse forms, not forgetting the hymn. But he matches form to feeling, rather than the other way around. So, instead of getting a stream of sly jokes and satirical cuts, we get poems whose high spirits and sharp observation are continually breaking off to admit the spirit of place and of character, the sadness of human beings and of things. The dangers in Betjeman's method are obvious. Some of his poems hang in a hair's-breadth balance between the success of sincerity and the failure of smartness. The tone of "The Arrest of Oscar Wilde at the Cadogan Hotel" is not quite a success. On the other hand, "Parliament Hill Fields" (a note of nostalgia, it must be admitted), "Death in Leamington," "Sudden Illness at the Bus-Stop," and the exquisitely satirical "Bristol and Clifton" are perfect examples of how emotion may be smuggled into the modern lyric without restricting its freedom or dulling its finish and point.

COLLECTED POEMS,
edited by Lord Birkenhead (1959)

Light verse, during the last fifty years, has come to be important in more ways than one. Its practice has provided a method of getting poetry (as Yeats put it) down from its stilts, ridding it of stiffness and pretentiousness, and forcing it to face up to contemporary reality. W. H. Auden, in his preface to *The Oxford Book of Light Verse*, which he edited in 1938, wrote a spirited defense of his subject. Poets major and minor, he remarked, given a settled and valued place in society, should be able "to express themselves in an easy manner, to use the speaking voice, and to use as their properties the images of their everyday life." The Industrial Revolution (by breaking the community of custom and belief) had, he held, made poets insecure, gloomy, and introverted. Yet in spite of everything, light verse in English not only survived but developed new resources, technical and otherwise, during the nineteenth century. Parody and satire ran side by side; after Praed's Regency *vers de société*, W. S. Gilbert extended the field in every direction, and Lewis Carroll and Edward Lear explored levels of fantasy and the subconscious. Writers of light and nonsense verse kept appearing, in bravura performances, until the end of the century (Kipling, Belloc, Chesterton, de la Mare), inventing unforgettable and semi-hypnotic metres and a fascinating new vocabulary as they went along.

A dividing line between light verse of pure wit (which tends to deal with topical subject matter, plays with language, and is rather heartless) and light verse with some emotional content has grown more definite in our time. Even in our day, when much form has dissolved, light verse in the first category is always written in the strictest form. The complication and finish of the metre, the structure of the stanzas, the rightness of the rhymes all contribute to the general effect; the sharper the wit the more impeccable the vehicle. Form may be parodied (as in Ogden Nash and William Plomer), but it must be acknowledged. In the second category, a little more leeway exists: certain kinds of satire, as in Osbert Sitwell, can override form, although even here a certain epigrammatic terseness and balance are usually kept.

That a poet writing light verse can open up areas of feeling that have become either suspect or taboo comes as an unexpected development in the contemporary situation. In England, John Betjeman, since the early thirties, has been producing light verse in which, very close to but not crossing the line of parody, he has revived a whole set of emotional attitudes that can only be called Victorian. His *Collected Poems,* compiled and with an introduction by Lord Birkenhead, have just been published in America, after having had an unprecedented success in England. There are special reasons for this British popularity: Betjeman has a deep and ineradicable love for Englishness—in architecture, religious belief (he is a practicing Anglican), habit, manner, and custom—wherever it is found, and in whatever outmoded or dilapidated manifestation. He mourns the disappearance and disfigurement of the countryside, but many of the encumbering and disfiguring works of man—villas, factories, railway lines— move his heart and stir his memory. He is quite openly nostalgic for a solidly Edwardian middle-class childhood; he is equally emotional about English virtues once generally practiced but at present held in little esteem. And he cherishes English eccentricity as well as English normality; all sorts of small, warped, and baffled lives rouse his pity and imagination.

His verse forms, elaborately varied, reproduce an entire set of neglected Victorian techniques, which he manipulates with the utmost dexterity and taste. His diction and his observation are delightfully fresh and original. And it is a pleasure to let down our defenses and be swept along by his anapaestic lines, with their bouncing unstressed syllables, and to meet no imperfect or false rhymes in the process; to recognize sentiment so delicately shaded, so sincerely felt, that it becomes immediately acceptable even to our modern sensibilities, grown used to the harsh, the violent, and the horrifying. We often, however, come upon a poem that brings us up short, to experience a melancholy, an irony that is close to Hardy or a pathos that is timeless. Betjeman has a passion for bells. To him they are a symbol of the ancient and unchanging; they remind him of worship and of death; they sound through his darkest moods (and he has them) of fear and self-revulsion; they center him in life. However light his means, his purpose is never trivial. His *Collected Poems* should attract American readers as they have already attracted British ones.

R. P. BLACKMUR

(1940)

CRXRXS

R. P. Blackmur, author of *The Expense of Greatness*, is a good critic because he is serious, and has both sensibility and intellectual subtlety. He has, it is true, in a marked degree, the faults of these virtues. His seriousness is often invalidated by the web of super-seriousness he tends to spin from it. His sensibilities are not always searching enough; he can hedge around with them, and miss the point, while using them with scientific precision. And his subtlety often enervates rather than reveals. He has, as well, extreme faults of style. It is important to deal with his virtues first, because they are the particular ones they are —rare at any time and practically extinct at the moment.

Although he can be completely wrong on matters situated on what he himself would call "the periphery," Blackmur is frequently beautifully right in matters situated at the center. He knows that a work of art is a complex product of human growth and suffering (although he does not quite manage to say this in his aphorism, "Death is the expense of life and failure the expense of greatness"). He is the direct opposite of the critic who throws off banal middle-class remarks to comfort a middle-class audience. He recognizes and admires "speed" in apprehension and expression, while he himself works with great patience and, sometimes, maddening slowness, around, above, and through his subject. He lugs in moral standards to strengthen his critical weight; but these really do not matter, because, as with all

59

sensitive critics, his reactions are at bottom instinctive. He knows what is serious even in American art; and there has been serious American art in spite of the tendency, at present, to push it back and keep it at folk level. Blackmur, fortunately, is the sort of person who instinctively knows that there is a difference between a lyric poem written by a great lyric poet and a Mother Goose song; between wrought-iron work of a high period and a well-made doorknob or frying pan; between Bach's B-Minor Mass and *Ballad for Americans;* between a song by, say, Hugo Wolf and the most beautiful folk song ever invented by anybody. He knows that the novels written by John Steinbeck, Richard Wright, Herman Melville, and Henry James differ greatly. He knows that "all things excellent are as difficult as they are rare." And he is the kind of person who would never be able to deny knowing all this.

Blackmur, however, has serious lacunae in his special knowledge. And he carries an impeding, almost crippling, amount of extra baggage in the form of a whole critical vocabulary taken over from the moral philosophy so popular in English and American universities since the last war. If Blackmur made a determined effort to throw out of his vocabulary such words as "synergical," "sordor," "anterior," "quotidian," and, most especially, "heuristic," it would be all to the good. The terms from moral philosophy, too, tend to reduce some of his passages to pure Swahili; the result of superimposing these terms on literary analysis is more befuddling than clarifying. And they are not native to Blackmur's cast of mind; when he lets himself go he tends to think in images. This philosophic apparatus, moreover, is manipulated, often, with a kind of swank unbecoming to a sincere critic.

As his perceptions, for some reason, are likely to be good or bad in alternation, his courage, too, often wavers. He can be courageously offhand and even—surprisingly—flip in dealing with obviously bad poets; on the other hand, he treads rather carefully, mincing every statement into the minutest segments, in order to get around saying something directly damning about someone who, by reason of established position or what not, is not quite attackable. Using his own methods alone, he can be triumphantly right and revealing, in the case of T. E. Lawrence (this essay, in spite of its almost impenetrable structure and style, is the best in the book), while remaining incomplete and even biased in the cases of Yeats and Hardy. He can be both wrong and right, as in the case of Emily Dickinson. Here he does stand up, with a good deal of spunk, for a decent edition of Dickinson's works. But on the other hand, because of what he does not take in, he misinterprets the reasons for her poetry; leaving out whole tracts of her circumstances, such as her psychic slavery to her father. He brings in James, Dostoevski, Gide, and Mann in discussing a novel by Frances Frost. On the other hand, he can write paragraphs of fine good sense and delicate analysis, such as the paragraph devoted to the proposition, "Assenting to experience is the basis of conviction."

A perusal of some intense, personal, non-philosophic criticism, of the sort contained, for example, in Flaubert's *Correspondance,* would do Mr. Blackmur a world of good. French criticism of all periods might help him to overcome the more annoying—to the reader—coils and tangles of his subtlety. But he is on the side of the angels, and only needs more impatience, more courage, and perhaps ten more years of varied experience and wider reading, to make him a critic of imposing stature and of the first order.

ELIZABETH BOWEN
(1939)

Modern fiction of the subtler kind when written by women is likely to depict at length the trouble resulting from unsuitable and complicated people falling in love. The stays and obstacles once provided by difference in social position, family feuds, missent letters, and trumped-up misunderstandings have narrowed into drama arising from the fact that the lovers have neuroses that do not match, are in love for the wrong reasons, in love too late or too soon, or are incapable of love at all. Elizabeth Bowen in her previous novels has described such combinations, and Colette has worked with them for years. Miss Bowen has also probed with great thoroughness into the reaction of sensitive children, sometimes the offspring of mismatings, thrown into situations of which they hold only one or two clues. *The House in Paris* successfully brought off an atmosphere of emotional tension, resulting when the past, present, and future converged on such a child, who was caught, between journeys, in rooms full of the tragedy to which he owed his being. *The Death of the Heart* turns on a girl of sixteen, the product of a misalliance, who, when introduced into the "edited life" of her half-brother's smart London household, throws upon it the full glare of her innocence, breaks through its surface, and shows the lack of human feeling on which it is based.

Miss Bowen's young Portia Quayne is the daughter of a late second marriage, following an impulsive liaison, between a middle-aged conservative Englishman and a silly but warm-hearted widow. The first Mrs. Quayne with rather mean nobility divorces her husband and casts him off. Mr. Quayne, cut loose from his pleasant country moorings, is forced to live shabbily on the Riviera with his new family. After his death and that of Portia's mother, his son Thomas takes the child into his home, knowing that his father wanted some settled, decorous English experience for her. Portia, still feeling grief for her mother, enters a household built up with great taste and care by Anna, Thomas' wife. Everything in the exquisite house overlooking the park—the aquamarine curtains, the furniture rubbed "so that you can see ten feet into the polish," the ritual of beautiful food, the series of delightful effects—depends upon Anna. Even the family friend—called St. Quentin and a novelist—is choice and seems picked to match the wallpaper. Portia's brother, sunk in the depths of passionate cravings which marriage has not solved, is Anna's. And Eddie, the neurotic, charming young hanger-on, to whom Portia gives the full weight of her innocent affection, is Anna's—not her lover, but her amusement and her foil. It is Anna who at once instinctively ridicules the child, as she ridicules anyone of awkward human worth. Portia, learning of an ultimate betrayal, runs first to Eddie, who of course, although he has worked off some of his warped tenderness on her, rejects her; then to Major Brutt, another misfit in Anna's *décor*. Major Brutt telephones the house and tells Thomas that Portia demands that they come to some decision about her. In a masterfully done scene the three disabused adults—Anna, Thomas, and St. Quentin—thrash the matter out at the dinner table. ("This evening the pure in heart have simply got us on toast.") They come to a decision. They send a servant, Mrs. Matchett, Portia's only confidante in the household, to fetch Portia back in a taxi, as one would send for a lost parcel.

Miss Bowen has elsewhere spoken of "the limitations of English narrative prose, with its *longueurs* and conventions dangerous to truth." In her novels she has taken every precaution to reduce these conventions to a minimum. The strokes come close, and every stroke tells. Miss Bowen is particularly good at reflecting one character in another, always making it clear that some people see things partially while others take in every detail.

Matchett, the self-contained upper servant, with her toughened sympathy and snobbery and her pride of the good artisan, sees everything. Eddie sees everything—in his way—and himself, "at once coy and insolent," only too well. Matchett can sum people up. Of the "sacrificing" first Mrs. Quayne she says: "I couldn't care for her; she had no nature"; of Anna: "Oh, she has her taste and dearly loves to use it. Past that she'll never go." Eddie says of Anna: "She loves to make a tart out of another person. She'd never dare to be a proper tart herself." Thomas has an occasional moment of insight into the society about him; "self-interest, given a pretty gloss." But Portia, not yet absorbed into "the guilty plausibility of the world," sees more than everything. She detects the impossibility of a natural human relationship between these people who write letters, go to dinner parties, talk at tea—always "stalking each other." She watches "thoroughly"; she tries to shake some human response out of Eddie; she importunes; she nags with the implacable fury of first love. At the end she gives the show away to simple, kind Major Brutt. "Anna's always laughing at you. She says you are quite pathetic. . . . And Thomas thinks you must be after something. They groan at each other when you have gone away. You and I are the same."

Miss Bowen's talent is so rich and so searching, and this novel stands so far outside the class of novels which resemble packaged goods put up for the trade, that one is tempted to give her nothing but praise. She sees deeply, but not widely enough. Corruption has not lately entered the class of which she writes; the heart is not dying in these people; it never lived in them. And her tone, too keyed up, never lets down for a moment; the *longueurs* are deleted to such an extent that they are missed. Beautifully done descriptions of times of day and the weather edge the action—to a tiresome degree. The backgrounds for emotions are chosen with care; one, an empty seaside boarding-house on a Sunday morning, is almost unbearably appropriate. Miss Bowen can cook the vulgar English to the same crispness to which she treats their betters. But *The Death of the Heart* is too packed, too brilliant, for its own good. What Miss Bowen lacks is a kind of humility. She has forgotten more than many novelists ever knew, but what Turgenev, for example, knew, and was chary of expressing, she cannot quite deal with. Once in a while the reader hears the accent of self-satisfaction, if not display, in the novelist. But for all that, *The Death of the Heart* deepens our view of the horrors experienced by open innocence up against a closed world.

C. M. BOWRA

(1949)

The scholar cannot always be trusted to be fair to a poet's outer work or inner aspirations, particularly when scholar and poet are contemporaries. For although the percentage among Ph.D.s (or their equivalent) of those who hate, despise, and distrust imaginative literature is surely small, there is, nevertheless, a large proportion of scholarly critics who would twist and transform the poet's work or intention into something nearer to a doctorate's desire. Condemnation of the poet on rational grounds is fairly common, and learned writers, at their most meddling and obtuse, will even step into the poet's place and rewrite his poem. The poet is, therefore, at times as badly served by the scholar as by the man in the street, and this is a pity, because the scholar, however unimaginative, at least knows history and can remember how crudely poets have been served by their contemporaries in the past, whereas the ordinary citizen, as he recoils from a work of the imagination, believes he does it for the first time and credits himself not only with tremendous common sense but with tremendous originality.

C. M. Bowra, whose new volume of essays concerned with modern poetry is entitled *The Creative Experiment,* is a scholar —Warden of Wadham College, Oxford, since 1938, and Oxford's Professor of Poetry since 1946. The book is a sequel to *The Heritage of Symbolism* (1943), wherein Bowra discussed, with much learning and liberality of approach, the post-Symbolist poets

Valéry, Rilke, Aleksandr Blok, and William Butler Yeats. In the new volume, he deals with men whose experiments with form, content, and language belong to a later period—the first half of the twentieth century. Two elements are outstanding in Bowra's treatment of his subjects. In the first place, he is so sympathetic to their aims that he often becomes belligerent about the essential rightness of their methods. In the second place, he is a linguist, with a broad knowledge of European literature in a variety of languages. Because of this breadth of choice, he is non-provincial and fitted to combat the suspicion, widely held in America, that modern poetry is a conspiracy composed entirely of writers who are members of the English-speaking world. The poets whom Bowra here presents as fruitful innovators are Constantine Cavafy, an Alexandrian Greek born in 1868; Guillaume Apollinaire (de Kostrowitsky), of polyglot origin but a Parisian by choice; the Russians Mayakovsky and Boris Pasternak; the Andalusians García Lorca and Rafael Alberti; and T. S. Eliot, British subject but an American by birth.

Bowra understands both the historic and the poetic processes. That action brings on reaction, that a stiffened convention immediately creates the need for the breaching of that convention are the facts that hold true in history as well as in aesthetics. Poetry must continually change, since it is close to the stream of life, which cannot for a moment remain stagnant, and it must change with increasing swiftness, and with a complete disregard for the past, in periods—like our own—of unceasing and shifting pressures. Light alloys have replaced cast iron; people no longer decorate their rooms (except in fun) with copperplate engravings of Landseer's dogs; young ladies no longer play "A Maiden's Prayer" on cottage pianos. Modern art is firmly based on a new sensibility. The aim of modern poetry, as of the other arts of our time, is, Bowra says, not to simplify or explain, not to soothe, console, or "give an ultimate sense of harmony," not to teach or exhort, but simply "to present." And this problem of presentation, he points out, is one that must be settled not theoretically but according to the circumstances in which the individual poet finds himself.

Conservative poets cannot cope with the situations of a period in which codes are breaking down, and experimental poets, too, sometimes make mistakes—Marinetti, for example, with his worship of power as embodied in the machine. But for the last fifty years there has been a flow of modern vitality only in the experimentalists. Whether or not an experimenter manages to keep to his chosen track or is catastrophically derailed by his temperament or his times depends upon a thousand contributing factors, ponderable and imponderable. Bowra follows the revolutionary and tragic career of Mayakovsky with the same understanding that he gives to the more pliable Pasternak. He emphasizes Apollinaire's rare power to absorb the modern world with joy instead of rejecting it with loathing, and he brings out two virtues often overlooked in Eliot—his exquisite ear, and his insistence upon dramatic balance as well as intellectual content. Bowra's exegesis of "The Waste Land," by the way, is the most nearly complete and rewarding of any written by Eliot's contemporaries.

Bowra is a good critic because he understands not only the aesthetic process (what the poet sets out to do, and how he does it), insofar as it can be understood, but also the aesthetic experience (what the sympathetic reader receives from the poem). And he is on the poet's side, since he realizes what infinite and inexhaustible vitality, spiritual and mental, is required in order that, in our time, as in any other, "the maximum of truth and of poetical effect" may be secured.

THE BRITISH IN BRIEF

LAWRENCE DURRELL (1960)

Lawrence Durrell has described how his collision with Henry Miller (and Surrealism) in Paris in the late thirties freed his emotions and his gift for language. He soon found his subject —the Mediterranean littoral, a region that has attracted writers and artists from the beginnings of Romanticism to our own day. Durrell has no fear of being a Romantic. Most of these *Collected Poems* (chosen from seven earlier books) evoke with full poignance ancient and modern moments of time and spirits of place. The impressions tend to slip away and evaporate, however; Durrell's convictions are floating ones, and his seductive verbal brilliance often frays out in a rather irresponsible way. He has intervals of sounding like a highly suggestible and articulate lotus-eater, as well as intervals when his intransigence of thought and feeling takes on a rather ugly satiric edge. But at their best these poems have both vividness and vivacity.

ROY FULLER (1958)

One would think that truthtelling was rigidly confined to the young. As a matter of fact, a good many difficult and complicated truths have been uttered during the postwar period by poets of the war and prewar generations. Geoffrey Moore brings this out when he speaks, in "Poetry To-day," of the poetry of Roy Fuller, a member of the group of Englishmen who began to write during the war. Fuller's recent *Brutus's Orchard* is a book of the utmost technical distinction, but the reader is soon made aware that he is being spoken to by a poet with a firm sense of life's tragic ironies, great and small—by one who can detect, through everyday appearance, the stain left upon existence (to use a thoroughly "large" figure) by "chaos and old night." The illusion of actual face-to-face speech is very strong from the first page to the last, and the details are so sharply indicated that one is drawn without difficulty through image and symbol to concept and conclusion, while the development of theme and of emotion gains by Fuller's habitual understatement. There are no disguised trivialities here; Fuller is dealing not only with the world of modern man but with the heart of experience and the terror and mystery of life. The volume, beautifully produced and printed, certainly stands as a manifestation of modern poetry in English in full complex vigor, and as far as truthtelling is concerned, the young have an example to emulate.

ELIZABETH JENNINGS (1956)

A Way of Looking, by Elizabeth Jennings, which won the 1956 Somerset Maugham Award, is the first collection by this young English poet to appear in America. Miss Jennings' cast of mind is speculative and contemplative to what sometimes seems a dangerously abstract degree. For it is the concrete that gives life to poetry, as Yeats spent a lifetime in asserting—the generalized idea must be meshed with the particular object or event, and emotion must be the beginning of vision—and it is the abstract that brings in stiffness, coldness, and artificiality. But Miss Jennings, it turns out, is really less concerned with the abstract than with the essential. The thread that ties her thought to her surroundings is often very nearly invisible, but it is always there. And however slightly connected with the physical world her poetry may appear to be, it never falsifies or bypasses the facts. It is not easy to grasp Miss Jennings' work at a first reading, because of her compression and simplicity—qualities we are not used to. A second reading helps to bring out her musical quality —everywhere present—as well as her meaning.

JAMES KIRKUP (1954)

At a time when an almost unrelieved mannerism and melancholy have taken hold of mid-century poetry, it is refreshing to come upon a book of lyrics which shows that "variety and range" may still exist within the mind and temperament of one individual. James Kirkup's *A Spring Journey and Other Poems* of 1952–1953 is the sixth collection of a young Englishman now in his thirty-second year, and the third to be published in the United States. Kirkup is not "unhappily in love with God" or with himself; he writes in form with ease and exhibits no sign of what may be called spiritual strain. He has that rarest of gifts—the power to transmute the ordinary into the extraordinary, and when he flies off into a piece of extravagance, as in "Rhapsody on a Bead Curtain," he makes the shift naturally. He is completely involved with everyday experience, describing the interior of a railway carriage with the same accuracy and interest that he applies to the night sky seen from an observatory. He likes to move about and examine the "special look" of places, the difference in times of day, and changes in the weather, and he often combines formality with exuberance. He has remembered two facts many of his elders have forgotten—that an important element in the poetry of our century is the poet's renewed faculty of interesting the reader, and that seriousness of imaginative aim need not rule out an occasional show of gaiety and high spirits.

THE MOVEMENT: JOHN WAIN AND KINGSLEY AMIS (1958)

A fair sampling of British verse has been published in American editions during the last ten years, but a complete picture of any literary situation, especially of one in a state of flux, cannot be assembled through scattered publication alone. A recent pamphlet, "Poetry To-day," written by Geoffrey Moore for the British Council and the National Book League, is therefore particularly interesting and valuable at the moment, because it gives an admirably concise account of the poetic scene in England between 1950 and 1957. Mr. Moore, surveying the situation broadly, has come to the conclusion that poetry in Britain is at present in full new bud, if not in flower. Shifts in social and cultural conditions have brought about changes in the poet's material and point of view. And the youngest generation (at least the poets belonging to what has come to be known as the Movement) have taken to heart Sir Herbert Read's requirement for poetry written in the fifties of this century: "It should not raise its voice."

The Movement started out with three members—John Wain, Kingsley Amis (a conjunction with the Angry Young Men group occurs here), and Philip Larkin [q.v.]. Other names were soon added, since it rapidly became apparent that a certain like-mindedness existed among the young in the university-intellectual world. The influence of two older poets, Robert Graves and William Empson, and of the late George Orwell was soon evident. Stress was put on intellectual virtues—upon detachment, irony, and common sense; upon honesty and integrity. They distrust, Moore goes on to say, all large systems of thought; they state what they know and feel personally, however much the statements stand against the traditional, respectable grain. But, he adds, they often fail to satisfy, owing to an inability to accept genuine ideals and emotions, because they are nauseated by false ones.

These limitations show up to rather a marked degree in John Wain's *A Word Carved on a Sill* (the title comes from Robert Graves). Wain writes with the utmost neatness and restraint; he is fond almost to addiction of crisp *terza rima* and the artful villanelle. Romantic subject matter is bypassed with care, and although human feeling of a mild kind and various items of the natural world are not absent, they are present in the most incidental way. Kingsley Amis' *A Case of Samples: Poems 1946–1956* is a collection edged with a penetrating cynicism that is broken into only rarely by something approaching tenderness and more often by a wild humor. Amis is technically less stiff than

Wain, and he is able to use the severe forms of light verse to express a far from light content. He, too, is bitterly unromantic and takes a tough attitude toward love, and his dislike of what he considers base types sometimes goes over the line dividing spleen from venom.

WILLIAM PLOMER (1956)

Borderline Ballads is a collection of satiric verse that, although written in plain British, nevertheless requires some adjustments by the American reader. Plomer is, as a matter of fact, what used to be known as a colonial, and we remember that satire has often originated at the edges of Empire. It is possible to classify him as a writer of "light verse" only if we extend the genre to include Swift and Byron, both of whom Plower in some ways resembles. There is nothing of the coy or the suburban about him. He is out for blood, and he pinks his subjects with an unbuttoned foil. Like Swift, his diagnosis of the symptoms of his human specimens is clinical and unerring, but, again like his great forerunner, he is saved from ultimate cruelty and meanness by an underlying largeness of heart and mind. He is also terribly funny. The rollicking skill of his verse, his diction (which continually shocks and refreshes), his quick eye and ear for the pretentious and the preposterous—these are contemporary British gifts that Americans can appreciate but are perhaps, at the moment, slightly too sanguine to share.

KATHLEEN RAINE (1954)

The Year One is Kathleen Raine's fourth book and her second to be published in America. Miss Raine knows the power of runes and spells, but her poetry does not approach nature by any hieratic, philosophical, literary, or historical path. Miss Raine is *in* nature, as simply as a shell on a shore or a bird in a tree; at moments it is clear that she feels herself to *be* nature. This is the sort of mystical identification that gets into poetry (or any other art) only through the most direct and most sincere means. Many of Miss Raine's poems are deceptively simple; they seem to have little connection with the tough, artisan side of writing. When her nicety of observation (and she can observe as closely as a professional naturalist) coincides with a deep level of feeling, her poems fuse spirit and substance in a remarkable way. Many of them have Scottish hills and the sea as a background, and these succeed in matching in their tone the loneliness and purity of the Hebridean wastes.

VERNON WATKINS (*1960*)

Born in 1906, a Welshman educated at Cambridge and an early friend of Dylan Thomas, Watkins never succumbed to the influence of his younger compatriot either in manner or in point of view. His poetry, disciplined from the beginning (he was first published in 1941), is completely free of ambiguity, irony, and skepticism. In his new book, *Cypress and Acacia,* he continually expresses his belief in the virtue of simplicity, and he shows a reverence toward nature and a sympathy for the various bafflements of mankind with an emphasis that might easily lapse into blandness and piety but that never does. He is quite willing to deal with the past and allows only one machine (a tractor in a field) to show up in his description of the present. This separation from the harsh modern scene has given some critics the opportunity to call him neo-Romantic. Watkins has certainly kept hold of the Romantic poet's right to reflect, meditate, and have intimations of one kind or another, and there are moments when his poetry seems distinctly nineteenth-century. Under the surface, however, a modern sensibility is at work. His experience is so genuinely felt, so exactly observed, and so freshly expressed that any initial sense of the old-fashioned and the *déjà vu* soon disappears. This is delightful poetry, whose subject and technique show a complex temperament and a craftsman's hand.

COLETTE

(1930)

Chéri and Mitsou are the first of Colette's novels to be published in translations in America. From the long list of her books, written in the thirty years since 1900, one could choose other titles of perhaps equal brilliance. Her first literary period began in 1900, with the publication of the Claudine series; her mature literary career started with the appearance of *La Vagabonde* and *La Retraite sentimentale,* some ten years later. For twenty years Colette has been the most widely read and most sincerely respected woman writer in France. *Chéri* was published originally in 1920; *Mitsou,* published in 1917, was her first really objective novel. *Chéri* and its sequel, *La Fin de Chéri,* have already become contemporary classics. *Mitsou,* whose last pages drew tears from the eyes of Marcel Proust, is hardly more than a sketch for a novel of character, yet it stands unmatched in subtlety in the literature of our time.

Colette's excellence, long recognized by a European public that includes her fellow artists, is not easy to define by English-speaking standards. That she is a born writer and an exceptionally sensitive woman is evident. Her full-bodied gusto, her fresh senses and compassion unspoiled as a child's, are immediately clear to the running eye. She is not erudite. Her pages are singularly free from allusion and echoes of literature. She can be compared to little but herself because she has written her discoveries down just as she herself made them. She has lived her life—as a provincial girl, the wife of a Parisian man-about-town, a dancer in music halls, a woman of letters—and written of it concurrently. She has not checked the development of her talents by regrets for the past or yearnings into the future. The steps of her life, the ripening of her perceptions, appear as clearly in her novels as in the facts and dates of her biography.

The novelist, and particularly the novelist writing in English, works in a dangerously malleable form. His narrative, roughly, must adjust itself to a rising action, a knot, and a resolution; through this diagram, and because of it, characters must appear and change. In this loose texture, under these few demands it is difficult to detect maneuvers and sharp practices. Animus, stupidity, inaccuracy, and condescension, if disguised by a neat and fashionable manner and a long wind, can easily pass unnoticed. The good novelist is distinguished from the bad one chiefly by a gift of choice. Choice, itself a talent, as taste is a talent, is not, however, enough. Only extreme sanity and balance of selection can give to prose fiction the dignity and excitement inherent in more rigid forms of writing: drama, poetry, and the exposition of ideas.

Colette makes perfect choices. She writes with the naïve freedom of the amateur who has only himself for audience, and with the artist's unwavering adherence to form. Her simplicity of manner seems odd to the English reader, accustomed to the extremes of romantic rhetoric and to banal situations put down by writers hardened to their medium and not open to their material. The dated touch of nineteenth-century attitudes of mind still lies heavy upon modern fiction. In spite of loud assurances to the contrary, novels infected by their audience, warped by their authors' biases, bleached by literary form and custom, are the novels that, with few exceptions, come from the presses. Colette, backed by a tradition that includes *La Vie de Henri Brulard*, puts down what she knows—what her sharp senses and hearty nature have told her as the truth. This, we can conclude, is her only secret.

The stories of Katherine Mansfield, so obviously influenced by Colette, illustrate the Frenchwoman's method of attack without giving a hint of her quality. For Katherine Mansfield's talent leaves off where Colette's begins. The Englishwoman's sensibilities could touch nostalgia, pity, and regret. They could not seek out the difficult human relationship, grasp it in essentials, reduce it to form. Where Colette struggles with the problem on its own terms, Katherine Mansfield shied away.

In *Chéri*, Colette chooses for her subject one of the most difficult situations in the rather limited gamut of relationships possible between men and women: the love of an aging woman for a young man; the dependence of a young man upon the passion and tenderness of an older woman. She makes her problem perfectly clear and does not slight its implications. Chéri is not a casual boy picked up by Léa late in her career. She has known him from childhood. She is the friend, contemporary, and confidante of his mother. Like his mother, she is a successful courtesan; unlike her, she is healthy, intelligent, and gay. Léa does not make the first move; it is the boy who chooses her. From the beginning, the psychological set is probable. And from the first kiss of these lovers, so ill assorted according to conventional standards, throughout the course of their love affair, Chéri's marriage, Léa's flight from unexpected sorrow, to Chéri's final rejection of her love and power, the mother-son basis of the bond between them is not for a moment forgotten. The last scene between Léa and Chéri is so complex and so moving that it stands beyond casual appraisal. These two, characters in a novel easily classed as scabrous, take on a tragic nobility, *"Léa,"* says a contemporary critic, *"se dompte comme une héroïne cornélienne."* This seems improbable, but is nevertheless true.

Mitsou is so lightly blocked in, so delicately developed, that it barely merits the heavy title of novel. Mitsou, the little singer in a music hall, is the only character that has a name; the others are known by titles, like the people in an allegory or a harlequinade. Brief stage directions report the action for the most part; the scenes are perhaps five in number. Mitsou before the mirror of her dressing room, dressing, under the eyes of the young officers, "with a cheerless ease and an absent-minded immodesty which banished all coquetry"; Mitsou in the apartment furnished according to her own taste, and paid for by the Man of Means, an apartment "extraordinary, in spite of her good intentions"; Mitsou at her desk, writing serious little letters, full of grammatical errors and the newly awakened gentleness of first love—that is

all we have, with the exception of Mitsou and her Lieutenant, in
a strangers' embrace, seen against the ornate jumble of ornaments in her bedroom. What more could one do for this sober,
well-meaning child, who does not miss her performance even
though her lover goes away tomorrow? Colette does not attempt
to do more. She defines her lightly, wakens her briefly, and lets
her go.

Turning the light formality of French fiction to her own uses,
Colette has colored French prose, for a long time rather grayed
by reflections from Parisian streets, with the varied green of
provincial gardens. Honest, sensuous, and witty, she has produced
a solid body of work that owes little to masculine attitudes. Other
translations of her books as excellent as these two should not be
long deferred.

IVY COMPTON-BURNETT

(1951)

The novels of Ivy Compton-Burnett owe much of their power to
the fact that each of them is a nightmare into which we are
drawn by degrees but from which we escape with reluctance. For
these are high-comedy nightmares. Miss Compton-Burnett belongs to the company of artists who, with the aid of the comic
spirit, are able to enlarge life by imposing inexorable patterns on
it. Within a straight Victorian world—which escapes being "period" because it lacks any scrap of fashionable ornamentation
—her three fixed circles revolve: masters, servants, and children.
And although the members of each circle are vocal to a degree,
communication among the groups is largely indirect. Children
spy on masters and servants; servants, on masters and children;
masters, on servants, children, and one another. Situation is
built up by the intrusion of some shocking reality in the masters'
world which soon filters, by eavesdropping, into the other two;
and the only weapon available to the majority of masters is the
weapon of convention. But natural reactions, suppressed in one
quarter, are allowed to the servants and to the young. Thus, humane generosity and simple love are allowed to break through
barriers of spite and hypocrisy; and the rigid pattern is at length
changed. Sex, in this closed universe, keeps cropping up in terms
of comedy. A prevalent background of illegitimacy exists; so that
masters are frequently faced with the results of their early
"stumbles" in the form of butlers who are their natural sons and

housekeepers who are their natural daughters. In *Darkness and Day*, the world of the bastard impinges so closely upon the world of the family that one of the masters believes for a time that he has married his own cast-off child. The child's mother (a servant) proves that this is not the case. But for a moment all three circles are menaced; and the one remedy seems to be silence. "Oedipus lost no time in going the full length," someone remarks. "Anything like that would make it very public."

Miss Compton-Burnett is certainly fixed permanently at the emotional level of childhood's most "knowing" and disabused stage. This is a point of fixation which breeds a hostility to life that great gifts of intelligence and style alone can alleviate. Miss Compton-Burnett, in many ways a female Swift of our day, constantly proves her possession of these gifts.

HART CRANE

(1933)

⚜

Hart Crane, whose *Collected Poems* have been edited with an introduction by Waldo Frank, was born in Garrettsville, Ohio, in 1899. He committed suicide by leaping from a boat bound north from Mexico on April 27, 1932. He began to write poetry at the age of fifteen; at the time of his death he was revered by many of his contemporaries as the greatest American poet since Whitman. The violence of his life had become a legend and the merits of his work a center of controversy. His poetry, incoherent, of emotional extremes compact, was seized upon as a symbol of the cultural chaos in which it was produced.

Mr. Frank's introduction is long, and, to anyone uninitiated into the metaphysical mysteries, rather puzzling. In it he exhibits one modern critical tendency: the desire to lift the poet out of his true place and ascribe to him the function of the seer; to accredit to a work of literature some mystic revelation. Thus, Crane was a seer, according to Mr. Frank, in spite of the fact that he possessed no "inner nucleus." Moreover, he was a product of "the great tradition," although "because of the time that fleshed him . . . he could not employ traditional concretions." And in Crane's long poem "The Bridge," according to Mr. Frank, in his guise of St. John, the symbol of American life finally appears. "The Bridge" offers us, as it were, the Word made Steel, for our spirit's consolation.

If we may be permitted to examine Crane's poems a trifle more

realistically, we see at once that the poet's quarrel with himself—
that quarrel which Yeats names the first cause in the poetic
process—was far more grievous than his quarrel with his world.
This inner feud was so intense that suicide was his only solution.
And in the matter of "traditional concretions," although Crane's
work undeniably bore the impress of the three great and inexplicable American romantics, Poe, Melville, and Whitman, it
took its immediate color from modern French writing: Surreal-
ism-out-of-Rimbaud-out-of-Victor-Hugo. One certain proof of
Crane's genius was his ability to build remarkable poetry from
the materials offered by a literary movement crammed with
blighting and senseless *blague*. He took over much of its form
and many of its attitudes, but impregnated it with the intensity
of his own powers. All questions of "the greatest since . . . ,"
of seerhood, of the voice out of chaos, the cave, or the cloud, put
to one side, Crane was a poet of genius whose untimely death
was a certain loss to American literature.

DETECTIVE NOVELS
(1944)

The modern detective novel originated in times physically, and perhaps spiritually, darker than our own. The *roman policier* was based on the invention, new and terrible to the French, of the political police, under Fouché and Napoleon. Later, Vidocq, an adventurer born under the Old Régime, managed under the new dispensation to make a transformation in which the chaos of the period is summed up: he became Chef de la Sureté and used his criminal career as a basis for his position on the other side of the law. His *Memoirs*, published in Paris in 1829, intersected the legend of the Byronic hero. Here was something new, a product of another social situation, the beginning of a new legend. Vidocq appears almost immediately in literature as Balzac's Vautrin. Meanwhile, and following closely in the steps of actual spies and *agents provocateurs*, Eugène Sue began to produce, in the thirties, his series of *romans-feuilletons*, which included *Les Mystères de Paris* and *Le Juif errant*. Jean Cassou has stated that the development of the *roman-feuilleton* and the creation of the social sciences is parallel. The secrets of "sordid and terrible Paris" were sought out, in the first, under the cover of darkness. The rich and the poor, the intriguer and his victim, were linked together. "The poor adventurer, the pariah, the *carbonaro*, the artist, the regenerator, the adversary of the Jesuits . . . these were the phantasmagoria projected by [the beginning of] the nineteenth century." They were symbolic of the strange desire that had manifested itself in the midst of chaos: "to pass beyond the political to the social revolution."

The earliest detectives worked by mystery and ruse rather than rapidity and force. Roger Caillois, in his intelligent study of the genre, *Le Roman policier*,* says that the detective is at first successful not through his logic but because of his disguises. He is, at the beginning, an inheritor of Fenimore Cooper, the infallible observer of the forest. The great city has become a new jungle, more dangerous than the solitudes of Canada. This pattern was soon abandoned, but it has returned in the spy and secret-agent stories of the present. But let us watch the closing in of the form, the development of "deduction," which at one point made the detective novel into an almost pure play of the logical faculties, a detached *jeu d'esprit.*

This tendency toward rules was observed in the detective novel while rules elsewhere in nineteenth-century literature were being progressively rejected. The detective novel splits off from the surrounding anarchy of form. And within its closed universe Poe further limits its locale by inventing the convention of the locked room. The detective now has completely rejected his bloodhound role. He becomes the scientist "coordinating indices," the artist-priest astounding the world at large as well as his rather stupid human foil. The crime becomes as isolated from life as a chemical experiment. Rules to protect the reader emerge: "Give the reader an equal right with the detective . . . no supernatural or scientific marvels . . . no tricky architecture . . . no factors brought in at the last moment." And the *acte gratuit,* the motiveless impulse, cannot function at this point; the diabolical machinery must work on the basis of accepted motives. Now, "the detective story must take from existence nothing but a frame. . . . It is not interested in passions or emotions except as a force to set the mechanism in motion. It is only interested in forming a complete and simple figure from incomprehensible and partial fragments. The novel attaches itself to the nature of man. This nature is a bother to the detective story, at this stage, and it supports it only unwillingly."

* I have followed the analysis of M. Caillois' *Le Roman policier* (Editions des Lettres Françaises, SUR, Buenos Aires, 1941) very closely. I am also indebted to *Quarante-huit,* by Jean Cassou (Gallimard, Paris, 1939).

M. Caillois' analysis now reaches a crucial fact. Here is this new form, coldly opposed to everything literature stands for. But the pure exercise of the intellectual faculty, the detachment from emotion, the devotion of the detective to the penetration of "an artificial miracle"—all this is brought up against the unalterable convention that a detective novel must be based on a corpse. It demands a murderer—a person who has killed and risks capital punishment; no other sort of malefactor will do. And because of this anomaly between crude subject and skilled method, the detective story cannot remain a pure puzzle for long. "The cards must be shuffled." Suddenly "neither the murderers are real bandits nor the searchers real police." Variations multiply; here, in a late development, is Simenon's Maigret, a detective with a compassionate heart. "An obscure necessity obliges these policemen to make reservations in their role. They have a liberal attitude or a liberal profession. . . . They occupy a marginal place in regard to society, in the manner of the sorcerer or devil in the ancient tales who appears in the guise of a stranger, a horse dealer, a doctor, an itinerant merchant."

The closed circle begins to break. The puzzle begins to widen back toward the novel proper. Now the criminal has become anyone. "The most unexpected person" is now any man or woman, of whatever age or condition. And the elaboration of the setting becomes inexhaustible. *Everywhere* has become the scene of the crime. No situation, however sacred or cut off from life by money, power, or prestige, has been omitted. As in a fox hunt, every modern type and modern locale has been "blooded" by the detective novel. But the detective story has not by any means merged with the novel. It has, instead, drained off from the other form many of its residues of "sensation." While apparently working with the most icy logical detachment, the narrative breaks off "complaisantly to recount scabrous scenes of cruelty or eroticism. The ambition of the intelligence is flattered while the appetite for sensation is satisfied."

The mention of death and dissolution has almost disappeared from modern middle-class and "folk" literature. The detective novel does not reject one detail of the macabre. And it openly accommodates fear and aggression, open or disguised. Certain authors specialize in the frozen will of the nightmare—or the neurotic symptom; their characters may not escape even if they could. The rat-in-the-trap, the spider-and-the-fly motifs recur. The baseless fears of the folk tale or the psychiatric clinic are endlessly repeated. And the inveterate reader of detective stories can soon classify his reading into stories written by and for sadists, by and for masochists; into stories in which someone, under a pseudonym, is working off some obsession or perversion or fear that is sure to link up with similar aberrations in some reader. On a higher level we get a complete picture of paranoia in Kafka's *The Trial*.

The obscure religious undercurrent in these dramas of sin and retribution cannot be overlooked. "One of the strange phenomena of the nineteenth century"—I quote a modern clergyman—"is the spectacle of religion dropping the appeal to fear while other human interests have picked it up." The Gothic novel that began in the late eighteenth century bore the marks of a broken-down, secularized, floating religion. It is the supernatural that intervenes. The trappings are Catholicism's ruined abbeys; the fumes are those of a Protestant personal hell. Ritual has dissolved. The detective story, on the other hand, has all the marks of a live cult, developing from primitivism toward complexity. The victim is always there, whether the sign of a brutal sacrifice or a more human oblation. And the priestlike character of the detective was once very clear: Sherlock Holmes, in whose human reality many people believed, is the supreme example of this type.

"The present-day individual," writes a psychiatrist, "is more and more called upon to give up his aggressions. The repressed and therefore unconscious criminality of the normal man finds few socially harmless outlets: dream and fantasy life, the neurotic symptom, and some transitional forms of behavior. . . ." The breakthrough of the submerged unconscious, the symbolic struggle between good and evil—in the detective story we find a re-enactment of these struggles. And the flight motif has returned, along with the tracking-down-of-the-fugitive role of the official or unofficial police. Graham Greene, one of the most intelligent and exciting writers of the modern "thriller"—because his imagination seems peculiarly sensitive to archetypal subconscious themes—has recognized the role of the conscience in these dramas; he gives one book in its English edition a title extracted from Francis Thompson's poem "The Hound of Heaven"—*The Labyrinthine Ways*. And it is Greene who has stated that the history of contemporary society is being written "in hundreds of volumes, most of them sold in cheap editions—the detective novels." The great and perceptive writers of the nineteenth century from George Eliot through Henry James accepted the material and announced the themes, in a period devoted to ideals of "progress" and bourgeois complacency. At the moment, continuous and sharp attention should be paid to this vehicle, in which every rejected and denied human impulse can be accommodated, from the petty but terrible *Schadenfreude* (joy in another's misfortune), bred from the poorer native qualities of the human heart as well as from the pressures of a competitive society, to larger evil schemes of power and ambition. The detective novel, now snobbishly cut off from the main stream of literature, reviewed flippantly if at all, may at this moment have within it secrets of what we are and shall be. And the future may look back to it, as it now exists, through great works engendered by it, as we look back through Baudelaire's poems to Sue's Paris, and back through Shakespeare to the crude horrors of the Tragedy of Blood.

EMILY DICKINSON

୧୨❀❀❀ଔ

LIFE AND LETTERS (*1945*)

The legend of Emily Dickinson has grown in America since 1890, when the first series of her posthumously published poems appeared. And this legend has not been confined to the literary field. The shadow of the spirited little figure, self-secluded in her father's "mansion" in Amherst, is known and loved by many people for whom the quality of her poetry would have little or no appeal. She has become a kind of secular saint. For she has redeemed and justified that former American type: the lonely and eccentric Old Maid. The Old Maid, formerly a character more comic than pathetic, became, in the person of "Emily," a mysterious and transcendent being. The desire to hunt up a definite lover for Emily, noticeable in several rather fanciful biographies written in the 1920s, was perhaps due to romantic hope that the legend could be fully rounded out in a conventional way. All old maids are disappointed in love. Who, then, disappointed Emily Dickinson?

The peculiar manner in which her works came before the public helped not only to promulgate mystery but to prevent the poems themselves from being closely attached to the life. Mrs. Todd, Emily's first editor, presented the poems under the headings, "Life," "Nature," "Love," and "Time and Eternity" (how we feel the breath of the nineties here!). Mrs. Martha Dickinson Bianchi, Emily's niece, taking over the role of editor in 1912, continued this classification in all subsequent "collected" volumes. Moreover, an underlying drama of family feuds and split allegiances kept the material itself in an incomplete state. *Ancestors' Brocades: The Literary Debut of Emily Dickinson,* written by Mrs. Todd's daughter, Millicent Todd Bingham, brings before us for the first time a full account of the circumstances connected with the appearance of the first three books of poems (1890, 1891, 1896), and with Mrs. Todd's edition of the *Letters* (1894). Mrs. Todd copied and collated hundreds of poems from the difficult and cryptic manuscripts; she gathered in letters from crotchety and non-cooperative correspondents. Her version of Emily's life is still a sensible piece of narration. She did not know everything and she did not understand everything; but neither did she throw dust in the reader's eyes, or make any effort to build up the facts into "romance."

Amherst, in the early and middle nineteenth century, far from being a community in which "revolutionary" Transcendental and Unitarian ideas could take root, was a provincial, principally Congregationalist town where Puritan emotions were passing over into Evangelical ones. Edward Dickinson, Emily's father, was a product of this stern and unyielding background: a man, as Emily said, who stepped like Cromwell when he went to gather the kindling. He was, it is becoming evident, a character of pathological harshness whose word in his family was law.

"I never had a mother," the poet remarked to Colonel Higginson. Edward's wife was allowed, it would seem, little voice in the management of her three children, Austin, Lavinia, and Emily. Austin, after making some futile early gestures of escape to the West, finally settled down in a house adjoining his father's and subordinated his career to his father's wishes. He married outside the clan—a witty and "worldly" woman called Sue—but this marriage was not a success. A coolness grew up between husband and wife and Austin spent more time in his father's house than in his own. Emily and Lavinia were from the first subdued by the paternal will. And Emily adored her father. She was always her brother's friend, although her friendship with her brother's wife was, it now appears, soon broken. Lavinia, in later years, guarded and protected Emily. It was to Lavinia that Emily tacitly entrusted her manuscripts; what now seem to be thousands of these turned up in the Dickinson house after Emily's death.

Mrs. Todd, pretty and disarming, managed to break through the poet's later reserve. It was natural, then, that Lavinia should come to Mrs. Todd for help in the matter of the manuscripts. Mrs. Todd was to devote years of her time to deciphering the material entrusted to her. The poems, and later the letters, once printed, had a certain success, and Mrs. Todd took to lecturing on the poet. Lavinia, to whom all the profits from the published poems accrued, saw her beloved Emily slipping from her. Austin, on the other hand, wished to reward Mrs. Todd in some way. He deeded to her a strip of land adjoining the Dickinson estate. After his death, Lavinia, now an eccentric and rather appalling spinster, brought suit for the land, and won her suit. Mrs. Todd at once stopped work on the manuscripts, locked them in a box, and never referred to the incident in her lifetime. After some years, Mrs. Bianchi began to publish poems from the original manuscripts, which had now fallen into her hands.

Mrs. Todd realized that the poems could be classified, according to handwriting, into three distinct periods. Mrs. Bianchi never admitted that these distinctions existed. Thus Mrs. Bianchi's collections, brought out in a haphazard way as the years went on, were notable for their carelessness and inaccuracy. Even the most cursory reader could not help being baffled by poems that did not make any kind of sense. This sort of presentation was unfair to Emily Dickinson. Whatever her oddities of style, she had the firmest notion of what she wanted to say and how she wanted to say it. The poems are never the babblings of a broken heart or the ravings of a broken mind. They show, even in their present disordered arrangement, a clear line of development: a classic line, rising through early sentiment and experiment to a middle ground of technical and spiritual control. Beyond this middle period the "great" expression begins. The compressed, direct force of the later work points to a spirit freed, as well as to a technique mastered.

So much can be puzzled out. Fortunately, the mass of published material is now so large that certain rough conclusions can be drawn as to both the life and the work. The newest collection, *Bolts of Melody* (more than six hundred and fifty "new"

poems), is edited by Mrs. Bingham from the manuscript copied
by Mrs. Todd. It is now perfectly apparent that there were two
personalities involved in the work and in the life: the poet whose
courage and spiritual fiber developed into a massive and im-
perturbable maturity, and "Emily," the child who never developed at all, but lived, even after her father's death, in her father's
shadow.

The letters show that this division was the result of some shock
undergone by the poet in her early twenties. The earliest letters
are gay and outgoing. Some shattering blow (which Mrs. Bianchi
glosses over) was then dealt. "It is extraordinary," Colonel Higginson wrote Mrs. Todd, "how the mystic and bizarre Emily is
born between two pages [of letters]—as Thoreau says, summer
passes to autumn in an instant." Whatever happened, the eager
young girl disappears, and a child and a "bizarre" woman take
her place. Both of these personalities became "poets." So that, in
1862, when Emily Dickinson wrote to Higginson, asking for
literary criticism, we are rather repelled by the "child's" coyness
of approach, but amazed at the maturing woman's already considerable powers.

The "roughness" of rhyme and obscurity of meaning, so
troubling to Mrs. Todd and Colonel Higginson, fall with perfect
naturalness on modern ears. The wheel of taste turned; and
"Emily's" sentimental verses, concerned with fainting robins,
waltzing butterflies, and the like, began to show up for the childish utterances they actually are. But now another layer of her
work came into view; and a new generation, with subtler ears,
and a sterner sense of poetic values, found this poetry exactly
suited to its taste. The influence of Emily Dickinson's "great"
period on the generation of Auden, if not that of Eliot, is inesti-
mable. She had instinctively, on her own, "wrung the neck of
rhetoric"; cleared out the trash from her versification; condensed
her observation to a sharp focus. She became one of the "ancestors" of the young; her poetry, in recent anthologies, stands side
by side with the poetry of Blake, George Herbert, Donne, Thomas
Hardy, Hopkins, and Yeats—with Shakespeare's songs and the
Border ballads. She is able to face up to Edith Sitwell as well as
to Christina Rossetti; and her influence is not yet wholly absorbed;
she still stands open toward the future.

Mrs. Bingham does not hope for a complete and competently edited *Works* for at least fifty years. The original manuscripts are still not available. For scholars, a grueling task lies ahead. Meanwhile, we probably have the heart of the work already in print. And now that the legendary, romantic side of Emily Dickinson's life has been pretty thoroughly canvassed, it is surely time for her readers to consider her as a writer and to assess her powers on the highest level of mystical poetry, where they should be assessed. Her insights are equaled in intensity only by the intuitions of the greatest mystics and visionaries. Her wit (as opposed to her "fun") is of a "metaphysical" kind. Her range is wider than the fragmentary manner in which her poetry has been presented would lead us to suppose. Her mature work, as a matter of fact, passes, in an amazing way, beyond the mystic poetry with which we are familiar; it is something quite new; it has infinite weight and infinite reverberation. Beside her triumphs, her habit of childish play with the idea of "littleness" and helplessness, her coy tricks and affected airs show up for what they are—some compensating or compulsive game. The quality of the great lyric poet continually enlarges and will not shrink as fashions change. When the myth of the saintly American spinster no longer has any appeal, the works of the poet Dickinson—the woman who possessed "the disenchanting and re-enchanting faculty of seeing the world in its simple truth"—will continue to attest to the one-time existence in America of a heroine, an artist, and a seer. "The summers of Hesperides are long."

THE POEMS (1955)

So many obstructions have turned up to hinder the posthumous publication of Emily Dickinson's poems that the appearance of a definitive edition, only five years after Mr. Gilbert Holland Montague's gift of important material to Harvard University, seems a scholarly miracle. Credit for this triumph over time and trouble can be wholeheartedly given to the editor, Thomas H. Johnson, whose discovery of the American "metaphysical" poet Edward Taylor was a literary event in 1939. *The Poems of Emily Dickinson*, in three volumes, includes "variant readings critically compared with all known manuscripts," and since certain poems exist in five or six sometimes differing versions, the grueling task of arranging and collating almost two thousand items might have turned out to be the work of a lifetime. Mr. Johnson not only has accomplished the physical work in an incredibly short time but, in his introduction, has brought sympathy and insight to bear in an illuminating way on several major Dickinson enigmas.

Students of Emily Dickinson have for many years suspected that a definite chronology of the poems (based on changes in the handwriting, and other evidence) was the missing key to the poet's development. This chronology, of course, had to be based on poems written in Emily Dickinson's own hand, and these autographs for years were scattered and divided; forty individuals are known to possess one autograph or more. Mr. Johnson discovered that fair copies gathered by the poet herself into little booklets, or "packets," constituted two-thirds of her work, and the handwriting of these showed discernible changes from year to year. (A series of holograph letters reproduced in this edition make these changes very clear.) His subsequently established chronology brings out one important point: that the poet's development followed a normal pattern—she was never a woman who compulsively scribbled on any scrap of paper that came to hand. The poems show apprenticeship, a period of full flowering, and a gradual decline in creative energy—the usual progress of a lyric poet who does not force or falsify his gifts. The work comprises seventeen hundred and seventy-five poems, of which forty-one are known to be unpublished, in whole or in part.

The chronology, moreover, sheds a clear light on Emily Dickinson's greatest emotional experience—her love for, and deep devotion to, the Reverend Charles Wadsworth. Dickinson biographers have accepted this situation in recent years and have dealt with it openly and conclusively. But here is the cold statistical proof: in the year following Wadsworth's removal (in December, 1861) from Philadelphia to a San Francisco pastorate, she began to write, Mr. Johnson remarks, "with daemonic energy." Her production since 1858 had been increasing, but in 1862, when she was thirty-two, she transcribed into packets "no

fewer than three hundred and sixty-six poems" in which a new
"quality of tenseness and prosodic skill" was uniformly present.
Three more years of "full creativeness" followed. Thereafter,
"throughout her life, the yearly average never exceeded twenty,
one-half of which never progressed beyond the work-sheet
stage."

Various other facts adduced by the editor confirm previous
biographical suppositions. The poet's seclusion was partly based
on her desire to have some control over her destiny, to impose
some pattern upon her situation that would give her talent room
to function. With shrewd intent, she sought out Higginson, in
1862, as a "tutor." Higginson, on the whole, was a poor choice
as a preceptor, but he was a reassuring professional anchor, and
we now understand how great her need then was for conventional reassurance. And if she refused a public during her lifetime, she built up with care a private audience of friends who
gave her a measure of scope and power.

To read Emily Dickinson in this new text, in which every
idiosyncratic habit of spelling, punctuation, diction, and local-
ism is reproduced, is to read her in a slightly different language.
But that language is at last her own. The sentimental figure built
up by editors from Higginson on (with the exception of Mrs.
Bingham) fades out, and we come upon a woman of timeless
genius—a visionary as well as a matchless observer of reality.
The frequent childishness and the surface eccentricities seem
unimportant. Working alone, without a vigorous culture to back
her up, Emily Dickinson nevertheless became, within limits, a
self-determined woman who made choices—rather than the
pathetic recluse of the legend—and an artist who more often
than not was right the first time.

A MYSTICAL POET (1959)

It has been suggested that I develop, on this occasion,* a statement I made in 1945, in an article published in that year—that
the time had come "to assess Emily Dickinson's powers on the

* The bicentennial celebration of the town of Amherst, Massachusetts,
Emily Dickinson's home.

highest level of mystical poetry, where they should be assessed."
Since then, the appearance of the *Collected Poems* and of the
Collected Letters, superbly edited by Thomas H. Johnson, has
made such an assessment less difficult than it formerly had to
be. For now, with the existence of these definitive works, the
stages of the poet's development are connected and clarified.
We are now faced, as we should be, with the career of a writer
who—we now realize—throughout her life made the most difficult kind of choices, many directed toward the protection of
her sensitive nature and of her remarkable poetic gift. It is the
poet Dickinson who has advanced into the full light of literary
history and now belongs not only to Amherst, not only to America, but to the world that reads her either in English or in translation.

Now, the term "mystical poetry" is a difficult one to deal with.
The words "mystic" and "mysticism" have become rather suspect
in modern, materialist society. So it is important to define and
place this term, at the outset. Mystics have appeared, it would
seem, with fair frequency at many periods, in many cultures; but
there is no doubt that when, in the West, we speak of true mysticism, we have in mind the example of the Christian saints. "In
Christianity," says Evelyn Underhill, "the 'natural mysticism'
. . . which is latent in humanity and at a certain point of development breaks out in every race, came to itself; and attributed
for the first time true and distinct personality to its Object"—
namely, God. True mystics do not indulge in diffuse pantheism
or hold to the aim of "the occult," which wishes to wrench
supernal power to human uses. In the words of another commentator: "The aim and content of Christian mysticism is not
self or nature, but God."

We can see at once that there is a difference between the
character, as well as the aims, of true mystics and of poets; and
we know that to come upon the two gifts in one person is extremely rare. But close points of resemblance do exist between
the mystic experience, at its purest and best, and the experience
of poetic—or indeed, any creative—expression. Poets down
the centuries, visited by that power which the ancients call *the
Muse,* have described their experience in much the same way
as the mystic describes his ecstatic union with Divine Truth.

This experience has been rendered at length, and dramatically, by Dante, as well as by St. John of the Cross; and certain poems in the literature of every language attest to moments when, for the poet, "the deep and primal life which he shares with all creation has been roused from its sleep." And both poets and mystics have described with great poignance that sense of deprivation and that shutting away from grace which follows the loss of the vision (or of the inspiring breath), which is called, in the language of mysticism, "the dark night of the soul."

Certainly one of the triumphs brought about by the emergence of the Romantic spirit, in English poetry, at the end of the eighteenth century, was a freeing and an enlargement of poetic vision, and in the nineteenth century we come upon a multiplication of poets whose spiritual perceptions were acute. Beyond Vaughan and Herbert (who, in the seventeenth century, worked from a religious base) we think of Blake, of the young Wordsworth; of Keats and Shelley; of Emily Brontë; of Gerard Manley Hopkins; and we can extend the list into our own day with the names of Yeats and T. S. Eliot. By examining the work of these poets—to whom the imagination, the creative spirit of man, was of utmost importance—we find that the progress of the mystic toward illumination, and of the poet toward the full depth and richness of his insight, is much alike. Both work from the world of reality, toward the realm of Essence; from the microcosm to the macrocosm. Both have an intense and accurate sense of their surroundings; there is nothing vague or floating in their perception of reality; it is indeed as though they saw "through, not with, the eye." And they are filled with love for the beauty they perceive in the world of time—"this remarkable world" as Emily Dickinson called it; and concerning death they are neither fearful nor morbid—how could they be, since they feel immortality behind it? They document life's fearful limitations from which they suffer, but they do not mix self-pity with the account of their suffering (which they describe, like their joy, in close detail). They see the world in a grain of sand and Heaven in a wild flower; and now and again they bring eternity into focus, as it were, in a phrase of the utmost clarity. In the work of Emily Dickinson such moments of still and halted perception are many. The slant of light on a winter day, the still brilliance of a summer noon, the sound of the wind before the rain—she speaks of these, and we share the shock of insight, the slight dislocation of serial events, the sudden shift from the Manifold into the One.

One of the dominant facts concerning Emily Dickinson is her spirit of religious unorthodoxy. Her deeply religious feeling ran outside the bounds of dogma; this individualism was, in fact, an inheritance from her Calvinist forebears, but it was out of place when contrasted to the Evangelicanism to which, in her time, so many Protestants had succumbed. She early set herself against the guilt and gloom inherent in this revivalism. She avoided the constrictions which a narrow insistence on religious rule and law would put upon her. She had read Emerson with delight, but, as Yvor Winters has remarked, it is a mistake to think of her as a Transcendentalist in dimity. Here again she worked through to a standpoint and an interpretation of her own; her attitude toward pain and suffering, toward the shocking facts of existence, was far more realistic than Emerson's. As we examine her chief spiritual preoccupations, we see how closely she relates to the English Romantic poets who, a generation or so before her, fought a difficult and unpopular battle against the eighteenth century's cold logic and mechanical point of view. The names of Blake and Coleridge come to mind; we know that to both these poets the cold theory of Locke represented "a deadly heresy on the nature of existence." It is difficult to look back to this period of early Romantic breakthrough, since so much of that early boldness and originality was later dissipated in excesses of various kinds. But it is important to remember that Blake attached the greatest importance to the human imagination as an aspect of some mystery beyond the human, and to listen to his ringing words: "The world of Imagination is the world of Eternity. . . . The world of Imagination is Infinite and Eternal, whereas the world of generation is Finite and Temporal . . ."—and to remember, as well, that "Blake, Wordsworth, Coleridge, Shelley and Keats shared the belief that the imagination was nothing less than God as he operates in the human soul." C. M. Bowra, writing of the Romantic ethos in general, brings out a fact which has been generally overlooked: that, although Romantic poetry became a European phenomenon, English Romantic poetry "almost alone . . . connected visionary insight with a superior order of being."

"There is hardly a trace of this [insight]," Bowra goes on to say,
"in Hugo, or Heine or Lermontov. They have their share of
longing, but almost nothing of Romantic vision. . . ." Hölderlin,
in Germany, tried to share a lost vision of Greece, but on the
whole it was the English who accomplished a transformation in
thought and emotion "for which there is no parallel in their age."
It is surely in the company of these English poets that Emily
Dickinson belongs. At its most intense, her vision not only
matched, but transcended theirs; she crossed the same boundaries
with a like intransigence; and the same vigorous flowers sprang
from different seeds, in the spirit of a woman born in 1830,
in New England, in America.

The drawing of close parallels between the life and circumstances of poets is often an unrewarding task. But in the case
of Emily Dickinson, because hers was for so long considered
a particularly isolated career, it is interesting to make certain
comparisons. It has been pointed out that there is a close resemblance between the lives, temperaments, and works of Emily
Brontë and Emily Dickinson. And one or two resemblances between Emily Dickinson and Blake (Blake taken as a lyric poet
rather than as a prophet) can be traced (quite apart from the
fairly unimportant fact that Miss Dickinson, in her apprenticeship, closely imitated Blake's form in at last two poems). Both
took over the simplest forms of the song and the hymn and
turned this simplicity to their own uses. Both seemed to work
straight from almost dictated inspiration (Blake, indeed, claimed
that his poems were dictated to him intact and entire), but we
now know, from an examination of their manuscripts, that both
worked over their original drafts with meticulous care. Both
had to struggle against hampering circumstances: Blake against
poverty and misunderstanding, and Dickinson against a lack of
true response in the traditionally stiffened society in which she
found herself. To both poets, limitation and boundary finally
yielded originality and power; they were sufficiently outside the
spirit of their times so that they were comparatively untouched
by the vagaries of fashion; they both were able to wring from
solitary contemplation sound working principles and just form.
T. S. Eliot, in his essay on Blake, speaks of Blake's peculiarity
"which can be seen to be the peculiarity of all great poetry. . . .

It is merely a peculiar honesty, which, in a world frightened to be honest, is particularly terrifying. It is an honesty against which the whole world conspires, because it is unpleasant. Blake's poetry has the unpleasantness of great poetry. Nothing that can be called abnormal or perverse, none of the things which exemplify the sickness of an epoch or a fashion, have this quality; only those things which, by some extraordinary labor of simplification, exhibit the essential sickness or strength of the human soul." Eliot then remarks that the question about Blake the man "is a question of the circumstances that concurred to permit this honesty in his work. . . . The favoring conditions probably include these two: that, early apprenticed to a manual occupation, he was not compelled to acquire any other education in literature than he wanted, or to acquire it for any other reason than he wanted it; and that, being a humble engraver, he had no journalistic-social career open to him. There was, that is to say, nothing to distract him from his interests or to corrupt these interests—neither . . . the standards of society, nor the temptation of success; nor was he exposed to imitation of himself or anyone else. . . . These circumstances are what make him innocent."

The circumstances which led to Emily Dickinson's very nearly complete seclusion are, of course, different from those which Eliot mentions as applying to Blake. It was physical frailty which put an end to her formal education. But later, as we read the record of her withdrawal, as this record appears in the *Letters* (and, of course, the full reasons are not given) we can detect the element of choice working. By the time she wrote to Higginson in 1862 she had made that choice, and only wanted to have it confirmed. She wished to know whether or not her poems were "alive"—if they "breathed." She received a certain confirmation that they were and did; and she kept to her solitude. This solitude was not harsh. Her love for her friends never diminished, nor her delight in their occasional presence; her family ties were strong; her daily round sustained her; and the joy she felt in the natural world—particularly in flowers and in children—continues. Until a series of tragedies (beginning with the death of her father) began to break down her spiritual balance, she held to that balance over a long period of years. Balance, delicacy and force—

fed by her exquisite senses and her infinitely lively and inquisitive mind—these are the qualities which reinforce her vision into the heart and spirit of nature, and into her own heart.

An added pleasure is given us, as we read Emily Dickinson's poetry from beginning to end, by the openness and inclusiveness of the work. Every sort of poem has been preserved; no strict process of self-editing has taken place, and we are not faced with periods in which much has been suppressed. The failures and the successes stand side by side; the poems expressing the poet's more childish and undeveloped characteristics and the poems upon which the sentimentality of her time left its mark, are often followed or preceded by poems which define and express the very nearly indefinable and inexpressible. There is no professionalism, in the worst sense, here; and it is interesting to note that, although she sought out Higginson's advice and named herself his "scholar," she never altered a poem of hers according to any suggestion of his. She had, at one time, perhaps been willing to be published, but, later, she could do without print.

We have, then, in Johnson's edition of the poems published in 1955, as complete a record of the development of a lyric talent as exists in literature. Scholars have busied themselves with the record; we know what color she names most frequently (purple) and what books she read (Shakespeare and the Bible well in the lead). We ourselves can discover, in the index to the three volumes, that her favorite subject was not death, as was long supposed; for life, love, and the soul are also recurring subjects. But the greatest interest lies in her progress as a writer, and as a person. We see the young poet moving away, by gradual degrees, from her early slight addiction to graveyardism, to an Emersonian belief in the largeness and harmony of nature. Step by step, she advances into the terror and anguish of her destiny; she is frightened, but she holds fast and describes her fright. She is driven to the verge of sanity, but manages to remain, in some fashion, the observer and recorder of her extremity. Nature is no longer a friend, but often an inimical presence. Nature is a haunted house. And—a truth even more terrible—the inmost self can be haunted.

At the highest summit of her art, she resembles no one. She

begins to cast forward toward the future: to produce poems in which we recognize, as one French critic has said, both the *voyant* faculty of Rimbaud and Mallarmé's feeling for the mystery and sacredness of the word. This high period begins in the early 1860s, and is not entirely consistent;! the power seems to come and go, but it is indubitably there. And when it is present, she can describe with clinical precision the actual emotional event, the supreme moment of anguish, and even her own death itself. And she finds symbols which fit the event—terrible symbols. The experience of suffering is like dying of the cold; or it resembles the approach of a maelstrom, which finally engulfs the victim; one escapes from suffering as from the paws of a fiend, from whose grasp one emerges more dead than alive. One poem, written about 1863, defies analysis: the poem which begins "My life had stood—a loaded gun," which I would like to read you.

> My life had stood—a Loaded Gun
> In Corners—till a Day
> The Owner passed—identified—
> And carried Me away—
>
> And now We roam in Sovreign Woods—
> And now We hunt the Doe—
> And every time I speak for Him—
> The Mountains straight reply—
>
> And do I smile, such cordial light
> Upon the Valley glow—
> It is as a Vesuvian face
> Had let its pleasure through—
>
> And when at Night—Our good Day done—
> I guard My Master's head—
> 'Tis better than the Eider-Duck's
> Deep Pillow—to have shared—
>
> To foe of His—I'm deadly foe—
> None stir the second time—
> On whom I lay a Yellow Eye—
> Or an emphatic Thumb—

Though I than He—may longer live
He longer must—than I—
For I have but the power to kill,
Without—the power to die—

Is this an allegory, and if so of what? Is it a cry from some
psychic deep where good and evil are not to be separated? In any
case, it is a poem whose reverberations are infinite, as in great
music; and we can only guess with what agony it was written
down.

This power to say the unsayable—to hint at the unknowable—
is the power of the seer, in this woman equipped with an ironic
intelligence and great courage of spirit. The stuff of Emily
Dickinson's imagination is of this world; there is nothing macabre
about her material (in the manner of Poe) and there is very
little of the labored or artificial about her means. If "she mastered
life by rejecting it," she mastered that Nature concerning which
she had such ambivalent feeling by adding herself to the sum of
all things, in a Rilkean habit of praise. "She kept in touch with
reality," someone has said of her, "by the clearest and finest of
the senses—the sense of sight. Perhaps the great vitality of
contact by vision is the essence, in part, of her originality."
How exactly she renders the creatures of this earth! She gives
them to us, not as symbols of this or that, but as themselves.
And her lyrical notation is so precise, so fine and moves so closely
in union with her mind, that she is continually striking out
aphorisms, in the manner of mystics, from Plotinus to Blake.
And as her life goes on, everything becomes whittled down,
evanescent. Her handwriting becomes a kind of fluid print;
her poems become notations; all seems to be on the point of disappearing. And suddenly all disappears.

"She was a visionary," says Richard Chase, "to whom truth
came with exclusive finality [and] like her Puritan forebears
she was severe, downright, uncompromising, visionary, factual,
sardonic."

"My business is to create," said the poet Blake. "My business is
circumference," said the poet Dickinson. And we know that the
physical center of that circumference was to remain the town
of Amherst, which almost exactly one hundred years ago (on
December 10th, 1859) Miss Dickinson described with great

charm and deep affection, in a letter to Mrs. Samuel Bowles:
"It storms in Amherst five days—it snows, and then it rains, and
then soft fogs like vails hang on all the houses, and then the
days turn Topaz, like a lady's pin . . ."—as delicate a description
as a New England town and New England winter weather have
ever received.

ISAK DINESEN

(1943)

We now know Isak Dinesen to be Baroness Blixen of Denmark. It was apparent from the first that the author who published, in complete pseudonymity, *Gothic Tales* in 1934 was a woman, a native of Northern Europe, and a person whose sources were in some manner attached to the feudal tradition. *Gothic Tales,* because of their exuberance (severely regulated as it was), their civilized bitterness, their brilliantly informed fantasy, were clearly an end product of some kind. They had the quality, under the surface classicism of their style, of that sparkling improvisation contrasted with melancholy reverie so usual in Romantic music; the romance of the incompletely lighted and fantastic nineteenth-century "soul," at the end of one thing as much as at the beginning of another; caught back into nostalgia for the past and filled with premonitory anguish. But unlike Romantic music, these tales came to some sharp conclusions. Their intellectual underpinning was sturdy. They were highly conscious productions. The author behind them was not one to be taken in, least of all by herself.

Out of Africa (1938) brought the unknown author before us in the round. An autobiographical account of Baroness Blixen's life as owner of a coffee plantation in German East Africa, later Kenya Colony, it showed exactly what a feudal heritage had given this woman, and to what use she had put inherited ideas of responsibility. Her growth as an artist is also described; so that the reader, having read *Gothic Tales,* with only the information he could deduce from it, comes to any later work knowing more than one usually knows concerning a modern writer. He knows, for example, the writer's courage, both physical and moral, having watched it at work in rude and isolated surroundings. He also knows by the facts and their manner of presentation that she is as tender as she is courageous, as profoundly perceptive as she is sensitively humane.

Winter's Tales is not *Gothic Tales* repeated. The inventive extravagance has been reduced; the stories do not multiply, one within another, in the earlier manner. They share the simplicity and background, often, of the folk tale. But unlike the folk tale, they do not repeat some obsession of the simple mind—fear, desire for power or wealth, or luck, or freedom from restriction. And it is interesting to see how completely they differ from those "fairy tales" composed by Isak Dinesen's fellow-countryman, Hans Christian Andersen. In Andersen the folk tale took on, for all his charm of treatment, elements of sentiment and "rise": The Ugly Duckling is a far more bourgeois character than Cinderella. The majority of the characters in *Winter's Tales* are not going anywhere, in the success-story sense. And those who have some selfish or insolent plans for themselves are soon taken down by unforeseen small circumstance. Destiny's plans, far more noble than any they could have invented for themselves, take over (as in the case of the young wife in "The Pearls" and the writer in "The Young Man with the Carnation"). These plans of destiny often have heavy justice in them and work on two planes. The cruel feudal despot who misuses his power ("Sorrow-Acre") is baffled not only by the selflessness of his victim but by the unfaithfulness of his wife, whose child by her lover will break the closed line of succession. And at the center of the book stands the child Jens, the pure poet and "comic fabulist" who knows his place in this world without having to be taught it; when he is transplanted from poverty to riches, he can look back on poverty with pleasure, accepting luxury the while, and remember the pleasing elements in the nature of his former friends, the rats.

The blunt and flourishing optimism of middle-class materialism could not have produced these stories. That we get them at this particular period of history is a remarkable thing in itself.

They are, it is true, from time to time informed with the sharp bite of the civilized fable. But they are not fables, but parables. They deal almost entirely with inner themes of "love, hate, and reparation," with spiritual, not "practical" truths. The witty yet profound treatment of the artist and his public in terms of God and Job ("A Consolatory Story") sums up the author's view of one problem of reconciliation. Here light is thrown upon a situation by means of irony. Elsewhere Isak Dinesen prefers to irradiate mysteries of conduct by mention of other mysteries, as when, at the end of "The Invincible Slave Owners," the perplexed lover, realizing that certain human situations exist which nothing can change, contemplates the waterfall and thinks of the fugue. As in all good parables, the lines of meaning are not pulled tight. The reader is left with the threads in his own hands, and can examine and combine them according to his own experience.

The period quality is exquisitely managed. The publishers, it is true, have built up all the fustian possibilities of this atmosphere. The book is very nearly bound in seafoam and stardust; and one must grin and bear the book-jacket surrealism which runs over onto the end-papers. The little blurbs provided by the publicity department on the jacket for each story should be ignored; their facts are sometimes wrong and their interpretation almost always queer. These are by no means special or bizarre stories. They belong to an old and great tradition and are worthy of it. That they have been written in English is our good luck, the chance of contact with European tradition at present being what it is. It is good to be able to read them early, even though they are certain to be around for a long time.

T. S. ELIOT

COLLECTED POEMS (*1936*)

The later poems of T. S. Eliot, for years fugitive and hard to come by, are at last joined to his early work in the recently published *Collected Poems*. So the record, up to now, of the poet who has changed the accent of poetry written in our period is at last completely available to us. We can trace Eliot's "horror of a life without faith" from its first complete statement in "Geron-tion," through its elaboration in "The Waste Land," to its logical conclusion in "Sweeney Agonistes." "Sweeney Agonistes," still a fragment and likely to remain one, twitching to music-hall rhythms, reduced men and women to gargoyles who gibbered in a world where even the comparative nobility of despair was not possible. Faith began to stammer in "The Hollow Men," and from that point on, Eliot's belief mounts beyond his irony and pessimism, not in an unbroken line, but in a line renewed when broken. It is now possible to read the beautiful poems of the transition period ("Journey of the Magi" through "Difficulties of a Statesman") in their proper order, as well as the latest brief lyrics, the nonsense rhymes, and the fine "Choruses from 'The Rock.' " The last poem in the collection, "Burnt Norton," rather long and, compared to the crisp early poems, rather vaporous, brings the later phase to conclusion that resolves on a note of balanced calm and even a mild sort of joy.

Of the quality of the poetry there is little need to speak. Eliot, the self-styled "minor poet," brought back into English poetry the salt and the range of which it had long been deprived. From Dante through the Symbolists, he took what he needed from the varied stream of poetic resources; he swung the balance over from whimpering Georgian bucolics to forms wherein contemporary complexity could find expression. The *Collected Poems* are more than a work of poetic creation; they are a work of poetic regeneration.

THE FAMILY REUNION (1939)

Eliot's plays and poems, subsequent to his espousal of the Anglican faith, have not been entirely joyful. They have been well streaked, in fact, with his early defeatism and despairs, and the social-satirical note has seemed to be vanishing from them by degrees. *The Family Reunion*, a verse play with a contemporary setting, will appear to the reader waiting for pure spiritual joy to sound, after the fanfares attendant upon conversion, almost too good to be true. The new play presents an integrated Eliot, completely in control of himself and so filled with insight that the old Eliot comes in for some pretty close dissection, if not caricature. It is no small feat to bring off a Christian (a Jungian, a Sophoclean) theme of reconciliation with the conscience (the unconscious sense of guilt, the Eumenides) and at the same time to expose, down to the last set phrase, the hollow conventions of an upper (in this case, English) class. It is no small feat to surround and examine an early phase of the self by means of a later one.

The play is divided into two parts of three scenes each. In the first scene of Part I, it is the social irony which first attracts the attention. The two non-ironic characters—Harry, the eldest son, who returns to his mother's house ridden by real or imagined guilt—and his aunt, Agatha, who is addicted to clipped sibylline speech and an occasional piece of late-Eliot incantation—sound definitely suspect. There has been just about enough sensitive foreboding in Eliot. Cellars and attics, "the noxious smell untraceable in the drains," "the attraction of the dark passage, the paw under the door" sound so like parody that one is put on guard. A new element, however, soon appears to exorcise the old horror. Downing, Harry's "man," who has "looked after his Lordship for over ten years," is sheer practical common sense, and this Figaro-like conception is reassuring. Eliot, one feels, cannot be planning to recede once more into neurotic terrors while Downing, offstage, cleans up the car. And a complete recession does not, in fact, occur. We are drawn, it is true, with the struggling Harry, right down to childhood and back, straight through the necessary confrontation of the Eumenides. Eliot probes from the outside into the neurotic's tendencies toward cruelty and suffering in a manner one would not have thought possible. Harry, able at last to face his pursuers and accept them, liberates himself. He is then free to escape the deathly house, his mother's relentless will, and the stupidity of his relatives. His sibylline aunt bids him Godspeed. Downing goes with him, and the spectacle of master and man riding off to spiritual liberty in a well-kept car is the play's one faintly ridiculous effect.

Eliot of late years has talked at great length about the value of religious experience. *The Family Reunion* is the first incontrovertible evidence that he has thoroughly experienced the phenomenon. It is interesting to note that other than traditional Church of England symbols have contributed to this play.

Any person who has ever experienced the smallest success in the struggle for spiritual reconciliation will recognize that Eliot here demonstrates in detail the uncheatable nature of the combat. And Henry James never flayed the upper-class English with more delicate skill.

FOUR QUARTETS (1943)

Four Quartets is the first T. S. Eliot volume of serious poetry to appear in America since his *Collected Poems,* published in 1936. The first three poems included have been in print for some time, however. "Burnt Norton," with which the book opens, is familiar as the final piece in *Collected Poems,* and "East Coker" and "The Dry Salvages" were published in the *Partisan Review* in 1940 and 1941 respectively. Taken together, the four rather long works—"Little Gidding" is the other one—show Eliot experimenting in his tireless way. They also show a crucial turn in his thinking, and in his general approach toward the Anglican religion, which he embraced, along with British citizenship, in 1927.

The four poems are linked together by two devices. First, the basic construction of "Burnt Norton" sets the form of the others. Each has five sections. Each has a lyric in its second section, followed without pause by a meditation—development of theme, as it were. A second lyric stands alone in each fourth section as a detached melody. These lyrics and reflections, falling in their allotted places, are supposed, no doubt, to have the effect of the changes in the sonata form. This intended effect comes through, although not, of course, as definitely as in music. The second device is the use of place names as titles to all the poems. Eliot being the subtle inheritor of the Symbolist tradition, these specific localities afford him points from which to range or on which to brood. Burnt Norton is an English country house with a rose garden. East Coker is the town in Somersetshire from which Eliot's forebears emigrated to America in the seventeenth century. The Dry Salvages, according to the author's note, are "a small group of rocks, with a beacon, off the N.E. coast of Cape Ann, Massachusetts." And Little Gidding is the site in Huntingdonshire where, in 1625 or so, Nicholas Ferrar set up an Anglican religious community, which flourished in a quiet way until its destruction by the Puritans about twenty years later. Eliot, therefore, weaves back and forth between his native America and his adopted Britain. He has touched his own presumably Puritan sources and also celebrated, as a convert to the Anglican communion, a shrine belonging to what has been called the golden age of the Church of England.

The form and background once straight in our minds—Eliot gives no explanation of either beyond the note quoted above—we can read the poems for mere enjoyment, for they are certainly as beautiful as anything he ever wrote. The lyrics, especially the second in "East Coker" and the two in "Little Gidding," show what the poet can do in the province of pure emotion when all irony has been eliminated.

It has been said that some of Eliot's utterances about religion have been suspiciously melodramatic. Eliot, in making religious tradition a frame for his art, chose—the artist's inevitable choice —cohesion and integrity. But a choice of form was evidently not enough. It is interesting to trace Eliot's shift from formal interest in his religion (its history, rituals, and so on) toward a far from formal interest in his own post-conversion spiritual development. The four poems in this book, together with his play, *The Family Reunion* (1939), are records of that development, wrung out of him despite all obstacles of reserve. Eliot's conversion was accompanied by a certain amount of pride and arrogance. In "Burnt Norton," however, the classic procedure of spiritual death and rebirth begins and "the dark night of the soul" is heralded. The poem bears all the marks of deep depression. It is faint and minor in tone, circular and repetitive in thought. A flight back to childhood is considered, and the way out, through darkness and mental suffering, is recognized to be necessary only in an academic way. Here, human sympathy is also academic, if not actually lacking. This is the middle Eliot manner fading out and running down.

But in "East Coker" the suffering has been faced, lived through, understood, and the poet is back on his feet. The old lamenting and beseeching have completely disappeared. This is a terribly bitter poem, but the bitterness has some of the early Eliot edge, and it is directed outward, toward reality. The passage on re-nunciation at the end of section three; the "wounded surgeon" lyric, in a wonderfully effective stanza form; the surprising and unexpected direct personal comment on self and career with which the poem ends—all these are new and fine. The key becomes major, the effects broader. The broadening persists throughout "The Dry Salvages," and in "Little Gidding" many of Eliot's themes—one could almost say fetishes—are brought together in a real feat of reconciliation.

Eliot here stands at a distant remove from the "aged eagle" role in which he presented himself, with considerable affectation, in *Ash Wednesday* thirteen years ago. He has learned lessons in patience and sympathy, a firm basis for renewed poetic strength.

PAUL ELUARD

(1939)

Paul Eluard, one of the original members of the Dada "school," moved into Surrealism, under the leadership of André Breton, when "the Dada anarchy" was outlawed. He has held closely to the tenets of Surrealism through all their hardening and stiffening, in spite of the fact that his gifts seem perfectly opposed to all that Surrealism once stood for, and all it stands for now. The reasons for his alliance with Dada would be somewhat difficult to determine. It was natural, certainly, that a talent like Eluard's—simple and sensitive, quite unclouded by the fumes of the macabre, and undisturbed by the sardonic horseplay and involved cynicism of his sturdier contemporaries—should be forced, during the twenties, to take on some kind of protective coloring, make some defensive alliance, in order to exist. Such a talent was of the exact kind to move his contemporaries to parody. Eluard's complete complaisance to Surrealist doctrine, before and after Surrealism's alliance with "the revolution," permitted him to go on writing; but his passivity has lapsed, at times, into a kind of masochism, vitiating his work and making his "thinking" ridiculous. He has never rebelled against Breton's manifestoes and excommunications; he is, in fact, the complete complement of Breton, who has been called the Saint-Just of Surrealism. He obediently became a Communist when Surrealism, the party wedded to complete non-utilitarianism and to the exploration of the wayward subconscious, automatism and the dream, developed a dogma equally unyielding, and in many ways paralleling Communist dogma. Eluard has obeyed, it is true, without once changing his fundamental poetic nature. He stands today in the peculiar position of a poet who has remained a depository of one kind of poetic expression (a kind, as we shall see, which is not particularly French), while paying more than lip-service to doctrines in every way inimical to the development of that expression.

Surrealism has received little analytical discussion in English. Because it cast back for exemplars through the 1870 generation in France (Rimbaud and Lautréamont), to Baudelaire, it seemed to gather up Symbolist functions, and, moreover, extend them by adding Freudian theory to the Symbolist base. Actually, this widening and deepening never occurred, and Symbolism was contracted rather than extended, by Surrealism. Since Eluard's poetry is so symptomatic of one result of adherence to Surrealist theory, it is necessary to outline briefly the nature of the Surrealist revolt against Dada, and the uneven history of Symbolism (which did not proceed in an unbroken line, as is generally supposed) after Mallarmé.

In 1898 Mallarmé's chief pupil, Valéry, entered the silence which was to remain unbroken for twenty years. And although the influence of Rimbaud was not entirely dead, it was subjected to traditional distortions, chiefly at the hands of Claudel and Rivière, who endeavored to prove Rimbaud a Catholic character and an embodiment of angelic (though fallen) innocence. A regression toward convention and traditionalism had set in. Marcel Raymond describes it in his *De Baudelaire au surréalisme:*

Writers seemed prisoners of their culture. Psychological or physiological drama, recitals of sociologists, physicians and geographers, poems by archeologists or men of erudition, the literary jests and *divertissements* of mandarins—all these [pre-1914] works rested on a base of positive knowledge, considered unshakable and untouchable. Literature was . . . limed in the mass of facts, laws and hypotheses which the remarkable development of human knowledge had heaped up . . . during the 19th century. The great majority of the works of the period proposed to demonstrate something, whether by describing, analysing, explaining individual or collective phenomena, or by decomposing them into rational elements. . . . These works were clear and satisfied the needs of a simple logic. . . . All were determinist or finalist. The creative freedom of the artist could not function except between walls of truth, utility or good sense. . . . Poetry, from the early epoch of Parnassianism, had been towed along behind philosophy and history. Hugo, Leconte de Lisle, Prudhomme and Hérédia had wished to condense in their verse a world of ideas and facts. It is true that the Symbolists, coming after the Parnassians, had . . . opened literary windows and allowed the fog of mystery to come into the study of the man of letters. But, after 1895, the Symbolists were violently attacked: neo-classicists . . . wrote erudite poetry. . . . All the writers joined in a common cult of the intelligence: between a poem by Mme. de Noailles and certain pages of the novels of Régnier, between the phases of Anatole France, Maurras, Barrés, and the poems of Moréas, between the tirades of Paul Adam, the invectives of Mirbeau and certain social poems of Verhaeren, the difference was only one of meter and rhyme. . . .

In this situation, it is interesting to remember, it was foreigners like Rilke and Yeats who received refreshment from whatever feeble sparks of Symbolism remained alive. (Villiers de l'Isle-Adam was such a spark for Yeats. Rilke went back to Baudelaire.)

The birth of Dada coincided with the renovation of the "conception" of the universe, and of the spiritual life, by the scientists whose work, conceived and tested before 1914, became generally available thereafter. "Relativist hypotheses made absolute truth recede far beyond the touch of human reason"; the Freudian hypotheses broke down and complicated "the grossly simplified analyses, in the moral field, of the preceding era." Art, always acting as a symptom, and always well before the event (even in its least energetic periods), had already announced the change (Rimbaud, two generations previously). An undercurrent of revolt against officially respectable literature, colored with occultism, interest in the supernatural, the erotic and the sadistic, had begun before the war. Jarry was its chief mystificator. Apollinaire, of Slav and Italian-Swiss blood, born in Rome, brought back into French literature a forgotten interest of the Symbolists: an interest in "popular poetry"—the literature produced by everyday life. Popular songs and the machines and apparatuses then beginning to change the technique of European living appeared in his poetry more often than the esoteric trappings of the macabre. He rarely tried to elevate his tone to match the sublimity acceptable to French writing. He worked best on the level of wit. He was able "to create an atmosphere wherein the banal, the daily, the threadbare theme was transfigured." He was also capable of true pathos, and it was his wit and pathos which were deleted almost entirely from the Surrealist movement whose name derived from one of his invented terms. "It was things themselves [which interested Apollinaire], happenings which ought continually to become 'the marvelous,' if looked at with a certain bias."

Dada, soon dead and denounced by Surrealism, was, in its beginnings, a far more vigorous assault against logic and the weight of bourgeois ideals than Surrealism, fixed, humorless, and from the beginning out for the dead-end effects of madness and mystification. Symptomatic of postwar derangement, hysteria, and despair, Dada nevertheless contained elements of control over and insight into its aberrations. Its working resembled the forms of hysteria, but it was the hysteria of an intelligent living entity suffering from shock. It never developed the paranoid symptoms of Surrealism. It was able to laugh at its own jokes, be cynical with its own cynicism and cruel to its own sadism, and its dogmatic and persecutory symptoms were mild, if they existed at all. It found room for Max Jacob's *macaroniques* and bold parodies, and for Eluard's pathos. Surrealism, on its first appearance, immediately showed signs of a sobering-up process. It was announced by a call to order, disguised as a manifesto for more freedom. Its championship of automatism, its great show of dives into the depths of the subconscious and flights into the empyrean of *le merveilleux* were accompanied by a reciprocal tendency to law-making, litany-singing, and the issuance of marching orders. Breton's litany on "the marvelous" might be set to four-four time: "*Le merveilleux est toujours beau, n'importe quel merveilleux est beau, il n'y a même que le merveilleux qui soit beau.*"

It would be simple to produce an analogy between the functioning of Surrealism and the mechanisms discoverable in a person suffering from a psychosis. The more the irresponsibility of the "subconscious" is given rein, the more an increasingly rigid and authoritarian set of rules is thrown up, which parallel the workings, in a psychotic individual, of a super-ego, or too harsh conscience. The "jacobin and jansenist logic" superimposed upon Surrealism allowed it to remain detached from reality, and worked off the guilt of artists who had reduced their art to a kind of collection of picture postcards or a parlor game. Art, under these conditions, must become more rather than less fixed; its forms become monotonous. The monotony extends to the work of those "rage types" who take it out in invective (Surrealism is rich in these); it shows itself in the reduction of form to the bleak list and the tiresome juxtaposition. Not only is growth impossible, but recession is probable.

Breton and Eluard at one time collaborated in the writing of a book of poems which imitated the speech of "victims of mental debility, acute mania, general paralysis, etc." They "hoped," in their notes to these productions, "that attempts to simulate the maladies for which one is usually confined, may one day replace the ballad, the sonnet, the epic. . . ." Breton wished his recitals of dreams to be stenographic, and his approach to "madness, the dream, the absurd, the incoherent, the hyperbolic and all that opposes the summary appearance of the real" is one of "precise experiment." The truth is, that in Surrealism, the dream is treated in the most primitive way: it is recounted or imitated; Surrealist poets have gone into the subconscious as one would take a short trip into the country, and have brought back some objects of grisly or erotic-sadistic connotation, or a handful of unrelated images, in order to prove their journey. It has not occurred to them that the journey has been taken many times, that human imagination has, before this, hung a golden bough before the entrance to hell, and has described the profound changes the true journey brings about. It is a journey not to be undertaken lightly, or described without tension of any kind. And the *aller et retour,* if merely approximated, produces approximate expression: the sulphurous, the sadistic, the luxurious macabre, the Grand Guignol; or the childish, fatuous game.

2

"Give the initiative to words," said Mallarmé, and if this command is followed to its logical conclusion, the subject disappears. It is (or has been) a Surrealist pleasure to take the kernel of meaning out of forms into which meaning is most closely compressed. Here are three surrealist proverbs by Eluard and Péret:

> *Les éléphants sont contagieux.*
> *Les cerises tombent ou les textes manquent.*
> *Les grands oiseaux font les petites persiennes.*

Or the definition. Here are two Eluard *définitions*:

> *Un homme vivant monté sur un cheval vivant rencontre*
> *une femme vivante tenant en laisse un chien vivant.*

> *Une robe noire ou une robe blanche? Des grands*
> *souliers ou des petits?*

If the fortuitous brings in (by chance?) a semblance of wit (as it does, certainly, in the above quotations), this wit must be countered by the "fortuitous" poem, dull as a flat joke:

> *Un grand feu dans la cheminée*
> *Un bon tapis par terre*
> *Quelques chaises autour de la table*
> *Des brosses des charrues des clairons des dentelles*

> *Le tout soigneusement enduit de glu.*
> (Cours naturel, 1938)

A fine fire in the fireplace
A good carpet on the floor
Chairs around the table
Brushes ploughs bugles laces

All smoothly covered with bird-lime.

It is plain that Eluard is not perfectly freely "giving the initiative to words"; the element of choice is working, if in a reverse direction. In the two early poems which follow, Eluard's purity of diction, his taste (comparable in many ways to the taste of the Parnassians), and his pathos are evident:

LEURS YEUX TOUJOURS PURS

Jours de lenteur, jours de pluie,
Jours de miroirs brisés et d'aiguilles perdues,
Jours de paupières closes à l'horizon des mers,
D'heures toutes semblables, jours de captivité,

Mon esprit qui brillait encore sur les feuilles

Et les fleurs, mon esprit est nu comme l'amour,
L'aurore qu'il oublie lui fait baisser la tête
Et contempler son corps obéissant et vain.

Pourtant, j'ai vu les plus beaux yeux du monde,
Dieux d'argent qui tenaient des saphirs dans leurs mains,
De véritables dieux, des oiseaux dans la terre
Et dans l'eau, je les ai vus.

Leurs ailes sont les miennes, rien n'existe
Que leur vol qui secoue ma misère,
Leur vol d'étoile et de lumière

Leur vol de terre, leur vol de pierre
Sur les flots de leurs ailes,

Ma pensée soutenue par la vie et la mort.
                    (*Capitale de la douleur*, 1926)

THEIR EYES FOREVER PURE

Slow-passing days, days of rain,
Days of broken mirrors and lost needles,
Days of eyelids closed to the seas' horizon,
Of hours all alike, days of captivity,

My spirit which still glitters on the leaves
And the flowers, my spirit is naked like love,
Its forgotten dawn makes it lower its head
And look upon its obedient and vain body.

Nevertheless, I have seen the most beautiful eyes in the world,
Silver gods who hold sapphires in their hands,
Actual gods, birds in the earth
And in the water, I have seen them.

Their wings are mine, nothing exists
But their flight which shakes off my unhappiness,
Their flight of star and light

Their flight of earth, their flight of stone
On the tide of their wings,

My thought sustained by life and death.

("No play with words," Eluard says. "Everything is comparable to everything, everything finds its echo, its reason, its resemblance, its opposition, its transformation. And this transformation is infinite.")

LA NECESSITE

Sans grande cérémonie à terre
Près de ceux qui gardent leur équilibre
Sur cette misère de tout repos
Tout près de la bonne voie
Dans la poussière du sérieux
J'établis des rapports entre l'homme et la femme
Entre les fontes du soleil et le sac à bourdons
Entre les grottes enchantées et l'avalanche
Entre les yeux cernés et le rire aux abois
Entre la merlette héraldique et l'étoile de l'ail
Entre le fil à plomb et le bruit du vent
Entre la fontaine aux fourmis et la culture des framboises
Entre le fer à cheval et le bout des doigts
Entre la calcédoine et l'hiver en épingles
Entre l'arbre à prunelles et le mimétisme constaté
Entre la carotide et le spectre du sel
Entre l'araucaria et la tête d'un nain
Entre les rails aux embranchements et la colombe rousse
Entre l'homme et la femme
Entre ma solitude et toi.

(La Vie immédiate, 1932)

NECESSITY

Without great ceremony on earth
Near those who keep their equilibrium
Upon this unhappiness without risk
Very near the good road
In the dust of serious people
I establish relations between man and woman
Between the smeltings of the sun and the bag of drones
Between enchanted grottoes and the avalanche
Between eyes surrounded by dark circles and the laugh of
     desperation
Between the heraldic female blackbird and the star of
     garlic
Between the leaden thread and the noise of the wind
Between the fountain of ants and the cultivation of
     strawberries
Between the horseshoe and the fingertips
Between chalcedony and winter in pins
Between the tree of eyeballs and verified mimicry
Between the carotid artery and the ghost of salt

Between the araucaria and the head of a dwarf
Between rails at a junction and the russet dove
Between man and woman
Between my solitude and thee.

It is a limitation in Eluard that he is aiming at one kind of
poetry and producing another. Loose form and the continually
changed image must have beneath them—or rather, must rise
from the very existence of—a ground-swell energy, wildness, and
ferocity in the poet. When the poetic gift is sensitive, and its
projection mild, on the other hand, it is form alone which gives
edge to its nuances. Eluard is far closer, as Jean Cassou has
pointed out, to the German poet's nostalgia and "suffering"
than to the French poet's sublimity and lucidity. And he is certainly more close, in nature, to the Parnassians than to Baudelaire, Rimbaud, or Lautréamont, in all of whom ferocity is
present. The French classic line intersected, in Baudelaire, with
the macabre and Gothic; classic form was used with passionate
feeling and imagination and the results are superb and inimitable
poems. Rimbaud and Lautréamont charged language with such
force that it broke through form; even Hugo's rhetoric was not
adequate for these personalities. Even in Mallarmé the reverberation of emotion sounds through his designs for fans, and his
preoccupation with his furniture and lace curtains; the grandeur
of glaciers, thunder, and rubies invades the poetry from which
actual "meaning" has been barred. When Rimbaud wished to
express pathos, he immediately and instinctively went back to
form (in the poems "Bonheur" and "Chanson de la plus haute
tour," for example). The results of imitating a poet, whose form
is distorted because it is bearing more condensed meaning and
emotion than it can bear, may be observed in the imitators of
Hopkins. The tricks are managed, but the true effects not in
any way approached.

Emotion, when it rises above pathos, immediately takes on
complexity. Eluard, well below the complex level, and attempting
to work with the automatic and hallucinatory, at the end is left
with his vocabulary (simple, exquisitely chosen), his syntax
(also of the simplest), and his one emotional effect: "an amorous
and dolorous obsession of an infinitely pathetic character."

Eluard is incapable of the poem of revolt. When he feels that such a poem is required of him, he writes the following undistinguished and adolescent lines:

CRITIQUE DE LA POESIE

C'est entendu je hais le règne des bourgeois
Le règne des flics et des prêtres
Mais je hais plus encore l'homme qui ne hait pas
Comme moi
De toutes ses forces

Je crache à la face de l'homme plus petit que nature
Qui à tous mes poèmes ne préfère pas cette CRITIQUE DE LA
  POESIE

(La Vie immédiate, 1932)

CRITICISM OF POETRY

It is certain that I hate the rule of the bourgeois
The rule of cops and priests
But I hate even more the man who does not hate it
As I do
With all my strength

I spit in the face of the man smaller than nature
Who does not prefer to all my other poems this CRITICISM OF
  POETRY

The kindest of Eluard's critics have warned him against the traditional French affectation into which his writing can so easily be led. He shows this tendency in his comparisons, which are likely to compare something of emotional weight to something pretty or abstract, or charmingly strange. Or delicate attributes are given to creatures and objects of a certain natural energy and strength:

> Birds perfume the woods
> Rocks their great nocturnal lakes

And it is possible, in Eluard, as in any poet, to detect the faked phrase, put in to make things harder, or to render matters, to

the casual glance at least, more profound. All the manifestoes
in the world cannot infuse import into "agile incest" or "fishes of
anguish." This sort of thing, if persisted in, becomes *mignardise
et confiserie*.

Eluard's virtues are apparent, and his influence, if not strong,
might be importantly pervasive. His basic naturalness, existing
uniquely among his contemporaries, preserves in French literature (at a time when such a delicate ingredient might be entirely
lost) a *pathétique* equally as valuable as the sublimity, wit, irony,
malice, and corrosive rhetorical splendors with which that literature has always been so well supplied. Apollinaire combined this
pathos with wit; he has moments which go back to Villon. Pathos
alone, or in combination, is contrary to the self-conscious, anti-
sentimental, and synthetically tough spirit of the time; but it is
a valuable civilized and salutary element, none the less. That
Eluard's gifts should have been forced, by the fashion or neurosis
of his period, to disguise themselves as "unconscious" (so that
their true imaginative flights will not lie open to scorn), and
be reduced to the level of a word game, is peculiar enough.
That they should have been twisted into the use of propaganda,
and made to function under manifestoes, literary and otherwise,
will certainly amuse future critics and diagnosticians of his era.

EUROPEAN POETRY
(1941)

Emery Neff's *A Revolution in European Poetry: 1660–1900* is described on its jacket as "the only short history of European poetry since the Renaissance." It is incredible that this should be true; but as one considers, it seems all too possible that it is. Dr. Neff traces the enormous influence of French literary taste, during and after Louis XIV's reign, upon the countries of Europe; and the ferments produced in this taste, in the eighteenth and nineteenth centuries, by German literature and thought, a revived interest in Greece and Rome and the Orient, and political dislocations. At the end modern poetry emerges, after the appearance in France of Baudelaire, Rimbaud, and Verlaine.

Such an account is long overdue, and one is grateful for a new emphasis, not usual in histories of literature written in English, upon the European scene as a whole, rather than upon what went on in England alone. And although it is addressed specifically to "students and teachers of comparative literature," the general reader can share in this panoramic outlook, and watch the interplay of forces which lead to increasingly complex expression in modern poetry. In America interest in these European sources was dropped when the 1930s arrived with their material difficulties. Edmund Wilson's *Axel's Castle* was not followed up, as it should have been, by further detached discussion and by translations of works cited. The result has been that

American poetry in the thirties, when not completely provincial, was muddled as to its derivations.

The subject, as the author states, is, of course, immense. His method, on the whole, is admirable. He condenses in a masterly way, and writes coolly and clearly. He has refused to use the tags "neo-classical," "romantic," and whatnot; and, these often academic partitions once removed, the narrative moves with breadth and sweep. J. G. Robertson has said:

> There is manifest danger in the ineradicable instinct of our minds to classify and schematize. We love our antitheses: Classicism-romanticism; idealism-realism; collectivism-individualism. But with fuller knowledge comes clearness that such antitheses are inherently unreal; the evolution of thought shows no such sharp contrasts, no such hard and fast lines. Nature makes no leaps; and the progress of human idea, far from being a geometric progression, is an infinitely complicated growth, where one thought passes into its antithesis imperceptibly, like a dissolving view.

The need for these antitheses seems most real in a comparison of the arts of language. Because language is the carrier of ideas, it is easy to believe that it should be very little else than such a carrier. Comparative histories of architecture, painting, music, and even of "taste," escape bias more easily than comparative studies of the arts of language. Then it must be remembered that there are barriers in language. Linguistics are not needed in order to appreciate Palestrina, Mozart, Couperin, Purcell; or Piranesi, Dürer, Watteau, Constable. With poetry the ear and eye are not enough.

It cannot be said that Dr. Neff does much toward clarifying the inner qualities of the poetry with which he deals. He tends to tie up the spiritual with the turn of events and historic processes: changes of government, wars and their aftermaths, industrial changes, and alternate political enthusiasm and disillusionment. It has been said: "The critic . . . to reach the essence of poetry, must realize that he walks into a domain where the essential does not coincide with the most general, but with the most 'interior.' " But when we grant Neff's slight set toward the idea that poetry stems directly from the specific event (or in reaction against the specific event), his account of the historic background is thorough in the extreme. And when poets can be directly related to this background, he seldom makes an error, and very rarely an omission. He gives as admirably concise a description of the nature of French seventeenth-century taste as of Goethe's development and the development of *Faust*. He is also brilliantly thorough with the post-Napoleonic period: the rise of money; the struggle for civil rights and the rights of labor, in England and France; and the reactions of certain poets to these upheavals and transformations. He does a splendid job of disentangling the beginnings of modern criticism, giving Lessing and Herder their just due; and he performs another service in bringing out and relating to their age the great and neglected talents of Hölderlin, Leopardi, and Vigny.

Historic events, however, can never completely explain poetry. Poetry is often generations in advance of the thought of its time. It is often a throwback. Many imponderables make up the climate of literature. The often irrational turns of taste—the almost religious currents of guilt, fear, desperation, and disillusion (or of peace and release)—must be taken into account in the study of any art. Comparisons must include differences as well as likenesses. The gaps in Dr. Neff's scholarly (and truly valuable) correlation of poetic works, important events, and sources of ideas are consistent lacunae where might appear the poet or thinker out of series: the man who carried the past in him unresolved, or the man, not of his time, who is to be a force in the future.

For example, the works of Vico (not mentioned) were known, according to Robertson, to both Goethe and Herder. In 1681, when Boileau's *Art poétique* (of which Neff makes much) was being translated into English, Edward Young, the first precursor of the English Gothic Revival (of which Neff makes little) was born. Gray's enthusiasm for Ossian is put on record, but there is no mention of Gray's friend, Horace Walpole (whose Strawberry Hill has been described as "less an archaeological reconstruction than the expression of a state of soul"). Neff, with partial truth, traces Gothic interest to Germany and Bürger's *Lenore* (1774). But Walpole was reviving Gothic in England twenty years previous to this; and certainly native English Gothic stands behind both "The Ancient Mariner" and "Christabel." (Neff does not speak of Gothic but of "Wonder"; but how much more than

"Wonder" was this secularized return of medieval Catholicism
into Protestantism, always accompanied by a mask of anti-
Papistry!) Byron paid open tribute to William Beckford, another
precursor, and to Beckford's *Vathek* and Johnson's *Rasselas,* as
sources of Eastern color. *Vathek* appeared twenty years before
"Kubla Khan" was written.

It is, of course, ridiculous to push back influences too far; but
should not that friend of Winckelmann, Piranesi—the "picturesque" artist who was, oddly enough, responsible for "Adam"
in England and "Empire" in France—be given some notice,
along with Winckelmann? And, if it is rather one-sided of Dr.
Neff to emphasize the classicism in eighteenth-century England
at the expense of the century's Gothic side (the two streams
went on concurrently, according to good authority, from 1750
to 1830), it is certainly impossible to explain how German influence got into France without mentioning Madame de Staël. (Neff
does not allow Madame de Staël in his text; merely in his ap-
pended chronology.) Madame de Staël, according to Thibaudet,
smuggled Romanticism into France "through the 'gulf' of Geneva
and Coppet." Again, though Dr. Neff states outright that his
method is necessarily selective, it is certainly odd that so much
is made of Hugo and Leconte de Lisle (both of whom, of course,
bring out a great many of the points Neff stresses: the political
enthusiasms of the one; the disillusion with politics, and conse-
quent "escape" into exotic themes, of the other) while nothing
whatever is said of Béranger, Gérard de Nerval, or Banville.
Béranger, the most popular post-Revolution poet in France, died
in the year of *Bovary* and *Les Fleurs du mal* (how ironically
these events complete one another!). Nerval was "the only French
poet able to bring the actual feeling of the German ballad over
into French poetry; the one French poet of the time completely
open to the legend and music of Germany." Banville, admired
by Baudelaire, far from being made gloomy by political events,
"mocked the Empire while adoring it," and wrote of exotic
subjects in the most cheerful way.

Dr. Neff ends his book with the usual sad thoughts on *fin de
siècle.* But in 1900 poetry in Europe was just about to pass into
a new era of brilliance: Yeats, Rilke, Valéry, Apollinaire, were
alive and soon to produce modern work unmatched in depth,

subtlety, and complexity. The true synthesis, of which Neff certainly has a conception, must not only range widely but plunge deeply under the surface of events. One need not be either morbid or a mystic to know that this is true; such syntheses have been accomplished time and again in histories of arts other than literature. Certainly it is in the direction of *Einfühlung* that the liberation and future of comparative literature lies. Meanwhile, Dr. Neff has written a valuable book which should serve as a rational point of reference for students and the general reader alike.

EXPERIMENTALISTS
OF A NEW GENERATION
(1957)

The work of a new generation of "experimentalists"—young men (and an occasional young woman) who have lately thrown down the gage against the formal and the academic in poetry—has been published almost without exception by small presses. The San Francisco group has received a good deal of attention, but the new anti-formalism is beginning to surface in more places than one—in North Carolina, New York City, Cambridge, and Texas, in Montreal and Toronto. Sensing that the little magazines long ago lost their vigor and interest, the young now favor the publication of small books and pamphlets, sometimes well designed but usually not designed at all. There is nothing of the shy, wilting violet in these poets. They admire Whitman, but they have added to Whitmanian exuberance a number of fresh elements: many individuals are students of Zen Buddhism; almost all are extremely knowledgeable about modern painting and music as well as the poetry of those French post-Surrealists who have not come to terms with life (Michaux, Queneau, Prévert); and they have an extravagant admiration for the poetry and drama of García Lorca. Many "dig" cool jazz and approve of the hipster's formalized speech and laconic candor to the point of direct imitation. They usually have—unlike the Surrealists in general—a highly developed sense of humor; in fact, when they let down their defenses they can be very amusing indeed. All are against conformity, pretense, and gloom.

At present, it is difficult to separate out from the crowd the worth of individual talents, but some general goals have been fixed in the movement—enough to prove that this is not a unplanned mutiny. A pervasive desire to get out into the open in order to breathe fresh, creative air (the being-trapped-and-smothered motif shows up again and again) exists, and these young people are looking for some large poetic form that can accommodate anything and everything—including ordinarily rejected and suspect material—and wherein all the difficult attitudes may be assumed. They are impatient with small patterns and regular metres, which they find niggling and hampering. It is this insistence on largeness that has swept them over to an interest not only in Whitman but in Hart Crane, William Carlos Williams' "Paterson," Ezra Pound's "Cantos," and, surprisingly, Vachel Lindsay. They want spontaneity; one of the elements in cool jazz that attract them is its improvisation. They are certain, and unashamedly so, that the poet's essential function is bardic. The poet should be *heard*. They are familiar with recording apparatus, both discs and the more easily handled tape, and are perfectly willing to use it, as well as to appear on platforms before an audience. They show an active dislike for "the academies," the quarterly reviews, and "taught poetry." They fear and detest any touch of suburban ideals and are drawn to the underside of American life—saloons, cold-water flats, and jazz cellars, where they hope to observe and experience American loneliness, violence, and desperation.

This sense of existence as crisis and paradox has, in spite of the fact that we seem to have been aware of it before, brought renewed vigor to the American experimental line, which, until this recent outburst of energy, had almost entirely disappeared in affectation and artificiality. Warnings of dangers ahead, at the moment, may sound reactionary in the extreme, but certain proved dangers can be named. In the first place, poetry, or any other art, cannot compete with mass media on the latter's own terms. Neither can it (at present) imitate folk with any success. Then again, contemporary experimentalists cannot hope to deliver shock, in either form or content, as shock was delivered to French poetry by Rimbaud in the seventies or to poetry written in English by Pound, Eliot, and Gertrude Stein at the beginning of this century. Once form has been smashed, it has been smashed for good, and once a forbidden subject has been released, it has been released for good. Nowadays, the only way of producing shock in poetry, in any Western language, is to try to outshock, and this process soon tires the audience and exhausts the poet. Spontaneity, too, has been explored and utilized, from Dada through Surrealism, on all levels, from the conscious to the deeply subconscious and even the "demonic." It is never enough to smash form; form must be continually refreshed and renewed. And, after experiencing the poems of Baudelaire, Mallarmé, Hopkins, Valéry, Pound, Eliot, and Auden, the sensibilities of the contemporary reader demand some subtlety, some actual largeness of concept, some interesting effects of language, and some true wit. Originality, now as always, depends upon individual powers of insight, individual intensity, and an individual way with words. Loud shouts, extreme stances, exhibitionism of one kind or another are not the means the imagination takes to let the light through.

But the creative gumption already shown by this youngest group—or cluster of groups—should not be overlooked. The young men who are now playing it for laughs and excitement may develop into satirists of the first order, and those who are at present going in for Zen and the Sutras may, in the future, contribute both to poetry and to metaphysics. Meanwhile, their poems should be read. The *Evergreen Review*, established by Grove Press, in its second number printed a dozen poets of the San Francisco Bay area, together with articles about them. The City Lights Pocket Bookshop, in San Francisco (which publishes as well as sells poetry), and Jonathan Williams' Jargon Press, in Highlands, North Carolina, will supply lists and fill orders; here in New York, the Gotham Book Mart has many small-press items in stock. Buyers and readers are at least showing some interest in a renewed poetic liveliness that may lead into renewed poetic life.

GUSTAVE FLAUBERT
(1942)

The most important novel to be published in English in 1941 was the first intelligent translation into English of Flaubert's *L'Education sentimentale*. This novel, first published in 1869, was written after *Salammbo* and just before the final version of *La Tentation de Saint Antoine*. It is now generally acknowledged to be Flaubert's masterpiece. A profound and sardonic comment on Flaubert's own generation and the France of his youth, it is in every way pertinent to the human and social dilemmas of our own day.

The novel was viciously attacked by the critics and neglected by the general public, at its appearance. Only a few friends—Banville, the Goncourts, George Sand—understood Flaubert's intentions or appreciated his success in putting them through. Sand realized that Flaubert's readers were still too close to the events described, and too involved in the Second Empire point of view, to wish to appreciate the book's ruthless analysis of social change and human motives. They recognized themselves too easily. And Sand complained that Flaubert gave no overt clue to where his sympathies lay. She wanted "an expression of blame . . . to condemn the evil. People do not understand that you wanted precisely to depict a deplorable state of society which encourages bad instincts." Flaubert had run into this sort of obtuseness in the French public and government before this. It had brought about the suit against the morals of *Madame Bovary*. He was incapable of agreeing with Sand's rather sentimental moralistic demands. His idea of the relation between the individual and society was far more complicated than hers. Society warped the individual but was it not individuals who had created, and blown up to enormous proportions, the governments which symbolized this hampering agency? Perhaps the basic evil lay deeper, in the constitution of the human heart.

Flaubert was depressed by the book's failure. He wrote in 1874 to Turgenev that he was still astonished that this work had never been understood. He finally decided that the book lacked "the falseness of perspective." "Every work of art," he said, "ought to have a point, a summit, make a pyramid . . . or better, the light should strike some point of the sphere. Now, there is nothing of that sort in life. But Art is not nature!" Here Flaubert partially understands that in this novel he has created a new genre. Critics, including Henry James, have misunderstood the book's conclusions because they were in no way dealing, here, with another *Madame Bovary:* not with "realism" or "romance," but with satire of a high but hidden order.

There is no doubt that *Sentimental Education* is a difficult book to get the hang of, at a first reading. The reader must have a fair working knowledge of reaction and revolution in nineteenth-century France. To use a figure of Lowes Dickinson's, France was, throughout the century, politically in a state as though tracked by the Furies. It was a century of nervous unrest and of new and untried theory. And all theories, once applied, backfired in the most appalling way. The revolt against the Orléans line brought in the July monarchy (1830) and Louis Philippe's dead-weight bourgeois rule. Universal suffrage, granted after 1848 and thought to be the instrument to establish the kingdom of God on earth, resulted only in Louis Bonaparte and, after three years of the Second Republic, the Second Empire. Paris fought for freedom; the provinces, fighting for the still unlaid ghosts of the old regime and Napoleon, finally voted away the newly granted franchise itself. Added to the political melee was the social one. The Industrial Revolution struck France in the thirties, in the factories of Lyons. All political parties were thrown into the rise of money, and the new concept of the right to work. The resulting confusion was severe. It is precisely this confusion, and its results, mirrored in the characters of the men and women who were at once its creators and its victims, that Flaubert here describes.

The book, written under the Second Empire, covers the period from 1840 to Louis Napoleon's *coup d'état of* December, 1851—save for the last two chapters, which form a coda to the whole. The action, excepting a few short passages, is seen through the eyes of Frédéric Moreau, of the provincial landed middle class, newly come to Paris, as the book begins, to pass his law examinations. A new spirit is in the air. The tradition of Romanticism and of the Bohemian painter, writer, and poet had worn almost completely threadbare. The period of the career based on money deals of one sort or another (*Enrichissez-vous* was said to be the counsel of Louis Philippe to his subjects) had begun. Art and industry, art and journalism, stood opposed, in spite of naïve efforts to reconcile their purposes. (*Industrial Art* is the name of the magazine run by Arnoux, the husband of the woman Frédéric comes to adore; the paper of the unprincipled Hussonet begins under the name *Art* and ends up entitled *The Man About Town*.) Stock-jobbing, loans, investments, and mortgages were the preoccupation of deputies and ministers. Borrowing a little money and making more, getting in with "influential" people, occupied the minds of law students, writers, painters, and hangers-on. The movement of opportunism elaborates and expands into a mounting frenzy. Notes fall due; debts pile up; the fate of men and women depends on the worth or worthlessness of shares. Bankruptcies, auctions, bailiffs finish the hopes of guilty and innocent alike. Underneath runs the theme of personal treachery. Friends betray one another; old men revenge themselves in their wills; women take it out on rivals by holding over them old debts and promissory notes.

The revolts of Republicans and the new Socialists against bourgeois rule form the book's secondary theme. The theorists make plans and hold to rigid formulas. Spontaneous outbreaks of the people link up with the planned action of the revolutionaries. Barricades go up; arms are requisitioned from the citizens. The crowd swarms into the Tuileries; grand pianos and clocks are flung out of windows. One of the book's great set-pieces

describes the Paris street fighting in 1848. And the book closes
with Paris again under arms; the dragoons, aided by the police,
galloping against the citizens under the gaslight with sabers
drawn—and the Second Empire has begun.

Senecal, the democratic dogmatist who develops by degrees
into a tyrant and member of the police, is the character which
has astonished modern readers by its deadly accuracy and contemporary pertinence. "Where are the labor poets?" Senecal
asks, when shown a library. He wants, in literature, content and
not form. He thinks *tableaux vivants* corrupting for the daughters
of the proletariat. As a factory overseer, he extracts fines ruth-
lessly. "Democracy," he remarks, "does not mean license for the
individual. It means a common level under the law, the division
of labor—order!" "You've left out humanity," Frédéric answers.
It is Senecal who kills Dussardier, "the good fellow," the honest
believer in Socialist virtue "who attributed all the evil on earth to
authority."

And Flaubert traces down "an insane desire for authority, of
whatever kind if only it be authority," in all these people who
have lost so many natural links to life. "France, feeling herself
without a master [after '48], began to cry out in terror, like a
blind man without a stick, or a child that has lost its nurse." And
the reader continues to recognize these characters. There is something startlingly familiar in Hussonet, the journalist who prints
gossip and slander as news, who "extols the fifth-rate and disparages the first-class minds." Arnoux, the intermediate type
between Bohemian and businessman, infected with the failings
of both—"his mind was not elevated enough to attain to art
nor ordinary enough to think solely of profit, so that he was
ruining himself without satisfying anyone"—is closely akin to
Frederic, who feels the resemblance. Arnoux is a gourmet and
gives little dinners "with ten kinds of mustard." Deslauriers,
Frederic's friend, in the words of the Goncourts, is "with his fond
envy, his intermittences of perfidy and friendship, his solicitor's
temperament, a perfectly drawn type of the most widespread
kind of scurvy humanity." Mlle Vatnaz, the emancipated woman,
venomous, the dupe of her passions, a literary hack and go-
between with a business head, is still not a complete grotesque.

Then there is the gallery of "conservative humbugs," male

and female, whom Flaubert does not spare. "Bigotry of the rich rivaled the frenzy of the starving. . . . Property began to be confused with God, and attacks on it . . . almost resembled cannibalism." But Flaubert was out to show up "the bourgeois in blouses as well as the bourgeois in coats." He examines with the same detachment social theorists, the hysterics, terrorists, and fakes on the fringes of the Socialist movement, and the conservative money and power jugglers and their "distinguished" circle, ready to grease the palm of any government that came into power. The stupidity of the workers' meeting and the complicated spite of the dinner party are both analyzed. Flaubert wished to clear the reader's mind of all "accepted ideas" concerning the supposed nobility of either group. Suddenly, at the end of the book, we look back and see how each category has received its touch of clear-sightedness: these liberals who are at bottom neurotic reactionaries; these members of a new middle class who not only "have no interest in the things of the mind," who do not act according to motives of patience, pity, duty, love, or generosity, but actually do not know that such qualities exist. And has Flaubert spared from his satiric justice of treatment the supposed prototype of a lifelong love of his, Mme Arnoux? She has been thought to stand in the book as an unclouded exponent of womanly sweetness and virtue. Is she not, rather, a sort of Madame Bovary in reverse—a woman who rejects passion because she pietistically fears God's punishment, whose virtue brings her to the pass of offering herself, in age, to a man who suddenly recognizes the true incestuous nature of his devotion to her?

The profound psychological truth of the book's two final chapters is unequaled in modern literature. For in these two scenes Flaubert's uncanny knowledge of the pathology of modern life becomes startlingly evident. The nostalgic reminiscence of Frédéric and Deslauriers, casting back to their youthful frightened visit to the prostitute's house, reveals the continuing infantilism of these two grown-up children who have never been able to lift themselves over the threshold of maturity, who cannot learn, who can only, in spite of some native decency and generosity, repeat, and flee life's consequences. The modern split between emotion and reason stands revealed. Flaubert elsewhere remarks: "You do not possess Christianity any more. What do you possess? Railroads, factories, chemists, mathematicians. Yes, the body fares better, the flesh does not suffer so much, but the heart continues to bleed. Material questions are resolved. Are the others? . . . And as you have not filled that eternal yawning gulf which every man carries in himself, I mock at your efforts, and laugh at your miserable sciences which are not worth a straw." *Sentimental Education* is a handbook to the present because the gulf of which Flaubert speaks, after seventy years, has not been filled but only widened and deepened. The thirst for some saving authority has grown stronger, the childish bigotries more complete. Let us examine our theorists, Flaubert says, and throw out their false premises. Let us enlarge the provable human data. Have these nervous insurrections accomplished anything; are we following the "advanced notions" of a parcel of "buffoons"? Should "the government of a country be a section of the Institute, and the last section of all"?

Some partial answers lie in this novel, panoramic and profound, written in the "ivory tower" of Croisset and published one year before the inauspicious events of 1870 which ushered in the Third Republic.

FOLK ART
(1943)

Will folk art save us from creative and moral aridity if we can find and use it? The reiterated insinuation that formal art is fraudulent because it is difficult to understand and makes no effort to appeal to the majority—that it is, in fact, somehow treasonable to mankind's higher purposes and aims—is a typical bourgeois notion that has been around for a long time. That formal art cannot be put to any immediate use also lays it open to materialist denigration. The conviction that the simple is straight and pure and true, while the complex is concocted and double-dealing, is a partially moral one. It is a conviction which shares room, in the minds and emotions of many people, with an unconscious yearning for a lost rural world. In America, just enough time has elapsed since real unbanization set in for this yearning to roll up to its present proportions and to have acquired its present rationalizations. In spite of these desires and beliefs of the middle-class subconscious, the fact remains that no civilization has ever produced a literature out of folk (either current or revived) alone. The formal artist cannot be outlawed. The whole question is muddled in the extreme. Let us examine it with as much detachment as possible.

It is true that the formal artist, at least twice within living memory, has succeeded in getting past modern barriers to a real folk tradition, and that remarkable literature has resulted in both cases from the intersection of the formal with the folk

line. Lorca's genius was ignited in the most brilliant way by
Flamenco tradition, and Yeats was fortified and refreshed from
the beginning by his close knowledge of the Irish peasant. Both
these poets received the experience of poetry still attached to
music, at the improvisatory stage; and of an audience creatively
involved (actually listeners, as distinguished from mere readers)
in what they as poets produced.

But the fact is that only the most abnormal situations, political
or otherwise, kept these two folk traditions alive so late in an
industrial and urbanized Europe. The turning toward the folk,
at the end of the eighteenth century, was not only preindustrial
but prerevolutionary; and the same sort of ferments were present
in Yeats's Ireland and Lorca's Spain. The current attempts in
America to get back to primitive material are natural enough,
but they are different. They are the desire of a far from revolutionary population to get back to some earlier fun, as well as
some earlier integrity. Certainly the material is there. We can
trace the line of the American folk song through the ballads of
English, Irish, and Scotch origin (broken away from their original
scene and transformed) through the work songs of all kinds (sea
chanteys, songs of the plantation and the cattle-range), the
hymns and spirituals, up to the beginning of town life. Then the
culmination of the American folk song appears. Stephen Foster,
the untrained and greatly gifted writer of "popular songs," managed to express fully the emotions common during this period
of transition. On the one hand, through him the loneliness as
well as the rough gaiety of a primitive society found its voice.
On the other, Foster gave expression to something quite new:
an emotion which was to become increasingly persistent in the
American spirit—the sense of profound nostalgia for an already
disappearing non-urban way of life. The strong sentimentaliza-
tion of Foster by his modern audience proceeds from the holdover of this crucial though hidden nostalgia into our own time.
Clearly, he was the end of one kind of American folk, the point
beyond which no unadulterated development of his kind of material was possible.

We begin to get the production of the urbanized folk after the
hymns and marching songs of the Civil War. The railroads building and having been built, we get the railroad songs. The cities

once made, we get the hybrid genteel, and the barbershop ballads, and what is more vivid and interesting, the songs of the "underworld": brothel, saloon, dope joint, and prison. The earlier tradition fell into neglect as the way back to the farm became more and more closed. It was rediscovered and refurbished, along with hooked rugs and pine blanket chests, when the 1914 war broke up American Victorian and aroused, in some not quite understandable fashion, the middle-class enthusiasm for the American antique. The folk tradition, as a result, has become thoroughly "bourgeoizified." At present there is no way for the artist to get at it, for it has been dragged into a region where nothing living or nutritious for his purposes exists. It can be looked at and listened to, admired and imitated; but it cannot at the present time be called upon to do any truly important task. Only a writer thoroughly immersed in middle-class values, and soaked through and through with the sentimentality of the middle, could for a moment believe that this mummified and genteelized folk could contribute any spark of life to his purposes.

The English and French tradition of town-folk (with a head start of some forty or fifty years of true industrialism over the United States) channeled itself into the music hall. "The supreme embodiment of the surviving character of the English working people," writes one chronicler of the English nineteenth-century scene, "was the music hall. . . . Springing spontaneously out of the sing-song of the upper tavern room and the old out-of-door gardens of the artisans of the pastoral past, it became for a space of time a British institution. Its morality was to make the best of a bad job; its purpose to make everyone free and easy. . . ." The authenticity of this institution, created by the first articulate development of urban folk for its own enjoyment, soon impressed itself on the artists and writers of the time. Through it, they were able to skirt the middle, find excitement and restorative energy, and make a point of contact with "life." But the music hall decayed. It was based on that period of "proletarian" existence when the workers were stiffly encased in the tradition of knowing their place and imitating their betters. This tradition exploded in 1918; and we hear Eliot making a final tribute to Marie Lloyd, with added gloomy prognostications for the future:

. . . It was her capacity for expressing the soul of a people that made her unique. . . . It was her understanding of the people and sympathy with them, and the people's recognition of the fact that she embodied the virtues that they most genuinely respected in private life, that raised her to the position she occupied at her death. I have called her the expressive figure of the lower classes. There is no such expressive figure for any other classes. The middle classes have no such idol: the middle classes are morally corrupt. . . .

Eliot then goes on to express his fear that, with the disappearance of the music hall, and "the encroachment of the cheap and rapid-breeding cinema, the lower classes will drop to the same state of protoplasm as the bourgeoisie," and, moreover, when this state has overcome them, that they may die off from sheer boredom! This essay, written in 1923, closes with words of deep dismay as to the possibility of the hastening of this general disintegration by the development of another mechanical device for transmitting entertainment—the radio.

Eliot understimated his "lower classes." The music hall disappeared only after it had reached a high point of breadth and elegance. Folk expression continually runs toward this elegance, contrary to the *idée reçue* of its being by necessity clumsy and "vulgar." (And this elegance is not to be confused with the empty slickness of the *revue* kind.) But as a rather stuffy set of prewar conventions broke, the urban crowd shifted toward a freer, less imitative and reverent habit of mind and manner. Something new began immediately; persistent energy released itself into new forms and new media.

The energy is now at a more primitive level than formerly; these shifts go back and forth, as this current of urban life or that is released and breaks; many reasons requiring specialized attention are here involved. But the fact remains that American folk has never been more vigorous than at this moment. In "hot jazz," words are attached to music, as in all primitive states of poetry and music. Improvisation (the "lick") is in every talented performer's power. The rhythm is the important matter; the music has all the harmonic tricks under control with which to surround and embellish the beat. The various mechanical devices which Eliot feared and deplored have served, as a matter of fact, to aid the development and dissemination of this folk art. The folk now gets exactly what it wants to listen to. If the radio does not give it what it needs in sufficient quantity, people have their records and juke boxes, and, of course, the live performers. The vigor of folk at present is shown by its tendency to raid over into "classical" and bring back whatever tunes please it. The juke-box repertoire is a thing in itself: there the hymn tune (disguised) shares popularity with the crooned ballad and with certain hold-overs from the open spaces of the past. Compared to the songs of the upright piano and sheet music era, even the most naïve songs are less awkward and saccharine, more vitalized. And the imitation "folk song," such as the really remarkable "Blues in the Night," has taken on a finish which always characterizes folk in a good creative period *of its own*.

It is interesting to note that at this particular stage, "popular" interest in accident, sudden death, and the morbid in general (unlike American songs of an earlier day) has very nearly disappeared, along with the "topical song," that sister to the broadsheet.

A proposition could be drawn up:

Folk crosses formal art:

1. When folk has reached a moment of comparative breadth and elegance (when it can express anything, from the grotesque through emotion and satire, well).
2. When formal art has become easy and secular enough to recognize just where folk lies; and, having located folk, understands what is happening there.

A long period of time must elapse before, in America, the demands of this proposition can be fulfilled. But Eliot's fears were unjustified; just as the present middle-class hope that L. Stokowski can be crossed with Disney, or some genteel poet with the songs of pioneering backwoodsmen, is at once previous and misplaced.

Let us now take a brief glance at the American intellectual. The intellectual is a middle-class product; if he is not born into the class he must soon insert himself into it, in order to exist. He is the fine nervous flower of the bourgeoisie. His task, ideally, would be the close critical observation of the field in which he stands, while keeping his attention alert for new movement in the landscape as a whole. That the intellectual fails in this

job is one reason for the wholesale mixture of genres, the unre-
buked mistakes of prize committees, publishers, etc., the general
insolence of entrepreneurs—in fact the general failure to understand what is going on which marks the small remaining section
of American life still interested in literature.

The intellectual, being nervous, is subject to all the floating
airs of modern religion (present in quantity, no matter how
fogged and misted into the semblance of something else). One
must not forget that religious enthusiasm (and intolerance) has
always been inextricably mixed with every materialist idea; has
been a concomitant of all material push since Calvin. Intellectuals
range through the finest gradations of kind and quality: from
those who are merely educated neurotics, usually with strong
hidden reactionary tendencies, through mediocrities of all kinds,
to men of real brains and sensibility, more or less stiffened
into various respectabilities or substitutes for respectability. The
number of Ignorant Specialists is large. The number of hysterics
and compulsives is also large. It is natural that the truly sensitive
intellectual should have spiritual needs; for such a person the
necessity for those moments in life when one is forced to see
reality without wraps and unrationalized is strong. This necessity
leads to a real breakthrough into maturity on the part of some
individuals. For the less sensitive, the spiritual necessity hardly
exists; they require not steadying insight but emotional outlet.
It is in this class that we find the hot-gospellers, the morally
pretentious, the reformers, and the seekers of closed systems of
salvation. These men and women are not entirely the products
of an imperfect culture (for the type appeared in quantity in
France in the nineteenth century) but of a culture somehow
blocked and mixed; and of the impact of this curious situation
upon natures more simply constituted than they themselves
suppose. Flaubert wrote down an approximation of the type in
Bouvard et Pécuchet. He gave the two simple-minded copyists
a set of manias which is still complete for the dislocated middle-
class mind of our time; manias ranging from the collecting of
antiques to an absorption in various forms of science and politics.
These two prototypes of the middle-class yearner with a few re-
touches could represent not only the modern lecture-listening

audience, but many of "the experts who tend the complicated machinery of modern civilization."

One characteristic of the Bouvard-Pécuchet sort of enthusiasm is the violent repudiation after violent interest of one craze after another when the satiation point is reached. The revulsion shown by the intellectual toward the artist, during recent years, resembles this sort of compensating tendency. The too-great emphasis of emotion and hope placed upon the artist in the preceding period is lifted and placed at an opposite point. The D. H. Lawrence, Proust, Hart Crane kind of semi-worship went over, for a time, to Malraux; and then became transformed into something else. The very complexity of the artist's equipment became as much a target for the subsequent badgering and denigration as the non-material quality of his aims. It is moral blame of the most childish kind that we find most frequently expressed; and real puzzlement, also at a childish level. The atmosphere of former religious paroxysms and squabblings returns; the old fights between established religion and the sects and between the sects themselves; the old tiresome yet dangerous extremes of the persecutory centuries.

Now, one would think that the unstable intellectual should stand out against all these moral acrobatics and tergiversations: if not as judge, at least as arbiter. If he cannot remain firm, he should at least be in another part of the field, out of the melee and ahead of it. But as things turn out, he is either squarely in the mix-up, name-calling with the best or making motions of advancing, the while he has managed rapidly to retreat into something truly comforting in the way of pre-Copernican scholasticism, or has made a full flight back to Aristotle. And if he is of no real use in reconciling embattled sects, perhaps he could do a little simple journeyman's work in keeping entrepreneurism in its place. But here he rather fails us, too.

At this point it is necessary to remember that the middle class has produced, at the expense of much time and effort, a whole literature of its own. Its own writers, bred out of its own bone and flesh, educated in its own schools and amenable to its own scheme of manners and custom, have fanned out into the middle region; adapted in every way to express the middle intellect, temperament, grasp of reality, powers of analysis and emotion. Some of these poets, novelists, critics, biographers, and belletrists were born middle; some either rose or sank to where they at length find themselves. The complicated but smoothly oiled machinery of the publishing business, the general run of reviewers, the committees giving out literary awards, the more benumbed mass of academics: all these agents function, for the most part (and changing the figure), inside the same structure. During certain short periods, certain wild individuals stay outside and throw rocks, but since these intransigents tend to disappear for long intervals, the easiest supposition is that they are absorbed. And the periods of almost complete absorption present a very amusing spectacle indeed. These are the times when the book sections produce, week after week, month after month, serious judgments on books, but when everything judged and the judges themselves are cut out of the same piece of medium material. The commodity books are being dealt with by the commodity critics—a spectacle which would be purely funny if there were not elements of rather tragic irony in it.

The intellectual should at least know the difference between kinds, and have the courage to speak up when matters get really out of hand. He should make some admonishing gesture when a particularly startling piece of mutual aid comes through. He should know how the literary mechanism works: the way blurb-writing and prize-giving, journalists and literary impresarios engage with each other. He should be able to sense, watching the open pulls and twitches given reputations, all the subterranean maneuvering which must go on so that certain effects are produced at eye-level. What about the distinguished specialists who write blurbs for dust-jackets? Is this a harmless bit of fun, or a plan to get around the subsequent remarks of the book reviewer? What about the American prize committee (situated rather disadvantageously, one might suppose, for anyone not a journalist, in a school of journalism) which, having ignored brilliant talent, young and old, falls back ever again upon old standbys? What about the extra-literary influences which manage, from time to time, to bring to laudatory view a book of gibberish? What about certain anthologists who teeter on the verge of being members of the vanity press: are all their contributors paid? Who is to deal with these matters but the intellectual?

Meanwhile, the cry rises that poetry has disappeared. This plaint often comes from the dead center, say from the core of the Sunday book section. It rises with particular sharpness during times of cataclysm. The middle wishes poetry to throb, as it were, under the historic processes without a break; to light up ambiguous terrain with continual succeeding flashes of "inspiration." But poetry cannot be counted upon to act as a sort of combination faith-healing and artificial thunder and lightning. Poetry of the lyric order disappears for a century at a time. It shifts. And when the formal line has in some manner been exhausted, the vigor goes back to the base. The middle must put up with what it has: their flabby little songs, their attempts at reviving the "golden" American past; and their more ambitious flights: those attempts to combine autobiography with *post hoc ergo propter hoc* comment on the world situation.

"The function of the great individual is to take up and transform what has been communally produced." For this function one must wait, when the folk material is in a transitional phase —unmalleable and too full of its own rough vigor to be handled, and when "great individuals" seem to be lacking. Even the artist may misjudge the time. In Eliot's "Sweeney Agonistes" and "Fragment of an Agon" the two lines—of formal treatment and "rough" material—are somehow artificially combined; the result cannot really move us. But there are times when the poet can deal with whatever comes to hand. And folk will not always remain ungraspable.

A few notes on the future direction of the poet:

The true hierarchic attitude as exemplified by some "inheritors of Symbolism" (Stefan George and to a lesser degree Valéry and Yeats) seems to be exhausted. George's "willed rationalism toward the antique, his aesthetic and individualist humanism . . . which seeks in the universe the exaltation of man"—this line we have seen warped and corrupted; it now leads nowhere. The lesser task of the poet at present is satire. But satire cannot be asked to bear all of the weight of the diversified and subtle modern spirit. There is another development of this century's early period of aesthetic experiment and moral explanation. This

proceeds from Rilke. "In Rilke (as opposed to George)," writes
Geneviève Bianquis, already quoted above, "exists the most absolute abandonment to the law of the inanimate; the need to unknot,
to detach the bonds of the individual; the need to love everything,
to absorb everything into himself and to absorb himself in all;
to channel toward God or toward things all happiness, all sorrow
and all emotion." This is the contrast between the will which
builds Ages of Faith and the act of faith itself; between compulsion and serenity; arrogance and humility; between the raw act
of force and the more complex refusal of force but openness to
spiritual power.

The foundation material is ready for this tendency. The only
really usable and incontrovertible modern discoveries are in the
spiritual field; and these have their everyday diagnostic and thera-
peutic uses. Truth has been told, experience undergone, and movement undertaken—"forward" as Eliot says; but this forward
has not its old "progressive" connotation. The number of individuals engaged in writing poetry of this order will not be large,
and, as is so often the case, may be unseen by their generation.
The forms will be kept clear and the tone uninflated. No more
rhetoric; no more verbalizing; no more exhortations or elegies or
eulogies. No more conscious and affected investigations of dark
corridors and deserted strands; no more use of the universe as
a backdrop against which one acts out hope or despair. No more
dejected sitting about. No more searching nature for an answer-
ing mood. . . .

This exploration and movement can go on without having
to search out the folk for refreshment. The more complex tasks
have been neglected for a long time; attention to them is overdue.
Compared to these at once subtle and difficult necessities the
reiterated standardized demands of the bourgeois yearner sound
incredibly stupid and outdated.

Is it possible that despite our discoveries and progress, despite our
culture, religion, and world-wisdom, we still remain on the surface of
life? Is it possible that we have even covered this surface which might
still have been something, with an incredibly uninteresting stuff
which makes it look like drawing-room furniture during the summer
holidays?
Yes, it is possible . . .
But if all this is possible . . . then surely, for all the world's sake,

something must be done. The first comer, he who has had these disturbing thoughts, must begin to do some of the neglected things; even if he be just anybody, by no means the most suitable person: there is no one else at hand. This young insignificant foreigner, Brigge, will have to sit down in his room five flights up, and write, day and night. Yes, he will have to write; that will be the end of it.

This was written at the beginning of the century; but nothing much seems to have been accomplished. Now that a good deal of the drawing-room furniture lies in ruins, there may be another beginning.

FORMAL POETRY

(1953)

THE PLEASURES OF FORMAL POETRY

Before I try to analyze out certain basic virtues of formal poetry, I should like to state, and to analyze, certain modern objections to form. The first objection to form that rises in our minds is that form binds. The second objection to the use of form in modern poetry is that poetic form has become exhausted.

The main tendency in poetry since Baudelaire, Rimbaud, and Whitman, would seem to be bound up with efforts to free poetry from formal restrictions. This tendency has been central, but it has never been, as a matter of fact, steady. Baudelaire, whom we now name the great ancestor of modern poetry, wrote in a form that was so strict that it was often Racinian. Rimbaud, who smashed the French Alexandrine and wrote the first French *vers libre*, was continually going back to form; he wrote exquisitely balanced sonnets and, even in the late *Saison en enfer,* the most delicate and evanescent sort of formal lyric. Mallarmé, of course, was a tremendous formalist up to and including *Un Coup de dés,* for in this late and seemingly experimental work Mallarmé (according to Thibaudet) "wished to produce a visual and typographic aesthetic, built on the difference between the kinds of type, the largeness of the white spaces between, the dimension of the lines—[on] the entire architecture of the page." The subtlety of the language and of the inner rhymes and echoes in this poem certainly bring it over to the side of form. Mallarmé is adding another "formality" to verse.

This alternate and gradual loosening and tightening of form continues, through Laforgue, who could write in the most precise "light-verse" style, through Pound, Apollinaire, and Eliot. As a matter of fact, as we look back on "modern" poetry as a whole, we find as much experimentation *in* form as out of it.

One cannot deny, however, that certain set forms in the verse of all European languages now seem to the modern poet either pedantic or trivial. Certain formal verse patterns, therefore, seem to have been exhausted. Certain modern poets cannot function, for example, in the sonnet form. Others cannot function in any form which has regular stress, or which is pointed up by any sort of rhyme. It is interesting to remember in what way, and for what reasons, this exhaustion came about. For the dislike of form, in many young writers, amounts to actual fear and revulsion. The matter of form as opposed to non-form or free form sometimes slips over from the field of aesthetics into the moral plane. Nowadays young poets avoid form as they would avoid some stupid or reprehensible action.

The exhaustion of formal poetry goes back to a complex of reasons, and some of these reasons are closely meshed in with the history of morals in the nineteenth century. In France, at the height of the French Romantic Movement, poets (notably Victor Hugo) began to load their form with fantastic emotion and with cloying music. The middle-class revolution in taste was bound closely in with all this; as well as patriotic fervor, political conviction, and so on. In France, however, an anti-Romantic reaction occurred early, in 1857, the year of publication of *Les Fleurs du Mal* and *Madame Bovary* to be exact. So that it was quite natural for Verlaine, years later, to demand that poets wring the neck of rhetoric, even while he made, at the same time, poetry into pure music. In England, poetry was taken over bodily by the middle-class assumptions, and there was no adequate facing up to the situation by any major poet known in the Victorian era. (Hopkins was not published until 1916.) And the more that serious poets became absorbed into the society which surrounded them, the more complicated and unfitting forms they devised. Poetry was *used:* as a means of consolation, to bolster up flagging spirits, to cheer on, to cheer up; to create optimism where optimism was cheaply applied or out of place; to back up middle-class social ideals as well as certain philosophical ideals concerning human perfectibility. And a split occurred between "serious" and "light" verse. The quick and varied metres and the witty rhymes which Byron had devised as carriers for satire were siphoned off from the main stream of serious poetry. Within serious poetry, poets like Tennyson, meanwhile, doggedly experimented with unsuitable (to English) metres, in order to give some show of variety to their repetitive and tiresome subject matter. These experiments reached a dead end in Robert Bridges'—a true upholder of Victorian tradition—experiments with quantitative verse. These experiments were dead because the breath of life did not exist in the poets themselves or in the material with which they were attempting to deal.

"Light verse" took up the entire satiric burden, and lost caste because of its involvement with *opéra bouffe* (as used by William Gilbert in combination with Arthur Sullivan's music); or because of its (to the Victorian mind) even sillier relationship to the nonsense rhymes of Lewis Carroll and Edward Lear. These are the two limits to which poets in English pushed form: dull imitation of Greek and Roman poetry on the one hand, and gay and complicated satirical "patter-songs" and nonsense verse on the other. Both limits are unusable, in modern poetry. But the best nineteenth-century poets soon realized that a reunion of these two streams was not only important but imperative. For complicated rhythmic patterns, and light and limber and dancing rhythms have existed in serious poetry since the Greeks. When Gilbert Murray wishes to give an example of a rhythmic pattern used in Greek comedy, he is forced to quote a Gilbert stanza. It is a breach in culture when such rhythmic effects are lost; and French poets realized this fact before English ones did. Rimbaud goes back to folk song; Laforgue goes back to "light verse," whenever they sensed some tone of emotion which demanded these meters; neither was too proud or too inflexible not to make use of any metre that successfully carried his thought and feeling.

It is still the task of modern poets to bridge the division between serious and light forms; to refresh the drooping and weary rhythms of serious poetry with the varied, crisp, and fresh qualities of light verse. In English Pound and Eliot have performed miracles of deflation and revivification. Auden, as well, has worked to break down artificial barriers of form and tone, between the lively and the grave subject and treatment.

What is formal poetry? It is poetry written in form. And what is *form*? The elements of form, so far as poetry is concerned, are meter and rhyme. Are these elements merely mold and ornaments that have been impressed upon poetry from without? Are they indeed restrictions which bind and fetter language and the thought and emotion behind, under, within language in a repressive way? Are they arbitrary rules which have lost all validity since they have been broken to good purpose by "experimental poets," ancient and modern? Does the breaking up of form, or its total elimination, always result in an increase of power and of effect; and is any return to form a sort of relinquishment of freedom, or retreat to old fogeyism?

Let us examine meter. Meter is rhythm. In the words of the Scots professor who, in the nineteenth century, edited, with a preface, Walker's eighteenth-century *Rhyming Dictionary:* "A little consideration will lead to the conclusion, that verse, in most languages, differs from prose in the *return* of certain number of syllables that have a peculiar relation to one another as *accented* and *unaccented,* or as long and short. It is universally felt that a degree of *pleasure* arises from this definite arrangement, and the origin of that pleasure is to be traced back to the sense of time with which men are generally endowed." (You will remember Yeats saying of himself: "I have the poet's exact time-sense.") Now, when I asked a group of students, recently, to name some definite bodily rhythm which might illustrate mankind's sense of time, and with which a definite pleasure might be said to be connected, they could think only of the dance. This answer is interesting, because it shows how many rhythmic habits and rhythmic effects have become rare either as observed phenomena or as direct experience, with the advent of the machine. Students in a former century would think immediately, I believe, of the rhythmic principles underlying the actions which the Scottish professor at once brings forward as examples. "It is this principle which regulates," he goes on to say, "the step of a man or the stroke of an oar; and hence the pleasure we experience in beholding the regular step of a company of soldiers in their march, and the simultaneous sweep of the oars of a well-manned boat." Marching as a sort of everyday ritual—as seen in the changing of a guard, in a religious procession, or in a funeral cortege—is now a fairly rare sight; and so is the spectacle of rowers in "a well-manned boat." The Scotch professor then illustrates his point by the *time*, as distinguished from the tune, in music; but I do not want to bring rhythm in music (or in language) into the discussion at this point. I want to keep on emphasizing the pleasure to be found in bodily rhythm as such. What else formerly went to rhythm? We think of certain tasks, the rhythm of which has become set. Sowing, reaping, threshing, washing clothes, rowing, and even milking cows goes to rhythm. The variety of rhythm in sea shanties depends upon the variety of tasks on board a sailing ship, with the doing of which a sailor was confronted. Hauling up sail or pulling it down; coiling rope; pulling and pushing and climbing and lifting, all went to different rhythms; and these rhythms are preserved for us, fast or slow, smooth or rough, in sailors' songs.

How far back can we push this sense of time? It appears everywhere in the most primitive cultures. It certainly springs from the fact that a living man has rhythm built in to him, as it were. His heart beats. He has a pulse. A pulse of some sort exists in all living creatures—in plants as well, I think scientists have proved —and man shares with the animals not only a pulse, but an attendant rhythm: his breathing.

So we see man, long before he has much of a "mind," celebrating and extending and enjoying the rhythms of his heartbeat and of his breath. He is still at the point, let us say, where he performs these extensions without speech, or with the most rudimentary form of speech. Even without speech, a great many rhythmic effects can be produced by a human being. He can clap his hands rhythmically and he can stamp his feet rhythmically. Here is the beginning of the dance, of ritual, of drama. Then artifacts began to increase the pleasure of rhythm. The first aids and abettors of human rhythm were undoubtedly percussion instruments. A beaten hollow log must have been a great aid. The clicking together of the chestnut shells from which castanets take their name was another.

Eliot has said that poetry goes back to a savage beating a tom-tom in a jungle. That is, it goes back to reiterative beat. The Greeks have no god of the drum, no muse of the drum, it is true. The Muses, when we first hear of them, are three only: one of study, one of memory, and one of song. But Greek poetry, when we first come upon it, is a highly sophisticated and complex affair: the fruit of centuries of trial and error, of matching rhythm to language and language to rhythm; of a complicated and civilized relationship between dance-and-song. When we come upon the epics of Homer, written in the infinitely resonant and infinitely variable dactyllic hexameter; or, later, when we read the no less fixed yet no less variable sapphics or alcaics of the Greek lyric, we have passed far beyond a stone age. Man has become a worker in metals; the cymbal and the bell have been added to the castanet and the drum; man is now a musician as well as a dancer.

One Greek word combines dance-and-song, the word *molpe;* and the word constantly applied to the *effect* of all good singing and harping (for the lyre was the purely Greek instrument, since the wind-instrument, the *aulos,* was always considered of Asiatic origin) was *himeroeis,* meaning "not merely beautiful, but possessing that sort of beauty which makes the heart yearn." "*Himeros* and *rhythmos*—longing and rhythm—are the two special elements which the voice finds strengthened in the movement of the body. *Metron* means measurement; and the things measured are the *feet* or *steps* on which the words of the song move. For the words had to dance with the dancers . . ."

Why are Greek rhythms now unusable? Why does the Greek hexameter, which managed to pass over into Latin poetry, remain forever outside any feasible use in English? The chief reason is that both Greek and Latin, being inflected languages, are nearer to each other than either of them can ever be to English. "A highly inflected language," Gilbert Murray says in his valuable study *The Classical Tradition in Poetry,* "must have each syllable clearly spoken, because each syllable up to the last may seriously alter the meaning. This is perhaps the reason why, in Latin and Greek pronunciation, *quantity* was the chief variable; while modern uninflected languages have fallen back more and more on the easy careless method of stress." (And we should remember here

that certain rhythmic effects in modern poetry do indeed stem
from Greek rhythms. Gerard Manley Hopkins was saturated in
Greek. He was one of Jowett's brilliant young men at Balliol, and
many of the effects in Hopkins which we think of as triumphs of
"modern" compression are actually models of Greek compression,
as transformed into English verse by the hands of a master.)

I want to quote, at this point—before I quote some incisive
remarks by Eliot on the limits of freedom in verse—another passage from Gilbert Murray, a passage concerned with the inner
meaning of the Greek term *molpe*. Murray says:

> Love, Strife and Death and that which is beyond Death; an atmos-
> phere formed by the worship of Nature and the enchantment of
> Memory; a combination of dance and song like the sweep of a great
> singing bird; all working toward an ecstasy or a transcending of per-
> sonality, a "standing outside" of the prison of the material present,
> to be merged in some life that is the object of adoration or desire:
> these seem to be the subjects, and this the spirit and setting of that
> primitive MOLPE which is the foundation of ancient classical poetry.
> The tradition, if there is a tradition, rises there.

And this tradition, let us remember, goes back to *rhythm*, the
effect of which attracted the adjective *himeroeis*: "not merely
beautiful, but possessing that sort of beauty which makes the
heart yearn."

Here, perhaps, I should make a few remarks on that other element of formal poetry as we know it today: rhyme. Rhyme becomes necessary in poetry as rhythm weakens. The Greeks of the
great period scorned rhyme; and so did Latin writers, although
certain internal rhymes can be detected in Ovid and later Latin
versifiers. Rhyme has probably always been present in folk song
and folk poetry (we know how pleased children are when they
strike upon two words that rhyme); but high formal art for a
long time dismissed and ignored it. But as rhythm began to break
down, and when what we now think of as "monkish Latin" began
to appear, rhyme appears as well. As soon as the ordinary speech
of the people—the so-called "vulgar tongues"—began to build up
a body of formal literature rhyme became usual. The Provençal
poets elaborated and extended the use of rhyme to a remarkable
degree; so that by the time Dante began to write in Italian, his
native vulgar tongue—having had as his master the Provençal

poet Arnaut Daniel—he had at his disposal a great variety of rhymed forms, the sonnet among them; and Dante used the sonnet, and later *terza rima* as a *rhymed* carrier of his long poem *The Divine Comedy.* "Greek and Latin could do without rhyme because they had clear meters. Rhyme is needed to mark clearly the end of the line, and to provide the ear with fixed resting places. Without such divisions the metrical form would become dull and obscure. The hearer would not be sure where one line ended and the other began; he might not even be sure whether he was listening to prose or to verse. It is worth noticing that Latin took to rhyme when it had begun to lose the sense of quantity. Chinese insists on rhyme because it has no meter." This is still Murray, who says a little farther on: "The renewed popularity of rhyme in the time of Dryden followed upon an increasing looseness of the treatment of blank verse by the later Jacobean dramatists, and was part of a general reaction toward severity of form."

Every language seems to seek its own large meter—its own dramatic carrier, capable of long breaths, capable of bearing weights, capable of projecting maximum emotional power, and yet allowing for delicate variation; capable of assuming various speeds, and capable of letting through intricacy of thought and sharpness of wit; a meter suited to the syntax and the rhythm of any given language, to the preponderance within that language of actual vowels and consonantal sounds. The vulgar tongues have more light vowels and fewer massive clusters of consonants than the classic languages. A spoken language, from Dante on, seems to fall most naturally into an iambic line of one length or another. English poetry has for a long time been based on the iamb—a short followed by a long beat—an unaccented syllable followed by an accented one; and the classic and large carrier of English poetry has for centuries been the iambic pentameter or five-beat line (sometimes with an additional syllable at the end, as in "To be or not to be, that is the question"): blank verse.

Now, it was a tremendous task to smash the Alexandrine, as Rimbaud smashed it, when it had been recently charged with music and feeling by the Romantics. To smash iambic pentameter has not been such a tremendous task; for, all during the nineteenth century, as we have seen, the line was becoming more and more feeble, since no strong talent had taken hold of it and

filled it with refreshing power. (Browning's innovations were not
strong enough.) The line continued to dwindle; and, when it was
finally smashed, it was already at its last gasp, as it were. Now,
a dominant formal meter cannot become absolutely enfeebled
if the common language which surrounds it continues to feed
it. If the common, everyday language itself changes, the dominant meter must also change. If the accent shifts in the common
tongue, then the accent in the dominant meter must shift, too.

Certain Victorian poets sensed this shift—Browning particularly; and in Bridges and in Swinburne, the iambic beat is broken
by the introduction of trochaic, dactylic, anapestic, and spondaic
feet. These innovations went back, in part, to Milton, who, in his
later works, had introduced a consistent trochaic variation; and
to Coleridge, who counted *only* the accented syllables in a line.
It was the introduction of a sense of rhythms foreign to classic
English, in three English-speaking "foreigners," that finally broke
the iambic hold. These poets—William Butler Yeats, Ezra Pound,
and T. S. Eliot—by their experiments changed the iambic line
so that it again became flexible and vigorous. The trochaic foot—
a long followed by a short—had become dominant in ordinary
speech. It has also become dominant in the formal poetry of our
day.

How far can this mingling of meters go? Soon we come upon
a mingling of meters—in sections of Pound's *Cantos,* for example—that is nearer the beat of prose than of verse: that *is*
prose. Prose has its own rhythm, certainly. But is not something
lost to us, being as we are, rhythmic creatures, in the disappearance of many "rich and exquisite" poetic meters? Free verse is
valuable only when it continues to broaden and enrich; and it
becomes as hampering as any rigid meter when it rules out *any*
return to form.

"It seems to be almost a necessity in good verse that the ear
should subconsciously expect a certain pattern, and have its
hope, alternately or varyingly, suspended and fulfilled." There
speaks the student of classical meters. But we hear very much the
same dictum in Eliot's remark that "the ghost of some simple
meter should lurk behind the arras in even the 'freest' verse; to
advance menacingly as we doze, and withdraw as we rouse." A
failure in any discoverable beat is a failure in tension.

Eliot himself, one of the greatest English metrists, has made other remarks on modern versification. He says, for example, "that no *vers* is *libre* for the man who wants to do a good job. The term," he goes on,

which fifty years ago [he was writing in 1928] had an exact meaning in relation to the French Alexandrine, now means too much to mean anything at all. The *vers libre* of Jules Laforgue, who if not quite the greatest poet after Baudelaire, was certainly the most important technical innovator, is *free verse* in much the same way that the latter verse of Shakespeare, Webster and Tourneur is *free verse:* that is to say, it stretches, contracts and distorts the traditional French measure as later Elizabethan and Jacobean poetry stretches, contracts and distorts the blank verse measure. But the term is applied to several types of verse which have developed in English *without relation* to Laforgue, Corbière and Rimbaud, or to each other. To be more precise, there are, for instance, my own type of verse, that of Pound, and that of the disciples of Whitman. I will not say that subsequently there have not appeared traces of reciprocal influence of several types upon one another, but I am here speaking of origins. My own verse is, so far as I can judge, nearer to the original meaning of *vers libre* than is any of the other types: at least the form in which I began to write, in 1908 or 1909, was directly drawn from the study of Laforgue together with the later Elizabethan drama; and I do not know anyone who started from exactly that point. I did not read Whitman until much later in life, and had to conquer an aversion to his form, as well as much of his matter, to do so. I am equally certain that Pound owes nothing to Whitman.* This is an elementary observation; but when dealing with popular conceptions of *vers libre* one must still be as simple and elementary as fifteen years ago [1913].

Eliot, in this passage (from his Introduction to Pound's *Selected Poems*) goes on to list Pound's Victorian "influences." "Technically," he adds, "these influences were all good; for they combine to insist upon the importance of *verse as speech* . . . ; while from more antiquarian studies Pound was learning the importance of *verse as song*."

"Verse as speech" and "verse as song": these are the two attitudes toward formal poetry—or rather in formal poetry—that die out first, and perennially need to be renewed. Formal poetry

* Eliot has come to speak "more respectfully" of Whitman; and Pound has paid homage to Whitman's power both directly (in a poem addressed to his forerunner) and indirectly (in prose comments).

should continually remain in contact with the speech and the life around it, but this it does not do; and this division is made easier by the fact that poetry has for centuries been encased—one might almost say embalmed—in print. The technique becomes rigidified and poets begin to write by the rules that scholars have deduced from this or that poetic canon. Poets become frightened of emotion and of the Sublime (young poets today, I have found, are particularly terrified of the Sublime, they want no part of it!). In this situation, we have the keepers of the canon, and we have the breakers of the canon. Let us listen to Eliot a little longer, as he fruitfully defines originality.

Poets may be divided into those who develop technique, those who imitate technique and those who invent technique. When I say "invent," I should use inverted commas, for invention would be irreproachable if it were possible. "Invention" is wrong only because it is impossible. I mean that the difference between the "development" and the "sport" is, in poetry, a capital one. There are two kinds of "sports" in poetry, in the floricultural sense. One is the imitation of development, and the other is the imitation of some idea of originality. The former is commonplace, a waste product of civilization. The latter is contrary to life. The poem which is absolutely original is absolutely bad; it is, in the bad sense, "subjective," with no relation to the world to which it appeals.

Originality, in other words, is by no means a simple idea in the criticism of poetry. True originality is merely development; and if it is the right development it may appear in the end so inevitable that we almost come to the point of view of denying all "original" virtue to the poet. He simply did the next thing.

Eliot then says that spurious originality usually gives the public a greater shock than true originality; and ends by stating that Pound's originality is genuine in that his versification is a logical development of the verse of his English predecessors.

The technical tradition, then, runs on unbroken. We now know more of the linkages which connect any art to human function; and this knowledge should make us take more pleasure, rather than less, in *form*. I again quote Murray:

The regular or irregular rhythm of verse [corresponds], as we now are told, to the various physiological rhythms of the living body, and derives therefrom a mysterious power over the emotions. There is also a quality of rhythm or architecture in the composition itself which is quite different from mere plot-interest and corresponds, I think, to the real rhythms of life, as revealed in one part or another of the Tragic Pattern. All these elements, and doubtless others also, combine to make the felt but indefinable contrast with reality or truth, conveyed by the poem . . . Poetry tries to convey truth concerning those subjects about which we care most and know least, or at any rate are least able to make explicit statements. These mysteries were the subjects with which the Greek MOLPE was concerned—Love, Strife, Death and that which is beyond Death.

We still celebrate these subjects and face these mysteries, and formal art—art in which the great tradition is still alive and by which it still functions—is as modern as this moment, and as ancient as the farthest antiquity. This is the formal art fragments of which we should not only as readers "shore against our ruins," but keep as a directing influence in whatever we manage to build—to create.

ROBERT FROST

COLLECTED POEMS (*1939*)

Robert Frost's *Collected Poems: 1939* brings together six books, beginning with *A Boy's Will*, first published in England in 1913, and ending with *A Further Range* (1936). A preface called "The Figure a Poem Makes" describes Frost's experience with a poem's beginning and development ("There is a glad recognition of the long lost and the rest follows"). *A Boy's Will* should bring back to some readers the freshness its delayed American appearance let into literary parlors: a fragrance wholesome as the smell of new hay, which, more than twenty years ago, showed up the sad, unaired condition of American poetry. The lambrequins and antimacassars then disturbed have been put aside and all sorts of new and foreign breezes have since flowed in and out. Frost's first book was close to English prewar Georgian verse (also bucolic), but was saved from that school's sentimentality by the sensitive accuracy (akin to Thoreau's) applied to the long-neglected New England landscape.

North of Boston, which also had to be imported, as it were, from England, did something more: it put New England speech into literature. Reading these poems again one is struck by their solidity in comparison to even the best of a thousand poetic narratives derived from them. Frost never stretched his narratives to any great length. His good sense has kept him from running any of his tendencies into the ground. That same good sense, on the other hand, has kept him from developing, in any broad way, beyond his first work.

Frost has for a long time been one of the most popular poets of our day. Some of this popularity can be put down to the fact that he has always expressed, with imaginative sincerity, American nostalgia for a lately abandoned rural background. His love for the soil, his intimate knowledge of "country things," and his rejection of an industrial civilization's special values appeal strongly to readers who have been compelled to accept these values. If Frost had allowed his philosophy to remain completely implicit in his poetry, he would have escaped the occasional querulous tone apparent in his later books. It is not the province of the pastoral poet directly to preach. If one has chosen nature and eschewed cities, the choice must be absolute and unrationalized. If the pastoral poet sees fit to defend his chosen mode of life, he immediately lays it open to criticism in turn—is it not a backward and recessive development of the civilization he has thought to escape? Frost has broken out every so often in diatribe against the city and its machines, although, since his recognition by the public—late enough, one admits—the results of his successful dealings with that machine, the printing press, have enabled him to live as he pleases.

The best of Frost's lyrics are immune to criticism. They appear in his latest book as surely as in his first. But one reads *Collected Poems: 1939* waiting for a crack of upheaval, with some roughness of unforeseen growth thereafter. The tone is curiously static throughout. The emotion in the best lyrics, and particularly in Frost's greatest lyric, "To Earthward," does not "broaden down" from youth to maturity; it sounds intermittently. And the reader who holds these lyrics in deep respect somewhat feels that Frost's later carping and conservatism should never have appeared in his work at all.

"More than once I should have lost my soul to radicalism if it had been the originality it was mistaken for by its young converts," Frost says in his introduction. For the poet, the point is to lose his soul to whatever wisdom or folly, and then to regain it. "The best way out," he once said, "is always through." The ordinary man may be able to conceal his evasions; in the poet, the evasion shows. In the later Frost, the mold, unbroken, has stiffened a little.

A MASQUE OF REASON (1945)

Published near the occasion of Frost's seventieth birthday, this short verse play deals with the Job story in a spirit of good middle-of-the-road grassroots conservatism; Frost speaks in the language, and with much of the point of view, of the "dry" cracker-box philosopher. Job, a reasonable farmer at heart, has never been really satisfied with the elaborate explanation of the reason for his misfortunes given to him, on an unforgettable occasion, by God out of the whirlwind. Now safely dead, and granted the company of his beautiful but sleepy wife, Job decides, when God appears in the desert of the afterworld, to get down to facts, to face up to Mystery with Reason. Job's wife, too, has a few questions. God hems and haws but finally comes out with the explanation familiar to us all along: He did it to show off to the Devil. Satan's lieutenants act only for hire, but God counted on Job's free will and Job did not fail him. Job's integrity, it is true, leads to near despair and permanent puzzlement, but Job holds out, and a great moral turn occurs in the affairs of both God and Man. In the course of this little drama, many asides on present-day matters appear, and a charming ending, that will not puzzle, shock, or bemuse anyone (that will, indeed, bring down the house in a gathering of, say, the Ladies' Aid Society), gives Mrs. Job the last word, as she lines up God, Satan, and her husband for a photograph to commemorate the occasion—a photograph in which she will not appear but for which she asks them to smile.

We cannot bear down heavily upon this little divertissement. Frost, bringing us up against the problem of Pain and Evil, adds nothing to our insight into the subject. But it would not be in character for Frost to startle us with some new concept or to throw dangerous light into the shadowy corners of his scene. It is interesting to note, by the way, that Frost deletes Elihu. Re-

reading the original story, one is struck by the modern wisdom of this enthusiastic and invigorating young son of Barachel the Buzite. Here is a character for a modern poet to take hold of. Elihu's remarks would delight T. S. Eliot: Elihu's insight into the power of dreams, no doubt, long ago delighted that student of religions, Jung. Elihu urges Job to give up and give in, to forget about his stiff civic righteousness and his sense of moral pride. Frost, like Yeats and Stefan George, has a strong belief in Job's kind of individualism. Elihu is on the side of Rilke, Eliot, and (at present) Auden. Frost's God is thrifty, crafty, and non-experimental. (He wagers only on a sure thing.) God according to Elihu brings briefly before us Imaginative Immanence, which deals out, with one hand, mystery and suffering and, with the other, instruction and grace. Frost, too, reduces Satan to what he calls a "sapphire wasp," and an emaciated one at that. He makes Evil a rather slight and annoying malicious force, whereas certain modern poets, from Baudelaire on, have magnified the power of Evil. It is interesting to trace the line of reasonable conformity in Frost's little *jeu d'esprit* and to recognize how difficult it is, even in an era of the utmost tragedy, for a poet who has chosen the middle road to be serious in tone and searching in intent.

A LIFEWORK (1962)

The career of Robert Frost, the American poet whose popularity, in his seventies and eighties, came to exceed that of any of his contemporaries, presents a number of paradoxes. For most of his life his reputation came to be based on the figure he presented to his audience: that of a New England poet who lived close to the land, and whose principal interests, apart from writing and teaching, were rural ones. Yet he spent his formative years—until the age of eleven—in San Francisco, where he was born in 1874, and his years of adolescence and young manhood in industrial New England towns and cities—chiefly Lawrence, Massachusetts. His direct forebears, moreover, on his father's side, were town-dwellers. His paternal grandfather was an overseer of a cotton mill in Lawrence, and his father, William Prescott

Frost, Jr., after graduating from Harvard, moved west to become a newspaperman and politician in the growing city of San Francisco. His mother, Isabelle Moodie Frost, had come to America from Scotland as a girl of fifteen. She met Frost's father at Bucknell Academy in Lewistown, Pennsylvania, where the young Easterner on his way west had taken a teaching position, and where she herself taught mathematics. She, too, was city-bred (in Edinburgh) and it is apparent that many of the poet's characteristics—his intuition and imagination, as well as his belief in the importance of positive aims and values—were derived from her.

But there is no doubt that Frost's lifelong affection for the land was central and genuine. He possessed from the beginning the individualistic and independent nature which was, at one time, common not only in New England—where the Frost family had long been established—but in the rural areas of America as a whole. The elder Frost's streak of Yankee intransigence expressed itself in his youthful espousal of the theory of States' rights and the cause of the South; and he proved himself a member of the post-Civil War generation by his restless move toward the new opportunities lying westward. Frost's own temperament, as W. H. Auden—a knowledgeable admirer—has pointed out, was that of the "small-holder," of the farmer who owns and works his land. In Frost, the inheritance of the Yankee countryman and of the Scottish crofter met, and reinforced each other.

2

In his later years, Frost has described to biographers the difficulties of his childhood in some detail. They were difficulties which contributed to many of the tensions of his adolescence and young manhood, as well as to his choice, at an early age, of a responsible pattern of behavior. His father's character, it would appear, had more of Yankee gregariousness than Yankee reserve, and as a newspaperman and a dabbler in politics, the elder Frost's free and untrammeled participation in San Francisco's ebullient frontier atmosphere was frequently shared by his son, who went along as his companion—missing school and catching glimpses of the growing city's rougher side. Frost's mother exhibited courage by keeping the family and the household together during the San Francisco years, and by persisting in her independent attitude toward Frost's rather grim and hard-fisted grandfather when, after Frost's father's death at thirty-four in 1885, she returned, with Robert and his younger sister, to Lawrence. Her Scottish inheritance included a respect for learning and an aptitude for teaching, and she soon took charge of a district school, in nearby Salem, New Hampshire. Here she put into practice her teaching methods—original for the time—seating her pupils according to their grades of excellence, giving them individual instruction, and getting them to commit to memory passages of poetry or prose which she read aloud. This harking back to an oral tradition—usual in a society where books are scarce— made a strong impression upon Frost, whose ear, as it turned out, was unusually true and accurate. Her dealings with her pupils were easy and natural; she was remembered singing children's ballads to the youngest, as she held them on her knee. Her religious interests were also marked; once a Unitarian, she later became interested in the mystical doctrines of Swedenborg.

Frost's devotion to his mother was complete; he willingly took on any small job that would "help out." He entered Lawrence High School—having been his mother's pupil up to that time— in the fall of 1888, at the age of fourteen. Here he acquired the rudiments of the old-fashioned classical education then prevalent in the New England public high schools. Latin, Greek, and ancient history were subjects in the curriculum, and he made good marks. It was now that he met Elinor Miriam White, the charming and talented daughter of a former Universalist minister, who was to share with young Frost the honor of being Valedictorian on their graduation in June of 1892. By this time Frost had published poems in the school paper, and had made plans to go to Dartmouth on funds contributed by his grandmother.

From this point on, the progress of young Frost toward what he began to sense as his true interests—the interests of a poet and perhaps, on his own terms, an instructor of the young—ran into a series of obstacles. His stay at Dartmouth was brief. His interest in poetry was becoming more definitely centered as his reading broadened, and he was writing verse. But his creative enthusiasm was baffled, rather than aided, by academic routine.

Moreover, he felt that his mother—who had opened a small school in Methuen, Massachusetts—needed him. He left Dartmouth without giving official notice, and spent the winter of 1893 giving his mother the help she needed in managing her sometimes recalcitrant pupils. Mill work claimed him during the following summer and winter. It was at this period that he sold his first poem—"My Butterfly"—to the *Independent,* then a leading weekly, and attracted the attention not only of its editor, William Hayes Ward, but of the editor's sister, Miss Susan Ward. Part of the correspondence between the youthful poet of twenty and this learned spinster has been preserved at the Huntington Library, and Frost's positive belief in his talent comes through clearly (". . . I have but recently discovered my powers"). Frost now turned his back on the mills, for good.

Meanwhile, the relationship between himself and Elinor White was undergoing rapid changes, not always fortunate ones from Frost's point of view. Miss White had become a student at St. Lawrence, a Universalist college in upper New York State. She was therefore, except for summer visits home, out of direct communication with her young friend—whose devotion to her was constant. Moreover, Frost's inability to attach himself to any conventional way of making a living did not appeal to her family and her academic mentors. Frost, on a visit to St. Lawrence in the autumn of 1894, with a sheaf of privately printed poems in hand, felt himself to be severely rebuffed, and he reacted to this crucial disappointment by flight—to Maryland, Virginia, and North Carolina. His feeling of desperation at this time was to be recorded in a poem of his late maturity ("Kittyhawk 1894"), and he speaks of the "desperately absorbing experiences" of this journey in a letter to Miss Ward. This is the only break with a pattern of strict accountability to demands made upon him that the hard-pressed young poet allowed himself, in these transitional years.

Matters then took a better turn. The *Independent* gave "My Butterfly" a prominent place in its issue of November 8, 1894, and he became engaged to Elinor White at the Christmas season. Elinor returned to college for her final year, and Frost occupied himself with tutoring, teaching, and a short spell of reporting for the Lawrence *Sentinel.* The young couple, after their marriage in December, 1895, together took up teaching duties, again in Frost's mother's school, now situated in Lawrence.

The next five years were crowded ones. Frost's friendly relations with the Wards continued, and two other poems were published in the *Independent* in 1896 and 1897. The Frosts' first child, Eliot, was born in September, 1896. And it was now that Frost made his second effort to enter college. The advantages of a college degree to a man whose talents and background seemed to fit him for a career as instructor to the young were evident; and Frost, after correspondence with Dean Briggs, entered Harvard in the fall of 1897. His grandfather paid his tuition, and Elinor Frost's mother took a house in Boston in order to make matters somewhat easier for the young family. As a freshman he "was too mature for [the required] English A and hated it." And, although he received high marks in the classics, in his sophomore year "nothing went well." In addition, his duties as a son, a husband, and a father, proved to be overwhelming. "Harvard," he later wrote, in the *Harvard Alumni Bulletin,* "had taken me away from the question whether I could write or not." He resigned from the sophomore class at the end of March, 1899. The next month, his daughter Lesley was born.

A way of life which was to prove over a long period of time a background for some of his most remarkable work was about to become possible, but a double tragedy was to intervene: Frost's mother was stricken with cancer, and in July, 1900, his little son Eliot died. Elinor Frost, in spite of her grief, made the sensible request of Frost's grandfather that he buy them a farm, which the young husband and wife had "found for themselves" in West Derry, New Hampshire—"thirty acres, rather run down and poor, but with orchard, fields, pasture, woodland and spring." "Shall I give you a year? Will you settle down if I give you a year to try this out?" his grandfather asked. "Give me twenty!" Frost replied, and, as he said later, "that is just what it took. . . ."

Frost's mother died in November, 1900, soon after their move to the farm. She was fifty-six years old.

3

In 1900, when Frost and his young family first settled in West Derry, it was not so difficult for a man to leave an industrial environment to seek out a subsistence living on a "one man, one horse" farm, as it would be today. But it was difficult enough, especially in New England, where the land was poor, and where the native Yankee stock had lost much of its vigor through the losses of the Civil War, the trek to the West, and the flight to the cities of many of its more adventuresome sons. For Frost, the step was drastic. He was going, it is true, toward a way of life he believed, instinctively, to be his: toward true, old-fashioned values, outside— and opposed to—the period's ethos of competition and "success." And he was saving that poet's part of himself which he had believed in from earliest adolescence. He and his wife were putting a touching trust in what they must have sensed was ultimately an impossible way of making a living. To persist in their desires for a world of their own, in which they could bring up children beyond the reach of mill-town blight and the interference of hard-fisted relations, took courage. This courage, and the idealism which existed at its center, proved to be the source of the most original, moving, and sincere poems of Frost's early work—very nearly all the poems in *A Boy's Will* and *North of Boston,* as well as much of *Mountain Interval.*

The farm, as it turned out, could not produce even a subsistence living for the Frosts. After six years, and the birth of four more children, one of whom died in earliest infancy, Frost turned once more to teaching, this time as a part-time teacher of English at the nearby Pinkerton Academy—"a good two-mile walk from the farm." His teaching methods were somewhat unorthodox, but his pupils remembered his genial informality, his "admirable" direction of certain Shakespeare plays, and his interest in botany and in baseball. The family now began to spend their summers in Bethlehem, in the White Mountains, for reasons of Frost's health—"a high, free mountain world." In 1910, they moved from the farm nearer to the academy, and in the fall of 1911, to Plymouth, where Frost began to teach psychology and education at the state normal school.

The lyric poems later to be collected in Frost's first volume, *A Boy's Will* (1913), continued to be written; and Frost has said that as early as 1905 he had discovered a new dramatic vein which was to result in the blank-verse poems in *North of Boston*

(1914). Early in 1912, the impulse to break away from teaching
—at which he was having a good deal of success—and to prove or
disprove his faith in himself as a writer, took hold. The farm
was now his to sell, and he sold it. With its price in hand, along
with a small allowance from his grandfather's estate, he bought
steamer passage for himself, his wife, and his four small children
—destination, England—and sailed, in the early autumn of 1912,
at the age of thirty-eight, from Boston to a country where he
knew no one.

4

Frost's departure for England roughly coincided with two major
publishing ventures, which heralded the beginnings of a new
serious attitude toward poetry written in English. In October,
Harriet Monroe, in Chicago, published the first number of
Poetry: A Magazine of Verse, and in England, in December,
under the generous patronage of Edward Marsh, the first *Georgian
Anthology* appeared. The Georgian group, whose admiration for
the poetry of Thomas Hardy and of Robert Bridges was marked,
included, at the time, Walter de la Mare, John Masefield, W. H.
Davies, and Rupert Brooke. And in London, The Poetry Bookshop,
which was to become a center for poetic activity, had recently
been opened by Harold Monro. Frost knew nothing of any of these
developments upon his arrival in England. His first preoccupation
was to find a country place where he and his family could settle
and farm. On the advice of a writer of a country column in a
newspaper, he found a first home in Beaconsfield, Bucks. He
then set about finding a publisher, and here good luck played
into his hands.* Late in 1912, he was able to arrange for the
publication of *A Boy's Will* with the firm of David Nutt.

A Boy's Will, published in his thirty-ninth year, made an immediate impression upon those critics to whom it was sent for
review, and Frost began to meet, and to know, many members
of the Georgian circle. Among these was Edward Thomas, who

* Frost's publication in American magazines, through 1912, had been
severely limited: several poems in the *Independent,* two in the *Youth's
Companion,* and one in the *Forum.*

at the time was struggling with the pressures of a journalist's career. Thomas, like Frost, was a lover of the countryside and an amateur botanist. At the beginning of their close friendship Thomas had never written a line of verse. Frost advised him to begin, telling him that "he had been a poet all his life." Thomas, who had undergone periods of depression for many years, found in poetry a tremendous release, and he was a frequent visitor of the Frosts throughout their English stay.

Soon after *A Boy's Will* appeared, Frost met Ezra Pound. Pound's own career was beginning to expand into many areas. Already for some years established in London, with several books to his credit, the young Pound was beginning to take on his role of instigator and innovator, and in 1913 was actively engaged in formulating rules for the Imagists—a "school" with more experimental aims and interests than those of the Georgians, and he had already appointed himself foreign advisor to Harriet Monroe. Pound's review of *A Boy's Will* appeared in *Poetry* in May, 1913. Pound discovered, in Frost, a salutary attention paid to the truth, as well as compression and clarity of expression. "This man has the good sense to speak naturally and to paint the thing, the thing as he sees it." Another American poet was helping to clear away the falsity and fustian of Victorian verse.

Pound's friendship with Frost was short-lived; the young enthusiast soon found that his older compatriot was intent on going his own way. But Pound expressed his admiration for Frost's rendering of "the natural speech of New England" in a review of *North of Boston*, published in *Poetry* late in 1914 under the title "Modern Georgics." "Mr. Frost's work is the work of a man who will make neither concessions or pretenses. . . . His book is a contribution to American literature."

North of Boston, published by David Nutt in April, 1914, again impressed English reviewers. Edward Thomas, who was soon to die in the war, wrote of this collection of New England "eclogues":

This is one of the most exciting books of modern times, but one of the quietest and least aggressive. . . . These poems are revolutionary because they lack the exaggeration of rhetoric. . . . Many, if not most, of the separate lines and separate sentences are plain, and, in themselves, nothing. But they are bound together and made elements of beauty by a calm eagerness of emotion . . . . [The best poems in the book] are masterpieces of deep and mysterious tenderness.*

5

It is interesting to come upon a portrait of this man of thirty-eight in the reminiscences of his English friends, just as he is emerging from his years of obscurity and isolation. Frost had evidently reached a point of spiritual equilibrium by the time of the English journey. Eleanor Farjeon, a close friend of the Thomases, speaks in Book I of her memoirs † of Frost and his family after they had settled near Little Iddens, in Herefordshire, in beautiful orchard country. Here

the Frosts were poor, and indifferent to the conditions of poverty. Frost had [evidently] always taken life as it came where he found it. . . . Whatever he did he made worth doing. . . . His manner was friendly and undemonstrative. He looked at you directly; his talk was shrewd and speculative, withholding nothing and derived from nobody but himself. His New England speech came readily and leisurely, and of all the writers of worth I had met, he spoke with the least sophistication. [He was] unhurried in all he said and did. The Frosts did not live by the clock . . . their center was out of doors. Meals were taken at odd hours.

And when there were visitors, talk and the reading of poetry went far into the night, by candlelight, in the home the poet and his wife had made of "a labourer's cottage standing in a rough plot of ground planted chiefly with potatoes."

The difficulties brought on by the outbreak of the war in August, 1914, proved insuperable, and the Frosts returned to America in February, 1915. An American publisher, Henry Holt & Company, had already brought out a small edition (150 copies) of *North of Boston* from imported English sheets; the first "strictly American" edition of it and of *A Boy's Will* appeared in March, 1915. Frost now experienced his first taste of success. At forty-one, he emerged from almost total obscurity into best-seller status, thus receiving from his new audience the kind of

* The London *Daily News* and the *English Review* (August, 1914, unsigned review).
† Eleanor Farjeon, *Edward Thomas: The Last Years* (Oxford, 1958).

encouragement which proved, in his case, to be the source of fresh energy. The scars of his difficult youth and young manhood were still there, but, as it turned out, these were not irremediable. They became, in fact, important and available parts of his richly creative nature, which was to remain vigorous for many decades to come.

And Frost did not disappoint his audience. He began to publish regularly and at length. *Mountain Interval* appeared in 1916, and *New Hampshire* in 1923. Both volumes were filled with a variety of interesting and original work, although neither approached *North of Boston* in power of dramatic concept or depth of tragic implication. *New Hampshire* marked a revival, and even extension, of the poet's early lyricism. And the long title poem signaled the beginning of a new Frostian manner: the direct and open assumption of the role of shrewd Yankee sage; the translation of aphoristic Yankee wit and the charm of the born talker into poetic terms. This role, this manner, was to become, over the years, a perhaps too insistent one, but on its first appearance it was delightful.

Frost did not alter his way of living; he kept to the simple pattern of his early days. Having bought a farm near Franconia, he continued to live, if not as a farmer, at least as a thoroughly non-urban citizen. Soon he began to lecture and to teach; his connection with Amherst College dates back to 1917. He remained faithful to his native bent and worked, as far as possible, on his own terms. As the years drew him more and more into the circle of academic life, he continued to talk more than he wrote, and kept his published prose to a minimum. He left it to his listeners—some of whom were his warmest disciples—to take notes on his discourses, formal and informal; even the Charles Eliot Norton lectures which he delivered at Harvard in 1936 were never published. In this way, with an instinctive regard for both his gifts and his limitations, he recreated, in fairly unfavorable circumstances, the ancient oral tradition of the bard, as well as the refreshing legend of the "dry" Yankee sage.

6

Close critical examination of Frost's work has been slow to appear;

it is only during the last decade that we find any sustained attempts at detached appraisal in appreciable quantity, as distinguished from the fulsome praise which certain colleagues and fellow poets have lavished on Frost, the man and the poet, since his work began to be known. Several factors explain this critical lag. In the first place, Frost, in a period of extreme experimentation with form, continued to write conventionally, and in a manner which presented to the reader no prosodic difficulty of any kind. Again, Frost's poetry, at a time when symbol and myth had become important carriers of meaning, was allusive only in a restricted way; it offered few leads into elaborate subtlety; it did not encourage "close" reading or fine-drawn explication. It stood outside those currents of avant-garde poetic theory which restlessly absorbed diverse ideas from many adjacent fields —those of anthropology, medical psychology, history, and religion. Finally, Frost's popularity with a large audience—a popularity, it is true, based on a very limited selection of his work —rendered the quality of his appeal suspect to those who believed with Edwin Muir "that the imaginative writer today can be widely popular only by writing falsely."

Frost's diction has none of the "richness and virtuosity" characteristic of modern writing at large. But Frost's very limitation of means often leads the reader into the poet's most striking effects, and an inspection of his general poetic practice brings to light a very real power and control over language which is one basis of his incontestable originality. His mastery of formal poetics is remarkable from first to last; he is a trained and meticulous craftsman. His lyric style is flexible, musical, and completely natural. His form, moreover, is remarkably varied and never seems in any way to have been cut to fit the emotion. Each poem, from short lyric to longer dramatic blank verse, has its own "given" form, and the authenticity of the poet's gift is everywhere apparent.

Frost has put down, in "The Figure a Poem Makes," one of the most interesting and intelligible summations ever made by a poet of the genesis and progress of poetic composition. He describes the poet's ready passivity, open to the initial subconscious impulse, which must be undeviatingly followed and only lightly controlled, at the outset, by conscious ways and means. It is clear that Frost served a long technical apprenticeship. Actual influences, however, even in his early work, are difficult to trace. He had read, and admired, Edward Arlington Robinson's *The Town Down the River* (1908), and his Introduction to Robinson's *King Jasper* (1935) clearly shows his admiration for the work of the older man. Robinson, born in Maine in 1869, belonged to the cultivated New England town tradition (which had produced Emily Dickinson)—a tradition which had begun to dissolve and decay during his youth. His attitude toward this dissolution—of standards and manners as well as of material prosperity—was not entirely nostalgic. Robinson possessed an honest and unerring eye, and a talent for the "simple accuracy" that he admired in George Crabbe. He described his townsmen—particularly the failures, misfits, and outcasts produced by a society in transition—in sharp and tragic detail, and with insight, and he everywhere avoided the soft blur of outworn poetic terms. He turned toward the rhythm of the spoken idiom of his time and place—"Mr. Flood's Party," a favorite poem of Frost's, keeps closely to the turns of native speech.

But there is a great difference between Robinson's occasional approximation of the colloquial and Frost's final success in fitting the "cadences" of common speech to a regular verse pattern—perhaps his central contribution to modern poetic procedures. Poets contemporary with, or slightly older than Frost—among them Swinburne, Kipling, and Robert Bridges—had tried to vary the rhythms of English verse,* finding "the old, dull iambic Wordsworthian measures" tedious. Masefield, reviving the Chaucerian couplet with much success, had dealt boldly with the rough diction of the English working class.† Frost had evidently tried out one method after another (he has said that he tried to write "The Black Cottage" in rhymed couplets, while at Dartmouth). "We must write with the ear on the speaking voice," he later remarked. To that end he had worked in complete separation from the feeble and genteel American literary tendencies of his time, in the ten years from 1902 to 1912. His choice of blank

---

* See Swinburne's "A Forsaken Garden," Kipling's "The Law of the Jungle," and Bridges' "London Snow."
† In *The Everlasting Mercy* (1911) and *The Widow in the Bye Street* (1912).

verse proved to be exactly right for his special purposes. Through this unrhymed five-beat iambic line—which, since the sixteenth century, had been established as the most workable long carrying-line in English—the American poet was given a measure of freedom. The New England manner of speech—at once laconic and meandering—could be caught into this pattern without distortion, and with completely natural emphasis. Frost had, indeed, instinctively put into practice an Imagist tenet (" the natural words in the natural order") before that tenet was formulated (around 1913) by the Imagists themselves.

Certainly, at the time, a new, direct, and truthtelling attitude toward reality, as well as a complete refreshment of poetic diction and use of form, was in order, in poetry in English. The Romantic tradition—which had begun with Blake and ended with Keats—had become threadbare. The Romantic poets had made a conscious effort toward simplicity and clarity of expression; at the same time, their belief in the power of the imagination had enabled them successfully to describe strong and complex emotions. The Victorian era was one of uneasy compromise. The Victorian audience—largely unenlightened aesthetically and unsure of its moral values—began to demand from poets, and from artists in general, reassurance and consolation; and even Tennyson and Browning partially acceded to this demand. By the end of the nineteenth century, English poetry, in spite of isolated efforts, such as that of the Pre-Raphaelites, to bring life into a moribund situation, had become feeble and monotonously minor. The opening stanza of "By the Statue of King Charles at Charing Cross" by Lionel Johnson (1867–1902) illustrates one prevalent style:

> Sombre and rich, the skies,
> Great glooms, and starry plains;
> Gently the nightwind sighs;
> Else a vast silence reigns.

Here, the inflated emotion has drawn to itself language equally false. It was against such falsity that the best of the Georgians, together with the small but highly intelligent and articulate group of Imagists—with several Americans in their number—had begun their revolt. Frost, working in America in provincial isola-

tion, with little but his instinct for sincerity and a sensitive eye
and ear to guide him, had already succeeded in clarifying
language and intensifying form.

It is difficult to speak of Frost's first two books with detachment. The harshness, bafflements, loneliness, and grief of his
childhood and adolescence here have been made to surrender
their meaning at the same time that the tragic aspects of a neglected countryside have been absorbed and created by an eager
young sensibility. The tone, though often tender, is never romantic. C. Day Lewis speaks of Frost's preoccupation with "hard
fact": "no working farmer is romantic—not about nature, at any
rate." * And W. H. Auden has written: "[Frost's] qualities of irony
and understatement, his distrust of fine writing, are those of the
practical man. His poems on natural objects . . . are always
concerned with them not as *foci* for mystical meditation, but as
things with which and on which man acts in the course of his
daily gaining of a livelihood." † And both Day Lewis and Auden
speak of the quality of "good gossip" which the blank-verse poems
often take on. "[These] anecdotes," says Day Lewis, "are told in a
discursive, racy, countryfied way, which may cause us to overlook
their psychological penetration, the technical skill of their verse
. . . and the economy of means behind their apparent rangi-
ness." And he then singles out for special praise the poems "where
Frost broods and comments on familiar country things, imperceptibly weaving a pattern, catching a truth in it almost absent-
mindedly, like a conjurer reaching down a penny out of the
air."

The dramatic monologue of Browning—which was to undergo
a vigorous rehandling in the work of more than one of Frost's
contemporaries, notably in Pound and T. S. Eliot—reappears in
this most unpretentious of settings; and Frost's dialogues and
monologues often resolve into talk so disarmingly natural that it
seems to be overheard. This simplicity is by no means naïve;
it involves a highly trained ear as well as the utmost probity of
choice. "The Pasture," the lyric which served as an epigraph to
North of Boston, written with a controlled and distilled simplicity,

* C. Day Lewis, Introduction to *Selected Poems of Robert Frost* (Penguin,
1955).
† *Recognition of Robert Frost*, ed. by Richard Thornton (1937).

is a love song, among other things—surely one of the loveliest in the language.

As has been pointed out, Frost's power of close and accurate description, in which all the senses are involved, at times approaches clairvoyance. The early books, like many of the later ones, are scattered through with details from the natural scene; things seen, heard, caught in motion, breathed in, touched. "The slow wheel that pours the sand"; the blue berries of the woodbine and its "littered leaves"; the leaves of the hardwood grove that "fit the earth like a leather glove"; the brook's "slender tinkling fall"; the "tattered and swift" line-storm clouds; the "thawing wind" that invades the house—these are things brought into focus by flashes of piercing vision.

In the West Derry years Frost came to take pleasure in—and derive courage from—the varied patterns of character in people whose circumscribed way of life was becoming increasingly difficult to maintain. This isolation was often burdensome, to a crippling degree, but they were on their own, and managing in some way to survive. Far from being "an isolated, brutish and taciturn peasantry" these New England farmers were, on the whole, gentle, high-minded, and articulate. Frost presents a range of their emotions, often in first-person narratives, from the normal, sympathetic, and humane—"The Black Cottage," "The Death of the Hired Man"—through degrees of comedy— "A Hundred Collars," "Blueberries"—to hatred, terror, and incipient madness—"The Housekeeper," "The Fear," "A Servant to Servants." Both "The Fear" and "Home Burial" describe extreme states (of panic guilt and obsessive grief, respectively) with clinical exactness.

Frost continued to explore, through several books, the possibilities of his blank verse, although the later short dramatic vignettes are less grim in subject and tone than those in *North of Boston*. Two narratives, "The Witch of Coös" and "The Pauper Witch of Grafton" (which appeared in *New Hampshire* (1923) under the covering title of "Two Witches") mark a high point in Frost's use of the form. In both, the mania of extreme old age is described, with the utmost insight into, and sympathy with, woman's nature and character beset by time. As Day Lewis points out, "The Witch of Coös," "all the more sinister for the homeliness

and disturbing visual precision of its similes" (the skeleton
mounts the stairs "like a pile of dishes"), is projected—in spite
of its grisly detail—in a delicately established tone of high
comedy. "The Pauper Witch of Grafton," a re-creation of a love
story in the most fantastic terms, ends upon a note of true pathos,
with a passage which is one of the most memorable in Frost.

7

Frost's early relation with the machine, and with man as a
machine-tender, had left an indelible mark on his character,
and understandably so. The relation of young people to the New
England textile mills was a difficult and crucial one. Children
went into the mills and, very often, remained in them throughout their lifetimes. Sarah Cleghorn's famous quatrain (1919)

> The golf links lie so near the mill
>   That almost every day
> The laboring children can look out
>   And see the men at play.

records a fact that Frost, who was later to write the Preface to
Miss Cleghorn's *Threescore: An Autobiography* (1936), could
verify in his own experience. The adult uneducated artisan, too,
was trapped into long hours at a mechanical grind, under the
crudest of labor conditions. Not until the Lawrence strike of
1909 were these conditions brought into general notice.

Frost's experience implanted in him not only a dislike of
supervised mechanical tasks, but a nightmare image of the
machine as menace—an object to be viewed with fear and
dread. The locomotive, the buzz saw, even the stones of the
primitive grist mill, become, as it were, centers of evil force
which override, kill, and maim ("Out, Out—," "The Self-Seeker,"
"The Vanishing Red"). "The Lone Striker" is the single poem
which brings a textile mill into sight (with certain of its processes
meticulously described)—but then only as a trap which the
young man in the poem must escape from at all costs. Frost is
never concerned (as many poets and men of letters have shown
themselves to be, since the beginning of the Industrial Revolution) with the blighting results of industry upon human beings

in general. His is a personal feud, with the machine as adversary. "The Egg and the Machine," for example, which presents a singularly inept one-to-one encounter between a man and a locomotive headlight, occurs fairly late—in *West-Running Brook* (1928). And the long poem "New Hampshire," while it lists many of that state's charming and diversified features, omits all mention of its mills and factories, which had flourished in numbers along its principal rivers for decades.

A central criticism brought to bear on Frost's middle and later work is pointed toward such omissions of ugly fact from the New England scene. Do these omissions constitute actual evasions; is Frost, at times, involved in the propagation of a kind of false pastoral? The scene to which he had become emotionally committed from youth on—the background of small town, village, and of isolated farms beyond the village—was, in fact, changing with great rapidity during his mature years. The railroads and the telegraph poles had already penetrated deeply into rural areas in the time of Thoreau, whose attitude toward both was not completely hostile. But with the appearance of the automobile and the telephone, the older concepts of speed and of communication were drastically altered. Certain features of the countryside and of local custom were gone for good; the tractor was soon to supersede the plow. And certain appurtenances and tools of the older way of living suddenly became completely obsolete. At the same time, a deeply felt nostalgia for a vanished way of rural existence began to manifest itself in a generation that had experienced the transition. It cannot truly be said of Frost that he catered to this nostalgia. His material was his by virtue of hard-won experience. His meticulous attention to his own craft was closely linked with the handcraftsman's love of method and material, so tellingly described in "The Axe-Helve." If a large proportion of his readers preferred to separate out from his work those poems which satisfied their yearning for some version of a lost American Golden Age, the fault was theirs.

It is true that Frost's conservatism—a natural trait in those who live on the land, "closely bound to the wheel of the seasons" —became more marked with the passage of the years. Although many of his admirers wished to think of him as "ordinary" to the core, Frost's nature, of course, was complicated in the extreme.

As a poet, he was a man of strong feelings, and strong feelings are bound to include resentments. A relapse into small-mindedness is, however, a danger lying in wait for any artist of a conservative cast of mind. Statements come to be built not only on emotional conviction, but on hidden prejudice as well. Ill-tempered disputation is then in order, together with a wrong-headed pleasure in holding "notions." The detachment of the artist disappears; the work begins to be in favor of this or that small conception or opinion; the thought becomes whimsical; ideas are no longer large and centered. Emerson and Thoreau, local exemplars from whom Frost learned much, do not coerce the reader. They express themselves with deliberate casualness. This is the philosopher's, and the poet's, way—a way which rises above pettiness and irritability. Any other must lead toward constriction of vision and asperity of tone.

The fact that Frost's more sharply edged comments on national affairs and the state of the world began to appear in years of economic depression brought against him the charge of callousness. Many of the poems written in these crucial years are bitterly opposed to the main tenets of the liberal thought of the time—particularly to collective action, of which even the extreme individualist, Thoreau, approved. Frost's confidence that the terrors of his time could be adequately dealt with by processes of will and determination alone, his lack of flexibility toward the shifts and changes of modern life and society were certainly limiting, especially in view of the efforts made by many of his contemporaries—Yeats, Pound, Eliot and, later, Auden—not only to understand but to remedy, restore, and repair. The fact that Frost was able to hold to his convictions, in a period of great confusion of values, testifies to a central force of character that he was never in any danger of losing. But now for the first time in Frost's work, nature appears as a refuge to which man must retreat, rather than as a natural environment which man can freely choose as his own. Frost begins to repeat injunctions to stand fast, ward off, dig in, take care.

The three later books, *A Further Range* (1936), *A Witness Tree* (1942), and *Steeplebush* (1947), were not, however, consistently given over to preachments concerning the paths mankind should follow, or the policies the nation should adopt.

Quick wit, apt comment, and true lyricism are present in all three, together with a continuing insight into human motives. There are traces, too, of a new melancholy—"The Wind and the Rain" and "Come In"—as well as a new tenderness—"The Silken Tent." Frost had undergone tragedy and loss in these years (Mrs. Frost had died in 1938 and his son Carol in 1940); and they marked his passage into old age. His limitations and self-limitations were now fixed and, in all probability, were to remain unchanged: his tendency, when forced into a tight corner, to lapse into the ambiguous parable; his occasional narrowing of perspective; his inability to establish "a hierarchy of values." In Frost's late career, the evidence increasingly showed, there would be no shocking confrontations, as in the later Yeats, and no profound spiritual insights, as in the case of Eliot. On the other hand, with his own weapons, the old poet was still capable not only of standing his ground, but of dealing some wicked blows. His will remained indomitable. If he consistently clung to the middle regions of mild faith and to a middle tone— which ruled out the noble, "lofty," and transcendent manner—he did not slip back into any false romanticism of style or of attitude; and he continued to avoid the plaintive, the inflated, and the confused.

The tensions, dark conflicts, and passionate involvements which must inform poetry at any level—and had been evident in Frost's from the beginning—in the later Frost were by no means entirely suppressed. When allowed to come through, they pervade certain poems with almost nightmare intensity. The strangely projected pathos of "The Lovely Shall Be Choosers" (a poem in memory of his mother); the suggestions of planned evil in "Design"; the thwarted and maimed human passions described, with the utmost compression and subtlety, in "The Subverted Flower" and "The Discovery of the Madeiras"; the strange timelessness and horror of "The Ingenuities of Debt"—these are unforgettable examples of the imagination working in deep psychic regions. Recurrent moments of anguish and of spiritual doubt and alienation in the later work, as in the earlier, are indicative, as one of Frost's more perceptive critics has pointed out, of "Frost's capacity for a kind of power frequently ignored or underestimated by his admirers." It is a power springing from the poet's close relation to the untouched, the wild, and the primordial: to nature's pure but terrifying springs; to unobstructed height and depth; to snow, stars, darkness, and storm. And Frost has often been able to describe in unflinching terms the precarious balance in man, as in nature—the always imperfect resolution of conflicts in the human heart and mind. That this power and insight have persisted proves Frost extraordinary, in spite of his basic countryman's caution and his frequent shrewd assumption of the mask of "the ordinary man."

But, although Frost in age has maintained his creative energy past the crucial point where many poets decline into repetition or subside into silence, he has failed to achieve that last extension and renovation of thought and emotion—that masterful ordering of experience—which we constantly find in the later poems of Yeats, up to the time of his death in 1939, and in Eliot's *Four Quartets* (1935–1943). Frost's *A Masque of Reason* (1945) and *A Masque of Mercy* (1947) seem extremely light in weight compared to these.

8

Frost's apotheosis in his middle eighties—his final emergence as an ideal manifestation of American character as well as of American poetic genius—has resulted, on the whole, in a happy and beneficent relation between the poet and the population at large. His honors—literary, academic, and, finally, national— were evidently a source of pleasurable satisfaction to the man who had experienced obscurity over a singularly extended period of time. The honorary degrees conferred by Oxford and Cambridge Universities in 1957 brought him back to England, where he had first met positive encouragement and warm literary friendships. Resolutions of the United States Senate on his seventy-fifth (1950)* and eighty-fifth (1959) birthdays, conferred on him a kind of unofficial poet-laureateship, and this standing was accented and reinforced by the invitation extended by John F. Kennedy when newly elected to the presidency in 1960, that Frost read one of his poems at the inaugural ceremony. Frost responded by writing "Dedication: For John F. Kennedy

* The year 1874 was established as his correct birth date after this time.

His Inauguration," which, on the occasion itself, merciless winter sunlight prevented him from reading. He then, quite unperturbed, proceeded to recite "The Gift Outright" (from *A Witness Tree*)— "by heart."

A Witness Tree (1942) takes its title from trees "blazed" by early surveyors of the American wilderness to mark the corner of each square mile. As Edwin Way Teale explains, "When the bark that has grown over these scars is pried off, its inner side reveals, in a perfect negative, the scratches of the code-marks put there a century before." It is understandable why this symbol was chosen by an elder Frost—poet by gift, countryman by nature, and frequent explorer of the wilderness by choice.

STEFAN GEORGE
(1943)

A selection of poems by Stefan George, translated from the German by Ernst Morwitz, a friend of his later years, and Carol North Valhope, has finally appeared in English. George has held the position, in some enlightened opinion, of being the greatest European poet of the start of the century and of our own times. Interest in his work, however, has lagged far behind interest in Rilke's, a fact which would have caused George himself (he died in 1933), and has caused surviving members of his circle, considerable anguish. George consistently ignored Rilke, and George's followers have on occasion been ruthless and unfair to Rilke's achievement and ideas. George had, it is certain, a streak of the megalomaniac in his nature, and that Rilke's poetry should have insinuated itself into the hearts of English, French, and American readers was a development that he could not foresee.

Mr. Morwitz and Miss Valhope have chosen work from seven George volumes, beginning with *Hymns* (1890), published in his twenty-second year, and ending with *The Kingdom Come* (1929), published in his sixtieth. The original poems stand on pages facing the translations. The full sweep of a career extraordinary in its nature is rather fully recorded. Mr. Morwitz, in a long preface, attempts to give American readers some inkling of the reasons for George's impressive life and art. This exegesis partly fails, as have so many explanations written by men who knew the poet. The addition of a portrait would have been enlightening. It is always a shock to the student who has begun the study of George without knowing what he looked like to be confronted with the almost brutal planes of the poet's skull and jaw, the thin, ascetic mouth, and the ecclesiastical costume he affected. Americans have seen this sort of face before, but usually it is the face of a prizefighter or an impresario, rarely of a creative man. There is something rather fake, moreover, to my view, in this clerical getup. The rigorous, serious, completely dedicated hierarchic figure and the consistently ordered and almost stage-managed life we do not understand because in America we do not yet produce such people (at least in the field of literature) or such careers.

Rilke is on record as making a kind and sympathetic explanation of the high-priest act George indulged in. "When a great poet is born into a time inimical to him," Rilke said, "he must protect himself." It is still a puzzle just where the George protective mask ended and his vanity and power drive began. Underneath all this rigidity, strangely enough, existed not a particularly complex nature but a rather simple one. "A simple soul," as a disciple has called George, certainly produced those lyrics of which the expression alone is complex. What saved George and what made him powerful, apart from the impression his very looks must have made on the beholder, is the manifest sincerity and profound depth of his emotions. George drew everything into himself, but his temperament changed the world he so seriously absorbed into verse ranging from the most lucid songs to poems glittering with the religious pronouncements of the seer. It is his magnificent language combined with his simple heart which save him in the end.

Born in 1868 of peasant and petty-bourgeois Rhineland stock, George was given a good formal education and soon left Germany to study with Mallarmé. Naturalism was in full swing in Germany and throughout Europe, and George made a determined stand against the ideals of the society in which he found himself. As he grew older, he felt a traditional German pull away from lyricism toward seership, ethical ideas, and religion-making. He has been accused by some of thinking Hitlerian thoughts before Hitler. His friends, however, including the present translators, have cleared him of any views even remotely National Socialist. It is true that the Third Reich tried to claim him, both in life and after his death. He died in self-imposed exile at Locarno, but I have seen a volume of his selected poems published of late years in Germany in which the place of his death is given as Munich. Many facts will become available after the war ends. Meanwhile anyone interested in the comparative literature which is becoming so important in our day should try to understand George while remembering to enjoy him.

ANDRE GIDE

IMAGINARY INTERVIEWS (*1944*)

It is a good omen that the first book to come through from France, in translation, after a silence that gripped that country from the 1940 invasion on, is a piece of literature—and one so fresh and vigorous that it might have been written by a man in his vigorous prime. It was written, as a matter of fact, by a man in his early seventies. André Gide was born in 1869, a date difficult to credit in this connection. Malcolm Cowley, who has done an excellent job of translation with these nineteen dialogues, two short essays, and a brief journal written at the fall of Tunis, brings out in his introduction to *Imaginary Interviews* the presence of certain passages concealing hidden fire to smoke out treachery. These passages exist, it is true, and no one can bring off such subtleties with the same ease and *brio* as Gide. At the same time, it would be a mistake to take this book as a piece of writing whose value lies solely in its hidden polemic. The remarkable thing about it is its openness. By comparison, much of the writing to which we have been accustomed in an uncensored American literature, these last heavy years, seems closed and stifling. It is the final answer to those opponents of Gide—and how numerous and vocal they once were—who prophesied for him final sterility. It is the final proof that his "Christianity without dogma," his belief in harmony and

187

joy, his determined belief in individuality, had firm bases. It is also a proof, as Cowley says, that a wholehearted devotion to the literary art may in itself constitute political action. The *Interviews* appeared regularly from November, 1941, to the spring of 1942 in the literary supplement of *Le Figaro*, one outlet for serious writers in the unoccupied zone.

The works of André Gide have been presented to American readers in the most haphazard way. *The Counterfeiters* came out rather promptly after its French publication; but detached completely from Gide's career as a whole, it could not but puzzle many readers. *Si le grain ne meurt* . . . , the key book to Gide and one of literature's great confessions, appeared in its first French public edition in 1924; it was published here in an expensive limited edition (*If It Die*) in 1935. The two lives of Gide in English to which Mr. Cowley refers in his preface are valuable, but nothing is so valuable as reading Gide himself, from beginning to end, in his proper order. He has, from the first, possessed the rare faculty of being able to make more or less disguised autobiographical material a continuing basis for his writing. This accomplishment—for autobiography is the most dangerous, and can be the dullest, material in the world—proves an actual underlying development. His vivid grasp of his own experience has been put into the service, moreover, of his moral ideas.

This man, whom readers without French will have to piece together from the scattered books available to them—they have his *Dostoevski*, his African travel notes, his books on Russia, and *The Counterfeiters*, as well as certain short pieces of prose —became a center of influence only after 1918. He had purposely kept his early productions small and varied, in what his opponents considered a perversely baffling manner. His opponents were intelligent and formidable. To Catholics especially he came to represent corruption and secret-keeping: the result of a truly demoniac possession. What was manifesting itself in Gide was showing up in several isolated individuals at the time—Freud, Havelock Ellis, Shaw. The fact of the unconscious was breaking through European thought. Gide's basic tenets, upon which he acted with, to others, an infuriating tenacity, were actually rather simple. Combining in himself opposing elements of the most irreconcilable kind—a Protestant upbringing and a passionate nature the sexual organization of which differed from the "normal"—he early broke, through action, from the illness and misery imposed upon him by seemingly implacable forces. He refused to continue the endless and sterile struggle "against a conformity to which all nature was in contradiction." "It dawned upon me at last that this discordant duality might be resolved into harmony. And then I saw that harmony must be my supreme object, and the endeavor to acquire it the express reason of my life." Many years later he repeats his conviction—the conviction that defeated, for him, the anxiety which so afflicts modern man: "When I made the discovery that joy was rare and more difficult and more beautiful than sadness, joy became for me not only (which it is) a natural need but even more a moral obligation."

In order to give his "dangerous thoughts" some kind of circulation in the heavy pre-1914 world in which he found himself, Gide resorted to ruses. He wrote his books under the protection of the myth. It is difficult fully to understand Gide without a knowledge of these small early works. They are filled with a diffused wit, gaiety, and freedom. They brought into French literature something completely opposed to the heavy work of Barrès—in its own way "mythical." They gave release from deadly compromise and pervasive hidden or open pressure. They "decompressed," in the phrase of one modern French critic.

It is this faculty for "decompression" which gives life and vigor to everything Gide writes. It is present in his criticism—in France the criticism which comes nearest to the warm humanism of Montaigne. It is a releasing touch that operates under the cool and pure classic style that Gide has made flexible, while keeping about it "an odor both resinous and dry." Under this serene surface exists an intellectual and emotional organization fully conscious of "the winds from the abyss." Gide has never allowed his need for reconciliation to blind or deafen him to the terrible contradictions of life, to the often insane tensions functioning in the human spirit. It is the appreciation of the force of these terrors that has drawn him to Dostoevski, Blake, Flaubert, and Shakespeare. He believes in the validity of the extreme, of the sincere, of intense limitation.

The crucial importance of Gide's thought at present is that he has discovered, and long acted upon, the fact of each man's personal responsibility for evil.

What a sad need for hatred [he wrote in his *Journal* in 1937] I see on all sides today! . . . the need to oppose all that should be understood, completed, enriched, united. These conflicts I have felt working in myself, before having come upon them in the outer world. I know them; and by this personal experience I know how one uses oneself up in the struggle. . . . [A day came] when I said: What good does it do? when I began to look, not for struggle and partial triumph, but for accord: to understand that the more separate and different are the parts composing this accord, the richer the harmony. And in the same way in a state—it is a somber kind of Utopia, this dream of smashing one part by another: this dream of a totalitarian state where the subjugated minorities cannot make themselves heard: or, what is worse, where each and all think the same. It cannot be a question of harmony when the choir sings in unison.

It is inevitable that this translation of *Interviews imaginaires* should bear some marks of being printed for an immediate use; of being enlisted to a hard-hitting purpose, with a special target in view. This sharp direction of appeal has resulted in one or two faults. The first translation into English of a set of Gide's essays should be more fully annotated. Some footnotes exist, but not enough. Such annotation would tie these essays firmly into a background of reference, as well as stand as a reassurance that the time will come when literature will again move freely over long open spaces, without fear of traps or ambushes.

The sly, the sinuous, the demoniac Gide: can his opponents find him in this book? I do not think so, any more than his admirers can find an infallible guide; for Gide can make mistakes in literary judgment. The important thing is that they are never mistakes of sympathy. He can be wrong about American writers, but for interesting reasons. And we search in vain for the stiff old figure, loaded with years and evil—the end his enemies prophesied for Gide long since. This man who, during the fighting in Tunis, walks the streets happy in the radiant spring weather, who falls into a happy conversation concerning the respective merits of George and Rilke with the first British staff officer he meets, who lies at night with his window open on "a field of stars," is an aged man. It is impossible to remember this as we read him. His trust in life has not been an empty hope; he is free; and he hands an unambiguous key to freedom to us all.

JOURNALS (1947)

The publication of this first of a projected three-volume American translation of Gide's *Journal: 1889–1939* should mark a fresh start, rather than a continuation, of Gide's reputation in the United States. The *Journals* draw Gide's other works into focus; but do many people now read the scattered American translations of Gide? The latest work published in America was Malcolm Cowley's translation of *Interviews imaginaires*, in 1944.

The *Journals* provide a firm basis for judgments of Gide's character and place in letters. For they are the central pier upon which the imposing edifice of his work is built. Gide from the beginning of his career has been a diarist. The regular, often daily record of thought and event has provided him with a form at once exigent and large, wherein his desire for stability as well as for movement and change, his detailed inquisitiveness as well as his wider curiosity, could be satisfied. Bored with the "big machines" of French literary form, incapable of filling in conventional backgrounds or of inventing stock figures, wary of technical tricks not based on actual emotion, happy to change his mind concerning the worth and direction of his material while that material was still in the process of composition, Gide has always preferred the short form, where effects can be brought off with full spontaneity, before the impelling emotion is exhausted.

Gide's most unfriendly critics have never been able to attack him in respect to his style. The present volume of the *Journals* shows us that style in the making, from the days when the young Symbolist had not yet decided to write "without metaphors," to 1913, when the accomplished man of letters had evolved a manner of writing so clear and flexible that it was a matter of pride to himself and of emulation to his disciples.

The youthful admirer of Chateaubriand has "sharpened his beak" upon Stendhal. The *Journals* soon come to be based upon sincerity of feeling. In this way they never become a mere record of events. Neither do they fall into the errors and *longueurs* of the *journal intime*, since Gide effectually skirts the endless introspective self-indulgences of the intimate diarist. Experience and interest continually enliven the record: books read, music played (Gide is an "intellectual" who can use his hands with precision and speed), journeys undertaken, gardens planted, friends met, meals eaten, daylight walks and midnight prowls described, methods of work delineated with the same care as the most obscure of passing moods, the weather, and the scenery enjoyed. Gide's advance into maturity is by no means in a straight line, without forced detours or periods of circuitous progress. But he soon found his pace and his road. He writes, in 1905: "I escaped early from that world in which, to appear proper, I had to watch myself too closely."

Gide's courageous moral stand, which had so much influence on the post-1918 generation, is not indicated very clearly here: he has written his "confessions" elsewhere. The first exposition of his moral theories appeared in *Les Nourritures terrestres* in 1897, in the last decade of the nineteenth century, at a time when, in French intellectual life, all that was not "determinist" or "finalist" was suspect. A rigid positivism had penetrated French thought to an excessive degree. The only escape for "sensitive souls" was into the refuge of an equally strict and confining religious dogma. In this situation, through bitter personal suffering, after a stay in North Africa and a friendship with Wilde, Gide dared to reconcile irreconcilables. He brought emotion over into the moral realm, declaring the experiences of the flesh to be of equal value to those of the mind and the spirit; and he affirmed that spiritual values could operate in a life-giving manner outside the rituals of religion. Always claiming a basic Christianity, he began his meditations on the figure of a Savior who stood for man's joy rather than for man's tragic and deforming frustration.

As the world of affairs begins to claim more of his attention, Gide meets people and events head-on; he does not take anyone's opinion as his own; he analyzes character and motive with a penetrating combination of intuition and acumen. His dislike of virtuosity in art parallels his impatience with the deviousness and pretentiousness of human beings. The tension between the oppositions within himself continues; perfect balance between impulse and scruple, asceticism and sensuality is never entirely achieved. There are breakdowns, nervous crises, and capitulations, as well as spiritual and physical convalescences and reanimations. By keeping the poles of the tension clear, however, Gide escapes most of the enticements of self-deception. His life and relationships must be kept, so far as possible, vital and necessitous. All must be natural in the area of the senses while at the same time the will must function with a kind of "supple obstinacy." Gide's dealings with his colleagues and friends never lack an edge of critical sharpness; but shows of ambition, jealousy, rancor, and spite never occur, and small gossip and downright malice are relatively rare. His chief desire is to have friends who "exist behind and beyond what [they] reveal to us." He does not neglect "the insulted and injured."

Take upon oneself as much humanity as possible. That is the correct formula. . . . Absence of sympathy equals lack of imagination. The most gifted natures are perhaps the most trembling. . . . As soon as an emotion decreases, the pen should stop; when it continues to run on just the same—and it runs on all the more easily—writing becomes detestable. . . . The wonderful thing on this earth is that we are forced to feel more than to think.

These are the words of a man and an artist who has detached himself from killing and "glacial" abstractions and moved into a world where the modern divided spirit is at least partially healed, where there are provable and classic linkages between the timeless and the time-bound.

Nothing has been spared—neither good-quality large paper nor an intelligent and meticulous editor—to make this American edition impressive. The French *Pléiade* edition (1939 and 1940) on which it is based still retains a peculiar charm, however. Complete in one volume, printed on thin paper, its 1,352 pages compactly yet flexibly bound, this French edition resembles some object delightful and usable: a convenient missile, let us say, against "the Philistine"; or a concentrated form of nourishment, on which one could maintain life over a long period.

JOURNALS *(1948)*

The reader who advances into the second volume of Gide's *Journals* in English translation can be sure of a very nearly complete record of sincerity on all levels. The style takes its tone of truth from the material; the material is clarified by the style. In spite of our romanticisms the classic ring of absolute sincerity in writing is happily recognized by modern ears. The broad, generalized biographical work, as well as the emotional "confession," now leaves us more or less unmoved. We can easily detect that false smoothness and serenity which echoes a "maturity" achieved through the repression of a whole side of the personality. We also suspect, as Gide points out, the finicky style, as in Amiel, or the self-satisfied style, as in the Goncourts. Gide's *Journals* are one biographical work of our period where modern "truths" are discovered, and then openly presented in a manner equal to their complex demands.

The second part of the *Journals* also disproves the assertion of Gide's enemies that he is always ready with a specious formula that might at any moment be transposed into its opposite. We see only too clearly in the entries between 1914 and 1917 how Gide, harassed by the paradoxes of his own nature, as well as by the historical situation in which he found himself, and the object of critical attacks from all sides, was often compelled to improvise some way of life, and some means of spiritual survival, from day to day. It is one of the virtues of the *Journals* that these desperate improvisations have not been deleted from it. Gide often allows himself to sound like a lost soul—or like an ordinary human being whose control is snapping and whose will is petrified.

The search for equilibrium in a highly organized modern man, the theme which runs through the long work, is particularly apparent in this second section. Gide, at the beginning of the 1914–1918 war, was able to envisage his own worth and the moral and aesthetic tasks which lay before him, but only intermittently and in a partial way. He was forty-five, an age when the spiritual nature is impelled toward some comfortable orthodoxy, when the physical being begins to lose energy, and when the creative mind is assailed by fears of depletion and dryness. It is a period, moreover, when manias and compulsions may seize hold of the personality and force its acts into some repetitive pattern. It is an age when one must learn patience, without losing drive. "I cling desperately to this notebook; it is part of my patience; it keeps me from going under" (February, 1916).

The *Journals* at this time of doubt and loss become confused and begin to stammer. Long periods are filled with entries that are empty and dull. Gide finally consents to their mediocrity. He also consents to any diversion which will give him a little peace; piano practice, reading and translating, pets, botany, household tasks, and gardening. This is a time of the sharpest analysis of people. Whatever "life offers must be scrutinized with care"; and Bourget, Cocteau, Valéry, Proust, Maritain, alive and in the flesh, are so examined along with crowds of the non-illustrious. We now recognize in these activities the attempts at "therapy" of a man whose more minatory side has taken the upper hand, and who is convinced that part of his nature is "abominable." Later Gide could write: "Arrogance and boredom are the two most authentic products of hell. I have done everything to defend myself against them and have not always succeeded in keeping them at a distance. They are the two great provinces of romanticism."

Gide finally made two decisions, with what difficulty the contemporary entries show. First, he rejected any sort of orthodox religion, in spite of his belief in God and the proselytizing efforts of his converted friends. Second, he decided to put down his "childhood recollections," in the first person singular, with as much frankness as possible. He also decided that the time had come to publish his study of the place and importance of homosexuality (*Corydon*) in a signed commercial edition. His dissatisfaction with his work continues (". . . it all lacks tremor, elasticity, and richness . . ."); but soon the days of real desperation are over, even though the necessity for constant self-discipline continues. "I must go right on even if I have to write in the margin: to be re-written." By 1917 Gide has made himself capable again of love and joy. The periods "when my mind [is] much concerned with ridiculous anxieties that fatigue and dim it" lessen and then almost totally disappear.

The Gide who in 1921 begins *The Counterfeiters* has come into that state of equipoise where original, because unfrightened, assessments of human nature and morals can be made. *The Counterfeiters,* published in 1926, begins where most novels leave off. The conventional theme of adultery becomes only an ironic detail in this survey of the neglected sides of human existence: the tragedy of senility, the sadism of childhood, the latent or real criminality of adolescence, the irresponsibility of the romantic. By 1927 all Gide's secrets were out. The man who had for a long time projected his ideas in the form of parables was now able to step forward with open statements.

This volume ends with Gide convinced, as one of his best critics has said, "that evil is a force which can become a factor of progress"; that "the real value is hardly ever the apparent value"; that "life destroys individuals, but, on the other hand, individuals bungle life." At fifty-eight Gide tells us that self-satisfaction on the anxiety level is both stupid and a waste of time. There is a world elsewhere. If he has not formulated the approaches to that world in neat metaphysical language— which he abhors—he has allowed us to watch the full spectacle of himself living them through.

GOETHE

(1949)

A general eagerness to wring some usable wisdom from Goethe, preferably in condensed form, on the two-hundredth anniversary of his birth, has pushed the great man from the company of the poets into the company of the philosophers, for the twin barriers of language and of time do not matter so much in the realm of philosophy. Metaphysics, by reason of its airiness, can seep from one period to another, and when one deals in abstractions, the partitions of language are fairly thin and yielding. But poetry, and particularly lyric poetry, is forever stuck fast in its original tongue. And although Goethe from youth on was surrounded by philosophers and knew them as close friends and as correspondents, and although his liking for abstractions, symbols, and enigmas steadily increased, he remained a poet *pur sang*. Schiller, who, Goethe said, "cared more for speculation than for the direct vision of things," found him but an indifferent Kantian, and if Goethe showed a strong sympathy for certain portions of Spinoza's thought, it is doubtful that he followed through to the end Spinoza's complicated and geometric arguments.

Being a poet, Goethe thought in images, trusted his intuition, and, in his own words, dwelt "in the truth of the five senses." This innate empiricism prevented him from being thrown off his course by the metaphysics all about him, and he boasts, in one of his lighter verses, of having achieved splendid results because he never lost his way "thinking about thought." We must not be led astray, therefore, into believing, because of the enormous range of his interests, that he possessed a variety of approaches toward his subjects. One approach—that of the interpretative imagination—underlies all Goethe's researches, from the theatre through the plastic and graphic arts, from the nature of the universe through the conduct of life, from religion and sociology through botany, mineralogy, and optics. Thomas Mann has spoken of the combination in Goethe of true naïveté with extraordinary intellectual power. Goethe's was the poet's naïveté, and this pleasing gift never dwindled.

Language is the insuperable barrier between Goethe and ourselves. Translations are not much help to the poetry, and Goethe's thought, at its purest and most forceful, is embedded in the poetry. "Goethe was particularly unfortunate in his English translators," D. J. Enright truthfully observes. "All along [his] natural, idiomatic German is debased into some or other kind of awful synthetic poesy. . . . The modern reader . . . after he has glanced at one or two of the *Faust* specimens [in English], may be led into abandoning Goethe on the ground that no really great poetry could ever look quite so dreadful in translation. But it can." C. F. MacIntyre's version of the first part of *Faust,* published in 1941, has helped dispel this unhappy tradition. One way of getting at *Faust* is to get it onto the stage. The ideal celebration of Goethe's bicentenary this year would have been a full-dress production of *Faust,* in the exciting manner of Reinhardt's production of the Second Part in Salzburg in the early thirties. It would have put Goethe's poetry where it belongs—in the mouths of living and breathing characters.

The barrier of time is difficult to overcome. For Goethe is the epitome and one of the prime movers of a cultural period that was not only short-lived, in contrast to its importance, but, when it was over, was gone for good. It was the period between the charming yet rather sinister excesses of eighteenth-century German Rococo and, on the other hand, the "Biedermeier," a German version of English Early Victorian. It was the period of the informal "English" park, midway between the stiff, formal parterres of the past and the hideous, formal, geranium and begonia beds of the future. It was the period of "bourgeois classicism" so well described by C. L. Laing when, writing of Beethoven, he says:

The sentimental irrationalism of the *Sturm und Drang* emptied into
the quiet world of ideas. . . . The genius [of the times] recognized
the validity of objective norms; boundless humanism gave way to a
humanism which recognized its own limits. This moderation and
equalization ripened into a classicism of which the German phase is
the very symbol. Classicism beatified life and gave it lastingness by
viewing it from the heights of the ideal. . . . Its art was devoted to
the ideal of plastic beauty which it believed to be absolute; its principal object was man living in consort with nature, man beautiful in
body and soul . . . man who became aware of his inner harmony,
and who was the measure of all things. The result was an aesthetic
world-picture, a Germandom reborn from the spirit of Hellas.

It was this idealism of an enlightened burgher class headed
toward freedom that provided the climate for the time's "explosion
of genius." Goethe, the young bourgeois from Frankfurt, all fire
and temperament, was one of the constructors of this ideal and
point of view. The gradual development of his feeling for classic
depth, clarity, and equilibrium showed itself in his growing
control over his life and impressed itself upon his surroundings.
Far from being "a Prince's valet," he was the guide and teacher
of his Weimar duke, and succeeded in making a humane man
and ruler out of an irresponsible boy. We must look back at this
period, of course, from across the Romanticist period that followed it (and that Goethe distrusted), and it is not easy to keep
focus on the distant scene. That the period had its effect beyond
the borders of Germany is proved by the reverence and admiration
given it, during its brief existence, by the rest of Europe and
even by America. It is the only cultural bridge between the
eighteenth and the nineteenth centuries, at a time when France
was exhausted by its fit of power and England had retreated from
eighteenth-century "liberalism" into reactionary anti-Jacobinism
and the small and dull frivolity of the Regency.

Goethe, except for Carlyle, made no great impression upon
English thought or letters. English industrialism was a going
concern long before Goethe's death. His point of view appealed
more to Scotch moral idealism and American transcendentalism
than to British hardheadedness. And soon, all over Europe and
in America, Romanticist doubt, melancholy, and soul-searching
began to negate the classic ideal. Goethe's age was at an end,
and the poet for whom every living and evolving thing had

importance, who was an enemy of the dry specimens of the museums, was turned over to the scholars and the commentators to be explained, ticketed, and mummified.

When we look for modern writers who have understood and profited from Goethe's poetry and ideas, we come upon an unexpectedly lively list. We find, to begin with, a young man who, visiting Rome in 1851, linked Goethe, quite naturally, with Dante, Shakespeare, and Michelangelo. This was Gustave Flaubert. We find continual references to Goethe in Flaubert's *Correspondance*. He defends Goethe against detractors, and everywhere tenders him admiration and praise, and one Goethian maxim helps him to run his life: "*Qu'est-ce que ton devoir? L'exigence de chaque jour.*" The influence of Goethe upon Flaubert was a creative one as well; the first *St. Antoine* derives directly from *Faust II*, and the first *L'Education sentimentale* from *Wilhelm Meister*. In our own time, we find Gide, in his *Journals*, constantly referring to Goethe. He reads the poetry with delight and attempts to translate it. He notes that "nothing in life so calms me as the contemplation of this great figure," and that "the greatest influence to which I have *submitted* is that of Goethe." We find among modern critics, philosophers, and historians who have submitted themselves to Goethe's intelligence and intuition the names of Santayana, G. Lowes Dickinson, Valéry, Toynbee, Albert Schweitzer, and, of course, Mann.

A Study of Goethe, by Barker Fairley, published in 1947, is the best modern critical work in English and should be consulted by anyone truly concerned with the poet's achievement.

To those who, although permanently baffled by German, can read French, a new and complete translation of *Faust,* published in 1947, can be recommended. It includes the Gérard de Nerval version of *Faust I,* together with *Faust II,* translated, with absorbing comments, by Alexandre Arnoux and R. Biemel. For those who can cope with German, a neat and well-printed pocket edition of *Faust,* in two volumes, has recently been published in New York.

The best introduction to Goethe's lyric poetry for the non-German reader is through music. Forgetting all the attempts of Romantic composers to deal with Goethe's work—from the sweetenings of Gounod, Tchaikovsky, Thomas, Massenet, and others, to the horrification of Berlioz—he can turn to three songwriters, two of whom were Goethe's contemporaries and one of whom is a modern. Beethoven's songs and incidental music for *Egmont,* and Schubert's songs written to Goethe's lyrics, bring us close to the poet's own music. The most extraordinary evocation of Goethe's power and poetic range, however, comes to us through the fifty-one songs written to his lyrics by Hugo Wolf. "Music as such," a learned critic says of Wolf's settings, "was never an aim to him, only a means to enhance the poem." Anyone who has listened to the wild longing of the Wolf-Goethe "Kennst Du das Land?" or to the noble and transcendent beauty of their "Prometheus" and "Ganymed" has experienced the only world it is important to share with any great poet—the world of his intense emotion and his piercing vision.

ROBERT GRAVES

POEMS (*1946*)

"I write poems for poets and satires or grotesques for wits," says the English poet Robert Graves in an uncompromising short foreword to *Poems, 1938–1945*. "For people in general I write prose and am content that they should be unaware that I do anything else. . . . To write poems for other than poets is wasteful."

Let us allow for some satire and grotesques in Mr. Graves's pronouncement. Modern poets, nagged and harried as they frequently are by critics, often fall into a self-deprecatory manner; they run for cover and mumble apologies and fumble for explanations. Some, however, like Mr. Graves, stand their ground and refuse suggestions that they distrust their gifts, hate their art, and denigrate their colleagues. In the same week that Mr. Graves's book appears, Mr. Norman Rosten, a younger man and an American, reiterates his conviction that poetry for poets is no go. "I do not belong," Mr. Rosten says, on a slip of paper tucked into the review copies of his long narrative poem *The Big Road*, "to that school which holds to the curious belief that poery is written for poets and should be as difficult and obscure as possible. Poetry should neither exhaust nor confuse, but invigorate and clarify."

Now, it would be easy to place Mr. Graves's and Mr. Rosten's books beside one another and proceed to run one down in terms of the other. Because the two men are working in completely different genres, it is more important to get beneath their dissimilarity of form and aim to what they share in common. And it is more important, in view of their opposed poetic positions, to try to estimate the clarifying and invigorating qualities in each, for the present and for the future.

Mr. Rosten's narrative deals with the building, during the war, of the Alcan Highway, from Dawson Creek to Fairbanks, by forces of United States Army Engineers. "Here in tremendous reading," says the book's jacket blurb, "is a poet's challenge born out of bold yesterday and the roaring techniques of today." The narrative's own technique owes a good deal, let us say at once, to W. H. Auden and T. S. Eliot, two poets; Mr. Rosten may not have written for *them*, but they certainly wrote for *him*. The overwhelming influence is that of radio (sections of the story have been presented over national and armed-forces networks). And how Mr. Rosten loves power! Strong men succeed strong men: Roman empire builders, Spanish conquistadors, American pioneers, and Russian navigators. Power conquers and regenerates; by rough methods alone are slaves transformed into free men. Clean, true-hearted, tender-hearted toughness, which breaks into folk music and psalm-singing from time to time— there's an ideal for you, fit for any radio network at any hour. "All things vanish but the road," says Mr. Rosten, thus summing up the entire contribution made to civilization by the Roman world.

It is fatally easy to make fun of such a tale, and, at this point, one could seriously begin to extoll Graves's exquisite small effects and deplore the splash of Rosten's large ones, to praise Graves's wit and note Rosten's lack of humor, to point out the older man's quiet complexities as opposed to the younger's loud simplicities. But the real difference between the two men, and between their respective works, does not lie in detail; it centers in the large underlying fact that while one is wrapped up in his time, the other is outside it, observing it in a detached and chilling way. Rosten is giving "the public," during a transitional period, what he and that public believe it needs: romantic braggadocio to comfort it (for it is sad), to reassure it (for it is bewildered), and to needle it (for it is exhausted). Graves is merely using a

trained ear and eye and a mature set of emotions to note certain
striking features in the strange set of circumstances in which
he has found himself; to set down in musical language the
unusual turns of thought that come, in crisis, into a sardonic
mind. Graves uses the sharp edge of satire to cut toward the
future through a mass of accretions that belong to the past.
History, the facts of which Rosten sentimentalizes with so much
vigor, has its distilled truths, and one of these is that satirists
alone see through confused, transitional times. It is difficult to
hear them—or to believe them, once heard—but they are there,
and it is their insight which marks out lines as definitive and lasting as any wilderness road.

NEW POEMS (1964)

It seems at present dangerous and almost wicked to acclaim the
virtues of the traditional. Academies of all kinds have been in
disrepute for decades, and form in the arts has come to be
thought of by many people as a sort of trap. But the fact remains
that when high, lively poetic talent appears, operating in conventional form, crowds run toward it, though often in the belief
that they are running toward something else. The late Dylan
Thomas, for example, was a formalist of the first order—in
youth, we have been told, a student of Milton and George Herbert,
and in maturity one of the few moderns writing in English who
could face up to the intricacy, and the exaltation, of the ode. It
is difficult to remember, in periods of experiment, that form was
invented to produce pleasure and that poets (young Sidney,
young Shelley) once hotly defended their right to speak in numbers. Yet in spite of the loud, rebellious cries that are being
continually raised by this or that partisan of poetic freedom,
conventional delights still count. Even that wonderfully con-
temptuous brickbat epithet "square" goes off course when aimed
at pure lyric endowment. It hits the barnyard fowls but misses
the nightingales.

   As a matter of fact, the amount of brilliant formal poetry
written in English at the moment is striking. The favorites of the
Muse are ever the Muse's defenders, and Robert Graves can be

considered a shining instance of how the goddess seems to continue to take care of her own. Graves, in his *New Poems*, is still able to write memorable lyrics at an age when in many poets the impulse to song has lessened or totally disappeared. Although his tone frequently slides over into the incantatory and his gods and demons are recurrent and slightly obsessive, they are beings whose power we are made to recognize by the sheer practiced skill of Graves's writing hand.

NATHANIEL
HAWTHORNE
(1960)

The Scarlet Letter, first published in 1850 and the author's first work of any length, established Hawthorne's reputation. Henry James, then a child living in New York City, was "to remember dimly the sensation the book produced, and the little shudder with which people alluded to it, as if a peculiar horror was mixed with its attractions." James, upon whose writing the example of Hawthorne was to leave a strong imprint, in 1879 produced the first important critical biography of his forerunner. Here he says of The Scarlet Letter: "The book was the first piece of imaginative writing yet put forth in this country. There was a consciousness of this in the welcome that was given it—a satis- faction in the idea of America having produced a novel that belonged to literature, and to the forefront of it. Something might at last be sent to England as exquisite in quality as any- thing that had been received, and the best of it was that the thing was absolutely American: it belonged to the soil, to the air; it came out of the very heart of New England."

Hawthorne at forty-six had experienced many aspects of the New England scene. He was born and had grown up in the town of Salem, Massachusetts, the son of a sea-captain's widow in straitened circumstances. A strong sense of the past was always present in this descendant of Puritan forebears, whose ancestors included several worthies prominent in the early days of the settlement. He had spent his youth surrounded by the atmosphere of Salem's most vigorous period—the era of the merchant ships whose trade with the Orient had brought to this small port an unexampled prosperity. Young Hawthorne and his family had little or no contact with this new Yankee wealth and power, evidences of which can still be seen in Salem streets lined with impressive Greek Revival houses. An education was possible in spite of poverty and, at Maine's Bowdoin College, Hawthorne came to know Longfellow and Franklin Pierce. He returned to Salem, where he led, for twelve years, an almost morbidly secluded life as an apprentice writer. He also made himself, at this period, a close student of the history of the region. After modest periodical publication, his first sketches and tales were collected in the two volumes of *Twice-Told Tales*. He left Salem in 1836 to work in Boston, and five years later he joined the Brook Farm community, a Utopian Fourierist experiment. His stay was brief (his sympathy with Transcendentalist theory, never strong, was to become directly critical in later years). His marriage in 1842 with Sophia Peabody, whose devotion to Emerson was marked, brought him to the Old Manse at Concord, and into a rather cool friendship with the Concord group. The publication of *Mosses from an Old Manse* was followed by his short (1846–1849) tenure as port surveyor at the Salem Custom House. When the change of political administration brought this position to an end, Hawthorne suddenly found himself faced with the necessity of providing, with little or no means, for a wife, two children, and an ailing mother. Mr. Field, his Boston publisher, visited the author and has described Hawthorne's circumstances (he was living in an inadequately heated "modest wooden house") and his depressed state of mind. It was during this visit that Hawthorne gave to Field "the germ" of *The Scarlet Letter*. Field's enthusiasm encouraged Hawthorne to go on with the book, which, written at high speed, was finished in February, 1850. Hawthorne later stated in his *English Notebooks* that he was in an extremely nervous condition after finishing the book, "having gone through great diversity of emotion while writing it, for many months."

Hawthorne had chosen, for the place and time of his subject, the New England of a remote past—Boston during the period of the first Puritan emigrations, when the hard "iron" rule of a Calvinist theocracy was not in any way mitigated (as it later came to be) by humane considerations. This sensitive descendant of witch-hunting and Quaker-persecuting ancestors had built for himself, in his early maturity, both a literary method and a moral point of view. He was intellectually fearless and uncompromising; but a strain of whimsicality, and tenderness, together with a feeling for "the Marvelous," tempered his sterner qualities. He had not been swept over into the middle-class optimism and sentimentality of the time any more than he had been taken in by cloudy Transcendentalist hopes. A vein of Calvinist rigor—a sense of man's ultimate imperfectibility—had filtered down to him through many generations. Any open belief in immortality, in heaven and in hell, is either withheld or ironically made ambiguous. His belief in the final worth of the strictures of the moral law is more clearly evident. He was convinced that no true spiritual value could exist that was not based on suffering, and that sin brought down upon the sinner a crucial need for contrition and atonement. "The riddle of the soul's growth" was ever present in his mind; and his sense of the dignity of the individual was unshakable. The central tenet of his creed was his confidence in the importance of "the truth of the heart."

It is Hawthorne's insight into emotional complexity and the hidden depths of the human spirit which attracts the modern reader to him, and has helped to bring about the high critical regard accorded him today. Some critics at the turn of the century found him minor and passive, and he has been assigned, even today in some quarters, an overwhelming allegiance to the patterns of Puritan allegory. In general, however, the winds of critical controversy have set in his favor—so strongly, in fact, that his real virtues have often been lost sight of in elaborate modern interpretations of his method and purpose. He has been made a forerunner, for example, of the French Symbolists, and his "romances" are often approached more from the point of view of their hidden poetry than of their open prose.

The poetry exists; Hawthorne's central images have the impact of poetic condensation and intensity. His choice of "the romance" over the novel was a conscious one; he openly explained that "the romance" gave more scope for the play of imagination. In *The Scarlet Letter*, as frequently elsewhere, Hawthorne succeeds in focusing upon the grimmest of events a steady but warm light which at once illuminates and defines. He shifts his tone with the utmost subtlety in the course of outlining this "tale of human frailty and sorrow." He fully accepts the privilege of the ancient teller of tales, of coloring fact with fantasy. We now admire his exteriorization of inner conflict, but we must remember that ultimately he knew himself to be describing men and women (and a child) of flesh and blood, concerning whom there must be no omission or distortion of the truth.

The fact that we are not dealing with clothed abstractions becomes clear when we turn our attention to the figure of Hester Prynne—the first portrayal in American fiction of woman's nature in all its complication and contradiction. Hester is sustained from beginning to end by a recognizable feminine pride and courage. There is no trace (as has been claimed) of nineteenth-century feminism here. Hester engages only in feminine pursuits—needlework and nursing; she is practical and industrious; once she has taken hold of her terrible situation, she makes sensible decisions, and she is a watchful and devoted mother. Hawthorne gives her, it is true, at a late point in the story, serious moments of speculation concerning the hard position of women and the possibility of changing their destinies, but these meditations are not followed through. She is not a heroine in the large sense. She is a woman whose life, through adversity, has become "bare and harsh." But for a moment in the scene in the forest, Hester's original yielding and passionate nature is returned to her. "Her sex, her youth and the whole richness of her beauty came back from what men call the irrevocable past." We see her as she was before her tragic story began—as Hawthorne knew that she must, if only for a moment, be seen.

The perfect balance of the book's structure has often been described; Hawthorne's web of good and evil is classically worked out. And his glances into the heart's dark cavern are remarkable in their penetration. We see the power of repressed emotion when Dimmesdale, walking back from the forest, is presented with one fearful and perverse suggestion for action after another, and we witness his joy in this release. We recognize Chilling-worth's timeless knowledge of the power of suggestion and his skill (the physician's as well as the enchanter's) in diagnosing psychic ills by their physical manifestation. And the child Pearl, so puzzling to Hawthorne's contemporaries, in the light of a wider psychological understanding can be now taken as a closely observed example of the disturbed precocious child (she sees all; how much does she understand?) who projects its hostility even in play. In *The Turn of the Screw,* James was later to pattern upon Pearl that most malicious and enigmatic of little girls, Flora.

James, early in his own career, analyzed Hawthorne's in-heritance with perfect insight. He also recognized the importance of Hawthorne's contribution to the art of the novel—a contribu-tion which has not diminished in value with the passage of time.

He had ample cognizance of the Puritan conscience; it was his natural heritage; it was reproduced in him; looking into his soul he found it there. But his relation to it was only, as one might say, intel-lectual, it was not moral and theological. He played with it as a pig-ment; he treated it . . . objectively. He was not discomposed, dis-turbed, haunted by it, in the manner of its usual and regular victims who had not the little postern gate of fancy to slip through. . . . It was, indeed, to his imaginative vision, the great fact of man's nature; the light element which was mixed with his own composition always clung to this rugged prominence of moral responsibility, like the mist that hovers about the mountain. It was a necessary condition for a man of Hawthorne's stock that if his imagination should take licence to amuse itself, it should at least select this grim precinct of the Puritan morality for its playground.

"Be true! Be true! Show freely to the world, if not your worst, yet some trait by which that worst may be inferred!" This is the single "moral" which Hawthorne sets at the end of his profound investigation, in *The Scarlet Letter,* into the extremes of human impulse and conduct, and we respond to its continuing appeal.

HEINE

(1956)

The centenary of Heine's death was not celebrated in America in any marked way. In Germany, the definitive edition of the poet's letters, including three volumes of learned commentary, appeared, and two studies of his thought and feeling are currently available in England. The single biographical study of the poet published here this winter is not a new work but a reissue of Antonina Vallentin's *Heine: Poet in Exile,* which dates back to 1934. Mme Vallentin's life of the poet gives evidence of solid literary research, but her tone and approach show traces of Stracheyan methods, today a trifle dated, and she does not have Strachey's light hand.

The influence of Heine on poetry in English has long since been absorbed, so that little of it is perceptible today. A. E. Housman was the chief link between the poetry of the *Buch der Lieder* (1827) and English lyricism of the late nineteenth and early twentieth centuries, but Pound, somewhat later, recommended Heine (along with Sappho and Villon) to the attention of the Imagists. Heine's power, an anonymous critic in the London *Times Literary Supplement* has said recently, of creating the most poignant effects from a handful of conversational Ger-

man and the common experience of unrequited love was and
continues to be a kind of miracle. Housman took over not only
Heine's simplicity and directness of language but Heine's wit,
which could be warm and cold in turn. Many of Heine's songs,
in spite of their seeming casualness, are epigrams in the classic
manner; even effects of pathos are brought off by the very neatness and balance of the syntax, and a brilliant pointedness and
condensation are everywhere evident. Auden, MacNeice, and,
currently, John Betjeman have profited from Heine's example.
At the moment, however, the tendency of the contemporary
lyricist is to break away from Heine's miniatures into larger
frames. Out of their great sorrows, modern poets tend to make
more and more elaborate and extensive songs.

Heine himself, of course, was quite capable of enlarging his
form at the demand of his material; from "Die Nordsee" on, a
freedom that we would call experimental illuminates the work of
his middle and late periods. The author of "Lorelei," as Mme
Vallentin points out, was Germany's first satirist, and he invented
the *Zeitbild*, the poem that mirrors everyday settings and events.
Born in Düsseldorf while the city was still occupied by Napoleon's
troops, Heine experienced in his youth the spread of German
reaction (Metternich called him "this detestable writer") as well
as a growing hostility to the Jews. Exiled under official ban, he
found himself, in Paris, appreciated by a society that welcomed
international elements; he became a friend of Balzac, of Gérard
de Nerval, of Wagner, and of Marx. Like Byron (I am still
quoting the British critic), he was fascinated throughout his life
by "the poetry of politics"—summed up for both men in the
word "freedom." His life vacillated between extremes of courage
and of abject disorder, but his basic clear-sightedness made him
reject the dominant falsehoods of his own day to the extreme
of foreshadowing some of the sounder attitudes of our own.
Cruelly caustic, intensely skeptical, he nevertheless kept alive,
even in his tragic later years, a fund of mischief and of warmth;
neither poetry nor prose became artificial under his hands. Mme
Vallentin's account of the complicated European situation, whose
reactionary as well as falsely romantic tendencies Heine opposed,
is full and vivid.

GERARD MANLEY
HOPKINS

LETTERS (*1935*)

Gerard Manley Hopkins is without doubt the chief Providential
Influence (in the sense of where would they be without him?)
now acting upon the youngest generation of those who speak in
English numbers. The combined authority of Eliot, Pound, and
Yeats, supreme for so long, has begun to fade; the echo of their
measures is now the exception and not the rule. The young
have turned to a contemporary of their great-grandfathers for
prosodic guidance.

The main facts of Hopkins' career—his lifelong friendship
with Robert Bridges, which began at Oxford in the sixties, his
early conversion to Catholicism, and his subsequent induction
into the Jesuit order—are now generally known. His poems at
the time of his death, in 1889, remained in manuscript; the first
edition of his work, collected by Bridges, appeared in 1918. His
revolutionary prosodic theories and his extraordinary poetry
impressed, but somewhat unnerved, the friends to whom his
work was entrusted. All this comes out, along with the quality
of Hopkins' critical temper, in *The Letters of Gerard Manley
Hopkins to Robert Bridges* and *Correspondence of Gerard Manley
Hopkins and Richard Watson Dixon,* published this winter in two
volumes under the editorship of C. C. Abbott. These letters are

the most important recent addition to the annals of English poetry. They are the record of an intellect at once passionate, cool, sincere, and undeviating, and of a spirit fiery beyond description. Totally unknown to the great figures of nineteenth-century literature, Hopkins scrutinized their work with an intensity which allowed no stupidity or inexactitude of expression to escape unscathed. His remarks on the Brownings, for example, are brilliant. And the letters record, by implication, the progress of Hopkins' long poetic martyrdom: the conflict between his great gifts and his perfect and unquestioning obedience to the rules of his order. The two volumes are edited with a care which resembles reverence, and are illustrated with holographs and portraits.

FURTHER LETTERS (1938)

"It has always seemed to me that poetry is unprofessional," Hopkins wrote when he was twenty. Because he held, throughout his life, to the practice of his belief, his prose works come to the modern reader singularly pure: in the form of letters to intimate friends and notebooks. The *Further Letters of Gerard Manley Hopkins, Including His Correspondence with Coventry Patmore,* under the same reverent editorship of Professor Abbott, contains "all further letters which have come to light" since 1935, when Hopkins' letters to Bridges and the Hopkins-Dixon correspondence appeared. *The Notebooks,* edited by Humphrey House, were published in 1937. The letters in this volume are divided into three sections: miscellaneous letters to family and friends; a long-continued (1863–1888) series of letters to A. W. M. Baillie; and, at last, the Hopkins-Patmore correspondence in full.

Casual letters are at once a touchstone and a giveaway. They are certain to show all the cheapness and attitudinizing of a writer; rant, seedy thinking, sentiment, and obstinate prejudices come to the surface in such documents to be seen with great clearness. In the case of Hopkins, his letters prove, as his editor says, that the man was all of a piece; the letters "bear the imprint of the same rare mind and spirit, they have the same disciplined honesty and intensity of conviction" as the poems. So there is now disclosed to us for the first time the hidden stream of scholarly discussion which ran steadily beneath the public literary scene of the seventies and eighties. And here are the simply expressed but profound and hard-bitten conclusions reached by a man who had shut himself away from life—a man who feared his own nature, and, admitting his fear, took every precaution that that nature should not function freely.

Hopkins' remarkable scholastic record has not been fully emphasized. He was a brilliant student of Jowett's at Balliol, a fact which his superiors in the Jesuit order took into account when they appointed him Lecturer and Examiner in Greek to the University College in Dublin. His interest in Greek metrics never flagged, and his technical theories, as well as his technical practice, have opened, and will continue to open, new doors into poetic richness and freedom. Even more impressive, in these letters, than his scholarship are his unfailing curiosity and poetic insight. He was a man "for whom the visible world triumphantly existed." His eye microscopically took in every detail of the objects upon which he fixed his attention. His love for appearance was so great that the worst penance he could impose upon himself was to turn his eyes away from nature. His ear, sharp and interested, picked up turns of speech peculiar to a countryside. He was excited by ecclesiastical architecture no more than by the architecture of swallows.

In the field of the arts his musical interest ranged from Purcell to Wagner (about whose works, since he had no opportunity to hear them, he desired detailed accounts). His remarks on paintings are often profound. ("I have invented a Canaletto with genius: his name is Guardi.") And his critical insight into literature flashes out in a comparison, anticipating many like comparisons made in recent years, between what Keats might have lived to be, with what Shakespeare was. And again, his ideas about the "overthought and underthought" in Greek tragic poets ("underthought conveyed by choice of metaphors, etc., and only half-realized by the poet himself") foreshadow recent ideas of scholars concerning the underlying symbolism in Shakespeare's plays.

Baillie was not a poet, but his learning and sensitiveness and his interest in what Hopkins had to say often brought, from

Hopkins, a full rush of explanation and exposition. Hopkins' theories concerning the kinds of poetry—an account which proves him to have been, at twenty, a critic of the first order— were sent to Baillie.

The Patmore correspondence, which occurred during the last six years of Hopkins' life, when he was thirty-nine and Patmore sixty, has been published in part elsewhere—in Basil Champneys' *Life of Patmore* and by Father Lahey in his *Life of Hopkins*. Champneys hesitated to publish the letters in full, on the ground that they were too technical for the general reader. Patmore during this time was preparing the revised (third collected) edition of his *Poetical Works* (1887). Patmore's reputation had gone into eclipse. *The Angel in the House*, a generation earlier, had been second only to Tennyson's poems in popularity. Since Hopkins had expressed his admiration for the later "Odes"— attracted by their free form and intense emotion—Patmore asked his advice on revisions. The younger man's comments, in every case, go straight to the heart of Patmore's basic faults of style and tone. Hopkins' respect for Patmore (who, like himself, was "curious and learned in prosody") kept him from delivering a criticism in the bald manner of Tennyson, who once said that some of Patmore's lines seemed to be hammered up out of old nails. Hopkins not only points out Patmore's ambiguities, incomplete sense, and bad phrasing, but attacks his lack of true ear, frequent lack of taste, his affectation, insincerity, and Tory tub-thumping. Patmore took all this, it must be said, in good part. He saw, as might be expected, nothing but "strangeness" in Hopkins' poems. However, he wrote to Bridges, after the death of Hopkins:

. . . there was something in all his words and manners that was at once a rebuke and attraction to all who could only aspire to be like him . . .

and added that Hopkins' genius was unmistakable.

These letters bring out, finally, the tormented plans—almost amounting to manias—of Hopkins' later years. His discussion, with Baillie, of the probable derivation of Greek words from Egyptian (which led nowhere) and his determination to write music show the beating about of a rich nature against the rigidity of the rule it worked under. Much sympathy has been poured out concerning the conflict between Hopkins' character and the severity of the Jesuit life. But where could this fiery spirit, these delicate sensibilities, have fitted in the Victorian world, big as it was with ideas of optimism and progress, and punctuated as it was by the suicides of sensitive young men? "Great from the hard forming hand" Hopkins had chosen in youth "he triumphs, utterly defeated." Seen from our time, the design, the "instress," of Hopkins' life is so clear that it seems not only that life's best, but indeed its only possible, pattern.

ISOLATED CASES

LEONIE ADAMS (*1954*)

Léonie Adams, in her new volume, *Poems: A Selection,* has chosen poems from her first two books, long and ununderstandably out of print, and added to them a group of more recent lyrics. Miss Adams, like Marianne Moore, has affiliations with poetry of high periods of the past; in her case the tie between Jacobean drama and seventeenth-century English lyricism is close. She has moments of cousinship with Webster and Tourneur, with Vaughan and Traherne, and her later poetry is so charged with meaning that it sometimes slips out of syntax, in the manner of the later Mallarmé. She expresses a few major themes, of which the entrapment of the spirit in the flesh and the shadow cast by eternity upon time are two. She interprets nature more than man; her emotions are meshed into the turn of earthly seasons, but the light of the universal constantly sheds across her landscapes a strange and phantasmal gleam. The large and crucial divisions of time as we know it are her constant subjects. In "Winter Solstice" and "Light at Equinox" she brings to their evocation extraordinary powers of description. An essential gravity and nobility of thought and feeling run through her work without a break; she is everywhere committed to the difficult task of outwitting conscious powers in order that subconscious ones may operate as pervasively as possible. The reader is made aware that Miss Adams' "difficulty" depends not upon any surface play with words but upon the tension and complication of her initial poetic impulse. Poems such as "Companions of the Morass," "For Harvest," "Grapes Making," and "The Runner with the Lots" spring from and are indications of a poetic endowment as deep as it is rare.

ELIZABETH BISHOP (1946)

It is a hopeful sign when judges unanimously and with enthusiasm make an award to a young, fresh book of verse instead of to an old, stale one. In 1945, the three judges of the Houghton Mifflin Poetry Prize Fellowship did just that in the case of Elizabeth Bishop's *North and South*. Miss Bishop's poems are not in the least showy. They strike no attitudes and have not an ounce of superfluous emotional weight, and they combine an unforced ironic humor with a naturalist's accuracy of observation, for Miss Bishop, although she frequently writes fantasy, is firmly in touch with the real world and takes a Thoreau-like interest in whatever catches her attention.

She can write descriptions of New England and of Florida seascapes, of a mechanical toy, or of a mysterious pile of old boxes. And she has unmistakably her own point of view, in spite of her slight addiction to the poetic methods of Marianne Moore. Like Miss Moore, Miss Bishop, thoroughly canvassing all sides of a central idea, will make a poem out of one extended metaphor (as in "The Imaginary Iceberg"). Or she will bring into imaginative relation with one central theme a variety of subjects, making a poem out of a list of things or out of attributes related to a title (as in "Florida"). She often starts with a realistic subject, which, by the time she has unravelled all its concealed meaning, turns out to be the basis for a parable—the poem "Roosters," for example, contains all manner of references to war and warriors. Miss Bishop is a natural lyricist as well, but she does not use her lyrical side as often as she might. None of these thirty poems gives up its full meaning at once, so it is a pleasure to read them repeatedly. Miss Bishop has evidently put in eleven years on their composition; the first appeared in print in 1935. It is to be hoped that we shall get thirty more, equally varied, unexpected, and freshly designed, in rather less than another decade.

ABBIE HUSTON EVANS (1961)

All styles sooner or later become ingrown and monstrous. Writers and critics alike, in their eagerness to produce (and appreciate) work in an accepted style, by degrees come to overlook the importance and value of the unaccepted. Such a fatal closed system appeared in the dead center of the nineteenth century in Victorian England, when self-satisfaction about ways and means led to an almost total rejection of any aesthetic criteria but those then current. At present, signs of official and strangling convention are showing up in what history may or may not call mid-century American verse. Eclecticism is, at the moment, extreme, but it is often an eclecticism based on what have become modern clichés, in attitude or technique. The modern movement has proved over and over, as far as poetry is concerned, an eagerness to grasp reality and to acquire technical virtuosity. What it has failed to explore, except in rare instances (and a deep-rooted fear of Romanticism partly explains this failure), is variety, depth, and delicacy of emotion. Delight, tenderness, and a continuing refreshment of the ancient attitudes of wonder and awe have become unfashionable and very nearly unapproachable. The limiting of feeling to hostility (open or disguised), violence, guilt, anxiety, and fear has brought about a situation in which the gentler emotions have become suspect, not only in the work of the middle-aged but in the work of the young.

It is not, it is true, a period for hymns to joy. But this narrowing of the emotional field has its artificial side; it has become a convention. Whole areas of reality once open to the poet are being placed out of bounds. Not only is Nature also becoming suspect but Baudelaire's humane and compassionate vision of the modern city has very nearly disappeared. Poems define and explain, and poets skirt the true difficulties of response by planned excursions into rigidly marked-off territory. And poets of all ages too often succumb to an "insolent and trivial" style and tone that, as Miss Moore stated many years ago, they should stand above.

At the same time, the publication of poetry is no longer confined to a thin stream; verse flows out broadly, in every kind of print. Paperbacks have partly solved production costs, and poets have acquired a new audience, having become visible and vocal on lecture platforms and in classrooms, on discs and on tape. This new abundance is all to the good; little chance remains of talent being neglected or obscured. Yet in spite of all surface signs to the contrary, a certain monotony prevails. Skills are often remarkable, but brilliance of technique often covers the emptily discursive, the false and self-consciously symbolic—means and attitudes that stem from shallowness of experience and a contracted emotional range.

A turn into renewed freshness and vitality is due, and in fact, scattered evidence of change has lately appeared in unexpected quarters. For instance, in Abbie Huston Evans' *Fact of Crystal,* we discover something intense and rare—mystic apprehension. Miss Evans' body of work is small—she has published only three books: *Outcrop,* in 1928; *The Bright North,* in 1938; and the present volume—and her utterly distinctive quality has gone virtually unnoticed. Yet here is a New England woman (she was born in New Hampshire and grew up on the Maine coast) whose sensitive and strong perceptions pierce deep into the heart of things, whose sense of "inscape" can be set against Hopkins' and Dickinson's. Her Welsh inheritance, grounded in the stern landscapes of her childhood, has been disciplined, and defined, given grandeur and depth. These later poems, written in her sixties and seventies, include work of such profound inspiration that small modern categories and classifications fall in confusion before them.

JEAN GARRIGUE (1960)

Jean Garrigue, whose poetry up to now has been somewhat muted, exhibits in her fourth book, *A Water Walk by the Villa d'Este,* a new ability and eagerness for open virtuosity and even extravagance in diction and design. The long poem that relates to her title, "For the Fountains and Fountaineers of Villa d'Este," is a true tour de force—a brilliant display of light, sound, color, and motion that pushes language to its limits without resorting to distorting tricks of any kind. Miss Garrigue is now attracted to extremes, in nature and in art; she describes Alpine landscape and the elaborate art and artifacts of the High Renaissance with equal enthusiasm. To derive poetry from works of art of whatever kind is a difficult business; artificiality is a constant danger, and Miss Garrigue has moments when she floats and rambles. This failure in directness does not often happen; she soon returns to effective syntax and the exact phrase. Her rendering of the detail of Vermeer's interiors (in which everything is static) is as striking as her spirited treatment of the ordered confusion of the Italian fountains. And she manages (this is not an easy thing to do) to bring her high and glittering subjects into relation with each other and with ordinary existence; at her best she is exuberant to some purpose, spectacular for the right reasons—and a pleasure to read.

ANTHONY HECHT (1954)

A ruling desire of Dylan Thomas', partly derived from the tenets of Surrealism, was "not to interpret, record, or comment on life but to transform it." Anthony Hecht's first volume, *A Summoning of Stones,* illustrates this attitude, at the moment so attractive to the young. He sets forth his position in the book's epigraph, taken from Santayana ("to call the stones themselves to their ideal places, and enchant the very substance and skeleton of the world"). Hecht, born in 1923, served as an infantry rifleman in Europe and Asia. He was awarded, in 1951, a writing fellowship to the American Academy at Rome. The second experience has evidently been more important in his poetic development than the first; he draws more freely upon the

Italian scene than upon any background of war. And his verbal and technical brilliance is directed toward the celebration, rather than the dissection, of what he has felt and observed. The releasing touch of Thomas is strong, as well as the influence of other modern masters, and the ancient shadow of Sir Thomas Wyatt turns up more than once. There is a good deal of interplay between art and nature—the first reminds Hecht of the second as often as the other way round. The shimmer of a virtuoso technique cannot entirely obscure the fact that many of the poems have very little content, emotional or otherwise. But surely the enjoyment of the sumptuous, the exuberant, and the theatrical is natural in a young man. If Hecht, often disturbed by disorder and death, is drawn toward ideal proportion, elegance, and color —to a description of a botanical garden, pictures on museum walls, or a fête at the Villa d'Este—he is yielding to promptings that at his age only a fanatically serious spectator would deny him.

BARBARA HOWES (1954)

Barbara Howes' second volume (her first appeared in a fine limited edition in 1948), *In the Cold Country*, announces the most accomplished woman poet of the youngest writing generation—one who has found her own voice, chosen her own material, and worked out her own form. Miss Howes is daring with language, but she is also accurate. Her originality stands in constant close reference to the material in hand, and although much of that material is fantastic or exotic, it is never so simply for its own sake. Her diction becomes more exact the more it is applied to certain dissolving effects in nature that attract her, and her poems are full of movement. She can unfold a landscape, or plunge through ordinary surfaces, as in her delightful poem "The Undersea Farmer." Her connoisseurship, always evident, is of an active kind that illuminates instead of merely skimming over this subject or that. In addition, she has strong positive emotions that continually resolve into a major key. Here, watching a cultivated sense of tradition work through modern attitudes and techniques, we sense the possibility of a new reconciliation in modern verse, for so long filled with division and dissent.

GALWAY KINNELL (1961)

Galway Kinnell's first book of poems, *What a Kingdom It Was,* is remarkably unburdened by this or that current influence. Kinnell (b. 1927) is direct and occasionally harsh, and he keeps his syntax straight and his tone colloquial. His chief concern, we soon discover, is the enigmatic significance, more than the open appearance, of Nature and man. "Freedom, New Hampshire," an elegy for his brother—a full realization of country boyhood, in ordinary terms, with a boy's confrontation of cruelty and unreasonable happiness left intact—is also an affirmation of immortality. Kinnell's longest and most pretentiously titled poem, "The Avenue Bearing the Initial of Christ into the New World," deals with a most difficult subject—life in a city slum. Here pitfalls abound—sentimentality, insincerity, the possibility of mixed and unresolved feelings of pity and guilt. Kinnell bypasses all these. City streets are for a time his home; he feels the vitality of their people; he responds with extreme sensitiveness to multiple sights, sounds, smells; without any furtive condescension, he places Avenue C in the human context. Sympathy, identification, insight sustain this long poem in every detail, and Kinnell chooses his details with startling exactness.

KENNETH KOCH (1963)

Thank You and Other Poems is not Kenneth Koch's first publication; it follows his "mock-epic" *Ko, or a Season on Earth* (1959), which was surrealist in spirit but not in form, being written in skillfully rhymed stanzas. This initial effort started out well but went on far too long. The poems in Koch's new book belong to the last ten years, during which his talent has not remained inactive. They are chiefly occasional, with a slight leaning in the newer ones toward lyricism. Koch is not basically a lyricist. At his most effective, he introduces into surrealist tactics (always close to the boring) a fresh note of farce—an open play for laughs delightful to come upon amid the prevailing violence and gloom.

His methods have dangerous limitations. Nonsense and parody must be grounded positively at some point or other: the *farceur*, like the satirist, cannot operate from a base of complete cynicism; neither is a clown. For some things Koch cares. He is against the maneuvers of the more corrupt and venal avant-garde—witness "The History of Jazz" and his wonderfully demented chronicle "The Artist." He protests the pretensions that unfailingly adhere to culture-yearning groups ("Fresh Air" does these little social clusters up brown); the stacking of useless facts; the restriction of natural impulses, whether of movement or of speech; humorless high-mindedness; monotony. His own inventiveness seldom fails. Having constructed a sure-fire comic formula in the zany lists of the title poem, he quickly shifts to other methods. He organizes some poems like a set of explosions along a fuse, each a little louder and more destructive, and funnier, than the last. Or he projects a deadpan parody to end all deadpan style in "The Departure from Hydra." Sometimes we seem to be in the presence of a witty, widely read child who deals in noises ("gloop gloop!") as well as words, of a poet who has intuitively been attracted to the comedy that is the other, and more hidden, face of the art of our time. Koch's reliance on surfaces can become irritating; under his wilder verbal assaults his major, more serious intentions disappear. But his fun is hilarious while it lasts.

STANLEY KUNITZ (*1958*)

Selected Poems: 1928-1958, by Stanley Kunitz, is the work of an older man who has proved himself an accomplished formalist over the years. Kunitz was writing in form before the newest generation of well-taught young men were able to hold pen in hand. He is also a dramatic lyricist, having learned an important modern lesson: that the short poem can be made to bear remarkably heavy weights. Kunitz has a fearsome edge to his imagination. Many of his poems are shocking; in the space of a given page, nightmare, disease, disaster, madness, or crime gets into action and leaps into forceful being. His wit, on the other hand, is oblique; we are not struck by it directly, and the result is a slight sameness of tone. And the dark side of existence consistently turns uppermost—as Kunitz remarks, with good reason in our day. But although the poet is allowed melancholy, dejection, and grief, he is expected to turn away from ultimate despair, and at times Kunitz seems to be trapped in or blocked into an area of almost unrelieved shadow. We read him with interest, nevertheless.

JOSEPHINE MILES (1956)

American satirists, at the moment, are few and far between, and when they do turn up, their line of attack is likely to be oblique rather than direct. Josephine Miles, for a good many years and in three books, has shown a satiric gift of the most subtle kind. That this gift has been nourished by a California background makes it all the more rare; Miss Miles teaches at Berkeley. Her new book, *Prefabrications*, is principally focused upon details of day-to-day life—those details that it is almost impossible for a poet of any time or place to get at without showing signs of pressure and strain. Miss Miles writes with ease and with insight about the parking lot, the motel, the Los Angeles high school, the building project, the supermarket, and the service station. Through some delicate imaginative adjustment, the intermittences of the heart and the clear light of the intellect become involved with these locales. Miss Miles is able to produce *Zeitbild* of a true kind, because to her the spirit comes first.

MARCIA NARDI (1956)

In her first volume of *Poems,* Miss Nardi's talent is inseparable from her emotional cast—from her temperament, to use an old-fashioned term. She reacts to experience so directly that every-thing she says can be recognized as genuine and genuinely felt, and she faces up to the sterner facts of nature and society. She often seems to be not so much writing poems as having them write her. This is a dangerous process, especially for a woman, but Miss Nardi, in nearly every one of her twenty-three lyrics, proves herself to be someone who should be written.

HOWARD NEMEROV (1961)

Howard Nemerov's *New and Selected Poems* can be taken as an example of the well-written, intelligently ordered poetry that has been termed "academic" by the experimentalists. Nemerov does teach, it is true. He is also a novelist and critic. Let us hold to the statement recently made by François Mauriac that, by and large, the poet loses nothing by being intelligent. Nemerov can think, feel, and see. Many of his subjects are "occasional" (vignettes with a dramatic or satiric edge) and some are "meta-physical" (meditations on time, being, essence). He can be shock-ing where shock is needed, and some of his best poems are composed according to the fantastic design of the dream. His images are bright and true, and he is seldom dull. This collection, work from four earlier books and some new poems, shows a steady progress from youthful indetermination toward a mature grasp of value and belief. Moments of doubt occur when, to the poet, things seem inconclusively to cancel out. But Nemerov does not lapse into that semi-official attitude of nihilism and gloom that deadens so much contemporary verse. The terror and pathos of existence are not passed over; there is a healthy turbu-lence at work under his unruffled style. This is the formal poetry (if it must be so definitely placed) of a young-middle generation at its best.

LOUISE TOWNSEND NICHOLL (1954, 1959)

The gift of that double vision which sees through, not with, the eye is rare in any period and in either sex; it has been a particularly rare phenomenon in the work of American women poets since Emily Dickinson. That this power is in our time not only scarce but neglected is a fact we realize when we consider the recently published *Collected Poems* of Louise Townsend Nicholl. Miss Nicholl, who has devoted an entire career to poetry that is contemplative in the truest sense—that, in other words, is always close to that nameless dimension where time meets the timeless— has not received her just due from either the critics or the public. Her work is never showy or discursive, and her form is conventional, although varied with more subtlety, to meet the demands of her difficult subject, than is at first apparent. Padraic Colum (with a Celtic use of symbolism that transcends the Romantic) has said of her, "She has seen a halo, and she has seen it round many things—people, trees, houses." It is obvious that Miss Nicholl is writing religious poetry, but of a kind that goes beyond any set liturgy and touches the sacred in man and nature.

The World's One Clock, her most recent volume, brings out the quality at the center of her work: her ability to tip reality over into a slightly different dimension, to imaginatively illuminate the material object to the point of transparence—the mystic's gift. She gives intimations of our relation to time and the timeless; she makes time shift, so that past, present, and future merge; she uses the most precise images (often from music and geometry) to express spiritual experience. All this is accomplished with a modicum of means and in a vocabulary that is so austerely conventional that to some ears it may sound old-fashioned. But every word counts, as in all contemplative utterance, and Miss Nicholl's basic idiom is that of the spoken word. This is religious poetry of a rare and special kind, which is sometimes overlooked in one period, only to be rediscovered in another.

NED O'GORMAN and W. D. SNODGRASS
(1959)

Many younger poets seem to have lost the power of laughter, along with other open emotions. Their poems are often ruminative or regretful, and they utter no cries of joy, fear, or grief.

They do not seem to be aware, often, of whole areas of human experience. This suppression of feeling frequently results in poems that resemble the scared dreams of neurosis more than the fruitful vision which at some point is usually linked with primordial emotions. Two recently published volumes by younger men break through this static and elliptical situation—*The Night of the Hammer,* by Ned O'Gorman, and *Heart's Needle,* by W. D. Snodgrass. O'Gorman, who won the 1958 Lamont Poetry Selection for a first book, has the kind of vitality that an active belief sometimes sets in motion; his religious poems sparkle with gaiety, and a true range of subject (and of feeling) underlies his virtuosity with words. Snodgrass, also technically expert, has an eye for telling detail; his poems invariably center on the event, and his emotion, though subtle, is straightforward. The autobiographical theme—here the relation of a young father to his daughter—is also marked, and produces true pathos whenever it appears.

MURIEL RUKEYSER (*1939*)

Muriel Rukeyser is interested in the state of society to the almost complete exclusion of any conscious "personal expression." She is highly gifted. She can range freely over the insane manifestations of a world infected with a suicidal death wish; she can fuse the early Auden manner with the brilliant snapshot technique of Surrealism. She is earnest, and she has language. After a single reading of her new book, *A Turning Wind,* one is uncertain what ingredients of life and poetry are lacking. After one has reread it, the suspicion arises that Miss Rukeyser is deficient in a sense of human life. A certain amount of rough joy and silly pleasure, of lying and lust and horseplay, existing in humanity, however ill it may be, is overlooked. Miss Rukeyser has rubbed off the soiled and silly edges which mean nothing, and everything. Her world is at once too nightmare and too noble; it is static and literary. She does not realize that such a world could not last overnight, that the sense of injustice is only relevant when applied to living human beings, and that human beings, although oppressed and

cruelly crazy, are also wonderfully funny and healthily vulgar
(even to themselves). The day of chaste and noble proletarian
myths should be about over. It has been recently proved that there
is something hideously oversimplified in crude oppositions and
blind idealism. Miss Rukeyser can write with great complexity.
She should come into herself completely when she lets down a
little, masters a wider range of feeling, and mixes some loud
laughs with her high scorn.

The decade which outlawed from poetry personal emotion,
individual insight, and straight looks into the flawed human heart
now closes. It has been a queer time. And, from all current signs,
patriotism and "public speech" have still a long course to run. Art
is slow and long, but there's nothing brisker and more vocal than
politics.

FREDERICK SEIDEL (1963)

In *Final Solutions,* a collection of fifteen poems by Frederick
Seidel, the satiric involvement of a young poet (b. 1936) with
his time and place is total. Like Juvenal, Swift, and John Wilmot,
Earl of Rochester (at his best), Seidel is angry, and his anger,
ultimately, is directed less against evils apparent in this or that
person or society than against the basic stupidities and depravities
of mankind itself. Seidel is in earnest. He radiates heat. It is
apparent that he has asked himself frightful questions and has
not dodged the implications of their equally frightful answers.
He presents his own anguish less often than he describes the
suffering of a number of protagonists who reveal themselves
fragmentarily in monologues—always at some high pitch of
terror, ecstasy, or despair. These men and women (and a single
ghost) speak, more often than not, in formal stanzas. Seidel
instinctively goes over into strictly controlled (although uneven)
metre and into difficult rhyming as his emotion gathers force;
he does not miss an effect. The terrifying aspects of the experiences he describes are outlined with clinical precision by means
of the rightness of his epithets and of his nouns and verbs, which
can be tender as well as shocking. He is a master of metaphor.
And each poem is compressed straight up to, and sometimes

beyond, the limits of comprehensibility—not as a trick but for a purpose. The scenes are those of the actual world: this is Boston, New York, a Maine island, Paris, and ancient and modern Rome; these are sidewalks, traffic signals, sirens, helicopters (and clouds and stars) placed and functioning normally, and not revolving in a surrealist dream. The poems concerned with delirium are done from the outside. And there is not a trace, throughout the book, of the usual slick response of cold coarseness or gratuitous brutality.

Whether or not Seidel's talent will come into the full power it now suggests, it is impossible to predict. But how extraordinary if it should.

WILLIAM JAY SMITH (1958)

Light and nonsense verse, which the Victorians used chiefly to work off their hidden tensions, has become part and parcel of the modern poet's equipment. It cannot be carelessly written and remain either edged or pointed; its effects depend directly upon the amount of skill the writer can call upon, down to the last turn of syntax. Its relation to serious verse has become so close that a hair's breadth often divides the two kinds, and light satire, which goes back as far as classic antiquity, has in our day regained some of its effectiveness. William Jay Smith has recently published, in *Poems 1947–1957*, a collection of lyrics wherein serious and light verse are about evenly balanced. Gaiety and lightheartedness are extremely difficult to express; they are also impossible to simulate. The slightest suspicion of affectation is immediately defeating. Mr. Smith's serious poems are filled with fresh observation and direct emotion. His light verse—"epigrams, satires, and nonsense"—sparkles and flies free, often straight to the center of a chosen target. He is also an expert translator.

MAY SWENSON (1958)

In her second book, *A Cage of Spines*, May Swenson is lively, ingenious, and fanciful. She enters the world of things, animate

and inanimate, without self-consciousness and with a rare sense
of play. She tells riddles, observes the weather, and turns her
mind toward pebbles, birds, and small animals as readily as
toward people. Her faults, by no means extensive, are perhaps
too continuous a sparkle and an occasional lapse in the sense of
scale, for some things *are* larger than others. She is an accurate
naturalist, however, and an imaginative one.

JOHN UPDIKE (*1959*)

The poetry of a young American, John Updike, exhibits all the
surface characteristics of verse at its lightest. The gift of wit, as
unmistakable (and as inescapable) as a gift for chess or higher
mathematics, has its limits and its dangers. It can be ephemeral
to a degree when it shows up in verse, since part of its appeal is
its timeliness. It needs stout underpinnings of neat thinking and
sturdy observation, combined with a wide range of interest, to
anchor it to reality. Updike's first collection, *The Carpentered Hen
and Other Tame Creatures*, possesses these fundamental requi-
sites. In addition, it is wildly original and charmingly perceptive.
Updike has an unmistakable voice, and it will be delightful to
hear more of it as time goes on.

PETER VIERECK (*1953*)

It was partly Viereck's ingenuity in the use of conventional form
that aroused so much interest in his first volume, *Terror and
Decorum*, which won the Pulitzer Prize in 1949. His attack on
the more arid and drooping kind of "modernism" has been frontal,
and his admirers have cheered his championship of a new and
rather reactionary poetic future wherein poetry, with Eliot and
Pound finally vanquished in open combat, could once more

"communicate" to a large and eager audience. Nothing much has come of Viereck's crusade.

In this third book, *The First Morning,* he still displays a strong belief in his own powers, both poetic and polemic, and he is still full of vigor and zest, but much of his originality seems to be stiffening into eccentricity. He overindulges in epigraphs, he pushes personification and allegory to boring extremes, and although he makes attempts to write in the American vernacular, he has no ear for it whatever. His vocabulary is not used with real sensitivity, and he is continually lapsing into shrillness. Viereck, in short, now appears to be a writer of verse that is fundamentally not serious, that verges not so much on modern "light verse" as on nineteenth-century *vers de société*—something quite different from what he was originally taken for. He works almost entirely from the conscious—intellect and will—and for this reason is forced to manipulate many situations that the unconscious alone is capable of controlling. Tricks come more and more into evidence; Viereck's puns, parodies, and typographical eye-games carry us back to the more amusing side of Christian Morgenstern. Surely a new era of poetry is not announced by poets who lack a tragic sense or who are consistently rude to the elders from whom they have learned much. A return to form has its hazards as well as its rewards.

EDMUND WILSON (1962)

Good critics love literature; good poets love language. Mr. Wilson, whose mastery of critical prose is well known, has now gathered together his verse, both light and serious, in a volume called *Wilson's Night Thoughts,* which proves, among other things, his delight in and knowledge of words. In the poet's way, he projects emotion and intensifies reality through these units of speech; in the way of the happy specialist, he plays games with them. The earliest poems—which are fine and serious—go back to Wilson's 1917–1919 experiences in France; the middle and latest include exercises in metre and rhyme, translations and parodies, satires with a really cutting edge, and a range of non-sense. Several prose reminiscences written in the twenties and thirties are put in for good measure. A distinctly civilized compilation by a writer who has proved himself over the years to be that rarest of American figures—a truc man of letters.

HENRY JAMES

THE PRINCESS CASAMASSIMA (1936)

For all the varied critical attention given, in the last twenty years, to the novels of Henry James, those of his middle period are seldom read. When they are read, their real intention is often missed or is interpreted in some peculiar, special way. F. R. Leavis has recently pointed out several flagrant misinterpretations of James (including the classic mistake made by the critic who thought Isabel Archer divorced her husband and married an American businessman at the end of *The Portrait of a Lady*) and has explained the neglect of the early and middle James by the fact that readers, steered toward the works of the late, "difficult" period, and baffled by these, make no further investigation. The three books which, appearing in the center of James's career, fully exemplify the virtues of his early manner—*The Bostonians, The Princess Casamassima,* and *The Tragic Muse*—are those most completely ignored.

The Princess Casamassima, it is true, has recently come in for some attention, since critics interested in novels concerned with revolutionary activities have discovered that in this book James deals with revolutionaries in the financially depressed London of the eighties. Although I cannot claim to have un-

earthed every scrap of material written about this book, I have
read a fair amount and can say that not one commentator has
shown signs of understanding the design James has so clearly
presented in it. Usually *The Princess* has been put down as a
melodramatic and rather fumbling attempt at a novel dealing
with a revolutionary theme.

Several good reasons exist for these critical misconceptions,
but before we deal with them, it would be well to get clear in our
minds, since one of the charges against the book is that its
material has not been thoroughly grasped, exactly what degree
of mastery over his material, of insight into his characters,
James had reached when he wrote it. *The Princess* was probably
written concurrently with *The Bostonians*. Both novels were complete failures when they appeared (in 1886). James believed in
both books, although for reasons that remain obscure he did not
include *The Bostonians* in the definitive New York Edition. But
The Princess was included, with a preface which delicately but
firmly pointed up the book's intention.

During the seventies James had produced no completely successful long work. And certainly *Watch and Ward* (1878) and
Confidence (1880) are not only the most clumsy novels ever
signed by James but the most clumsy pieces of fiction ever signed
by a man of genius. They display the unsure approach of the
writer who is doing it all from the outside—from the notebook,
the stiff plan, the bad guess. Through some spurt of development
James, in 1881, wrote the finely balanced, deeply observed *Washington Square* and *The Portrait of a Lady*. He was now able to base
his books upon his characters, as opposed to supporting the action
with some artificial diagram of conduct. Each character now
casts light and shadow and is in turn accented or illuminated by
the darkness or brilliance of the others. James had not finished
profiting from Balzac, but he was now Turgenev's intelligent
pupil as well. The realistic method was becoming more effortless
at the same time that the technique of suggestion took in more
territory with greater ease—so that the chance of James's
fumbling, at this period, any problem he put his hand to is small.

The Princess Casamassima, it is true, opens with a block of
Balzacian realism mixed with Dickensian melodrama that is
extremely hard for modern readers to accept. In the later chapters

of the book detail and suspense are to be brought in with sureness and ease; every part of the situation is to be elucidated by that sure technical skill so characteristic of the pre-theatre James. The first three chapters, however, are thick with underlining and filled with a kind of cardboard darkness. The characters are so overloaded with reasons that they closely approach the line dividing drama from burlesque. The delicate little boy called Hyacinth, the son of a French working girl who is also a murderess, and an earl, her victim; Miss Pynsent, the tender old maid who has raised the child; Mr. Vetch, the battered fiddler with leanings toward anarchism—at first glance these appear cut out of whole cloth. And in spite of a few flashes of insight, the scene in which Hyacinth witnesses his mother's death in prison is dated and overcharged. Thus balked at the outset, it is little wonder that the reader expects to find a measure of falseness everywhere in the story.

Given the remarkable figure of Hyacinth and the remarkable fact of his sharply divided inheritance, what use does James make of them? It may be best to give the story in bare outline. Hyacinth, grown to young manhood, is apprenticed to M. Poupin, an exiled veteran both of '48 and the Commune. (Hyacinth's own maternal grandfather, James tells us at an early point, died on the Paris barricades.) Poupin teaches him revolutionary principles along with the trade (James considers it a minor art) of bookbinding. The youth then meets the two people who are to bring about the crisis in his life. The Princess Casamassima, separated from her husband and foot-loose in London on her husband's money, first dazzles Hyacinth with her interest in revolutionary plots and then with her interest in himself. And Paul Muniment, son of a north-country miner, an active, realistic, and inscrutable worker deep in revolutionary activities, attracts the ardent boy. Hyacinth actually gives over his life to Muniment, promising in a moment of enthusiasm that he will be the instrument for an act of violence whenever the need arises. Muniment accepts his pledge and binds Hyacinth fully, by a vow taken before witnesses. Hyacinth tells the Princess, after she has given him some minor glimpses of the great world, of his origin and dedication. Miss Pynsent dies; her small legacy enables Hyacinth to go to the Continent. He comes back changed.

What he has seen has convinced him that certain objects, of which he had no former notion, should be preserved, not destroyed. The Princess has meanwhile met Muniment. She brings her charm to bear on him, with the secondary purpose of extricating Hyacinth from his vow; but primarily to get herself deeper into true conspiratorial circles. Hyacinth, whose determination to do what he can to further the cause of the people remains unchanged in spite of his secret change of heart, thinks that the pair have cast him off. Then the call comes: a duke is to be assassinated and Hyacinth is picked by the mysterious instigator of these affairs to be the assassin. The revolutionary group, at this news, splits into two factions: those who wish to save Hyacinth and those who are willing to let matters take their course. Muniment, although he professes sympathy for Hyacinth and says that he is free to choose, does nothing. The Princess rushes to save the boy and to offer herself in his stead. She and a kind, methodical German conspirator meet at Hyacinth's lodgings. But the boy has already shot himself, with the revolver meant for the assassination.

Critics have construed this story according to the set of their own convictions. Van Wyck Brooks, for example, although appreciative of James's success with Poupin, Vetch, Miss Pynsent, and others, considers Hyacinth an insufferable little snob. And Hyacinth is, according to Brooks, an embodiment of James's own yearning after the glories of the British upper classes.

> This unfortunate but remarkably organized youth . . . is conscious of nothing but the paradise of which he has been dispossessed. . . . In real life the last thing that would have occurred to a young man of Hyacinth's position would have been to "roam and wander and yearn" about the gates of that lost paradise: he would have gone to Australia, or vanished into the slums, or continued *with the utmost indifference* at his *trade* of binding books. But this attitude represents the feeling of Hyacinth's creator. [Italics mine.]

C. Hartley Grattan believes that Hyacinth's "sense of deprivation" vitiates the worth of his radical impulses:

> The conviction that it is senseless to do anything, no matter how small the act, to destroy the upper classes leads to the climax of the novel in Hyacinth's suicide.

But Grattan admits James's insight into his material.

When the social-minded young English disinterred the book

some years ago because of its theme, Stephen Spender wrote in *The Destructive Element:*

The observation of political types in this book is really remarkable and curiously undated . . . Paul Muniment . . . is a true revolutionary type. He has the egoism, the sense of self-preservation, the cynicism of a person who identifies himself so completely with a cause that he goes through life objectively guarding himself from all approach, as one might preserve for the supreme eventuality a very intricate and valuable torpedo.

Spender's evaluation of Hyacinth is this:

Hyacinth, with his strong leaning toward the upper classes and yet feeling that he is somehow committed to the cause of the workers, might today have become a Socialist Prime Minister: a Ramsay MacDonald who . . . would dismay his followers by going over to the other side and becoming the most frequent visitor at large country houses and of dinners at Buckingham Palace.

Now Hyacinth, in the very essence of his character as James with great care and at considerable length presents it, could never become what Spender thinks he could become, any more than what Brooks thinks James should have made him become. Before turning to Hyacinth, let us examine the character of the Princess. Who is she? What is she? What has she been, and what is she likely to be? The development of her character must have meant a good deal to James since she is the only figure he ever "revived" and carried from one book to another.

She was Christina Light in *Roderick Hudson,* the character in that early work who evokes the mixed feelings of admiration and exasperation that James was later to call up through many of his women. She is the daughter of an Anglo-American shrew and adventuress who forces her, by a threat of scandal, into a marriage with the highest bidder. James managed to bring out, even at a time when his art was still imperfect, Christina's marred idealism and ignorant pride, so that they freshen every page on which she appears. The coarser and weaker people, in contrast with her straightforwardness, show up in a sorry way. Roderick Hudson, with whom she falls in love and whom she tries to galvanize into some kind of manhood, crumbles, after losing her, in much the same way, James makes us feel, as he would have crumbled had he won her. Brought up to deadening shifts, she has one flaw. She is not truly courageous. She marries the Prince at once after receiving the shock of her mother's revelations.

In the later book she is the single person who is continuously presented from the outside. James never "goes behind" her. We are never told what she thinks or how she feels; we merely see her act. James clearly presupposes a knowledge in the reader of her early tragedy. To watch her casting her charm and enthusiasm about; to see her reacting more and more violently against her money and position; to see her—after Muniment has told her that it is her money alone which interests his circle, and has prophesied her certain return to her husband now that the Prince has stopped the flow of that money—rushing in desperation to offer herself as a substitute in the affair of the duke's assassination—all this can puzzle us if we know nothing of the beautiful girl who moved through the scenes of *Roderick Hudson*.

Now "the cleverest woman in Europe," she bears a grudge against society strong enough to force her into repudiation of everything her trained taste fully values. When Hyacinth bares his own tragedy to her, the relation of the two is lifted out of a stupid contrast between a revolutionary-minded woman of the world and a talented pauper. For what the Princess knows, as she listens to him, and what the reader should also know, is that she is herself illegitimate. James, far from being taken in by it, deeply realizes that the life she represents is as undermined by the results of cruelty and passion, for all its beautiful veneer, as Hyacinth's own. Having failed in her youth to face a crisis and see it through, she knows in her heart that when she thinks of herself as "one of the numerous class who could be put on a tolerable footing only by a revolution," she is thinking dishonestly. It is her despair and her defects which push her toward extreme revolutionary enthusiasm, as much as her generosity of spirit. But in Hyacinth she recognizes—after she has emerged from her first sentimental ideas concerning him—complete devotion, consistency, and fineness. This boy "never makes mistakes," and is incapable of going back on a given promise. She shows him specimens of English county families, toward whom her own reaction is: "You know, people oughtn't to be both corrupt and dreary." But what Hyacinth tenders them, as he tenders her, beneath his devotion, is a kind of gentle pity.

For this son of a criminal and an aristocrat is not, as he has been made out to be, a little snob, an affected artisan with a divided nature and ambitions beyond his station. James with every subtle device of his mature art, from the first sentence describing him to the last, shows the boy as an artist, a clear, sensitive intelligence, filled with the imagination "which will always give him the clue about everything." James has endowed him, indeed, with the finest qualities of his own talent; and this is what is meant when James says that Hyacinth had watched London "very much as I had watched it." Hyacinth is, like James, "a person on whom nothing is lost." If the character has a fault, it is that James has distilled too purely into his creature the sharp insight, the capacity for selfless devotion, the sense of proportion, the talent for self-mockery and gentle irony which seldom exist in genius without an admixture of cruder ingredients. But James wanted a cool and undistorting mirror to shine between the dark and violent world of the disinherited on the one hand and the preposterous world of privilege on the other. Such a clear lens (Maisie, Nanda) James was later to place in the center of psychological situations. He was never again to place it, and with the final polish of genius added, between social classes. For that matter it has never been placed there, up to the present, by anyone else, although Conrad, in *Under Western Eyes*, a book almost certainly modeled on *The Princess*, examined the revolutionary side of the picture through the clear spirit of Razumov. We are used, in fiction dealing with social problems, to the spectacle of the artist absorbed or deflected into one class or another. James kept Hyacinth detached to the end. And though the solution for the artist, in the insoluble situation James has constructed, is death, as the symbols of the two extremes he has instinctively rejected (after he knows that his own life must exist independently, apart from either) stand by his deathbed, we feel that what they both have been left to is not exactly life.

The book is full of wonderful moments. Short mention should be made of the ultimate opacity and brutality of Muniment, as he is shown in contrast not only to Hyacinth but to the more humane members of the revolutionary circle; of James's masterly analysis of Hyacinth's spiritual coming of age, resulting, on his return from abroad, in increased self-sufficiency and a more complete grasp of his work; of the complex rendering of Hyacinth's rejection of the thought of violence when his mother's murderous hands come before him; of the superb portraits of the solidly disillusioned Madame Grandoni, the morbidly jealous Prince, and those true fools and snobs—Captain Sholto and Muniment's horrible invalid sister. The scenes of submerged London have been praised. What is even more astonishing than these is James's knowledge of the relentless mechanisms of poverty—poverty's *minutiae*.

It is interesting to trace down the source of James's understanding of Muniment. We remember that the elder James was surrounded by socialists of the Fourier school, and that he "agreed with Fourier that vice and crime were the consequences of our present social order, and would not survive them." The younger James had, no doubt, seen Muniment's counterpart multiplied about him, in Fourier's more fanatical followers, in his childhood.

"Very likely . . . all my buried prose will kick off its tombstones at once," James wrote to Howells in 1888. After, it would seem, Stendhal's hundred years.

THE BOSTONIANS (1945)

The Bostonians, evidently written sometime between James's fortieth and forty-second years, serialized in the *Century Magazine* in 1885, published in both England and America in 1886, has never until now been reprinted in an American edition. Its non-appearance in the *Collected Edition* (1907–1917) has raised various questions, chiefly concerned with James's apparent later squeamishness toward the frank insight of his early work. Whatever the reason, James never rewrote the book, as he did some others. It stands, therefore, as perfect "early James." That it has not become, and will never become, a "period piece"—a novel irremediably of its time, an outmoded lump of costume drama—can be put down to the fact that James, even in his early forties, "knew the world." *The Bostonians* is shot through with the lights of humor, with the satire of a detached, experienced, civilized intelligence. Far away from the milieu he presented, James drew the picture of Boston in the seventies with the greatest variety of detail, the utmost vivacity of presentation. He is grinding no ax, shedding no tears, driving through points without fanaticism. His separation from his material gives him a freedom that is almost the freedom of an expert in some sport; James often, here, plays a wide, high, and handsome kind of game. The underlying tone of the book is gay—the tone of high comedy.

The title is not to be applied to the inhabitants of Boston in the large. James makes it clear that his "Bostonians" are two young women—Olive Chancellor, of a certain position and means, "a spinster, as Shelley was a lyric poet or as the month of August is sultry," living on the water side of Charles Street; and Verena Tarrant, the daughter of a mesmerist and all-round charlatan, who lives in a wooden cottage "with a little naked piazza," on an unpaved "place" in Cambridge. Verena has a "gift"—the gift of eloquence. She is able to move audiences, speaking inanities in a voice that James compares to both silver and gold. She is a kind of *reductio ad absurdum* of that influential American figure, the platform orator. Gotten up in a costume resembling that of a circus rider, she opens her pretty mouth and exerts her fresh and genuine charm upon a variety of audiences in the cause of women's rights. Olive is, by contrast, a far more complicated character. A woman of distinction (James insists on this throughout), no fool, completely in earnest in her desire to establish some contact with "the toilers"—the workers who, she senses, touch reality beyond and "beneath" the layer of middle-class vulgarians she despises—Olive is yet sterilized by an aridity of spirit, baffled by genteel prejudices, and warped by a nervous constitution. Set against James's portrait of a woman reformer of an earlier period—the warmhearted, eccentric, but touching Miss Birdseye—Olive Chancellor is a rather terrifying resultant of Puritanism gone to seed, a female organism driven by a masculine will, without the saving graces of masculine intelligence or feminine tenderness and insight.

These two young women move in a tepid atmosphere of post-Abolition idealism. It is an atmosphere still peopled by the cranks, faddists, cultists, evangelists, revolutionaries, and dogmatists so usual in America in the forties and fifties—the intellectual and emotional débris of the breakdown of faith, the beginning of the "scientific view," of the general ethos of still crude industrial and moral revolutions. James knew these visionaries, of all shades of sincerity and sanity, well; his father's New York home had been a sort of clearinghouse for them. It is James's background of plain experience and accurate youthful observation which makes the revolutionaries in *The Princess Casamassima* so modernly recognizable and the cranks of *The Bostonians* so sharply alive. In these two books, written almost concurrently, James pays these characters his clear-sighted and ironic *devoirs*, and leaves them for good.

The "ouside observer" in *The Bostonians* is, insolently and cleverly enough, a young man from the recently "conquered" South. Of first-rate intelligence, completely "unreconstructed," holding "unprogressive" ideals of manliness, courage, and chivalry, Basil Ransom, introduced into the midst of these, to him, vaporous ideas expressed by these decaying, except for Verena, personalities, has a civilized set of principles to fall back upon—principles that seem "medieval" to his cousin Olive and her "set." James's artistic and moral courage in contrasting, at the time, Ransom's "prejudices," Ransom's humorous and "feeling" nature, Ransom's underlying flexibility of outlook with the eerie and run-down New England prophets of "progress" and "change," cannot be underestimated. James had, it is true, Turgenev's example. Turgenev, earlier, had bent an artist's eye on the follies committed in the name of "progress" by the romantic Russian reformers and their allies in the middle class (he invented the term "nihilist"). *The Bostonians* loses nothing by being read along with *On the Eve* and *Rudin*, and Verena Tarrant often resembles a Turgenev heroine. But James, in describing her surroundings and giving her motives, is solidly on his own ground.

Ransom's pinpoint sharpness of eye results in a sort of continual sparkle in the first part of the book. The young Mississippian does not hesitate to put a name to things; he sorts out the real from the artificial instantly. He spots the self-sufficient sincerity of the little woman doctor with the same swiftness with which he puts down Verena's father as a "carpetbagger" and a "varlet." He sees through the pretentiousness of Mrs. Luna; and he does not fail to see true discrimination and actual passion for justice in Olive, in spite of his quick recognition of her manias. James succeeds in keeping Ransom free from a romantic emphasis. As Philip Rahv, in his preface to this edition, says, "In the figure of Ransom [James] created with remarkable prescience a type of intellectual who has only in the last few decades come to the fore in the English-speaking world . . . a type, exemplified in writers like T. S. Eliot or the school of Southern agrarians, whose criticism of modern civilization is rooted in traditionalist principles. Thus James anticipated . . . one of the major tendencies in twentieth-century thinking."

Behind the central figures—and how masterly is the introduction and first grouping of these—James has painted in with complete verisimilitude, combined with his own peculiar kind of poetic light and coloring, the New England social, spiritual, and physical scene as it has never been rendered before or since. Anyone who has grown up in New England during the last fifty years can vouch for the truth of these delineations of New England social and spiritual tremors. Here is the top layer shot through and through with the humanitarian feeling which must, rather guiltily, accompany utilitarian push and compromise— seeking for "roots" and reality. Here is the entire middle class yearning upward, toward "the fragrance of Beacon Street." James bares the many thin layers of provincial snobbery with scalpel nicety. Turns of both vulgar and affected speech; wrong entrances regretted; all sorts of little affronts taken as "liberties"; shabby genteel uneasiness; upper-class *idées fixes* and brutalities of placement ("it is as though [I] had struck up an intimacy with the daughter of [my] chiropodist"); the beginning of newspaper curiosity into private lives; the pushing tactics of the vigorous outsider—the whole brittle, energetic, shifting scene, filled with cruelty, uncertainty, nervousness, and "nerve"; here it stands in James as in our memory.

Nor does he scamp the scene's *décor* and backdrop. Note the poignant description of the period's American bleakness, seen in "the red sunsets of winter" from Olive's drawing-room windows. Remark the details of another Boston dusk, as Ransom walks the Boston streets before Verena's "big" lecture. Consider the exquisite description of the Cape—the background James puts behind the bitter struggle between Ransom and Olive for the "possession" of Verena. One sentence, beginning, "There were certain afternoons in August, long, beautiful, and terrible, when one felt that the summer was rounding its curve," can be set, for sheer power of evocation, against anything in Emily Dickinson.

I have always associated the little "Square," Union Park, in Boston, with *The Bostonians*. Set between two busy and now run-down avenues, it takes the form of a flattened oval—that shape dear to the nineteenth century. Great trees shade it, around a grass plot running its length, decorated by two small cast-iron fountains. The red brick houses, with their "salient" bulging fronts running from top to bottom of the façades, exemplify the first Boston architecture purely American-nineteenth-century in character. The naïve assumption, usual at the beginning of a period of technological and political triumphs, that anything sufficiently bold and powerful must last forever, is built into these "fronts" along with their brick and mortar. It was in such a house that Miss Birdseye lived, and that Ransom first saw Verena. But things change. Today—and for the last forty years or so—these houses have been shabby boardinghouses or "light-housekeeping" rooms. The roomers, armed with their paper bags of food and their milk bottles, return to them at night under the shadow of the gracious trees, mount the steps beside the flourish of scrolled iron railings, and enter the big doors under obsolete, elaborate "gasoliers." The materialist spirit that thought to build enduring mansions built, instead, the most solid and dismal furnished lodgings.

In *The Bostonians* James fixes the crudities and misapprehensions of that spirit. Far from identifying himself with Ransom, he uses this character to throw uncompromising light on a humanitarianism itself grown harsh, proud, and aggressive, cut off from the humility and the realism which must be charity's true base. He shows us perfectionists blind to their own imperfections, liberals neutralized by their "liberality," radicals bound by unyielding dogma to callousness; as well as the "moist, emotional" yearners and the hysterics of both sexes, unconsciously seeking a ritual and a master that they consciously reject. *The*

Bostonians is happily again available to those who have over-looked one of the greatest of American novels, which has existed, as it were, in the shadow of the very culture upon which it sheds light, since 1886.

THE LATER PHASE (*1944*)

F. O. Matthiessen's intelligent study of James's later period, *Henry James: The Later Phase,* appearing one year after the rather neglected James centenary, presages, it is to be hoped, other criticism directed toward the Works and produced by critics who do not hate James or misprise good writing. Matthiessen mentions at one point the present interest in the international scene as having some relation to a new interest in James. It would be one more queer twist of circumstance if Americans now come to an interest in their great compatriot because of reasons quite separate from the central values in James. What James really was—a great "poet" and a profound psychologist—and what he actually accomplished, is beyond any interest of a "timely" kind, no matter how pressing and serious such an interest may seem to be.

James's reputation has been affected by the turns of fashion before this. He has been earlier than his time, later than his time, and his work has fallen into neglect between "periods." He has been thought outmoded, when his modernity was notable; genteel, when he had become the sharpest critic of "gentility"; a dull expatriate, when his books flashed with incisive American wit; "fine drawn," when, at the end of his life, his writing was loaded with almost an excessive weight of insight and experience. He lost one audience at the end of the eighties. He gained a younger one in 1918, only to have it almost completely fall away during the experimental and eclectic decade of the twenties. The Parrington–Van Wyck Brooks sort of attack appealed to exactly the type of reader who, by nature and training, would decry James in any case: the middle-class mind dead set against anything it cannot "use" or "understand." James, being a shining mark, drew to himself all the concentrated vituperation such

minds are capable of producing. Every dictum of Flaubert's—and
there are many—concerning the hatred of the artist felt by the
rank and file of the bourgeoisie was proved as a deadly truth by
the attacks made, and the misinterpretations thought up, by such
critics, on the subject of James.

Matthiessen has made a choice among the works, and deals
at length with the three last novels—*The Ambassadors, The
Wings of the Dove,* and *The Golden Bowl*—published during
James's lifetime; together with, in passing, *The American Scene*
and the two posthumous and unfinished novels, *The Ivory Tower*
and *The Sense of the Past.* This phase Matthiessen calls "major."
It might better be called the "past-master" period, for James had
been "major" for twenty years or more before he entered into his
last and greatest powers of thought and expression. A period of
mature experimentation—with the theatre, with the strict dramatic form as applied to the novel, and with various special
viewpoints (notably those of the child and the neurotic)—in-
tervened, in the nineties, between the middle and late James. The
later novels have often been singled out for special praise—or
blame; they have never, however, been analyzed with the thoroughness they deserve, and we must be grateful to Matthiessen
for the attention he has paid to their subtleties, and the care he
has taken not to split their form and content into two unnatural
divisions. He is out to shed light, and direct attention not only
toward the master's "pattern" but also toward the magician's
enchantment surrounding that pattern and the fine mind's
relentless insight into it. This is the James, Matthiessen with tacit
irony reminds the reader, who has been accused of identifying
himself with his characters. This is the "snob" who was taken in
by the European scene. This is the dim-witted old man drawing
out a tangle of conclusions from desperately small premises. We
see, instead, the deliberate, immensely skillful artist in his sixties
adding to his effects; the clear-eyed man who can penetrate,
to the point of clairvoyance, almost every human obscurity. We
see James writing these last novels with a speed incommensurate
with their complexity. During the three years of their composition James also produced the life of William Wetmore Story, the
American sculptor, and several short pieces. The delightful Story
biography, revealing James's perfect grasp of the American

artist's problems during the period with which he deals, is a Jamesian success too little known. It is a pity that Matthiessen does not include a detailed estimate of it in his treatment of the last phase, where it belongs. Matthiessen has access to eight working notebooks, running from 1878 to 1914. Not a great deal of clarification of James's intentions is, however, drawn from this source.

One or two matters not accented by Matthiessen come to mind, together with what seems to me a real underestimation, based on imperfect analysis, of *The Golden Bowl.* Matthiessen believes that James's twenty years' absence from America, during a period of crucial American social change, made him uneasy with the "multimillionaire" Adam Verver. Do we not see, instead, in Mr. Verver, as well as in Maggie, James's recognition of a new American type? Surely some kind of maiming and distorting force, as well as increased powers of specialization acting upon basic American romanticism, aggressiveness, and naïveté, reverberate through *The Golden Bowl.* Mr. Verver and Maggie are at first grotesques. They are at once far too powerful and far too infantile. Maggie must learn that love and "help" cannot be bought, or called in, and later neglected; that these things turn out to be dangers to face up to. Matthiessen states that the dynamics of the book are provided entirely by Maggie. The exact opposite is true. Maggie is reduced to impotence and fear when she tries to go it alone; to run everyone. It is only when Charlotte steps out on the terrace with her silent offer to help that Maggie is deflected from her crass, childish, and neurotic course. And behind Charlotte is the Prince's "humility" and delicate sense of balance and form. In this book it is the Europeans who "save" the Americans; it is the Americans who have become corrupted by power, and "taste" pushed too far. Note should be made of Mrs. Assingham's extraordinary analysis, at the end of the novel's first part, of the relation between the four principal characters—an analysis securely based on the truth of modern psychology, and all done without benefit of Freud or Jung. James, in *The Golden Bowl,* had come to the point where he could hear aright, in spite of "stock" pretenses, the whole hidden story of the human heart, including its minor "intermittences." The reader is led, through small truths, toward stern, prodigious human facts. He experiences, not minor interpretation, but comprehensive wisdom.

From one point of view, *The Golden Bowl,* written in the same year (1905) as Debussy's *La Mer,* is one of Impressionism's triumphs. Both works are formal accomplishments "of magnificent scope" of that school. And the later James must be approached in the same way as one approaches music. Soon any surface stylistic oddity disappears. The center continually shifts, but the development of theme never stops for a moment and never errs. As in great music and in tragic life, the shifts are always toward the larger and unsuspected capacity, modulation, event; and toward a final major resolution.

James knew that democracy was diversity. To step into his world of Americans, Europeans, and every international combination of the two, is to find oneself in developing diversity. To read James we must follow "the silver clue . . . to the whole labyrinth of the artist's consciousness: his active sense of life." To understand James we must be the opposite of his "awful Mona Brigstock, who is *all* will, without the smallest leak of force into taste or tenderness or vision, into any sense of shades or relations or proportions—the thriftily constructed Mona, able at any moment to bear the whole of her dead weight at once on any given inch of resisting surface." The Mona Brigstocks, American or "international," should leave James alone. The non-Monas should go toward him without fear, if they have not already found him.

ROBINSON JEFFERS

SUCH COUNSELS YOU GAVE TO ME (*1937*)

The hero of Robinson Jeffers' latest set-piece of human savagery
walks off the stage acting in an unusual way for a Jeffers character. He is moved, because of pity, to a moral decision. He chooses
to shoulder another's punishment, after considering the advantages of suicide and escape. Previously he has acted in the
usual Jeffersian manner: abetted his mother's incestuous passion
for himself and stood by at his father's murder. He then turns
over in his mind the question of whether anything is anything.
Is there any crime, any innocence, any binding "human taboo"?
Finally he decides that modern man has certain duties ("life is not
rational"), and that retribution is one of them. So he turns away
from union with the "clean" California wind and the "sane" California mountains, and he chooses to expiate, not his own guilt,
but his mother's.

All this is very fine, or would be in a character less queerly
constituted than this young man is sure to be. Jeffers decides,
at one point in the action, that human taboos can be transcended.
God must have gone beyond human taboos. He is rather confused,
however, on the stand that both ancient and modern man have
taken concerning taboos. And he cannot, try as he will in this
case, force his characters to go beyond them. The mother-son

incest theme proves too much for him. Classically and primitively, this breach of taboo brings down automatic punishment on even the unwitting transgressor. The wrath of the gods winds up, as Cocteau has expressed the process, like an infernal machine and fells the culprits. Oedipus actually marries Jocasta, in ignorance. In modern and Romantic tragedy the incest-tainted hero, like Hamlet, is usually stricken with inaction. The hero of Jeffers' poem walks open-eyed into the beginning of an incestuous relationship with his mother. But at the last he sheers off. He talks as though he were capable of anything. In point of fact he is capable of nothing but a great many obscurely expressed wrong reasons for his traditional stirrings of conscience. And he arouses little sympathy in the reader. For he and his mother—who, like most of Jeffers' women, *is* capable of anything—seem not so much puzzled and depraved as simple-minded. And, perhaps unfortunately in the humanity Jeffers professes to despise, the moral struggles of idiots somehow do not count.

The Romantic poet should not continue, over a long period, to excoriate the humanity of which he is a member. The satirist can manage analysis and defamation of the human race. He stands outside. The Romantic is involved in the action. The more he strives to identify himself with clean and mindless nature, the more he must degrade his characters and increase the enormity of their crimes. Meanwhile, his own importance increases by leaps and bounds. He is soon no longer content to be chorus, commentator, or prophet. He tends toward the state of God himself. Jeffers says:

> I the last living man
> That sees real earth and skies
> Actual life and real death.
> The others are all prophets and believers
> Delirious with the fevers of faith.

And again:

> To be truth-bound, the neutral
> Detested by all dreaming factions, is my errand here.

Notions of this inflated kind now frequently appear everywhere in Jeffers. His lyrics, the forms he has many times successfully filled with the intense emotion and remarkable descriptions of natural beauty, are now vitiated by pronouncements. It is a pity that his mixed, parochial, and rather Presbyterian disgusts must thus gain headway. A man who has, from the beginning, turned away from the arts, "sports and gallantries, the stage, the antics of dancers," as childish nonsense, must at length grow peevish even surrounded by noble landscapes. "Bitter earnestness," for the dramatic poet, can be a faculty which cuts both ways.

"In very truth, the man who can see all creatures in himself, himself in all creatures, knows no sorrow." Such a man is also protected against ultimate confusion and obsession. Jeffers' great talents, allowed some humble relation to the race, which, whatever its faults, can at least laugh and change, might have escaped the limits that now increasingly distort them.

MEDEA (1946)

In *Medea: Freely Adapted from the Medea of Euripides*, Robinson Jeffers works for the first time within the actual frame of Greek drama. Jeffers has adapted Greek legend before this, and in 1935 he used the Medea theme in the poetic narrative *Solstice*, setting it against his California landscape. Now, keeping both his Romantic-Nihilist attitude toward life and his overblown rhetorical tendencies intact, he adopts a classic mold. Curious results naturally occur. Jeffers has chosen, it is true, a Greek tragedy which seems to call for his kind of shock-dealing hand, for the *Medea* is by no means a stiff and formal vehicle of classic "pity and terror." An early work of the highly original Euripides, it seems at moments to accumulate and to release only terror. As critics have pointed out, there is no tragic interlock between character and situation. Medea, the Asiatic princess and sorceress, brought to the Greek city of Corinth by the wily Jason and there abandoned with her children, reacts to the situation as she reacted to earlier events in her career—with vengeful guile and frightful cruelty. "If the only profit in the *Medea*," says a modern British scholar, "is the news that barbarian magicians who are passionate and villainously treated do villainous things, the demands on our tolerance cannot be met."

In the Jeffers version, very little in addition to Medea's villainous side comes through. Euripides, on the other hand, in this study of oppression and revenge, treats the dreadful story with the sharpness of psychological insight, the compassionate and truth-loving skepticism, the striking combination of realism and imagination, which characterize his work. He not only keeps before us, by exquisitely managed implication, the fact that "the passions and unreason to which humanity is subject are its greatest scourge"; he suggests as well the presence in the universe of implacable forces to which the wild nature of Medea is related. She is, of course, the granddaughter of Helios, the sun god, and it is the double potentiality—at once benign and destructive— of natural powers that Euripides stresses in the ambiguous final episode, in which Medea escapes by supernatural aid.

Jeffers ignores these implications. He changes Medea, by a process partly of cutting and partly of expansion, and by abrupt shifts in emphasis, from a woman who has some degree of control and some power of awakening our sympathy into a creature so obsessed by jealousy, pride, and a paranoid fear of ridicule that she passes from the normal world into the regions of insanity. From her first cry of inordinate rage, she is in an extreme of sadism. Euripides' Medea, however, is capable of a long, tender, relenting speech, in which we feel the current of human love, and she is surrounded by the poetry of the great choruses, in which, in spite of everything, love, and not fury, is the dominant theme. His Medea outlines her ghastly plans, is admonished, and plays out her frenzy against a background of understanding wisdom.

Jeffers, following the Romantic tradition, depends upon suspense for his big effects. And to the Euripidean horror, calculated with great nicety by a master in the field, he adds all manner of overwrought frightfulness. His Medea's mania for grinding, mashing, slicing, pulverizing, and beating her enemies into a bloody froth soon paralyzes and numbs our sensibilities. Jeffers' nightmare world, in which reality is squeezed and beaten into the shape of a brutal adolescent's dream, is, however, more relevant to our present situation than it was when it burst upon us, twenty years or so ago. If Jeffers now pitches his tone so high that it becomes a shriek of hysteria, he is only screwing up to their utmost the tensions of our scene. To compare this "free adaptation" of his with Euripides in a straight translation is to be brought up against the most shocking symptoms in our literature and life.

JUAN RAMON
JIMENEZ (1958)

We must blame history, in part, for the fact that so little Spanish poetry has been translated, successfully or unsuccessfully, into English. England, in the natural way of things, did not, after Elizabeth, spend much time or consideration on the literary works of a defeated rival, and after the early seventeenth century there was little in the way of brilliance or power to be considered, either in prose or in verse, Cervantes, Góngora, and Lope de Vega being contemporaries of Shakespeare. Spanish poetry of any interest or intensity did not exist in the eighteenth century, and it was negligible or imitative up to the end of the nineteenth. No constellation of Romantics appeared, and the themes of doubt, soul-searching, and spiritual turmoil in general, which occupied the Victorians, had no counterpart in a country almost totally closed off from the Industrial Revolution. Only with Federico García Lorca, born in 1899, did modern Spanish poetry come to international attention.

It was left to the 1956 Nobel Prize committee to bring to international notice two other modern Spaniards whose importance might otherwise have been passed over—Antonio Machado, who died in 1939, after having helped defend the Spanish Republic, and Juan Ramón Jiménez. Jiménez received the Swedish medal, but in its presentation the committee, by also naming Machado and Lorca, evidently took into consideration the merits of these two Spanish poets, now dead. For, as the uninstructed then came to learn, Lorca was by no means an isolated figure; both Machado and Jiménez had been, to some extent, his masters—Jiménez particularly so, because he had explored, in his work, much the same territory and material, although in a quite different way. Lorca's poetry, dramatic and highly colored, had some of the "Spanish gaudiness" that is a striking but ultimately superficial element in Spanish art as a whole. Lorca had emphasized, moreover, folk (chiefly gypsy) intensity and abruptness, and his poignant refrains, his ballad feeling, came over with greater ease in translation than Spanish verse written in more conventional forms. And Lorca's closeness to literary Surrealism in its most flourishing period linked him to poets writing in a like manner in French and English.

But it is now generally conceded that Jiménez, of a slightly older generation (he was born in 1881), has had the strongest influence on Spanish poetry written in the twentieth century. Unlike Rubén Darío, who first brought French Symbolism over into Spanish verse, he was not so much an imitator of this French poet or that as he was a writer of the same kind of poetry. His first poems, published when he was eighteen, were close to the heart of a native Spanish Impressionism, what has been called the "shimmering extravagances" of his native Andalusia. Jiménez later developed a style and attitude that could accommodate direct and detailed observation of the world about him; like Yeats, he worked himself free from any device that resembled applied ornament; for him, to be modern meant to be free. His rhythms became more individual as he moved away from conventional metres toward a kind of patterned vers libre. He has never lost, however, his special power over language, which has become— in his later years—increasingly transparent, shifting, and luminous.

At its most subtle, such poetry, of course, defies translation. It nevertheless seems a pity that the first attempt to make the work of Jiménez available in any large way in America turns out to be more baffling than clarifying. *Selected Writings of Juan Ramón Jiménez*, edited (with a preface) by Eugenio Florit and translated by H. R. Hays, breaks so many of the rules we are accustomed to have modern translators follow that very nearly all of the savor and point of the poetry is lost, while the prose—which should present far fewer difficulties—comes through in rather a blunted way. Translation has offered, in our century, refreshment to the poetry of all Western languages. So many crucial discoveries of both difference and relationship, and so many fruitful exchanges of material and method, have been made that it is difficult nowadays to think what modern poetry in English, for example, would be like if it had not received the exciting impact of Pound's renderings from literatures ranging from the Chinese to the Anglo-Saxon, of Eliot's translation of the Symbolist St.-John Perse, of the various translations of Rilke and of the French Surrealists. Modern versions of the classics of antiquity have also been turned into acceptable and readable modern speech, from Homer and the complete canon of Greek drama through Virgil and Ovid. These have been demanding labors, carried out with several rules in mind—strict adherence to the spirit and tone of the originals and the utmost simplicity and accuracy in regard to form and language, the natural words in the natural order. In the case of lyric poetry, modern translators have also been meticulous, wherever possible, about presenting the original poems on facing pages.

We are given no originals for Mr. Hays's translations, so we have no notion of the poems' basic pattern and coloration. His unsuccess can be gauged, however, by the frequent awkwardness and the pervasive weakness of the English. Here all the old, bad literary words, which modern poets have worked so hard and so long at eliminating, reappear. And here are the little extra (and unnecessary) turns of speech, at the same time that important touches are left out. And the syntax is disarranged, so that telling emphasis is lost. Granted that the translation of lyric poetry requires the most delicate tact and the most varied gifts of ear and insight, and granted that the Spanish language presents special hazards to the translator, surely today, after so much achievement in the field, it is difficult to bear what seems to be deafness on the part of a translator not only to the Spanish he is taking the poem out of but to the English he is putting it into. Hays's versions, taken on their merits as English poems, would most certainly never have seen the light of print.

Eugenio Florit, a poet who in his youth, in the thirties, knew Jiménez in Cuba, gives a most sympathetic and detailed account, in his preface, of Jiménez's development and influence. Florit emphasizes the poet's critical powers and his gift of Goyaesque caricature, for Jiménez has a biting sardonic side. What seems to be most striking in Jiménez, apart from his lyric gift, is his persistence and endurance, his impulse to advance and to explore. He is again comparable to Yeats in his mature insistence on examining every level and facet of his experience, of refining his expression down to essentials, of contemplating both appearance and essence. These two men, both from "backward" countries (and both close to the most primitive regions of those countries— Yeats to Sligo and Jiménez to Andalusia, a province where an ancient pastoral life continues to exist), brought over into the modern, mechanized world a sense of poetry as a part of primitive ritual, and of the poet as one who is still able to touch at their source human gaiety, melancholy, and enchantment. Jiménez's travels in North and South America and his present "exile" in Puerto Rico (where he has lived and taught since 1952) have not blurred or distorted his sense of origins. It is a heartening fact that even today "sensibility" is more tense and durable than one might suppose; that Jiménez, for all his uneven health and sensitive nature, has been able to hold to unchanging human values in a world that seems to turn more and more toward the concept of man as machine-tender or puppet. The slightest lyric of such a poet is a positive act against disorder of feeling and the falseness of the second-hand. Platero, the tough little Andalusian donkey, the beast of burden who is Jiménez's most touching creation, was made "of steel and quicksilver." His master shares these qualities, and would have poetry share them.

DAVID JONES
(1963)

American readers have had to wait for the publication here of
the work of David Jones. His first book, *In Parenthesis,* with an
introductory note by T. S. Eliot, appeared in London in 1937 but
was not published in New York until 1962, and *The Anathemata,*
"reshuffled and again rewritten intermittently between 1946 and
1951," has now reached America eleven years after its first British
printing. David Jones (born in 1895, of Anglo-Welsh parents),
veteran of the 1914–1918 war (Royal Welsh Fusiliers), poet,
engraver, watercolorist, and Roman Catholic convert, has accumulated high and even reverent praise from Eliot, W. H. Auden,
the late Edwin Muir, and others. *In Parenthesis* combined a kind
of war diary with a real and imagined past; the present "fragments of an attempted writing" reveal Jones's ardent desire to
uncover and restore sacred signs and symbols to a time and a
society that have lost the sense of living myth through negation
and neglect. Jones has inherited, in a pure form, the Celtic
religious temperament once so active in history, and this inheritance is reinforced by his unremitting scholarly drive. He
feels that his poem need not be finally impenetrable to a reader
who, not frightened by "mystery," is willing to read it slowly and

aloud. And it is true that in spite of this poet's plunges into the darkness of legend and the twilight of chronicle, of his liking for archaic words and circuitous syntax, of his finical glosses and occasional echoing of late-period Joyce, certain passages of haunting beauty and power come through. The book is finely produced (in format, it matches the earlier *In Parenthesis*), with nine pages of halftone illustrations of Jones's drawings and inscriptions.

JAMES JOYCE

PROTEUS, OR VICO'S ROAD *(1939)*

Joyce has been writing *Finnegans Wake* for seventeen years.
In 1922 *Ulysses* was published in Paris; this book was begun the
same year. *Transition* has brought out about half of it, intermittently, under the title "Work in Progress"; and a number of
fragments have appeared now and again in pamphlet form. A
whole school of imitators has clustered around its linguistic and
philosophical example, and its influence has been so strong
that critics have been led to write of it in, as it were, its own
terms. Something unheard-of and extraordinary was happening
to language, history, time, space, and causality in Joyce's new
novel, and the jaw-dropping and hat-waving of the front-line
appreciators were remarkable in themselves. Because this subjective, or rolling-along-in-great-delight-with-a-great-work-of-art,
school of criticism has had its innings with Joyce's books, the
plain reviewer might do well to approach the work at first with a
certain amount of leaden-footed objectivity, remaining outside
the structure and examining it from as many sides as possible.

Joyce himself, as we shall see, has given a good many clues to
what the book is about. The first thing that strikes the reader,
however, is the further proof of Joyce's miraculous virtuosity with
language. *Finnegans Wake* takes up this technical skill as it
existed at the end of *Ulysses* and further elaborates it. Then

262

Joyce's mastery of structure and his musician's feeling for form
and rhythmic subtlety are here in a more advanced—as well
as a more deliquescent—state of development. The chief reason
for the book's opacity is the fact that it is written in a special
language. But this language is not gibberish—unless it wants to
be. It has rules and conventions. Before one starts hating or loving
or floating off upon it, the attention might be bent toward dis-
covering what it is, and how it works.

This private tongue is related to what Panurge called the
"puzlatory," and it is cousin to the language of E. Lear, L. Carroll,
and the writers of nonsense verse in general. It is based on the
pun and is defined, by Fowler, as: "Paronomasia (Rhet.) 'word-
shunting.' Puns, plays on words, making jocular or suggestive
use of similarity between different words or of a word's different
senses." Upon this rhetorical device *Finnegans Wake* is borne, no
matter what limits of intelligibility or impenetrability it touches.
Two examples may illustrate it:

> For a burning would is come to dance inane.
> Glamours hath moidered's lieb and therefore
> Coldours must leap no more.

> But listen to the mocking birde to micking
> bards making bared!

Now let us examine the texture of the writing. This, as one would
expect, is firm. Moving for the most part in a private idiom,
Joyce keeps unerringly to style's economy, precision, and weight.
Through a thousand variations, through a confusion of tongues,
the fundamental sinew of the writing persists; the book can be
opened anywhere, and a page read at random, in proof of this.
The remark of Richard Strauss to a young musician comes to
mind: "Why do you write atonally? You have talent." Joyce is
not writing as he is writing to cover up inexpertness. Prosodically,
he is a master, as can readily be seen if he is compared with his
apprentices.

He is a master-musician and a master-parodist. Here, even more
clearly than in *Ulysses*, Joyce brings over into literature not
only music's structural forms—as exemplified by the fugue, the
sonata, the theme with variations—but the harmonic modula-
tions, the suspensions and solutions, of music: effects in words

which parallel a composer's effects obtained by working with relative or non-relative keys. Phrases and whole passages are transposed from a given style, mood, tempo, signature into a more contrasting one. Certain proper names—Finnegan, Earwicker, Anna Livia, Dublin, Phoenix, Howth, James and John, Lucan and Chapelizod—reappear in truncated, anagrammatically distorted, or portmanteau forms. The night-river leitmotif reads, at its most normal: "Beside the rivering waters of, hitherandthithering waters of. Night!" Its variants are numerous and remarkable. Joyce, the parodist, in *Ulysses* always effectively colored matter with manner. The number of styles parodied in *Finnegans Wake* is prodigious. But these present parodies differ somewhat from their predecessors; they are actually more limited. The punning language in which they are framed gives them all a mocking or burlesque edge (the prose poems, only, excepted). This limitation and defeat of purpose—for an immense book written in two main modes only is sure to grow monotonous—is the first symptom to strike the reader of the malady, to be later defined, which cripples *Finnegans Wake*.

Thus equipped, then, with his private vernacular, Joyce proceeds to attack what certainly seems to be every written or oral style known to man. A list of these styles would fill pages. The range and variety can only be indicated here. All forms of religious liturgy (Bible, prayer book, sermon, mass, catechism, litany); conversation; letters informal, formal, and illiterate; the fable, the examination paper, the chronicle; fashion notes and soap-box speeches; the hair-splitting argument and the sentimental narrative. And here are dialects and jargons—"every known *patois* of the English language." Slang, journalese, and specialized vocabularies: of heraldry, the race track, the courtroom, the nursery. Also uncounted foreign tongues, from Sanskrit through Anglo-Saxon to modern European, back to pidgin English, baby talk, and the sounds children make before speech. There are also just plain noises, onomatopoetically expressed, from bangs and howls to twitters and whimpers.

The "auditive faculty" of Stephen Dedalus has been expanded so that the functions of the other senses become subsidiary to it. Joyce has put down everything he has heard for the last seventeen years. We now can examine some evidence from Eugene Jolas, the editor of *Transition*, as to Joyce's method of work. Jolas says: "It was necessary [in compiling a complete MS for publication] to go through a number of notebooks, each of which had esoteric symbols indicating the reference to a given character, locality, event, or mood. Then the words accumulated over the years had to be placed in the segment for which they were intended." And what Joyce was up to in general—the underlying theme and philosophical purpose of the book—has been partially elucidated by Joyce to Jolas and others. Jolas says:

> We know that Mr. Joyce's ambition has been to write a book dealing with the night-mind of man. . . . We have tried to keep in mind that the dramatic dynamic is based on the Bruno theory of knowledge through opposites, and on the Vico theory of cyclic recurrence. . . . History being, in his earlier words "a nightmare," Mr. Joyce presents his phantasmagoric figures as passing back and forth from a mentality saturated with archetypal memories to a vision of future construction.

Another of Joyce's favorite exegetes sheds a little more light (and it can be definitely stated that light is needed, since the one actual fact which is clear to the reader, without exegesis, is that the action takes place in one night or one aeon of time, and is concerned with a man—a giant, an earth-force—asleep). Stuart Gilbert says:

> Joyce's new work is partly based on the historical speculations of Vico. . . . Vico held that there is a recurrent cycle in human "progress," as in the movement of the stars. Societies begin, continue, and have an end, according to universal laws. . . . Every nation passes through three stages, the divine, the heroic, the human. The prelude and aftermath of each cycle is complete disintegration. . . . Vico contemplated the writing of an "ideal and timeless history" in which all the actual histories of all nations should be embodied. . . . "Work in Progress" is, in many aspects, a realization of Vico's project. . . . It is interesting to note that an exceptionally intricate passage in Mr. Joyce's book is, in effect, a fantasia on the quinary scale. . . . Even the difficult passages of the "Anna Livia Plurabelle" fragment become lucid when read aloud in the appropriate rhythm and intonation by the author. In fact, rhythm is one of the clues to the meaning . . . for each of the polymorphous personages of the work has his appropriate rhythm, and many "references" can be located by reference to the rhythm of the prose.

With these few "clues" well in mind, the reader can only open the book, without further explanation, and battle his way into it. Life is too short to read all the glosses which have already multiplied around it and will continue to multiply. Some of its themes are perfectly clear. The pedestrian reviewer can add a few scattered notes, put down during her own two weeks' life with the literary monument.

There is every reason to believe that a *complete explanation* of the whole thing will come, after a longish lapse of time, from Joyce himself. This happened, it will be remembered, in the case of *Ulysses* after about nine years. . . . There is nothing whatever to indicate that Joyce has any real knowledge of the workings of the subconscious, in sleep or otherwise. Carroll has far more intuition than Joyce into the real structure of the dream. There are no sustained passages which give, for example, the feeling of nightmare. The punning style, as a matter of fact, precludes this. It is as though Joyce wished to be superior to the unconscious. . . . At one point he brings in a long apologia for his own method and language. The effect of this interpolation is very queer. . . . Some sections start off with indicated time, but these indications seem to be afterthoughts. . . . The later versions of the fragments already published seem to be changed out of sheer perversity: a clause is omitted leaving nothing but a vestigial preposition; a singular noun is shifted to the plural, and the meaning is thereby successfully clouded. . . . The most frightening thing about the book is the feeling, which steadily grows in the reader, that Joyce himself does not know what he is doing; and how, in spite of all his efforts, he is giving himself away. Full control is being exercised over the minor details and the main structure, but the compulsion toward a private universe is very strong. . . . Joyce's delight in reducing man's learning, passion, and religion to a hash is also disturbing. . . . After the first week what one longs for is the sound of speech, or the sight of a sentence in its natural human context. . . . The book cannot rise into the region of true evocation—the region where Molly Bloom's soliloquy exists immortally—because it has no human base. Emotion is deleted, or burlesqued, throughout. The vicious atmosphere of a closed world, whose creator can manage and distort all that is humanly valuable and profound (cunningly, with Godlike slyness), becomes stifling. . . . *Ulysses* was based on

a verifiable theme: the search for the father. The theme, or
themes, of *Finnegans Wake* are retrogressive, as the language is
retrogressive. The style retrogresses back to the conundrum.
To read the book over a long period of time gives one the impression of watching intemperance become addiction, become de-
bauch.

The book's great beauties, its wonderful passages of wit, its
variety, its marks of genius and immense learning, are undeniable. It has another virtue: in the future "writers will not need
to search for a compromise." But whatever it says of man's past,
it has nothing to do with man's future, which, we can only hope,
will lie in the direction of more humanity rather than less. And
there are better gods than Proteus.

APPROACHING UR (*1944*)

A Skeleton Key to Finnegans Wake, by Joseph Campbell and
Henry Morton Robinson, is the first full and painstaking attempt
to translate, page by page, the dream-language of Joyce's last
work into English. The authors have attempted to trace, further-
more, "in thin lines" the skeletal structure of the enormous and
baffling book. They have provided a synopsis of the whole, given
indicative names to the four large sections and to the chapters.
They have identified and translated many of Joyce's quotations—
those in identifiable human tongues. They have tried to keep his
alternately looming and dissolving characters straight; listed
references and cross-references in footnotes; have labored, that
is, to give the reader some intelligible ground to stand on and
some recognizable space to move around in. Like archaeologists,
whose tasks theirs of necessity so much resemble, they have uncovered one more layer of Joyce's extraordinary verbal buried
city. They also supply, in an introduction and conclusion, another
fairly impassioned defense of the book as a work of art, and of
Joyce as a great conscious artist.

The quality of being *closed* becomes more and more evident
as expert attention is directed toward *Finnegans Wake*. The book
docs not seem, like certain structures of great literature, to be

a tower or high place, built on earth and open at the top and on
all sides to the Nature about it. Into a limited locale (at its largest,
Dublin, on the island of Ireland) are brought all ages of man
and some of nature. In one narrow room and one sleeping mind,
the developing human faculties, from the brute upward, grow
and dissolve and reform. The circle of Vico's history is superimposed upon the circle of Dublin. Macrocosm and microcosm,
symbol and reality, inextricably mix.

The present "translation" proceeds page by page; but the
translators have of necessity chosen certain passages, and what
has seemed to them the core of these passages, for detailed comment. It is interesting to notice what portions of a knotty (or
merely repetitive) passage the elucidators have separated out,
and what portions—sometimes containing matter which another
observer might consider interesting or crucial—they omit. The
footnotes, too, while generally filled with the most helpful kind
of information, have moments of complete blankness as to what
the text seems to present in the most forcible way. The use of
this "key" is therefore stimulating to the thoughtful student in
more ways than one. It brings up new problems with every step
of ground it clears.

Time must pass, and thorough research be made, before
certain fundamental questions concerning *Finnegans Wake* can
be answered. One question that comes to mind is: are we dealing
with a work (always granting that it is a work of incontestable
genius) essentially small in inner meaning and even in essential
design, a work that has nevertheless exfoliated into a semblance
of growth and complexity? Are we dealing, that is, with a work,
the product of a man and artist who has never come into maturity?
Or are we dealing with an essentially great work, the product of a
man and artist who has suffered life and transcended his suffering; who is no longer the victim of his talent, his circumstances,
or the tensions within his own character, but has become master
of them all? Are we getting from this fantastically distorted and
interwoven speech, these amazingly contrapuntalized themes,
illumination and truth; or are we being led into the mystery of a
childish individual's dreaming game, with the rigmaroles and
jokes and tricks of the child (or immature man) presented to us
neat?

Joyce's lyric gifts, his full equipment as a trained realist, his ingenuity as a fabulist, his skill as a parodist, his sharp wit and Jesuit-trained learning, his innate musician's ear—these attributes are as clearly evident in *Finnegans Wake* as they are in any piece of writing he ever produced. What difference does it make if we are listening to the operations of sleep; we have heard such operations in great pieces of literature before this. Even if Joyce was a sick man, we are listening to a writer who was in many ways a martyr to his genius and to his age. But we want to penetrate the disguises he has had to throw about himself; or the symptoms he has been forced to assume. We have this desire not out of niggling curiosity, but out of real interest: that we may receive the help and refreshment that any true artist's struggle with his material gives us, particularly when we are caught with him into the same deforming time.

The poet and the "comic fabulist" are equipped with uncommon gifts by which they are able to get around interior "censorship." They have tricks, as it were, to get the information through. They transpose the dangerous and (actually) untellable truths of the subconscious into imaginative terms, not easy to bring, otherwise, into the light of day. What strikes the more detached observer when faced with the extreme opacities of certain portions of *Finnegans Wake* is the certainty that concealed beneath his very eyes is a submerged fable having to do directly with Joyce, with Joyce's relations to the world, with Joyce's attitude to his time. Is not the whole book a masked attempt at the fullest *apologia pro vita sua* that Joyce has yet given us? And this last confession and apology certainly must be more revealing (consciously or unconsciously) than anything written in his earlier career. Under the ostensible action, under H. C. Earwicker and Anna Livia Plurabelle, and Shem and Shaun, and the multitude of other clear or ambiguous figures, from time to time another drama shows: the drama of Joyce's own life, up to the writing of the book, and during the writing of the book. It is a drama terrifically malicious in expression; it flays one contemporary after another; it brings down all façades of learning and worship in one mass of mocked-at debris. Joyce is doing more than returning compulsively to the Dublin from which he is an exile. He is razing more than Dublin structures with the fires of his love and hatred.

What exterior situation, then, brought Joyce to the pass where, to get his secret across, he had to resort to a kind of desperate cunning? To resort, as well, to the often monotonous, often trivial, often brutal, ruses of the accomplished *farceur*? Or to the insistent sobbing minor lyric passage? (It seems at times that these two "tones" are the only ones in the book.) Does this work stand like a terrible half-buried monument, both to the recent past and the near future: outlining a deforming epoch when a work of art must become oblique expression—a joking show, a wry song, a cockeyed cinema-mythology—in order to exist at all?

"The price of virtuosity is abject slavery to a complaisant tool; that of creative artistry is wilful dominance over a recalcitrant tool." What do we finally see in Joyce: virtuoso or artist; compulsive neurotic or a writer with himself entirely in hand? This question requires a deeper analysis than has yet been dared by Joyce students and disciples. It is not a skeleton key we need, so much as eyes to see in spiritual (was it?) darkness; and ears with which to separate cunning (are they?) confusions.

PATRICK KAVANAGH
(1965)

The career of Patrick Kavanagh presents extraordinary features completely outside the usual literary framework. His *Collected Poems* reveals an astonishing talent—according to some enthusiasts, the finest not only in Ireland but in all English-speaking areas—that has kept on renewing itself not so much by a process of orderly growth as by a continual breaching of boundaries. Judging by his recent poetic practice as well as his comment on that practice, it is clear that Kavanagh now stands free of all obligations except the deepest and most demanding claims of the open imagination. The early work of this poet, born in 1905 in the Irish countryside, reflects a life close to the pieties and rude circumstances of the agricultural laborer. His disillusion with the lot of the Irish countryman came into being only after he had described that lot—in "The Great Hunger" (1942)—with mixed affection and loathing. His subsequent descriptions of Dublin literary life and politics were again filled with the blackest disillusion. Kavanagh's chief object of detestation has come to be the coat-trailing, charming, Irish semi-clown—a tragicomic caricature designed, according to the poet, for the foreign trade. Behind Kavanagh's intransigence stands a thorough understanding of modern traps laid on all sides for the bafflement of human dignity, as well as an unfaltering sense of some human innocence, marred but indestructible. His satire, cutting close to the bone, spares neither cause, nor institution, nor individual. He names person and place, and he can be as scathing in a sonnet as in a piece of parody or a stretch of doggerel. Since, as he frankly states in his introductory author's note, written in London in 1964, he now dislikes much of his early verse, the selection of the poems in the new volume, of nearly two hundred pages, was left to his friend Martin Green, who has carried out his task admirably. To come upon Kavanagh's spontaneity is delightful, and one understands the sober reasons that have kept him from being listed among the more official and solemn post-Yeatsians. Far from officialdom of any kind, Kavanagh survives and flourishes in that invigorating region where, without respectable let or hindrance, the wild rivers run and the wild timber grows.

PHILIP LARKIN

THE LESS DECEIVED (1958)

Philip Larkin, whose *The Less Deceived,* a volume of poems
written since 1945, was published in America this spring, has for
some time been considered the most gifted poet of his generation.
Larkin is a true dramatic lyricist, of the kind that modern poetry,
with its emphasis on dramatic presentation, has fostered. His
manner has been compared to Hardy's, and it is true that he walks
straight into his chosen situations and works them through step
by step with Hardian bluntness. Such an approach makes for
an order that at times seems merely logical, and Larkin's poetry
has been criticized for being "non-evocative." This criticism does
not take into account the rightness of his epithets, which are
always at the center of the matter; they have been aimed, and
they hit their mark. He has completely escaped the dry and flippant excesses of some of his contemporaries; he tells the truth
without resorting to the aid of wry similes or captious allusions.
If he recognizes limits, he also, it is clear, apprehends depths.

THE WHITSUN WEDDINGS (1965)

Countries, nations, states rarely get the kind of poets they hope
to get or think they deserve. Literary history is full of embar-

rassing (and sometimes tragic) examples of misjudgment—
when the true original, having been denied honor in his lifetime,
is discovered (sometimes by foreigners) after his death, or when
a mediocrity once honored for some popular timeliness continues
for a generation or so to blemish the pages of anthologies. One
rarely, moreover, finds in the chronicles any large agreement
in the case of the fairly young on the part of their contemporaries.
Recently, in England, such agreement has gathered around the
figure of Philip Larkin. His fourth book, *The Less Deceived*,
published inconspicuously by a Yorkshire press in 1955, when
Larkin was thirty-three, rapidly went through four printings, and
the author found himself the center of a group briefly known as
the Movement—young poets with an interest in detachment,
irony, and form. Larkin's own concerns turn out to be remarkably restricted both as to time and as to place; in a recent inter-
view he stated that he is not interested in any period but the
present or in any poetry but that written in English. Larkin's
present high standing in his native land is not based wholly on
this insularity, however. The reaction that set in a decade ago
against the excesses of postwar romanticism—against those poets
who had come to express continual highly pitched manifestations
of the hallucinatory, the apocalyptic, and the surreal—was also
involved. Human nerves, as Eliot once remarked, can stand just
so much irrationality; the mindless incantation loses power as it
begins to irritate, and the pleasure of having the imagination
work on recognizable facts is doubly welcome once it reappears
after an absence.

Larkin, on the dust jacket of his latest volume, *The Whitsun
Weddings*, disclaims any special love of form: "Form holds little
interest for me. Content is everything." But it is at once apparent
to the most casual reader that this member of what is now becoming a middle-aged British poetic generation possesses formal
gifts that are not only perfectly controlled and strongly sustained
but capable of wide and interesting variation. He is able to use
such gifts as they are seldom used, to describe the tough realities
of his time—those sometimes major and sometimes marginal
uglinesses that seem unassimilable in art unless they are cari-
catured: the hideous, the cheap, the wrecked object; the desolate,
the devastated locale. Larkin's realism (which has Hardy behind

it) is not inflexibly dour. A profound pessimism exists, but this bleak background is often unexpectedly broken to let through some calm and tender emotion.

One aspect of Larkin's work that often adds subtle reinforcement to his moments of pathos is his open assumption of the British sense of class. The title poem—one of Larkin's most striking successes—of the new book is based on a touching succession of insights into what must be taken as a working-class spring festival. Larkin reports with a direct first-person approach the phenomenon of young brides and their wedding parties as they appear at the railway stops during a journey he is making to London from the North. Written in stanzas large and free enough to accommodate minor variations in stress and speed, yet strict enough to give what can only be called an odelike dignity to awkward material, the poem releases, in its last lines, a restrained lyricism that reverberates in the classic manner. Touches and colorings of feeling keep recurring in Larkin, not set off in any sharp contrast but present as part of the general web of his response to the difficult details of his world—details he does not shy away from but attacks and resolves. And he openly examines his limitations. This frankness has troubled those of his readers who expect from him a more copious flow of work, perhaps more cheerfully expressed. And what about the disconcerting streak of wicked satire that appears from time to time? A great deal of truthtelling is projected by Larkin's intense dramatic lyricism.

D. H. LAWRENCE

BIRDS, BEASTS AND FLOWERS (1923)

D. H. Lawrence's early poems were the record of a terrifically focused personality embroiled with love and beauty. Heavy, packed almost to oppression with images conceived upon some intensest point of vision, these poems seemed to have been written out of that blood sense of which Mr. Lawrence has told us so often: that dark, unthinking stream which floods over and puts out the little scheming mind. There was little search for reason in them.

With *Look! We Have Come Through!* a break came. The poet, becoming sick of himself and of a world tainted wholly by his thoughts and emotions, is riven out of his old being by a passion at last greater than himself. He begins to give reasons. Men and women, he cries, in a long rhapsodic manifesto, must merge utterly in love, die in it, be slain. Yet each by some mystical process must nevertheless remain free from the other in a strict spiritual isolation. All must be fused, yet not fused. From this impasse—that it was an impasse the tortured figures of the novels seem to prove—Mr. Lawrence has turned at length.

In a novel, a book of essays, and a book of poems, published within the last year, the fusion has become less important than the escape. The poems in *Birds, Beasts and Flowers*, although they contain much of the old Lawrence's incredible apprehension

of eye and word, have, as well, the ferocious dogmatic quality
which has long since crept into his prose. They are poems that
cry, implicitly, for existence to have done. They ask an isolation
absolute, man's spirit to be a naked stalk, standing trembling and
alone in a lush physical world. Mr. Lawrence has turned his back
on humanity that strains for illusion, not identity, and gives his
allegiance to beasts (if they be strong, single beasts) and to fruits
of the earth.

When Mr. Lawrence left the Midlands he entered a wide and
terribly various world. He went toward it with a great thirsting
will to pare down beauty to its core. The prose of *Twilight in
Italy*, the first record of these journeys, contains passages which
cannot be outdone by any poem he has ever written. The seeds of
the later mysticism and philosophy are there, but Mr. Lawrence
was still the questioner. He still believed that in mankind there
could become "ecstasy of light and dark together": "Why do we
not know that the two in consummation are one, that each is only
part, partial and alone forever; but that the two in consummation
are perfect, beyond the range of loneliness or solitude?" Existence
had not yet been divided for him, like the apple in the fairy tale,
of which one side was white and sweet, the other glowing and
poisoned in every grain. The reasons for Italy's beauty were
secondary to the beauty itself, bright in his sentences as upon
his eyes. Lately India, Australia, and America have come before
those eyes. But they are more tired. A tightness has bound the
sight. And the world must no longer be light and dark com-
mingled. Light or dark, singleness or merging: in a kind of despairing didacticism Mr. Lawrence shouts that the choice must
be made.

With America he has quarreled because she does not make
the choice. Both Whitman and his country are flawed by the
same weakness. In *Studies in Classic American Literature* Mr.
Lawrence has smashed down one of his own idols—the poet who
in 1920 was to him the master of "the unrestful, ungraspable
poetry of the sheer moment—life surging into utterance at its
very wellhead." It is Whitman's philosophy that concerns him
now. "Whitman said sympathy. If only he had stuck to it. Because
sympathy means feeling with, not feeling for. He kept on having
a passionate feeling for the Negro slave . . . which is merging."

In *Birds, Beasts and Flowers* America comes under the same lash:

> You who in loving break down
> And break further and further down
> Your bounds of isolation,
> But who never rise, resurrected, from this grave
>   of mingling,
> In a new proud singleness, America.

Demos—"demon too"—is the madness by which Mr. Lawrence will never be possessed. He watches Socialists in yellow boots, on Italian Sundays, decked with hibiscus and salvia, and denies them equality with himself and the flowers:

> Never
> To be a Bolshevist
> With a hibiscus flower behind my ear
> In sign of life, of lovely dangerous life,
> And passionate disquality of men.

He wants the world burned and beaten down, but not by them. And though he seek out in escape an ancient equivocal fern world, where perhaps the grape was the rose, or a world withered with lava, or even plunging beneath the ground, "the winding, leaf-clogged, silent lanes of hell," yet the spell upon him of this earth is not quite dissolved. The almond tree flowers out from iron branches; there is still kingly fruit and flower—pomegranates:

> O crown of spiked metal
> Actually growing!

But the spell of love is dissolved. Those who once found in Lawrence a passionate clairvoyance into love, need not look for it here. To the integrated individual, love is not important. But Mr. Lawrence cannot yet state his thesis calmly. There is something slightly hysterical in his railing against the lusts of goats, the love-gluttedness of the little hairless Mexican bitch. He is more calm with his proud beasts. "Snake," the drama between a serpent and a man who sees it shouldering down into its secret kingdom, is one of the fine poems in the book. The mountain lion, the eagle, the turkey cock, the fish—rocked in a cold element "without love"—are each beautifully struck from the old power. And Mr. Lawrence has allowed "Medlars and Sorb-Apples"—after breaking it with two perversely flippant lines—to be a poem. It is soaked in the rotten-ripe scent of autumn, and chilled by separation's cold anguish. In it nothing is proven concerning isolation. It is isolation: "the intoxication of final loneliness."

Though Mr. Lawrence continue to write poems with corrections within them, poems in which deliberate inanity is set beside phrases which almost shock the mind with their perception, though he deny every human emotion in the world, he will never quite succeed in denying himself. The essential genius must remain, under the invective and didacticism that perhaps have become necessary as defense in this personality, at every point asking the essence, or else surcease, oblivion—at every point refused.

SELECTED POEMS (1948)

New Directions has done a real service to English and American letters by bringing out, in its "New Classics Series," a small book of D. H. Lawrence's verse, *Selected Poems,* an excellent job of editing by Kenneth Rexroth. Lawrence's poetry has been rather poorly treated by English and American publishers. All the single volumes, both early and late, are out of print, and the collected edition, in two volumes, published in America in 1929, is also unobtainable. It is, therefore, extremely difficult for anyone who has not, as it were, grown up with the poems to get a comprehensive view of Lawrence's poetry, of his development of poetic thought and feeling, or of the progressive refinement of his literary methods. Mr. Rexroth, in his introduction, analyzes Lawrence's purely poetic contribution, a contribution that can now be recognized as one of the most important, in any language, of our time.

The most striking characteristic of Lawrence's poetry, from the beginning to the end of his career, was, as someone has said, its extraordinary power of "intense, direct, personal, mystical apprehension of reality." He began to write poetry in a period when English poets were afraid of approaching Nature in any but the most sentimental and shamefaced way, and when human problems, unless they were of the most naïve order, were omitted from verse entirely. Lawrence's early work bears a few marks of the constricting conditions that prevailed at the beginning of his career. In an astonishingly short period of time, however, his burning curiosity and his insatiable taste for the compelling experience had lifted him far out of the ruck of his more timid contemporaries. Rexroth traces this rapid development with great insight. The early poems show the progress of a bewildered young man writing within the scope of "nice" values, whose worth he has not yet learned to suspect; of the "common" young man slicked up to look like a provincial schoolteacher, whose likeness, with a stubborn chin jutting out over a high white collar, we have seen in an early photograph. This conformity disappears when we come upon the tragic poems on his mother's death. In them, he pours out his grief so violently that it almost never again recurs. Thereafter, Lawrence is able to get at reality in his own way. He gets at it by direct contact with, and by sympathy for, Nature. Nature, to Lawrence, comprises more than "birds, beasts, and flowers." It includes the most complex human relationships. Lawrence makes a difficult and complicated marriage, and he writes down the steps of this mature love relationship (many of which had to be taken in the dark, for lack of adequate knowledge in the society around him) in the magnificent poems of *Look! We Have Come Through!* a title that makes unself-conscious use of the exclamation mark, from which modern taste tends to shy. These poems, written between 1912 and 1917, accomplished in English literature what Gide had accomplished some twenty years earlier in French literature; they affirmed the importance of human joy. "Feel grief," they say, "but give over guilt and anxiety. Only the materialist and madman is afraid of happiness."

Lawrence's insight into the "secrecy" of man and of things grew steadily deeper; because he was continually exploring new fields, he succeeded in keeping the barrier between his unconscious forces and his consciousness extremely thin. European history opened up before him; he reconstituted the ancient Etrurian domain and way of life. He gave us a prophetic vignette of modern Europe in ruins, and he gave us warnings against the "police State" and "spy government everywhere." His technical ease increased. Over two hundred short lyrics, aphorisms, and satires were gathered together in the volume called *Pansies,* published in 1929, the year before his death. In these, Lawrence had advanced so far into a future he saw with the utmost clarity that many of his more sentimental and dogmatic followers fell away from him in a state of shock.

Not enough poems from *Pansies* appear in the present volume. Mr. Rexroth has, however, on the whole done his sampling with a sense of proportion. What is needed, of course, is a complete collection of Lawrence's poetry. The importance of his later work will then stand out. This work, for various reasons, has been not only neglected but maligned. The young English poets who trod hard on Lawrence's heels learned some of their most valuable lessons from it. Lawrence taught them to be sensible, to be at ease, to be good-natured, to be sane. He taught them that no subject is closed to the poet who is himself truthful and free:

> Give, and it shall be given unto you
>   is still the truth about life.

> But giving life is not so easy.

> It doesn't mean handing it out to some
>   mean fool, or letting the living dead eat
>   you up.

> It means kindling the life quality where it
>   was not, even if it's only in the whiteness
>   of a washed pocket handkerchief.

Lawrence's poetry has been the portion of his work most difficult to appraise. Yet in spite of the striking contrast between his poetic successes and poetic failures (the contrast between Lawrence in command of his gifts and the victim of his obsessions—a duality his readers must reckon with in all his work, in whatever form), his collected poems stand as one of the most invigorating contributions to the verse of the early twentieth century. He was—at his best—original, fearless, and emotionally open. He disdained all masks and disguising personae; he could dissect with a cutting edge; and in his *Last Poems,* as Richard Aldington has said, he was finding "a new voice of grandeur and dignity."

FEDERICO GARCIA LORCA
(1937, 1940)

❦❦❦

Federico García Lorca, Spain's greatest modern poet, who was shot at the age of thirty-seven in Granada in the early weeks of the Spanish war, was, like Yeats, fortunate in having direct access to a living folk tradition. Again like Yeats, Lorca was open to the avant-garde movements of his time. Yeats came under the influence of French Symbolism; Lorca had his Surrealist period. The poems in the first section of his *The Poet in New York* (well translated by Rolfe Humphries from the poet's perhaps incomplete typescript) are thoroughly Surrealist. They were written in 1929 and 1930, when Lorca, already famous in Spain for his songs and ballads, lived in New York as a student at Columbia and travelled as far north as Vermont.

Lorca had a right to Surrealism as non-Spanish poets have not; his native literary tradition stems from Góngora. And the modern Spaniard has cut loose from the idea of a religious hell so recently that the private hell of the subconscious floats closer to the surface in both Dali and Lorca than, nowadays, in artists of other nationalities. These facts must be borne in mind by the reader who, like myself, distrusts Surrealism's worth and pretensions and the worth of any poet who adheres too rigorously to its tenets. In the case of Lorca, we have proof of his poetic worth in his non-Surrealist work. The brilliant and popularly inspired *Gypsy*

Ballads were published in 1928, and we have examples of them in the latter part of this book. His Surrealist period in America and Cuba followed. Later, Lorca published his "Lament for Ignacio Sánchez Mejías" (already translated into English by A. L. Lloyd as "Lament for the Death of a Bullfighter"), and in that late and superb poem we can see what the poet finally did with Surrealism. He used it as Baudelaire used "Gothic": he made it humane and the vehicle of emotion.

His ballads get at the nerve centers directly. Their oral tradition comes through at all points; we understand why this poetry is sung by illiterate people all over Spain. Objects in them move, glitter, give off heat, cold, and odor; expand and contract, glow and resound, and the heart of the reader goes through corresponding processes, is made to feel. They are grown out of the heart as wheat or grapes are grown out of the ground.

ROBERT LOWELL

LORD WEARY'S CASTLE (*1946*)

Religious conversion, in the case of two modern poets writing in English—T. S. Eliot and W. H. Auden—brought an atmosphere of peace and relief from tension into their work. But Robert Lowell, a young American who has forsaken his New England Calvinist tradition for the tenets of the Roman Catholic church, exhibits no great joy and radiance in the forty-odd poems now published under the title *Lord Weary's Castle*. A tremendous struggle is still going on in Lowell's difficult and harsh writing, and nothing is resolved. These poems bring to mind the crucial seventeenth-century battle between two kinds of religious faith, or, in fact, the battle between the human will and any sort of faith at all. They do not have the sweetness of the later English "metaphysical" writers; Lowell faces the facts of modern materialism more with the uncompromising tone and temper of the Jacobean dramatists, Webster and Tourneur, or of Donne, who (to quote Professor Grierson), "concluding that the world, physical and moral, was dissolving in corruptions which human reason could not cure, took refuge in the ark of the Church." (Lowell, it is clear, has not taken refuge anywhere.) He also bears some relationship to Herman Melville, the American with Puritan hell-fire in his bones. The more timid reader would do well to remember these forerunners, and the conditions that fostered them, when confronted with young Lowell's fierce indignation.

Lowell's technical competence is remarkable, and this book shows a definite advance over the rather stiff and crusty style of his first volume, *Land of Unlikeness*, published in 1944. This competence shows most clearly in his "imitations" and arrangements of the work of others, which he hesitates to call direct translations. "The Ghost" (after Sextus Propertius), "The Fens" (after Cobbett), and the poems derived from Valéry, Rimbaud, and Rilke reveal a new flexibility and directness. These poems might well be read first, since they show the poet's control of both matter and manner. The impact of the other poems in the book is often so shocking and overwhelming, because of the violent, tightly packed, and allusive style and the frequent efforts of nightmare horror, that his control may seem dubious. The extraordinary evocation of the sea's relentlessness and the terror of death at sea, in "The Quaker Graveyard in Nantucket" (an elegy to a drowned merchant seaman), is equalled in dreadfulness by the grisly emblems of "At the Indian Killer's Grave," a poem wherein successive layers of spiritual and social decomposition in the Massachusetts Bay Colony come to light through a descent into the King's Chapel Burying Ground in Boston. Lowell, again in the seventeenth-century way, continually dwells upon scenes of death and burial. He is at his best when he mingles factual detail with imaginative symbol; his facts are always closely observed, down to every last glass-tiered factory and every dingy suburban tree. To Lowell, man is clearly evil and a descendant of Cain, and Abel is the eternal forgotten victim, hustled away from sight and consciousness. And the modern world cannot reward its servants; no worthy pay is received by the good mason who built "Lord Wearie's Castle." (The old ballad from which the book's title is taken runs: "It's Lambkin was a mason good As ever built wi' stane: He built Lord Wearie's castle But payment gat he nane.") These are the themes that run through this grim collection. Lowell does not state them so much as present himself in the act of experiencing their weight. It is impossible to read his poems without sharing his desperation. Lowell may be the first of that postwar generation which will write in dead earnest, attempting to find a basis for a working faith, in spite of secretive Nature and in defiance of the frivolous concepts of a gross and complacent society. Or he may simply remain a solitary figure. Certainly his gifts are of a special kind.

LIFE STUDIES (1959)

The ability to face up to, and record, the raw contemporaneous fact has been one of modern poetry's great successes. Hardy was perhaps the first British poet who was able to use the everyday background of an industrial society (the railway station, the draper's shop) as a setting for his verse, at a time when most English poets were receding into a past—the Pre-Raphaelites into the Middle Ages, Browning into the Renaissance, and Tennyson into prehistoric Britain. (Whitman, in America, was, of course, superbly factual.) But it was Yeats who finally succeeded in getting himself, his ancestors, his enemies and friends into his work, and Auden learned from Yeats. This naming of names, once a device of satire (as in Byron's *Don Juan*), has given to modern poetry fresh liveliness and point. The modern poet's emotions have acquired emphasis by being attached to circumstance, and his memories, when kept strictly in line with actuality, have been freed from hampering nostalgia.

The poems in Robert Lowell's *Life Studies* gain much of their power and interest from the fact that they are almost entirely autobiographical. Lowell's need, at the age of forty-two, to reconstruct his past and his origins has been so strong that he includes an autobiographical essay, in prose ("91 Revere Street"), as a center around which he has placed the poems. And he describes in both poems and prose not only himself as a child, an adolescent, and a grown man but his parents and his grandparents, his own and his parents' friends. Few poets have subjected their childhood and their family situation to a closer examination. Here great dangers arise. To write almost exclusively of oneself and one's setting, identifying person and place, is a task that presents troublesome problems of tact and tone. To deal in this way with the shifts and bafflements of experience and social change, as well as, in familial terms, with the ugly elements of personal dissolution, requires balance, detachment, and consistent moral courage. Lowell exhibits these difficult-to-sustain qualities; he has not glossed over the hard parts. We are left with the feeling that more than a family has appeared and vanished before our eyes; we have followed a way of life and have shared the 'poet's apprehensions of an era. Lowell's new book shows him vigorously taking hold of intractable material that lesser talents would be incapable of confronting, let alone putting down in words.

FOR THE UNION DEAD (1965)

Proof that Puritan elements in the American character have never been entirely erased is the implicit demand from his audience that any American poet who at any time has shown signs of possessing a prophetic vein should continue with that vein, no matter what changes take place in himself or his situation. Robert Lowell's early poetry contained a good measure of Puritan brimstone. For the young Lowell, the seventeenth-century religious wars might have been fought yesterday, or, indeed, might still be going on. Lowell's later shift to closely personal subjects and looser poetic means has been deplored in some quarters. His latest book, *For the Union Dead*, is, in spite of its history-weighted title, largely a collection of personal memories, from which, evidently, much bitterness has been eliminated by the passage of time.

This turn toward the contemplation of one's past is natural at Lowell's age (the late forties), and he now is able to describe difficult transitional events with a compassion and humor that were totally lacking in his early writing. His later poems are expressed in loosened form quite different from his early high metaphysical manner. A contrast with Larkin is interesting here; whereas the British poet was both formal and idiomatic from the first, and at ease in describing his environment, the American had to approach the present by working through circuitous avenues of history and religion. Lowell, now the official poet of his generation, faces the various dangers of responsibility: the self-conscious attitude, the temptation to slip into a distorting nostalgia when dealing with the past, and the tendency to castigate every aspect of the present. Lowell, happily, has yielded to these dangers only in a minor way in these new poems. And if the custom of his country has eliminated for him the possibility of class pathos, it has presented him with the tragedy of race, which gives the book's title poem weight.

NEAR THE OCEAN (1967)

Is it possible for one individual, in one life-time, to combine the roles of *poète maudit* and *chef d'école*? A nice little thesis could be written analyzing this question, with examples ranging from Verlaine's early choices to the rare contemporary British and American poets who might just conceivably share both categories. A leader must remain on view, and he can have few secrets, "cursed" or otherwise. Robert Lowell, in his "confessional" poetry, has kept few secrets back. But confessions wear thin, and the attempt to keep them effective by artificial means must subject the talent of any poet, however gifted, to severe strain. The seven new poems (counting one in five parts) in Lowell's most recent volume exhibit a certain coldness and theatricality that often seem to spring from a will toward pure shock rather than from his earlier uncompromising intensity of presentation and courageous choice of subject. His translations—including three odes of Horace and Juvenal's "Tenth Satire"—are evidently meant to connect Rome ("the greatness and horror of her empire") to bruised and maimed aspects of America today. (Lowell has become more gentle toward the American past.) Sidney Nolan's horrifying illustrations (line drawings based on the text) rather disqualify the volume as a coffee-table object, although the large format and the perfectly acceptable and indeed rather romantic drawing (by Francis Parker) on the front of the dust jacket might help to place it in that class. An interim work in every respect.

HUGH MacDIARMID
(1967)

The *Collected Poems of Hugh MacDiarmid* contains, the author states in an introductory note, by no means all the poems he has written but only those he thinks worth including in a definitive edition. The volume, with glossary and index, runs to 498 pages and is in general chronologically arranged—1923 onward; twelve books have been drawn upon and a number of uncollected poems have been added. The early poems, chiefly lyrical, have great charm, in spite of the fact that they are written for the most part in a mixture of Scottish dialects—in a vernacular that at some point or other took to itself the name Lallans.

Like the Chilean Pablo Neruda, MacDiarmid has applied himself, in a perfectly open and often rather compulsive-seeming manner, to subjects that at present are neglected and even shunned by the majority of English and American poets and audiences. Both Neruda and MacDiarmid bring patriotic and political poetry again into view; they occasionally resemble not only Whitman at his most optimistic and orotund but Victor Hugo at his most grandiose and bardic. Both are capable, too, of mingling the emotions of nationalism with the philosophy of the international class struggle; Neruda has made no secret of his allegiance to Communism, and MacDiarmid's early intense admiration for Lenin has never lapsed. And neither poet has ever considered restraint a virtue. Both have written endless variations of their favorite themes; their allegiances have been forthright and their staying power has been enormous. And both, oddly, discarding their family and given names, have produced their work under pseudonyms.

MacDiarmid (b. 1892) is a native of Dumfriesshire, in Scotland. As one of the founders of the Scottish Nationalist Party, he began his campaign for the restoration of Scottish political rights and Scottish literary dignity when he was quite young, and a revival of Scottish speech was part of his earnest plan. The ghost of Robert Burns having been invoked, bitter satire against all things English and warm praise of all things Scottish poured fourth, in Lallans and to a great extent in strict metre and rhyme. Soon a small group of young admirers and imitators, talented and untalented, followed where MacDiarmid led, but no true revival of language came to pass. The heart of spoken Scottish dialects, as one observer has remarked, had long since ceased to beat, and the written language (a difficult mixture, which demanded the constant use of a glossary) irritated readers in Scotland no less than readers elsewhere. A newspaper controversy throughout Scotland brought on, in 1946, an almost total rejection of Lallans by the general public. Meanwhile, MacDiarmid himself gradually turned away from what he must have sensed was a moribund tongue toward English, and from lyrics toward long, discursive poems, in which a latent tendency toward teaching and preaching, an obsessive bookishness, and a harsh boastfulness came to light. MacDiarmid's egotism is only one side of his bold, inquisitive nature, and his obsessions are largely bound up with a gusto and an expansiveness that scorn the decorous side of man and society. By means of scandalous diatribes, literary and political, MacDiarmid has shaken friends and enemies alike from a national complacency. A group of friends have honored his seventieth birthday by presenting him with a portrait of himself, which is to go to the Scottish National Portrait Gallery. His *Collected Poems* constitutes a frank if frequently shocking portrait done by his own hand.

ARCHIBALD MacLEISH
(1939)

Last year Archibald MacLeish resorted to scaring people, over the radio, with air-raid noises and human screams in order to waken the population to "Fascist" dangers. Now he has published a small book of twenty pages with a similar end in view. *America Was Promises* traces, in Mr. MacLeish's languid and faintly eccentric style, the history of the American people sold out and misled by "the Aristocracy of politic selfishness." All hope is not yet lost, however. America is still full of lovely scenery, exquisite weather, "big fists," and strong hearts. "America is promises to Us To take them Brutally With love but Take them." And the poem ends with the plaintive imperative, "O believe this!"

This poem is Mr. MacLeish's saddest and most conglomerate attempt at "public speech" to date. It opens with a sort of crepuscular question and goes on through lines which faintly parody the now public poet's early "private" writing; there's some *Conquistador* in it, and even a little *Hamlet*. Mr. MacLeish is evidently aware of the dangers of appealing to the People with a capital "P." He partially skirts that problem by speaking of them at least once in lower case. Yes, Mr. MacLeish has heard of the sentimental come-ons and exhortations of demagogues and evidently does not wish to ally himself with such persons. The difficulty is that he is writing political poetry, even a kind of official poetry, and therefore the strict checks and disciplines of poetry written for itself (as a result of reality making a direct emotional impact

upon the unique temperament of a trained and exacting writer)
do not hold. If such disciplines were functioning, Mr. MacLeish
would certainly have realized, for example, that he was getting
off to a bad start with his title. *America Was Promises* is a sentence which even an untrained ear instinctively rejects; it sounds
ugly. But it also sounds impressive, and "public speech" is out
to impress.

Everything brought up by Mr. MacLeish sounds impressive:
the rise and decadence of American fortunes; the dead lying
in "Spain Austria Poland China Bohemia"; "the coarse ambitious
priest [leading] by the bloody fingers forward." Because of his
relaxed form, his righteous anger comes through so feebly,
however, that all we are moved to do is sit down and join the
author in a good cry. Bury his gifts though he may, Mr. MacLeish
is a private, a lyric, poet through and through; it is somewhat
of a loss that he did not allow himself to remain one. Evil conditions need a satirist to pin them down and flay them clean.
Official poets are seldom satirists. A pity. So we may look
forward to many poems from Mr. MacLeish which bear the
same relation to the art of poetry that Blashfield murals bear to the
art of painting, and we may look forward to a new and better
world announced by the rhetorical generalities peculiar to a low
level of writing in the old.

LOUIS MacNEICE

(1964)

The dazzling early lyric performance of Louis MacNeice remained unmatched in his generation. MacNeice's sudden death, at the age of fifty-six, last summer, followed closely upon the publication of his *Collected Poems 1925–48*. What proved to be his final volume, *The Burning Perch*, appeared posthumously last autumn. The *Collected Poems* should, although not so arranged, be read in chronological order, for it is an added pleasure to watch the opening out of a true lyric gift and of one so clearly illustrative of the subtle shifts and adjustments that have occurred within English poetic tradition during this century. The exuberance and inventive gaiety of MacNeice's early poems helped to break up a tendency of the time toward dead seriousness. His Greek studies kept him on balance and metrically ingenious, while he faced up, at a young age, to his era and place—being able to construct, at least once, a long poem ("Autumn Journal," in 1938) that brought together a dramatic account of public events and a candid record of personal crisis. A growing bitterness and melancholy appear in the later work, but MacNeice's eye for detail and his Anglo-Irish wit never quite failed him, and they reappear in his last book, faultlessly projected, as always.

KATHERINE MANSFIELD
(1940)

John Middleton Murry, in his preface to this collection of Mansfield miscellanea (*The Scrapbook of Katherine Mansfield*), promises a further substantial publication of unpublished letters soon. The present volume of unfinished sketches, notes for stories, quotations from books read, and pieces of direct personal analysis, adds little to the Mansfield canon. It stands, it is true, as another "book," and we know that it was Katherine Mansfield's great wish to leave work of some bulk and substance. But perhaps it is not a service to her character and talents to emphasize the more fragmentary side of her work.

For the great difference between Mansfield and the Chekhov she admired and in some ways resembled was that Chekhov had more time to develop; and that he was forced, by the fact of his doctor's profession, to deal in the ordinary way with his experience and surroundings. Mansfield, on the other hand, had only the world of childhood to back her up. Whatever sorts of rough reality she had known, she repressed; or inducted only in a "sublimated" form into her writing. The everyday side of life to her was "too crude, too ugly." It was not merely childishness, but the neurotic's love of childishness which gave poignance to many of her effects. "She had the privilege," wrote her French translator, "of living in a fairyland, in the midst of a strange little phantasmagoria of which she was at once the creator and the dupe; in a little universe of her own where familiar objects . . . took on unexpected roles." And Francis Carco, in his reverent memoir, speaks of "her natural taste for the poetry of the rain, of the night, of absurd and dangerous lives . . . and false situations. . . . It amused her to frighten herself . . . to have fear and pain at the same time. . . . She was hurt by living in the midst of so much ugliness and corruption. . . . Mysteries of the [pure] heart of a child!"

It was this purity which makes her finest stories what they are. But childhood, prolonged, cannot remain a fairyland. It becomes a hell. This Mansfield came to know, and the greatness of her letters and journals is based on her efforts to escape from this prison. It was her tragedy that she saw into her situation when it was too late to do anything about it which took time. The Gurdjieff offer to waken her "will" seemed to her the quick way out, and she chose it, without hesitation. She knew exactly what she wanted to find on the other side (see the entry in the *Journal* for October 10, 1922). Isolated passages in the present book also testify to this perception and it is a pity that, broken away from a context, they often sound snappish and petty. "Peace of mind? What is peace of mind?" she asked, early. Later she sensed what it could be; and a younger generation of writers was to take from her the phrase "a change of heart" and the sentence: "To be rooted in life, that's what I want."

As an artist, it is clear that Mansfield was a forerunner, in English prose, of a new kind of sensibility which, up to our day, has been imperfectly and brokenly expressed in the prose of all European literatures. She was nearer to Lawrence and Joyce in this than she wished to admit (she disliked the cruder aesthetic explorations of both Joyce and Lawrence, and thought sensibility artificial in Turgenev). This sensibility comes through, in a distorted form, in Lewis Carroll; and has always been present in lyric poetry, folk song, and proverbs; and turns up in isolated letters and journals during the nineteenth century. To it nothing is closed; the sharpened mind and sense reflect all. "Ordinary human consciousness," says I. A. Richards in his study of Coleridge, "may not, until recently, have had a form that could thus be represented. On one interpretation of the change, Katherine Mansfield [and others] have improved the descriptive technique of prose, have caught something always present which writers in the past could not (or did not wish to) catch; on another interpretation, something new in the modes of perception had come into being for them to describe."

From this point of view, anything left by Mansfield, no matter how incomplete and disconnected, becomes important.

EDNA MILLAY
(1939)

Edna Millay's new book, *Huntsman, What Quarry?*, is "the first book since the publication of *The Buck in the Snow*," her publishers say, "in which [she] has brought together a new group of her lyrical poems." This statement seems to pass over the appearance, in 1934, of *Wine from These Grapes*, a collection of lyrics and sonnets which showed signs of Miss Millay's successful passage from the emotions and point of view of a rebellious girl to those of a maturely contemplative woman. The present book, although it bears marks of the poet's magnanimity of nature and her basic poetic gifts, is a strange mixture of maturity and un-resolved youth. What further complicates its expression is the influence of the hampering and sometimes destructive role of the unofficial feminine laureate which Miss Millay has had to play for so long to her American public.

It is a dangerous lot, that of the charming, romantic public poet, especially if it falls to a woman. The temptation to repeat effects continually reappears; there are "occasional poems," which it seems necessary to write; and it is almost impossible for the poetess, once laurelled, to take off the crown for good or to reject the values and taste of those who tender it. Certainly

Miss Millay has never completely granted the demands of groups whose favorite she has remained for so long. But it is difficult to see why she still writes certain kinds of poems. The delightful ballad, peppered with colorful place names; the poems built on picturesque and faintly feudal situations (the hunter and the acorn-gathering girl; the princes and the handsome groom); and the numerous poems which describe pride trampled, though never actually defeated, by an unworthy object of affection—a time and place exist for these, but it is not in the middle of a career. It is difficult to say what a woman poet should concern herself with as she grows older, because woman poets who have produced an impressively bulky body of work are few. But is there any reason to believe that a woman's spiritual fibre is less sturdy than a man's? Is it not possible for a woman to come to terms with herself, if not with the world; to withdraw more and more, as time goes on, her own personality from her productions; to stop childish fears of death and eschew charming rebellions against facts? Certainly some fragments of Sappho are more "mature" than others. And Christina Rossetti, who lived an anonymous life and somewhat resembled, according to the cruel wit of Max Beerbohm, "a pew-opener," explored regions which Miss Millay has not yet entered. And there is the case of Emily Dickinson.

Miss Millay has always fought, and is still fighting, injustice. She is still subject to moods of self-disgust as well as to moods of mutiny against mankind's infringements on its own human decency. Once or twice she contemplates a truce which "slackens the mind's allegiance to despair." And twice—in the poem just quoted and in the recessively titled "The Princess Recalls Her One Adventure"—she writes as beautiful lyrics as she has ever written. But what has happened to the kind of development announced in *Wine from These Grapes*, the most kindly disposed reader cannot say. If Miss Millay should give up for good the idea that "wisdom" and "peace" are stuffy concepts, perhaps that development might be renewed.

THE MINOR SHUDDER:

Horace Gregory, Randall Jarrell,

Richard Eberhart, Theodore Roethke

(1952)

When Goethe stated that the shudder expressed mankind's best side, he was thinking not of the Gothic atmosphere fashionable in his day so much as of the general feeling of awe at the mysteries of the universe, to which the most hardened materialist is not entirely immune. In modern poetry, this larger emotion is rare indeed; the whole emotional set of the period is against it. The minor Gothic shudder, on the other hand, appears with fair regularity. The Surrealists revived it while exploiting the dark marvels of the subconscious, and traces of Surrealist influence continue to crop up in modern verse, although the movement, on the whole, is exhausted. Four poets who have published recent volumes illustrate the methods—precarious at best and open to failure more than to success—by which the modern imagination tries to project feelings of mystery and awe.

One method involves a putting on of masks, or *personae*, through which the poet speaks. This seems a simple procedure; Browning was good at it, as well as Pound and Yeats. It is, nonetheless, a difficult feat; as Yeats quickly discovered, "there must be a living face behind the mask." The poet, that is, must take infinite care not to stiffen into an effigy of the character he assumes; he must remain integrated, alive, and himself behind his disguises. And if he holds to this method, he will soon be forced to provide landscapes for his figures, thereby involving himself with growing problems, both imaginative and structural.

Horace Gregory, from the beginning of his career, has occupied himself with building up an allegorical world. He derives his scene from the most diverse sources: from the reality of the furnished room and the corner bar-and-grill, to the artifice of settings drawn from art, literature, or myth. He has peopled his backgrounds with a crowd of characters, ancient and modern, real and imagined. His later work, as it appears in *Selected Poems,* has taken a slightly different turn; his backgrounds tend to be real enough while his characters become more and more ghostly and decorative—passive *figurants* rather than actors. Gregory, too, is now fascinated not only by ghosts but by other kinds of magic. In his later poems, some final, transcendent, hair-raising event seems imminent. That it never occurs is not because of his lack either of ingenuity or of expressive range, for he has both. What is lacking is an ultimate daring that would crack the surface of his too carefully manipulated world, wherein the mask has come to disguise the face only too well.

Randall Jarrell, in his new volume, *The Seven-League Crutches,* is another poet who is obsessed with problems of reality and non-reality. Much of his recent work is wrapped in gauze—in the dreams and fantasies of childhood, in literary allusiveness, or in the distorting light of the legend or the fairy tale. His "adaptations" of poems by Rilke and Corbière are more vivid than his original writing; he catches the tone of both men and is particularly successful in bring over into English Corbière's roughness, deliberate dislocation of meaning, and alternate coarseness and tenderness. But when Jarrell attempts these effects on his own, his suspension of ideas, quirks of language, and tenuous dramatic sense show signs of artificial inducement. There is something not so much eerie as bloodless in Jarrell's world, inhabited almost exclusively, as it is, with beings too young to have known life or too baffled to act in it. These creatures revolve in a limbo of pain and fear. It is difficult to animate such shadows or to attach any dramatic substance to them.

Richard Eberhart, on the other hand, is a poet who can turn the cube of reality (in William James's phrase) so that another facet comes into view. At his best, he does this with the mystic's ease. His *Selected Poems* finally brings his gifts into focus. Eberhart, possessing the innocent unself-consciousness of one to whom the spirit is a reality, in earlier volumes displayed the faults of his virtues in tendencies toward diffuseness of language and dilution of idea. The poems in this collection are concentrated, both in mood and form, and the total effect is remarkable. "The Groundhog" and "The Fury of the Aerial Bombardment," already justly famous in the annals of modern verse, are by no means solitary successes. Eberhart continues to be original because his vision is constantly self-refreshing, and he needs no masks to enhance either his meaning or his impact.

If Theodore Roethke's poetry in *Praise to the End!* seems at first glance more consciously produced than Eberhart's, it is soon evident that the two poets share an unforced power of imaginative penetration into the obscure, the hidden, and the inarticulate, and that they are both capable of that larger awe of which Goethe spoke. Roethke has added several long poems to passages from *The Lost Son*, published a few years ago, and these additions accent his original theme—the journey from the child's primordial subconscious world, through the regions of adult terror, guilt, and despair, toward a final release into the freedom of conscious being. Roethke's description of this progress attaches itself to recognizable myth and legend hardly at all; his rendition of a sub- or pre-conscious world is filled with coiling and uncoiling, nudging and creeping images that often can be expressed only with the aid of nonsense and gibberish. But it is witty nonsense and effective gibberish, since the poet's control over this difficult material is always formal; he knows exactly when to increase and when to decrease pressure, and he comes to a stop just before the point of monotony is reached. Behind Roethke's method exists the example of Joyce, but Roethke has invented a symbolism, in his searching out of these terrors, marginal to our consciousness, that is quite his own.

MARIANNE MOORE

⚜

NEVERTHELESS (1944)

Marianne Moore's fifth book of poetry, *Nevertheless*, is her best. It contains six poems of no great length. The small format is delightful—a proof that a commercial publisher need not badger a poet to pad a volume with second-rate material in order that some outmoded publishing tradition be kept up. This little, firm, profoundly beautiful set of poems is an event for which a country more conscious of the importance of the good artist would crown Miss Moore with official laurels. As it is, officialdom has never seen fit to give her the Pulitzer Prize.*

Many of the facts about Miss Moore's quality and importance have already been set forth in T. S. Eliot's preface to her *Selected Poems* (1935). Eliot speaks of her service to the living language "in maintaining its strength and subtlety and preserving its quality of feeling"; of her appreciation of the individual word; of her success in startling us into an unusual awareness of visual patterns with something like the fascination of a high-powered microscope; of her elegance and form. Eliot also speaks of two characteristics of Miss Moore's earlier work which have baffled many readers in the past—her lack of out-and-out poetic "music" (her rhythm is basically that of good prose) and her intellectual detachment, which sometimes seemed to stiffen into actual cold-

* This oversight has since been corrected.

303

ness. During the nine years which have passed since Eliot's preface, Miss Moore has become both more "musical" and more openly warm-hearted. The warmth was always there, but it is now more noticeable because it is more personal, tender, and even playful. It is a humane, humorous, imaginative warmth that satisfies the heart and mind equally. Neither wistfulness nor that self-pity which often attacks women writers when they let down their guard has invaded these self-possessed poems.

Miss Moore's love of animals, fruit, flowers, and beautiful artifacts, once shown rather obliquely, at present touches her subjects with a subdued but penetrating light. The poems are like fables, giving new point and meaning to certain necessary virtues of mankind. The fortitude bred by mutilation or deprivation ("Nevertheless"), the tragic bases of equanimity ("Elephants"), the beauties of stalwartness and skill ("A Carriage from Sweden"), the need for every man to search out, in time of war, the arrogance and division in his own heart ("In Distrust of Merits") —these are the things Miss Moore brings before us—few, but of terrible importance. Added to these is her charming poem on the ordinarily comic skunk ("The Wood-Weasel"). This little animal, suddenly detached from cheap jokes, is restored to its dignified place in Nature by a few words from the imaginative and kind heart and by a merciful look from the just eyes of Miss Moore. Marianne Moore acts according to the rule she herself has demanded in art—that it should be "lit with piercing glances into the life of things . . . acknowledge the spiritual forces which have made it."

Marianne Moore is now our most distinguished contemporary American poet. Her talents should be guarded and encouraged, so that we can expect from her a long career, rich with the superb poetry she is able to compose.

THE FABLES OF LA FONTAINE (1954)

Miss Moore's eight years' labor of translating into English *The Fables of La Fontaine* would have gone for nothing if she had succeeded only in giving a fair replica of the French poet's form without being able to catch that most subtle factor in any poet's work—his underlying tone. In general, success in this sort of reproduction depends primarily upon success in recognizing hidden intention as well as open character, and this recognition must be based on a certain sympathy between the translator and his subject. It is clear that any likenesses between two poets, one a modern American and the other a seventeenth-century Frenchman who spent much of his life either close to or within the court of Louis XIV (the twelve books of the *Fables* first appeared between 1668 and 1694), must exist on the deep levels of poetic temperament or on the high levels of technical brilliance. There will be critics who will deny to Miss Moore any success with La Fontaine's limpid and seemingly effortless music, but no one can deny that she shares with the great French fabulist an idiosyncratic view of man and nature, a delicate irony and humor, and on the technical side, stylistic gifts at once elegant and inexhaustibly fertile. Both poets, moreover, share the desire to break bonds and to express themselves in their own fashion, for it must be remembered that La Fontaine was as much an original in his own day as Miss Moore is in hers.

Miss Moore mentions in her preface the governing principles of style she has adhered to—"the natural order of words, subjects, predicate, object; the active voice where possible; a ban on dead words, rhymes synonymous with gusto." These are almost invariably the rules of the best modern poetic procedure, and Miss Moore has been faithful to them. It is with her style that she has captured her subject, but not with her style alone. Her humor resembles La Fontaine's humor in the closest way; both are laconic, insidious, and "dry," and on the ground of intelligence, wit, and taste she and her forerunner meet again. These likenesses overshadow the superficial divergences between the two—the fact that La Fontaine's moral sense is more materialist and pragmatic than Miss Moore's and that while Miss Moore in her own work observes animals in detail as part of nature, La Fontaine uses them as symbols illustrating the foibles of mankind. But time after time the small, condensed phrase, the releasing epithet that encloses entire a turn of the Frenchman's thought has risen to Miss Moore's mind, and suddenly, in a flash, we get the La Fontainean quality complete. As for music, there is more

of it in these versions than would at first appear. The exact trans-
fer of the music of the *Fables* from French into any language, by
anyone, is an impossible feat. But there is no doubt that Miss
Moore has opened to us the heart and mind of the most humane
and perceptive poets of all time, a poet who presaged some of
mankind's most courageous efforts toward self-understanding,
which were to develop in the centuries succeeding his own. Because of Miss Moore's gifts of serious yet witty precision, we now
have La Fontaine in a modern English idiom, and we may well
apply ourselves to the lessons he has to teach.

AMERICAN TO HER BACKBONE (*1947*)

Impressionist critics, because they have attributed to Miss Moore
many of their own manias and virtues, have left her actual virtue
—her "secret"—untouched. She belongs to a lineage against
which the impressionist and the "modernist" have for so long
rebelled that by now they are forgetful that it ever existed. In Miss
Moore two traditions that modernism tends to ignore meet. She
is, on the one hand, a nearly pure example of that inquisitive,
receptive kind of civilized human being which began to flourish
during the high Renaissance: the disciple of the "new" as opposed
to the "old" learning, the connoisseur, the humane scholar—to
whom nothing was alien, and for whom man was the measure
of all. Her method, in her "observations," has been compared, and
rightly, to that of Francis Bacon and Sir Thomas Browne. But we
soon come upon in her work another, angularly intersecting, line.
Miss Moore, child of Erasmus, cousin to Evelyn, and certainly close
kin to the Mozart who refracted *Don Giovanni* as though from a
dark crystal, does not develop, as we might expect, toward full
Baroque exuberance. She shows—and not to her demerit—a definite influence derived from that Protestantism against whose
vigor the vigor of the Baroque was actively opposed. Miss Moore
is a descendant not of Swiss or Scotch, but of Irish presbyters. She
is, therefore, a moralist (though a gentle one) and a stern—
though flexible—technician.

It is not an infrequent American miracle, this combination of civilized European characteristics in one gifted nature. Miss Moore, American to her backbone, is a striking example of a reversion toward two distinct kinds of heritage; of an atavism which does not in any degree imply declension or degeneration of the original types involved. She does not write *à la manière de . . .* ; she produces originals. She does not resemble certain seventeenth-century writers; she might be one of them. She stands at the confluence of two great traditions, as they once existed, and as they no longer exist. "Sentiment" and the shams of the *pasticheur* cannot touch her, since she ends where they begin.

Examine her passion for miscellany: it is a seventeenth-century passion. "Academic feeling, or prejudice possibly, in favor of continuity and completion," she wrote in 1927, "is opposed to miscellany—to music programs, composite picture exhibitions, newspapers, magazines, and anthologies. Any zoo, aquarium, library, garden, or volume of letters, however, is an anthology, and certain of these selected findings are highly satisfactory. . . . The selective nomenclature—the chameleon's eye as we might call it so—of the connoisseur, expresses a genius for difference." There speaks a sensibility unmarked by the flattening pressures of an industrial age. Alive to the meaning of variation, Miss Moore can examine what the modern world displays, with an unmodern eye. This is her value to us. She sees as a specialist trained and bred sees. She is never, therefore, indifferent to what might strike her contemporaries as either precious or rubbish. Advertisements, travel folders, yesterday's newspaper, the corner movie, the daily shop and street, the fashion magazine, the photograph and the map—these phenomena are gathered into her art with the same care with which she "observes" small mammals, birds, reptiles; or with which she microscopically examines details of human artifacts: "sharkskin, camellia-leaf, orange-peel, semi-eggshell or *sang-de-boeuf* glaze" in Chinese porcelain, for example. Unlike a magpie, she is not attracted by any kind of glittering swag. She is never in danger for a moment of appearing either a dilettante or a snob. She is occupied with the set task of imaginatively correlating the world's goods, natural and artificial, as a physician correlates "cases," or a naturalist, specimens.

The tone of her poems often derives from her "other," Protestant inheritance. Are not many of her poems sermons in little, preached in the "plain style" but with overtones of a grander eloquence? Are not many of them discourses which are introduced, or subsumed, by a text? Note the frequent cool moral that she extracts from her poems' complexities; and the dexterity with which, from disparate and often heavy facts, she produces a synthesis as transparent and as inclusive as air. Her sensibilities are Counter-Reformation; her emotion and intellect, Protestant.

She has immensely widened the field of modern poetry. She takes the museum piece out of its glass case, and sets it against living animals. She relates the refreshing oddities of art to the shocking oddities of life. The ephemeral and the provincial become durable and civilized under her hands. She is a delayed product of long processes. She is at once a contemporary American, a seventeenth-century survival, and a native of those timeless and pure spiritual regions

> where there is no dust, and life is like a lemon leaf,
> a green piece of tough translucent parchment.

EDWIN MUIR
(1956)

The poetry of hallucination and dream is as common and usual in our day as what was once called "poetry of the spirit" is rare. The line of the first, running from Rimbaud, through the Surrealists, to the poetry of Dylan Thomas, depends almost wholly upon language; it tends to be rhetorical, enigmatic, and rather terrifying; it pushes expression to its limits and beyond. But now, as always, poetry that deals with a sensed reality beyond appearance keeps to limits, and modern poets, surprisingly, have written a good deal of it, from Rilke to Eliot and Auden (in their later work), but it is currently scarce. Such poetry cannot be successfully imitated or counterfeited, which is one reason for its not turning up very often. Its material, sometimes lying within the bounds of orthodox religion and sometimes not, is as difficult to project as its tone is difficult to sustain. Special gifts of perception and intensity are involved, and such poetry must have humility, that most uncommon of virtues, at its source.

At least one volume of new poetry this season shows marks of a particular adherence to things of the spirit. Its author is a Scot, Edwin Muir, who has already put on record his development as man and poet in a remarkable autobiography. Born in the Ork-

neys, a resident of Central Europe for many years, and the translator (with his wife) of Kafka, Muir continues to develop, in his
most recent volume, *One Foot in Eden,* a spiritual temperament
in a very nearly pure state. His symbols, largely derived from Old
Testament and classic Greek sources, are perfectly adapted to his
thought and feeling, and his poems rise out of these symbols with
an even pace, a slow tempo, and a delicate delineation of inner
light and darkness. He is a master of form (as mystics tend to
be), but it is not his "literary" skill that at once strikes the reader
so much as the quality of his insight. "The Days," surely one of
the great lyrics of our time, starts practically in a whisper, although it deals with the tremendous Biblical myth of creation.
Muir then proceeds from line to line, with sure direction, to fill
the original emptiness and loneliness with the astonishing facts
of nature, along with touching details of the life of man, circling,
at the end, into a vision of unchanging eternity. In another dramatic lyric, "The Horses," Muir demonstrates his ability to face up
to the idea of mankind's almost total destruction. And in "Telem-
achos Remembers," he outlines, in seven brief stanzas, an ageless theme of fidelity and love and brings a Homeric parable to
rest, as it were, securely in the present. These poems should con-
vince the most disabused reader that modern poetry has not come
to a complete spiritual impasse.

MYTHOLOGIES

THE SECULAR HELL (1946)

Was, von Menschen nicht gewusst
Oder nicht bedacht,
Durch das Labyrinth der Brust
Wandelt in der Nacht.
—Goethe: *An den Mond*

The "classic" myth is fresh, subtle, and varied. Its variety is the result of a long process of accretion, stratification, and absorption. Its subtlety is the crystallization of "mankind's deepest emotions." It is saturated with meaning; no matter how deeply we explore it, an irreducible residue of unconscious allusiveness remains inexplicable in any terms but the original legendary ones. The luminous primordial scene surrounds it; in a light that is still large, mankind's earliest awe before, and pleasure in, natural phenomena appears. The details are often, to use the Victorian term often applied to them, "repulsive" in the extreme. We can still respond, however, in spite of our modern knowledge of the myth's darkest sources, to Schlegel's definition: "The myth is a hieroglyphic expression of environing nature under the transfiguration of imagination and love."

Even a partial listing of the labors of Herakles, for example, shows the broadness and richness of the imaginative forces involved. "The capture of the Cerynean hind; the procuring of the girdle of Hippolyte; the cleaning of the Augean stables . . . the fetching of the red cattle of Geryon"; and then, with "the procuring of the golden apples of the Hesperides," we are transported into a climate of pristine beauty. The labors are translated into a region outside the material world, and the material world is exquisitely changed thereby.

The Hero as Transcendent Breaker of the Taboo stands at the center of many myths. But the taboo is not broken at once, or without previous bafflement. Before the hero takes on full responsibility, full guilt, he must at least once face up to insoluble mystery, be completely humiliated, or be changed into a compelling "opposite." The myth does not set up a series of material barriers only. One test is never actually passed; through and around it we hear the laughter of the Powers. It is when we see Herakles a prisoner of Lydian Omphale (who wears his lion-skin) that the story begins to vibrate with mystery and passes over into the "truth" of the dream. Beyond the crisis—and it is always great and compelling—of the final assumption of guilt, lies the irreducible strangeness of strength face to face with a spiritual or physical Force it cannot move, change, or understand. Oedipus before the Sphinx, Christ in the Wilderness and in the Garden, Herakles among the women: it is at these points that the myth opens another dimension to our view—a dimension to which we can as yet give no name, with which religion and poetry themselves can deal only tentatively and in part.

It is the rite which enables the individual to participate directly in the myth. The myth always moves toward the rite. It can only be *lived* through the rite. Religious ritual codifies, stiffens, and rationalizes. But the rite also reassures and shares; sometimes, it would seem, its operation is almost entirely fear-dissolving in character. But, as Roger Caillois has pointed out, in his interesting survey of the "sacred" (*L'Homme et le sacré*, 1939), a religion at a high point of health and effectiveness often allows, within whatever culture it operates, the occasional functioning of "permitted license" of an extreme kind. The institution of the festival (the feastday, the holiday, the *fête*)—during which rules are broken, sacrilege is at least ritually allowed, the profane is permitted to break into the stronghold of the holy, and authority is mocked— brings into a religion bound by the strictness of rules, not only a relief for pent-up energies, but a refreshment based on a return to older, and otherwise disguised, rites of fertility and "creation."

When a religion begins to lose health, it is always the releasing rites which are the first to disappear. The threatened organization puts increasing pressure upon rituals of *atonement,* and begins actively to persecute "the heretic." The ideas of the Sublime and the Numinous dwindle into superstitions ever proliferating into smaller details. Meanwhile, the dammed-up energies of "the faithful," once provided for by the ritually controlled "festival," break out in a persecutory manner toward any activity which seems to duplicate "the festival." The "myth" begins to float freely in the culture into which it has been loosed. It turns up in unexpected places—not only in literature and art, but in the general ethos of the society. And it is always "Hell" which breaks loose, as "Heaven" fades out. The magic which religion straitens and controls for its own purposes; the "will" that religion tames; the fear and guilt which religious practice resolves and accommodates— all these escape into "the profane." The magician and sorcerer (who "wish to coerce nature, instead of allying themselves with it") take up the priest's power. The individual conscience, meanwhile, is asked to bear the full weight of the individual's transgressions.

The dispossessed festival and the fertility rites now become obsessions. Malice and envy walk freely abroad. No force is available to confront Evil but more Evil. It is the Time of Demons, as well as of new—unrecognized—"mythmaking" power.

The witch and the warlock stand as twin "mythical" figures at the beginning of the modern world. A "white-witch," Jeanne d'Arc, is burned at the stake in 1431; but it is the figure of her comrade-in-arms, Gilles de Rais—the child-killing "Bluebeard"— that continues to fascinate the popular mind. And soon the terror and fascinated dread of sorcery and witchcraft is codified and fixed in the *Malleus Maleficarum* (1486 or a little later): a work which "spread widely and became for centuries the great formulation of the Catholic attack on sorcery." And now the figures of

the witch and the heretic merge. The repetitive pattern of the
witch-coven rituals is faced by the repetitive pattern of the witch
trials. When, late in the seventeenth century, after prolonged and
multiplied horror, the belief in witchcraft died out, it was more
from pure exhaustion than because of the light of reason newly
shed upon it. The last English witchcraft trials occur in 1717; the
last Scottish trial in 1722; and finally we hear Tam O'Shanter's
healthy drunken laughter as he watches the still-feared witch
revels "through the Gothic window in the ruins of Kirk-Alloway."

Lines of origin of the witch myth reach back to the Old Testament and the Greek and Roman worlds; yet there is little doubt
that its later European manifestations were rooted in the post-
medieval breakdown of religion. The persecutions in England, for
example, reached their height after Elizabeth. It is when a myth
of this kind seizes the imagination, and affords an outlet for the
passions of a whole society, that dangerous things happen. "Historic and social facts" then cease to be "the envelope in which the
myth lies" and become instead the bases of power on which it
feeds.

At the heart of an "age of reason," look for a counterdevelop-
ment of irrationality. It is interesting to consider the character
and career of John Wesley in this connection. Wesley's life
roughly coincided with the years of the eighteenth century. He
succeeded in channeling the religious "enthusiasm" present in
England since the Reformation, in one form and degree of intensity or another, into a compelling "personal" religious movement: the Methodist Revival. This "great, practical religious manifestation" was considered by Leslie Stephen to be the most
important event of the eighteenth century in England. Methodism
took into account the deprivations, spiritual and material, of the
English lower classes. It gave them an outlet, in the revival meeting, for their emotions; and, if not a ritual, at least a new kind of
permitted license. This, too, was the great age of the English
hymn. Wesley, a practical man and a great organizer, was, on
one side, according to the records, a witch-hunter *manqué*. "A
firm believer in ghosts and apparitions," he was opposed to the
repeal of the witchcraft statutes (1735) and he wrote, when over
eighty, an account of the haunting of his father's Parsonage at

Epworth by a "noisy ghost," or poltergeist, ascribing these peculiar disturbances to witchcraft. He thus sums up, as a transitional figure, many of the floating myths of a transitional age.

"The word *enthusiasm* was anathema to the polite in the eighteenth century." The English upper classes were totally immune to the revivalism of the poor. Yet from the middle of the century through Napoleonic times the class which, in Gibbon and Hume, had thrown up extreme examples of "the skeptic and infidel" was swept into an "enthusiasm" of its own—an interest which became a mania: the passion for "Gothic" and particularly for the "Gothic romances." The "graveyard poets" opened the path for Bishop Hurd's *Letters on Chivalry and Romance* (1762) and Walpole's *Castle of Otranto* (1764). At the end of the century the flood of Gothic novels was in full spate. The preoccupation of these productions with the "trappings" of an outlawed Catholic ritual was marked. The cloister, abbots, monks, nuns, friars, convents, priories, and anchorite's retreat crowded out other wild and gloomy preoccupations, such as bandits, robbers, and spectres. *The Confessor, The Haunted Priory, The Horror of Oakendale Abbey, The Hermit's Cave, The Children of the Abbey*, and the tremendously successful *The Monk*, by Matthew Gregory Lewis; ruins, underground passages, midnight—all these expressed "the triumph of chaos versus order" in the fiction of the period.

The thoroughness with which the Gothic romance—in a time when the feeling against superstition ran high and anti-Papist riots broke loose—canvassed every smallest detail of a former religiously based age, indicates that some life-giving forces had been omitted from "enlightenment." The imagination alone knew what had been lost. From the ruined halls, the broken monastery arches, the toppling and devastated churches, a life-giving breath of hell arose, and the reasonable man turned again and again to his brother, the fallen angel and the proud fiend.

"The liberal ideal," says Croce in his *History of Europe in the Nineteenth Century*, "contains what is essential and intrinsic in every religion: a concept of reality and an ethic that conforms to this concept. It excludes the mythological element, which constitutes only *a secondary differentiation between religion and philosophy.* The concept of reality and the conforming ethics of liberalism are generated . . . by modern thought, dialectical and historical. Nothing more was needed to give them a religious character, since personifications, myths, legends, dogmas, rites, propitiations, expiations, priestly classes, pontifical robes and the like *do not belong to the intrinsic* [italics mine]. . . . But the religion of liberalism showed itself to be essentially religious in its forms and institutions, and, since it was born, and not made, was no cold and deliberate device."

Let us oppose to this rather shallow misconception of the nature of "liberalism" and the modern worthlessness of the myth, a passage by Jung (*Psychology and Religion,* 1938):

In the last two thousand years we find the Christian Church assuming a mediating and protective function between "supernatural" influences, and man. Protestantism, having pulled away many a wall that had been carefully erected by the Church, began immediately to experience the disintegrating and schismatic effect of individual revelation. . . . As soon as the dogmatic fence was broken down and as soon as ritual lost its efficiency, man was confronted with an inner experience, without the protection and guidance of a dogma and a ritual which are the unparalleled quintessence of Christian as well as of pagan religious experience. . . .

"The hero as implicated in mythical situations is he who finds a solution: an upshot, an issue, fortunate or unfortunate. For the individual suffers above all from not being able to get out from the conflict of which he is the prey." The role of active hero comes to a point of stasis in Hamlet. The chosen breaker of the taboo is now baffled by the taboo. Beyond Hamlet, Faust begins a new role, a role which, in the modern "liberal" world, has become usual and "archetypal." Faust acts; but he must be split in order to act. "In Faust the crisis of modern thought is very clearly reflected," says Croce (with more insight), "when, having shaken off traditional beliefs, it began to perceive the emptiness of the rationalistic philosophy which had taken their place. . . . Two souls dwell in Faust, and the one wishes to separate itself from the other. His condition is the condition of a sick man."

A refinement of this splitting of the hero's "soul" occurs when the opposing forces begin a grim action of flight on the part of one, and pursuit on the part of the other. This theme is as old as the myth of Orestes. But from the beginning of the nineteenth century to our own day, this pattern begins to absorb other myths in great variety. And as the modern myth becomes less "repulsive" in detail, it becomes increasingly ambiguous, and weighted with both guilt and fear. Caleb Williams, in Godwin's cautionary tale, is *pursued by the murderer*. The shift in roles between Jean Valjean and Javert (who finally is pursuer or pursued; who at last is hero or hunted?) fixes a symptomatic situation from which the modern mind does not seem able to escape.

Society has been seen ostensibly to move in one direction toward certain "ideals" and goals, when actually it was unconsciously being drawn in a totally opposite direction. The birth of a new myth lets free new springs of energy. "The passions are good": this was the truth, spoken in "the language of Satan," that the nineteenth century, through the ferment of the Romantic Movement, was finally forced to learn. For the myth is never completely contemporaneous. As we have seen, it can regress, in order to gather up suppressed material needed for new life. It is also supremely capable of shooting ahead. It may point toward the region wherein some enlargement of the human consciousness is about to occur. Even the "Gothic" exploration of the "nightside of Nature" and the Romantic emphasis upon an (at the time) outmoded demonic, fatal, "insatiable" hero pointed inexorably to unconscious complexities and needs which only a later century was equipped to face, and find analytical means to explain and resolve.

It is now mainly to literature and art that we must look for clues to the unconscious processes. Does our need for "the numinous"—"the fearful, the uncanny, the dauntingly 'other' "—become fixed, and, as it were, trapped, in our crime novels and "murder" stories? "It is curious," says a contemporary observer, "how the great Victorian writers moved instinctively toward a tale of scandal and spiritual corruption. . . . The preoccupation grows stronger as the great bourgeois period becomes self-confident." Compared with the richness, fullness, and solidity of the Romantic and the Victorian imaginative productions, we are currently presented with dryness, thinness, fixity, and attenuation. Where is the valuable and revivifying darkness in the glaring seashores, the empty horizons of Chirico, Dali, and the Surrealists? Nature is dead; we are pushed to an extreme verge of the physical and spiritual world, our only companions a litter of half-human furniture, of wrecked bare forms, of amorphous abstractions.

By attending with intense and detached interest to what the imagination (at all levels) presents to us, we may hope to catch at times a hint concerning the myth that is forming at the heart of our world. The hero, for example, reaches crucial modern expression in Kafka. *The Castle* and *The Trial* show to us a nearly unbearable extreme of powerlessness in the face of the unknown. Here everything "means something"; we share the obsessive suspicions of the insane; everything whispers, cunningly cajoles, and promises hollowly; accuses and waits. In "crime novels" we are continually confronted with the "victim." Are we building up a symbolical kind of *printed* bloodless shedding of blood (a sacrifice being defined as "the giving of life to promote and preserve life, to establish union between the individual and the unseen forces that surround him")? What quiver of meaning, present and future, stirs in the hunting and "detecting" malice, in the fugitive's panic and guile with which our "popular" (and unpopular) literature is saturated?

Dread, in literature, has now shifted from the outer to the inner scene. Terrible events now take place in the most usual surroundings to the most ordinary people. Here is the suppressed personality as antagonist (in Conan Doyle, John Buchan, and countless others). And from time to time we see the myth, formed and whole, in a piece of fiction whose surface and conscious intention is rational or didactic: a birth-myth in a fantasy concerned with orthodox religion; the "father-found-and-murdered-underground," in a novel on a "social theme." And in Graham Greene we encounter the hero conscious of inner guilt, who draws to himself the outer guilty situations as a magnet draws iron.

Instinctively, "liberal" man has built around himself half-formed ritual, and occasions for vicarious expiations and propitiations. He has turned toward healing mystery and "the shudder."

> Das Schaudern ist der Menschheit bester Teil.
> Wie auch die Welt ihm das Gefühl verteuere,
> Ergriffen fühlt er tief das Ungeheuere.

It is Goethe who speaks these words, to explain the possible virtue inherent in our modern compulsive patterns of panic, terror, and flight.

THE GODS CONTINUE TO ARRIVE (1960)

The new and impressively large *Larousse Encyclopedia of Mythology* devotes nearly half of its five hundred pages to descriptions of the primitive rituals and beliefs of historic, prehistoric, and contemporary mankind. This emphasis on non-classical material reflects the strong modern interest in the forms and meanings of primitive religions, which has been growing in breadth and intensity since the beginning of this century. Nietzsche was many years ahead of his time when, in his first book, *The Birth of Tragedy* (1871), he separated the Dionysiac element from the Apollonian, thereby rescuing the pagan "classic" gods from "the noble simplicity and calm grandeur" assigned to them by Winckelmann and Goethe. Today, after a half-century of research by archeologists, ethnologists, anthropologists, students of comparative religion, and medical psychologists, not only has nearly every extant primitive culture been examined and interpreted but the gods of classical antiquity have undergone a return to primitive origins. And recently, with the discovery of the cave paintings of France and Spain, our knowledge of the primitive has been carried back to neolithic and even paleolithic thresholds.

The remarkable illustrations, chiefly photographs, are the most valuable feature of this impressive volume. The text, although it ranges widely, does not dig very deep, and there are signs here and there that certain of the more shocking features of ancient myths (notably homosexuality and incest) have been played down, if not actually suppressed, in accordance with the taste of a middle-class audience. And since the enormous accumulation of material is presented in a series of long articles by various hands and not divided under subject headings, the term "encyclopedia" is somewhat misused. The more scholarly reader will find flaws in the index. But the illustrations make up for a good many of these faults; they sweep from the sculpture of Assyria and ancient Persia to the artifacts of Oceania, from Mesopotamia to North, South, and Central America, from Egypt,

Greece, and Rome to the Negro Africa of today. What would be the response, we may well ask, of certain nineteenth-century philosophers, poets, and cultural historians to the more terrifying of these representations of the gods, these magical ceremonial objects and fetishes, these demonic masks? What would Matthew Arnold (who wrote of Persian and Teutonic heroes as well as of classical ones) make of the god Quetzalcoatl, in black stone, in the form of a plumed serpent? Or Swinburne, who was constantly calling upon the pagan gods, of the Hindu goddess Kali, hung with human skulls? Would not Herder and Goethe be appalled by the great-winged painted wooden Indian totem from Vancouver Island, and Tennyson (whose "Tithonus" and "Ulysses" dealt so movingly with classical themes) unnerved by the carved prow of a pirogue from the Solomons that glares out at the sea with the black pupils of its pearl-shell eyes? Nietzsche might have accepted them all, but there is no doubt that Thomas Bulfinch (1796–1867), the great Boston architect's son, who in 1855 published *The Age of Fable; or, Beauties of Mythology*, would, if presented with the Larousse compilation, be seriously shaken. It is unfair to discredit Bulfinch—he produced a charming and sound little book, which has become a minor classic— but certainly the shift in attitude toward mythology between his time and ours is touchingly apparent in his dedication of his work to Henry Wadsworth Longfellow: to "the poet alike of the many and of the few, this attempt to popularize mythology, and extend the enjoyment of elegant literature, is respectfully inscribed."

Speculation about the meaning and relevance of myths and detailed interpretations of mythical content have gone on since the appearance, in 1890, of Sir James Frazer's monumental study in comparative religion, *The Golden Bough*, which was followed by Jung's *Wandlungen und Symbole der Libido* (1912) and Freud's *Totem und Tabu* (1913). A group of British classicists who soon succeeded Frazer—F. M. Cornford, the Misses J. E. Harrison and Jessie L. Weston—applied many of his findings to their studies of Greek and medieval legend. Robert Graves, more recently, has produced, in *The Greek Myths*, a formidable piece of historical research. Mr. Graves is opposed to the theory of a collective unconscious, which Jung and Jung's followers support; he holds fast to the theory of an original and basic matriarchy existing in pre-history, and furnishes a considerable weight of evidence to prove the existence, and persistence, of the power of the Great Mother and of the vegetation gods throughout history. Now, in a rather summary introduction to the *Encyclopedia,* Mr. Graves defines mythology as "the study of whatever religious or heroic legends are so foreign to a student's experience that he cannot believe them to be true [a fact that accounts for] the omission from standard European mythologies, such as this, of all Biblical narratives . . . and of all hagiological legends." We do not get any view, therefore, of Judaism (the original monotheism) or of the Christianity that supplanted and (sometimes imperfectly) absorbed the pagan cults of Europe after Constantine. Certain other living religions are described, however—the Shintoism of Japan, the Taoism of China, and the Buddhism of India and China. There is no mention of Zen.

The analytical psychologists of our day, particularly the students of Jung, ascribe many of modern man's psychic ills and anxieties, in the words of Heinrich Zimmer, to his loss of contact with "the spiritual power . . . symbolized as gods or demons, or as images and holy places . . . The gain which the rejecting of this magic conditioning has brought to modern man, the increase in our rationally directed power over the material forces of the earth is paid for by the loss of control over the forces of the soul. The man of today is helpless before the magic of his invisible psyche." This *Encyclopedia,* although rather heavily written and undramatically organized—we are often given lists of this or that pantheon of gods, goddesses, demigods, and heroes, without any surrounding interpretive insights—is yet an amazing record of primitive man's imaginative power and of the resourcefulness with which he sought to deal with "the crises of life, death, unhappy love, and unsatisfied hate," using magic ritual as a no less (to him) powerful weapon than his ax and spear. In the East and the West alike, the themes of ordeal and of initiation, of quest, of metamorphosis and regeneration are repeated. Mythologies and cosmologies, over the centuries, become more and more complicated, for they come to record, as Graves points out, not only imaginary but actual events—conquests, inventions, and heroic feats—and foreign deities are taken over

from time to time. Their late manifestations are extremely complex—demigods and *genii loci* proliferate; the Hindu pantheon,
in luxuriant fantasy, goes to such lengths of multiplicity that any
attempts to codify it presents (for a European) an impossible
task. The Graeco-Roman mythology, as it has been handed down
to us, also presents complications. In Celtic and Teutonic legend,
as Graves points out, the scene is to some extent simplified, and
the myth builds up its hieroglyphic record of mankind's fear and
awe before the untamable forces of the universe in a more open
way.

Man's efforts to introduce some order into his precarious
existence and to give it conceptual framework; his success and
failure in bringing his brief existence into some accord with the
ineluctable facts of birth and death; his spirit's yearning after
immortality—all these acts and impulses find their symbols
within a magical structure. For primitive man cannot work
without the magic that propitiates and controverts the gods. And
now the heroes appear. They stand close to the gods, and share
their nature, but are recognizably human. They overcome obstacles by strength or cunning and are able to snatch from the
jealous and unpredictable deities that which they consider to
be rightfully man's. Beginning with Herakles, who freed Prometheus from his terrible bondage, the history of heroes is in
part the history of some actual human being's seemingly
impossible accomplishment. Hunting magic, as man's skill
extends to tools as well as to weapons, gives way to agricultural
magic. Certain animals are domesticated, and others put into
harness (the invention of the bit is praised by later poets, along
with that of the oar). The land comes to be watered and planted
to crops; grain and the vine flourish (protected by their
proper gods). Cloth is woven on the intricate loom; ore is
smelted. The silent air begins to fill with the music of the drum,
the harp, the lyre, and the flute. The "literate cities" begin to
rise. The gods help and hinder, but Nature begins to calm
down, under man's hand. Meanwhile, the gods multiply, and
their attributes shift and merge, or split off, as man's situation and his ideas of good and evil become more elaborate
and more profound. In late, highly civilized cultures (such
as the Hellenistic), the gods become frivolous in the extreme.

But under their new superficiality the primitive originals continue to exist—the gods of the sun, the sea, and the underworld, the goddesses of the harvest and of the hearth, the vegetation gods, and the gods of the crafts and of the arts. And behind them all looms the Great Mother—Ishtar, Isis, Kali, the Diana of Ephesus—whose sign is the moon. The primordial themes remain and are repeated—of loss, search, and restitution (Isis-Osiris, Demeter-Persephone), of the descent of the hero into the region of death (Gilgamesh, Herakles, Theseus, and Orpheus), of rebirth and regeneration (Tammuz-Adonis). The lost is found; the dead seed springs up again; the moon returns, after its three days of darkness.

Malinowski has spoken of "the ever-nascent myth [that] unchains the powers of the past and casts them into the future," and we have seen in our day the dangers attendant upon the willed use of a false and fabricated mythology when employed solely for ends of power. "It is not true," said Nietzsche, "that there is some hidden thought or idea at the bottom of the myth, as some in a period of civilization that has become artificial have put it, but the myth itself is a kind of style of thinking. It imparts an idea of the universe, and does it in a sequence of events, actions, and sufferings." "Myth is the secular dream of the race," according to Freud and his followers. For Jung, myth stands as a source of those archetypes of the collective unconscious which, in his view, constantly renew themselves "in all peoples in all times in an identical and analogous manner and arise just as spontaneously . . . from the unconscious of modern man."

Throughout the Christian centuries, the gods have gone through more metamorphoses than Ovid dreamed of. Transformed into demons (or mere men in disguise) by the early Church, they did not entirely disappear during the Middle Ages but survived as spirits of place, as hobgoblins and figures in fairy tales. The Renaissance brought them back in full panoply. And today, in spite of our thorough interest in the primitive, the classical pantheon of the Greek and Roman deities still has its strong attraction, and their legends, along with the classic situations of the Greek dramatists, appear again and again in modern literature. We still continue to find poignance in the

Homeric legends, in the story of the House of Atreus, in Theban Oedipus and Antigone—as though, in the Bronze Age, certain crucial human situations had been tragically worked out once and for all. The present *Encyclopedia* has an unexpected value in that it is a source book, now that classical education is dying or dead, for an astonishing array (as one finds if one begins to list them) of contemporary works in music, the theatre, poetry, the ballet, and literature at large that stem from a classical base. The Diaghilev Ballet produced, in its early years, not only Stravinsky's "Sacre du Printemps" (a modern theatrical and symphonic enactment of a primitive rite) but Ravel's "Daphnis et Chloé," Debussy's "L'Après-Midi d'un Faune," and the Chopin "Les Sylphides." (Stravinsky went on to compose "Oedipus Rex," "Apollon Musagète," and "Perséphone.") In modern opera we find Richard Strauss's *Ariadne auf Naxos, Elektra,* and *Die Aegyptische Helena,* as well as Milhaud's *Les Malheurs d'Orphée* and Carl Orff's *Antigonae.* The French theatre continues to be rich in classically derived plays: Cocteau's *La Machine infernale* (the Oedipus story) and *Orphée;* Giraudoux's *Amphitryon 38, La Guerre de Troie n'aura pas lieu,* and *Electre* (with Anouilh working close in his steps with *Eurydice, Antigone,* and *Médée*). Gide returned again and again to classical legend, from his early *Le Prométhée mal enchaîné* and *Corydon* to the later *Oedipe* (1932) and *Thésée* (1946). Classical reference in Valéry runs through his poetry as a whole, and supplies the framework for a good deal of his prose. Colette retells in modern dress the tale of Daphnis and Chloë in *Le Blé en herbe.*

In English, the modern account is again rich in classically derived themes. Housman, a classicist by profession, translates Horace's "Diffugere nives" ode (with its lovely references to Hippolytus, Theseus, and Pirithoüs; Diana and the Nymphs); Yeats, after having revived Celtic mythology in his early poems, in his middle and late periods turns toward a full use of Greek myth. (His Leda poem is one of his finest.) Pound's knowledge of the classical tradition shows up in his early lyrics and is one basis for his *Cantos.* Eliot, in *The Waste Land,* made the first dramatic and poetic use in our century of ancient nature rituals transposed into medieval legend, and his later plays are constructed along the lines of Greek drama—the Alcestis theme in

The Cocktail Party and the Orestes theme in *The Family Reunion*. And in Joyce's *Ulysses* we find a Homeric epic used as the underlying design for what is perhaps the greatest novel of our time.

"The myth transforms to the age." The gods continue to arrive.

PABLO NERUDA

(1969)

We are not likely to get, in English, a more detailed, subtle, and sympathetic analysis of the complicated and enigmatic poet Pablo Neruda than the one we come upon in the recent bilingual edition of the *Selected Poems*, edited and translated by Ben Belitt, with an introduction by Luis Monguió. In a deeply perceptive analysis of Neruda's career and achievement, Monguió, a professor of Spanish at Berkeley, looks beneath the influences the poet absorbed from the Europe of his time—"modernism, surrealism, communism"—to uncover Neruda's Indian heritage, absorbed in childhood and youth from the frontiersman's world of the Chilean backwoods. And Belitt, a professor of English literature at Bennington, a translator of Lorca, and a poet in his own right, has done a remarkably able job of editing (cutting down an enormous *œuvre* to "a profile of sixty poems"), interpretation, and putting into English.

The selection covers the period from 1925 through 1959, thus omitting the romantic and formal poems on which Neruda's first reputation was based. After he had begun "Residence on Earth" (in 1925), the Surrealist influence took hold. But it is apparent that the young South American inheritor of this style was more violent and daring than his masters. Neruda eliminates the Surrealists' boring lists and repetitions, neurotic verbal games, and infuriatingly irrational *non sequiturs*. He seizes directly upon reality in sharpest detail, and forces his apprehensions through by means of conflict and of rhythmic compulsion—"panting and strenuous rhythms." Rational impulse is almost wholly lacking. Neruda does not order or contrast events, in the manner of Brecht, and his disinterest in art and artifacts is very nearly total. At his worst he is coldly threatening, but even his most machine-made pieces of propaganda (which Belitt does not include but does not fail to mention) have the virtues of close and accurate reporting and a tone of sincere *engagement*. The finest of these poems deserve the care Belitt has expended upon them; they circle round from the pole of man's politics to the pole of man's fate.

ST.-JOHN PERSE
(1938)

American readers may now examine T. S. Eliot's translation of St.-J. Perse's *Anabase,* the poem which, both before and since its first apperance in England in 1930, has influenced many poets, including Eliot himself. The present edition, like the earlier, presents the French text opposite Eliot's version and is introduced by the original preface, wherein Eliot makes some attempt to clear up the poem's impenetrability. Because poetry, since 1930, has tended to become more impenetrable rather than less, and because we are now familiar with several watered versions, by American and British imitators, of this particular poem, we are more free than Mr. Eliot once supposed we could be to appreciate the power of the original work and to enter into enthusiasm about it.

Anabasis, as it is called in this translation, deals with the beauty and terror of the earth, and with the beauty and brutality of the civilizations man imposes upon it. It deals as well with what lies beneath and extends beyond man's ingenious arts and plans: his spiritual journey, begun and continuing in isolation, and at last faced with that symbol of further mystery, the sea. Perse's poem is filled with that special Asian exoticism of which our time approves. The sentiment projected onto the East by the nineteenth century (which populated the desert with Byronic heroes and multiplied, in copperplate vignettes, gazelle-eyed maidens diaphanously swathed, under palms) has now been supplanted by something quite different. It is Eastern harshness, barrenness, Eastern cruelty and strength that appeal to heightened and disabused modern taste. *Anabasis* encloses these qualities, as *Seven Pillars of Wisdom* enclosed them. Effects of violence, severe and barbaric splendor, and terrible solitude are here compacted into sentences which seem dislocated by the intensity of the material they are made to bear. St.-J. Perse is the pseudonym of M. Alexis Saint-Léger, an ambassador of France, who as a diplomat spent many years at the French Embassy in Peking and as an explorer has made journeys into the Gobi Desert. It is the work of a many-sided personality. The spiritual and the actual, bathed in hard, open light of arid lands, are combined to produce the poem's special atmosphere.

The original French often rises into sonority and ecstasy (never purely rhetorical) that are sometimes flattened and deadened by Eliot. For example, "To the scale of our hearts was such vacancy completed!" certainly does not adequately render the feeling of "*A la mesure de nos cœurs fut tant d'absence consommée!*" But an occasional stiffness of phrase is better than the complete softening the poem has been subjected to in the hands of other manipulators. *Anabasis* is difficult, like all excellent things. But it repays, to put it materialistically, careful examination. For it is easy to forget, at present, things undertaken in "the darkness of the spirit," in a world "given over to explanations."

KATHERINE ANNE
PORTER
(1930)

Katherine Anne Porter's stories, here collected for the first time, have appeared over a period of years in *Transition, The American Caravan,* and in commercial magazines appreciative of distinguished writing. In each of the five stories in the present book, Miss Porter works with that dangerous stuff, unusual material. Two stories have a Mexican locale. Two contain passages which describe lapses into the subconscious and the dream. "Magic" briefly explores the survival of frayed but savage superstition. "Rope" follows the rise and fall of an hysterical mood, and "He" sets against simple human devotion an idiot's non-human power and suffering.

It is to Miss Porter's high credit that, having fixed upon the exceptional background and event, she has not yielded, in her treatment of them, to queerness and forced originality of form. With the exception of "Magic" (which I should prefer to think of as an experiment, since its effect is false, for reasons only too easily defined—the use of the fustian maid-to-mistress monologue, for one), the stories do not lean upon the doubtful prop of manner for its own sake. Miss Porter has a range of effects, but each comes through in its place, and only at the demand of her material. She rejects the exclamatory tricks that wind up style to a spurious intensity, and trusts, for the most part, to straightforward writing, to patience in detail, and to a thorough imaginative grasp on cause and character. She has "knowledge about reality," and has chosen the most exacting means to carry her knowledge into form.

The fact, and the intuition or logic about the fact, are severe coordinates in fiction. In the short story they must cross with hairline precision. However far the story may range, the fact and its essence must direct its course and stand as proof to the whole. The truth alone secures form and tone; other means distort the story to no good end and leave within the reader's mind an impression far worse than that produced by mere banality. Joyce's "Ivy Day in the Committee Room" depends wholly upon the truth of the fact; Chekhov's greatest stories, say "The Duel" and "Lights," have command of reasons in the first place, of emotion, taste, and style secondarily. The firm and delicate writing in Miss Porter's "Flowering Judas," a story startling in its complexity, were it not based on recognizable fact, would be to no purpose. As it is, its excellence rises directly from the probity of the conception. It is as impossible to question the characters of the fanatical girl and the self-loving man—the "good revolutionist," who, softened to a state beyond principle, is fit only for a career—as it is to find a flaw or lapse in the style that runs clear and subtle, from the story's casual beginning to the spectre of life and death at the end. "Rope," after "Flowering Judas," is perhaps the most remarkable story in the book. It makes no claim; its integration becomes apparent only when the reader tries to recount it to himself in any other form than its own. The mood is put together so accurately that its elements cannot be recombined.

"Maria Concepcion" does not entirely come up to Miss Porter's standard. A slight flavor of details brought in for their own sake mars its intensity, and one does not entirely trust Maria's simplicity of motive. For the most part, however, the stories in *Flowering Judas* can claim kinship with the order of writing wherein nothing is fortuitous, where all details grow from the matter in hand simply and in order. Miss Porter should demand much work of her talent. There is nothing quite like it, and very little that approaches its strength in contemporary writing.

EZRA POUND

GUIDE TO KULCHUR (*1939*)

The English edition of this volume is called *Guide to Kulchur*.
Because this title so perfectly sets the tone of the book, it is odd
that the American edition is called merely *Culture*. Certainly
Pound is the last person to wish a cold, unironic title set at the
head of his irreverent remarks. The extreme oddness of these
essays, to the reader inexperienced in Pound, may automatically
invalidate many of his conclusions, some of which are valuable.
It would be a good thing, therefore, if the new title at the outset
were canceled and the old title written in.

Pound's ideal reader is a person who has experienced real
discomfort on being shut up, in a railway train, lecture hall, or
concert room, with well-modulated voices expressing careful,
well-bred opinions on the subject of the arts. Such a reader will
remember his own impulse to break into argot and obscenity.
This is exactly what Pound has done here, for 349 pages. He
has published in the last ten years a number of diatribes against
the canned reverence accorded literature. He now goes for
reverences pertaining to the whole field of culture, including
mathematics, philosophy, painting, and music. He is against
the pious respect which "stiffens around mankind's achievements

in all fields—the religion of culture well adapted to the emotional
needs of polite societies." He is all for breaking up, throwing out,
biting the thumb at, pulling the beards of, disinterring, fresh-
ening, "making new." He refuses to attack moldy but sacred
academic rigmaroles from a distance. A critic like Roger Fry,
from whom Pound has learned much, is content to pin down the
pretensions of Philistines, culture addicts, and avant-garde snobs
with well-bred wit. Pound walks into the field armed with stink
bombs. He fronts the "specialists," running to seed in their
limited circles, with his own eclecticism, which makes free of
many. He is at times shallow, misinformed, inaccurate, but he
smashes his way through the fences and pulls down the walls
between archives.

Pound is a provincial American who, after receiving degrees
from two provincial American universities, went to Europe and
never came back. He combines in himself at present two strongly
marked and—one would suppose—completely irreconcilable
types: the brilliant American village atheist, and the European
dilettante to whom "novelty is a positive virtue." At the beginning
of his career, sick to death of the hangovers from the English
nineteenth-century critical and artistic values then infecting
American poetry, he determined to exhume poetry in general
from the grave into which scholars and moralists had lowered it.
He was after poetry in all languages, poetry of all ages. The
preface to *The Spirit of Romance* (1910), "a book which never
had a public," announced this ambition. Recently he has added
a passionate belief in the theories of Major Douglas to his belief
in pure poetic values. He is now a soldier of an Economic Faith
Militant, as well as a fighting aesthete. His unexpected jumps
between these poles of enthusiasm, his uncontrolled and frequently hysterical attempts to link the two passions together,
his tub-thumping for Mussolini's planned economy make it a
simple task to cull ridiculous and half-baked statements from
his text. Certainly Pound has few disciples at present, and every
critical observer has had a period of disliking his methods. The
only way to be fair to a man who, in spite of all his faults, has
spent his life cutting away dead wood in the sacred grove is to
read *Guide to Kulchur* with an eye alert for its virtues rather
than its defects.

"Great literature," Pound has said, "is simply language charged with meaning to the utmost possible degree." One of the sternest of Pound's English critics has admitted this statement to be "a very good corrective to the academic and general habit of discussing literature in terms of Hamlet's and Lamb's personalities, Milton's universe, Johnson's conversation . . . and Othello's or Shelley's private life." In contrast to academic failure to see, or acknowledge, the human vigor at the center of human art and thought, here are some sentences from Pound:

In my student days no senior had the faintest inkling of Dante's interest, Shakespeare's interest in living. . . . The history of culture is the history of ideas going into action. . . . You can write history by tracing ideas, exposing the growth of a concept. You can also isolate the quality or direction of a given time's sensibility. That means the history of an art. . . . Properly, we shd. read for power. Man reading shd. be man intensely alive. The book shd. be a ball of light in one's hand . . . I suspect that the error in educational systems has been the cutting off of learning from appetite. . . . How to see works of art? Think what the creator must have known and felt before he got around to creating them. . . .

Snap judgments, wrong insistence, and, although this is rare, lack of ordinary common sense lie scattered about on these pages. On the other hand, the book is almost completely free from *idées reçues*—except, of course, economic ones. What is lacking is the increasing mellowness and the real, as opposed to hysterical, breaking through into new thought one expects, not entirely sentimentally, from a seasoned artist of fifty. Pound's original substance has not been tough enough to go forward, in spite of and through struggle, into great originality. His taste for the obscure and the esoteric has ultimately weakened his gifts. He likes to fiddle around; to translate Latin translations of Chinese ideograms into English; to put a phrase of Aristotle's, in the original, under a Chinese character. (But it must be remembered that the only interesting and profound discussion of Chinese ideograms in English comes from Fenollosa, through Pound.)

All sorts of memories of Pound's real service in clearing up the aesthetic-moral muddles of the last thirty years must be referred to while one reads this book. And two sentences might be added to its title:

To express anything at all is a crime with the philistine; to express anything vital is a crime with culture. (Roger Fry)

I am trying to use not an inch rule but a balance. (Ezra Pound)

CANTOS LII–LXXI (1940)

Ten years ago it was the custom for avant-garde critics to call those people who were puzzled by Ezra Pound's *Cantos* imbeciles. Such people then were beneath both explanation and contempt. Now it is different. Pound's publishers have gone to the trouble, as they publish his new volume, *Cantos LII–LXXI,* to provide a neat little explanatory brochure, which slips into a neat pocket pasted on the inside back cover of the book. This brochure, entitled "Notes on Ezra Pound's Cantos: Structure and Metric," contains two well and clearly written essays, one on Pound's matter and one on his manner. A photograph of Pound, making him look even more scowling than he frequently sounds, embellishes its cover.

Pound's moral ideas are based, we are told, on the discipline of Confucius; his economic ideas, on those of "certain of the Canonist writers on economics," "certain of the economic theories of the corporate state," Major Douglas, and the obscurer economist Silvio Gesell. Pound believes that everything in the modern mess could be fixed up if "the democracies" would "finance their war and defence with statal economy"—this in spite of the fact that Pound is against war. Pound is no Fascist at heart, we are told, although he likes to live in Italy; and the Chinese have taught him the use of "extreme ellipsis." Also, the *Cantos* actually are not based on the fugue form but may have been strongly influenced by the structure of Dante's *Commedia.* Pound has already given us an "Inferno" in the early *Cantos;* in the present "American Colonial and Chinese cantos," we are in the midst of his "Purgatorio." At any moment, as his apologist puts it, Pound may "plunge into the Empyrean." On the metrical side, we are assured, Pound is breaking up the iambic metres, usual and often monotonous in English poetry, with trochees and spondees.

After Pound's long and rather insolent cultivation of opacity and ambiguity, it would be easy to become hilarious at all this blueprinting. And it would be easy to poke fun at Pound himself, since he seems to be almost totally without humor. But one must realize that he is many ways a great figure. He did an extraordinary job thirty years ago of bringing life to English verse, and his influence has not yet petered out. He has written beautiful poetry. That he now sounds less like a poet than like a case history is tragic rather than comic. Faced with these new *Cantos*, one's warmest charity is certainly called into play. The dullness and brutishness of the Ming and the Manchu rulers, described in the first section, are equalled only by the fustiness and mustiness of John Adams' notations on life and business conditions with which Pound deals in the second. We are given, in this latter part, not "the idea and ideal of democracy as it was conceived in the mind of one of the founding fathers," which the publishers rather sentimentally promise us, but the atmosphere of American Colonial laundry bills and old promissory notes. Pound's early ability to open up gaps in his narration, through which we saw tranquil sea- and landscapes and lovely, cool forms of antique beauty, has totally disappeared. The only asides are scatological ones, of an extremely childish and petulant kind, and a few yelps of pure race hatred. As for the metrics, they often are those of prose (which is a mixture of iambs, trochees, and spondees).

Perhaps this is Purgatory. If so, we can only hope it is to be brief. For if Pound plans to make "plunges" into Paradise, he must be able to put aside his hatred, as Dante managed to do. If one hates anything too long, one not only begins to resemble what is hated but one forgets, one becomes incapable even of imagining any longer, what it is that one could love. What Pound would do in a paradise unencumbered by old bills of lading and growls about usury, it is becoming difficult to think. Moral indignation is one thing; *l'amor*, which Dante said moved the sun and other stars, is something even more difficult.

The ideograms occurring here and there in the text are certainly beautiful, and it is a great pleasure just to look at them.

THE PISAN CANTOS (1948)

Official justice has now dealt with Ezra Pound, and this autumn New Directions has again taken up the task of publishing his works. Two volumes announce the beginning of this program: *The Pisan Cantos,* twenty poems written by Pound while he was a prisoner in the Italian city awaiting trial as a traitor, and *The Cantos,* which includes not only the Pisan section but all of his "epic" (in Pound's view, any poem that contains history is an epic) that he has written to date. The initial sixteen cantos first appeared in book form in 1925, when Pound's reputation was at its height. At the start, this "epic" exhibited in full the range of Pound's genius. It is a late work, begun when he was nearly forty and firmly in command of his difficult style. T. S. Eliot's *The Waste Land* (1922), dedicated to Pound, had given the modern world its first major poem in English. It was time for Pound to commence gathering together the fruits of his already long career: his scholarship in medieval Romantic literature (chiefly the literature of Provence), and his interest in the culture of the Italian and French Renaissance, in Greek literature from Homer to Callimachus, and in Chinese poetry and ideogram. His episodic and disjunct style suggested cinema technique, or so critics have decided, for it involved the flashback, breaking up the sequence of time and of place. Each item made sense but had no apparent connection with any other. And from the first Pound employed his most obvious trick: the use of classical tags, often in languages, such as Greek and Chinese, that need transliteration, or in dead tongues, such as *langue d'oc.* As we look back with time's perspective, we realize that his various devices, if often used legitimately, were frequently the result of his mystifying, or sorcerer, side. The not clearly understood creates wonderment and awe, but bafflement and irritation as well. There is something hypnotizing, even for the initiate, in being confronted with a language one can barely pronounce, and the uninitiate are likely to be bowled over by words as simple as "to agathon" when they come at them in large black Greek capitals.

But it was the Chinese ideogram which really offered Pound the
chance to become a master magician. The ideogram is lovely
beyond belief, yet it thwarts almost any attack made upon it by
non-Chinese reason. There it is; one is impressed; the spell takes
hold, and Pound has the reader in his mage's power. These
Poundian procedures had their good aspect, however. The poet
was breaking down prejudice against forgotten or neglected
cultures. He was striking across the lines of specialist scholars,
so strict and so snobbish in our day. He was presenting the past
as though it were all simultaneous and were still going on; he
was making the point that in art this synchronization and timelessness actually exist.

Pound's streak of charlatanry, in *The Cantos* as a whole, was
so interwoven with valuable insight that it was fairly negligible.
What became really annoying was his growing tendency toward
obsession. The obsessed always lack that final ingredient of
greatness, humility. They are also invariably bad-tempered and
vituperative. They hammer and they scold. Finally they stop
making sense, and end up ranting in an exasperated gibberish.
Pound never reached the gibberish stage, but at his worst he
presented a picture of a fanatic who must always be in the right,
who cannot turn a hairsbreadth from the small and concrete
toward the large generality, who bores by quoting from documentation, and who sets up a pattern that gradually hardens,
until we get nothing but deadly repetition. In the cantos written
just before the war, Pound seemed to have lost his ability to
control his manias, and his increasingly vulgar presentation of
them often made him sound less like a lover of the highest
cultures and more like a rude inheritor of none. But he could,
at his best, revive, in lines of the most exquisite weight and the
purest flow, the classic world, the crystal beginnings of men and
gods.

Pound's imprisonment in Pisa seems to have brought him back
to art and to life. *The Pisan Cantos* shows a new sense of proportion. He begins to feel pity and gratitude, and he begins to
smile wryly, even at himself. I cannot think of any other record
by an artist or a man of letters, in or out of prison, so filled with
a combination of sharp day-to-day observation, erudition, and
humorous insight. The diatribes against usury (Pound's King

Charles's head) occur, but they are now a minor theme. The gibes at enemies continue, but they are now mixed with the memories of friends—and what great and brilliant friends! And Pound cannot give enough gratitude to the Negro soldier who secretly made him a desk out of a packing box, to get him "offen th' ground" (he was living in a tent). He speaks with tenderness of a visiting lizard, and he jots down reminiscences of his art and life, beginning with the moment when, as a young poet, he thought of dumping the entire edition of his first book into a Venetian canal. All this may help us to understand the stresses that beset this American poet, whose art time will in the end surely honor, and without whose influence and energy we should not have modern poetry in English as we know it today.

SECTION: ROCK-DRILL 85–95
DE LOS CANTARES (1955)

Section: Rock-Drill 85–95 de Los Cantares is the title Ezra Pound, now in his seventieth year, has given to a group of eleven new *Cantos,* the first to appear in book form since *The Pisan Cantos,* of 1948. New Directions has printed the text with meticulous care, and certainly care was necessary because of the presence not only of many Chinese ideograms and a great scattering of Greek but of words, phrases, and sentences from almost every living European language, as well as from one or two dead ones. *The Cantos,* Pound long ago remarked, are "a poem containing history." Notoriously, he has never been content to present history cold; he has made his hot and frequently obsessive insistences perfectly clear as the work has progressed over the years. Now "the truth must be hammered home by reiteration, with the insistence of a rock drill." (I quote from the book's jacket.) If this motive had been developed to its full implications, the present section would have been unreadable. Fortunately, it has been only partly carried through. Pound, even in his later years and in his continuing tragic situation, has kept one part of his work free from the rigidity of dogma; the fluidity of poetry keeps breaking into the fixed design.

The new *Cantos* show some surface changes. They are shorter and more compressed, and a visual dimension has been added to mere words-in-print not only by the now familiar ideograms but also by a few Egyptian hieroglyphs, a stave of medieval musical notation, and even, on one occasion, the signs of the four playing-card suits—heart, diamond, club, and spade. These symbols often serve as a sort of shock and refreshment to the eye rather than as an aid to meaning, for although the Chinese written characters are frequently transliterated, we are given, almost always, their sound and not their sense. Because of this new concision of language, however, which amounts to a verbal shorthand, the shifts between Pound's themes are at least quite easy to follow.

These themes tend to overlap, but we can separate out three major ones. First, there is the repeated statement of large principles of sound human law and effective human action; second, the celebration of art and life at its purest and rarest (always in examples taken from a real or legendary past); and third, the theme—if it can be called such—of small, idiosyncratic obsession (the evils of usury and debased currency). This third one is peppered, as always, with Pound's malice and bad temper. These three areas of the poem dissolve into one another as do patterns in a natural element, like water or cloud, instead of proceeding in straight lines according to logical degrees of argument. The first theme opens the new work, and the disciplinary adages on which, according to Pound (and Confucius), high historic periods are built alternate with praise of *paideuma*, a favorite Poundian concept, which involves a living tradition leading into a living culture—teaching, training, discipline, correction, letters, knowledge, science. At the beginning of Canto 90, the exploration of *paideuma* disappears for a time, along with every sign of personal pique, and we find ourselves in one of Pound's magic circles, with an antique landscape of extreme loveliness unfolding before us. Praise of poetry at its source (the Castalian spring), of the sea and moon, groves and altars, fauns, nymphs, and sirens, of leopards and carved stone, of pines and birds, brings into view the poet who has every effect of evocative language under perfect control. This innocent natural beauty (a kind of lost *Paradiso*) washes over into Canto 91, but soon not only history but Pound's most shocking interpretation of modern history are upon us again; the old bad words reappear, the thought and emotion become darker and more turbulent. From this point on, Pound's power of exquisite imagery is evident only in single lines or even in single phrases, but there are still moments of passionate tension, and the quotations—chiefly from Greek poetry—are always, although fragmentary, pertinent to their context. In spite of everything, the main impression of these *Cantos* is far from that of a rock drill. At the end, a Homeric motif briefly reappears—a breath of loneliness felt by a man far from home, with a long journey still ahead. Pound now presents to us the shadow, as it were, of a personality, but one from which every layer of self-interest and self-pity has been burned away. It is sad that traces of small and bitter vindictiveness still remain. "A man of no fortune and with a name to come."

At present, Pound has no direct imitators. The contemporary generation writing in English has learned from him, it is true; the rules he formulated for the Imagists, more than forty years ago—directness, naturalness, precision—still hold. The actual form of the *Cantos*, however, now seems slightly fossilized— worthy of note as origin and as process but with no truly invigorating aspects.

DOROTHY RICHARDSON
(1967)

The beginning and middle years of Victoria's reign were marked in England by grotesque excesses of male control—social, political, and familial. One student of the period has given, in recorded statistics, the number of benighted governesses (21,000 in 1851) and of ill-paid and sweated seamstresses who struggled at that time for some sort of livelihood. We also have the number—in six figures—of the domestic servants who, in 1841, waited on the Victorian wives, whose husbands, quite generally, had forced them into an enervating idleness. Idleness had become, for the middle-class woman, a class badge; if you were the wife of a prosperous man, you did nothing. The demand of the Victorian male for innocence—and ignorance—in a wife left the Victorian woman untrained in the practical conduct of life. The "bustling Chaucerian housewife," the Renaissance manageress of estates, had largely disappeared.

Girls and women, except in the rarest instances, took on the servile, flattering manners of the slave. Women became past mistresses of the cosseting gesture and the seductive wile. Their insanely hampering clothes made them into puppets. They were almost helpless under the law, trapped by father and husband. But soon they began to break into open, or half-concealed rebellion. Florence Nightingale raised nursing to an honorable profession. Miss Barrett ran away with Mr. Browning. "George Eliot" entered into a long, fruitful extra-marital relationship with George Lewes.

And they began to write. A very nearly complete documentation of the life and surroundings of the nineteenth-century English-woman has come down to us. From the mills of the Midlands to the parlors of the high bourgeoisie; from the Yorkshire moors to the governess's shabby little realm, we have it all, written by women who were learning to cast brave and penetrating glances into their surroundings and into their own hearts.

Dorothy Richardson, in making her first break into the pupil-teacher and governess pattern at seventeen, was following the Brontë tradition. A season in Hanover, used in *Pointed Roofs* (1915), was followed by two later teaching stints in England, described in *Backwater* (1916) and *Honeycomb* (1917). She then, barely twenty-one, moved into the beginning of a career that was to hold her for over a decade: she became a dental assistant for a group of Wimpole Street doctors, oddly combining the duties of nurse and secretary. At the beginning of *The Tunnel* (1919), the fourth "chapter" of her long prose work, *Pilgrimage*, we find her established in this post.

Merely to get at Dorothy Richardson's novels—the twelve "chapters" of *Pilgrimage*, published separately between 1915 and 1938 and in a four-volume collected edition in England and America in the last-mentioned year—has, of late, become so difficult that the waning of her reputation may be partly put down to the absence of the books themselves and data on their author. Moreover, she gave the public, or the occasional inquiring journalist, little help. After her marriage in 1917 to Alan Odle, an artist and illustrator, she lived, evidently with the thought of her husband's frail health in mind, principally in Cornwall, with a few months in London lodgings each year. This marriage, it is clear, was a sustaining one, which brought out, until Odle's death in 1948, a latent maternal emotion of a particularly deep nature —an emotion which had appeared only fragmentarily in her account of Miriam Henderson (the *persona* she had assumed in the closely autobiographical account of her early years).

It now turns out that the account did not end with *Dimple Hill* (1938). A later manuscript, *March Moonlight*, was discovered after her death in 1957. The journey of "Miriam Henderson" from the point when she was "thrown out upon the world," at seventeen, to the moment when, a woman in her thirties, she is about to be given, by a patron, a year of freedom in which to write, is now complete. But at the moment when she has found, after many false starts, her subject and method, Dorothy Richardson becomes so absorbed in recovering the experience of her young alter ego that she herself vanishes from sight.

Early on, Richardson's method was described by the novelist May Sinclair, in a phrase of William James, as "stream of consciousness." Richardson herself, in later years, repudiated this label, and it is true that she did not hold to a single method after her first experiments. Impressionism in the novel was soon to be pushed to extraordinary limits; but Richardson owes nothing to either Joyce or Proust, or to Virginia Woolf, who took over much but invented nothing. Two innovations are truly Richardson's. She used Henry James's viewpoint person, and she made that person—unchangeably—a woman: herself, at one remove. The character of Miriam Henderson is the mirror in which all is reflected.

As first this reflection is exquisitely clear, with the senses of the female perceiver unblurred. Later, Miriam becomes more tendentious; the arguments multiply and the lines dividing pure creation and repetitive obsession begin to show. For there is no doubt that Richardson was obsessed, concerning what to her was the irreducible gap between the nature and motives of women and men. But there is also little doubt that her findings had truth in them; modern psychological insight has confirmed many. And Miriam, as part of her gradual enlightenment, is finally able to recognize and acknowledge her deep and compulsive psychic scars.

Her variations on the man-woman theme are often extraordinary. It is evident that she has heard of the myths, as well as the historical facts, of matriarchy, and of the worship of the Great Mother; and, to her, it is with the bonds of a strong secret sisterhood that all women are bound together. It is fascinating to watch her sensibilities operate in a region which, though at first glance seemingly frivolous, is undeniably women's: the world of clothes. She has written a whole grammar, a whole history, of the costume of the late nineteenth and early twentieth centuries; she builds up, little by little, what can only be called an elaborate mystique of dress. Not only the cut of garments but their differing fabrics are described, and she is often naïvely delighted with the details of what has come to seem the ugliest period of fashion known to Western man.

She often takes direct leaps from perception of character through dress to perception of character through height, weight, bone structure, and tricks of carriage. She is merciless to "the common"; and it is almost always spiritual commonness that repels her. And commonness had, of course, its own undeniable sound. She can detect the nuances of this sound in three languages (French, German, and English) with zones of *patois* in between. She can not only detect the smallest peculiarity of speech, but she can reproduce it in an almost ventriloquial manner. The reader will remember a minor character—come upon once, and never to reappear; Richardson is full of such characters —by the shape of a forehead, the manner of getting in and out of a chair, or a flattening of vowels.

All this is feminine. It is feminine "reality" she is after; and she soon finds that this reality can be most tellingly presented in a condensed, episodic form. She is not recounting it to us retrospectively; she is sharing it with us in a kind of continuous present. Not *this is the way it was,* but *this is the way it is.* Irritation caused by this condensed, elliptical approach has been repeatedly expressed by masculine commentators. A gap between male and female sensibility then exists? Not an abyss, as Richardson came to believe, but certainly a temperamental disjunction from which irritation and misunderstanding can and do spring.

But she receives high praise from men. J. C. Powys, in a long study of her work published in 1931, says of her: "She works with memory, and what must amaze most people is the apparently willful choice of unpicturesque, unpromising, unideal and in many instances actually unpleasant aspects of reality. Yet all these queer things . . . arc treated by her with their ramifications and convolutions as if they were carefully selected ideal symbols of human life." These "queer things" were the material circumstances of her youth, and she did not shirk any difficulty in outlining and projecting this portrait of a young woman living in an attic room on £1 a week. She is recording feminine heroism, as well as feminine insight and subjective perception.

Particularly subjective and feminine are the waves of euphoria that wash over her again and again. Sudden radiance will illumine some dull task; a London street—the line of its houses against the sky, its traffic, its people—will begin to open out into timelessness. As with all true mystics, her vision is based on the sharp apprehension of reality. Later in the work, it is true, the half-impression begins to replace the full delineation, and the hint and the veiled anecdote can become rather tiresome. She begins to bypass crises. That she evaded any direct description of her mother's suicide, at the end of *Honeycomb* (1917), we now know; it is one of the facts put before us by Mr. Horace Gregory's meticulous biography, *Dorothy Richardson: An Adventure in Self-Discovery.*

At the same time, she does not scant descriptions of certain hysterias and neuroses of the transitional time she is dealing with —pathological states which were to disappear, or take on another coloring, in the post-1914 world. Here is the "born spinster," the "born bachelor," the pathological child, along with morbid jealousy and emotional tyranny in various disguised forms. It is freedom Miriam is out for, not power. She is fighting every step of the way, not only for social justice, but for the right, as a woman and a growing individual, to stand clear from the shams which had tortured her as a child; from her father's double-dealing and her mother's subservience and final despair.

Her diction, from the beginning, is fresh and alert. There is no "period" or deadening language; she places, often, epithet beside epithet in her effort accurately to give the true innerness of people and events. She possesses, Powys says, "a certain obstinate, humorous, massive, deliberate approach to life which is not in the least ashamed of being pedantic." She is capable of slashing out at women; and she is never taken in by the then-prevalent feminist notion that men have been continuously, throughout history, out to conquer and enslave women. Women have a birthright, which they should claim, as beings whose knowledge of, and intuitions concerning reality are profound.

Politics and the vote touch the surface only. "These women's rights people," she says in *Deadlock* (1921), "are the worst of all. Because they think women have been subject in the past. Women have never been subject. Never can be. The proof of this is the way men have always been puzzled and everlastingly trying fresh theories; founded on the very small experiences of women any man is capable of having. . . . [Men] must leave off imagining themselves as a race of gods fighting against chaos, and thinking of women as part of the chaos they have to civilize. There isn't any 'chaos.' . . . It's the principle masculine delusion. It is not a truth to say that women must be civilized."

Mr. Gregory's well-organized and perceptive study is extremely valuable in setting the rather confused record straight. He has had access to late correspondence between Richardson, her occasional patrons, and her many friends; and at last the dates are put right (1873–1957)—for at the time of her marriage, the forty-four-year-old woman had fibbed, in a rather endearing female fashion, about her age. Mr. Gregory quotes brilliantly from *Pilgrimage* and rightly describes it as a rare example of a woman's restless, yet profound, spiritual quest.

And in the beautifully printed, new complete edition, comprising, at last, the entire thirteen "chapters" of this remarkable and original prose chronicle of our time, we finally have Richardson through "Miriam" complete: the brave, if not entirely fearless (for she is often racked by fear), little wrong-headed-to-the-majority partisan of her own sex (and of living as experienced by her own sex), in her high-necked blouse and (before she took up cycling) long skirt, from which the dust and mud of the London streets must be brushed daily; working endless hours in poor light at a job which involved physical drudgery as well as endless tact; going home to a tiny room under the roof of a badly run boarding house; meeting, in spite of her handicapped position, an astonishing range of human beings and of points of view; going to lectures; keeping up her music and languages; listening to debates at the Fabian Society; daring to go into a restaurant late at night, driven by cold and exhaustion, to order a roll, butter, and a cup of cocoa; trying to write, learning to write; trying to love and yet remain free; vividly aware of life and London. And continually sensing transition, welcoming change, eager to bring on the future and be involved with "the new." And reiterating (on the verge of the most terrible war in history, wherein all varieties of masculine madnesses were to be proven real): "Until it has been clearly explained that men are always partly wrong in their ideas, life [will] be full of poison and secret bitterness."

RAINER MARIA RILKE

IN HIS AGE (1937)

Rainer Maria Rilke, the Austrian poet who died in Switzerland in 1926 at the age of fifty-one, is a rare modern example of the poet who, "having learned to give himself to what he trusted," finally "learned to give himself to what he feared"; an artist who neither became stunted through, nor desired to escape from, the demands of his nature and his art; a poet whose work grew with him. In a period when the facing of inner truth is in no way a popular occupation—since too many flights away from the task, from war to suicide, are not only accessible but even morally respectable —a dedicated career like Rilke's becomes an heroic career. His talent for detachment, his distrust of the state of being loved ("*être aimé, c'est vivre mal et en péril*"), have laid him open to the charge of neurotic irresponsibility. We have only his work to assure us of the ultimate hollowness of this charge, and that work is strongly reassuring. Rilke was often exhausted, often afraid, often in flight, but he was capable of growth and solitude, a process and a state denied to the coward's or the delinquent's existence. And he stands as an example of integrity held through and beyond change—one of the few examples of such integrity that our times have produced.

The steady growth of interest in Rilke has brought on several attempts to make him available to English-speaking readers. Four

349

of his prose works have appeared in English translation: *The Journal of My Other Self* (originally *Die Aufzeichnungen des Malte Laurids Brigge*), *The Life and Death of Cornet Christopher Rilke, Stories of God,* and *Letters to a Young Poet.* His last and greatest group of poems, the *Duineser Elegien,* have been translated by E. and V. Sackville-West in a finely printed and limited edition published by the Hogarth Press in 1931. As early as 1918 Miss Jessie Lemont translated some of the earlier poems with more awe than skill, and Ludwig Lewisohn and Jethro Bithell have done other renderings. Lately Stephen Spender has tried his hand at the difficult task.

It is always a question what use translation of any poetry serves. And the greater the poetry, the more closely it is limited to existence behind the barrier of the language in which it was originally written. When the work is subtle in meaning, intensely accurate in perception, profound in feeling, and the product as well of great technical virtuosity, the translator may well hesitate before attempting his task. Rilke may be classed with Baudelaire and Valéry as a poet complete appreciation of whom demands some knowledge in the reader of German and French.

J. B. Leishman, whose devotion to Rilke's work is undeniably deep and sincere, began to produce, in 1931, his series of translations with a volume of selections from all periods of Rilke's career, entitled *Poems.* Whatever his native qualifications for the task (and to lift Rilke into English requires extraordinary qualifications), and whatever his failure and successes, there is no doubt that the earlier book, together with the two volumes now under discussion, with their meticulous notes and long biographical and critical prefaces, give for the first time to the English reader a comprehensive notion of the quality, the range, and the power in one of the great poets of our time.

Requiem and Other Poems (1935) contains, among other things, versions of seventeen poems from the two volumes of *Neue Gedichte* first published in 1907 and 1908—the books wherein the great and mature Rilke for the first time came into view. The period which produced this poetry began after Rilke's meeting with Rodin. Rilke's early work had been filled with the mysticism, the sentimentality, and with that "unwillingness to renounce the attractions of the obscurer depths of the soul," which are peculiarly German. As he later expressed it, until he met Rodin nature had remained for him "a general occasion." His religious feeling, his seeking for God, had been at its worst a kind of adolescent *Schwärmerei* which his visits to Russia had fostered. The poems written immediately before his first visit to Paris (in spite of their great sincerity of tone and their growing mastery over effects) contain poems dangerously near religiosity of feeling.

He was born in Prague in 1875. His father's family was of German peasant stock which claimed some distant aristocratic admixture. From a rather pampered and enervating childhood he passed, at the age of eleven, to the hard life of a military school, which he endured for five years, an experience he never fully recovered from, and to which his distrust of close human relationships may perhaps be traced. He began to write—and publish—very young, and in 1899 and 1900, after an abortive attempt at training in the law and an unfortunate and silly early love affair, he made two visits to Russia. There he met Tolstoy and felt some vague sympathy with the tenets of Tolstoyism. In 1901 he married Clara Westhoff, a young sculptress, and through her became interested in Rodin. He first went to Paris in 1902, and on his second visit lived with Rodin as secretary for a year (1905 to 1906).

Malte Laurids Brigge (1910) and the *Neue Gedichte* (1907) are the direct products of the influence upon Rilke of Paris and of Rodin. Rodin taught him that the moment of inspiration must not be waited for but must be summoned and seized; and in Paris he learned to live "that simple life of a love that has endured, that without ever praising itself on that account, advances to everything, unaccompanied, inconspicuous, worthless. Proper work, abundance of tasks, all begin for the first time beyond this endurance."

Malte Laurids Brigge takes up, with extraordinary courage, the spiritual dissection of a modern city where it had been dropped by Baudelaire. (It was by reading Baudelaire that Rilke comforted himself during his first terrible Paris days.) In the Paris streets Rilke laid himself open to the strongest impacts of fear, horror, and loneliness. The cripples, the beggars, the madmen, the paupers, the terrible sick in those streets, became for him the door-

ways to meaning, to the secret which must, he believed, be hidden
from mankind. He instinctively used "that mental pathology
which seeks to understand human personality by studying it in its
rare or morbid states, states in formation or deliquescence." And
he not only looked upon suffering people in search of the secret.
He went to "things"—sculpture, flowers, cathedrals, paintings, an
open square, or a countryside. He detached himself from a subjective approach; for the first time he became objective. "His
former tone . . . had been that of prayer, of the examination of
conscience, of the act of faith. It had been an interior monologue
which looked for God." He now looked upon "the thing" with the
intensity which had earlier produced that profound and moving
poem "Der Schauende" (Mr. Leishman's translation of which, in
the *Poems* of 1931, is, up to now, his most inspired version of
anything in Rilke). He was granted access to that "inscape"
which Hopkins and the great mystics have felt to be present in
all objects in nature.

The *Neue Gedichte* (1907)—short, closely written, compressed
into most exigent form, using the most sutble possible powers of
language, rhythm, rhyme, and assonance—are of course ultimately untranslatable. The grace in them, the light which seems
to fall from the depth and height of the universe upon them, their
tenderness and precision, can exist only in the original German.
Mr. Leishman's methods of approximation have their moments
of success and failure. His extreme respect for Rilke's work has
led him to use the simplest and most direct English, singularly
free from rhetorical padding. But his keeping to the side of simplicity often makes the language too light and too ordinary: he is
hardly ever successful in rendering Rilke's extraordinary nouns
and verbs, the structure of the refracting crystal of his style. The
poems are always given, however, in their original scheme of
rhyme and rhythm, and the complications of the German (that
language *"si malléable, si capable d'abstraire et de personnifier à
la fois"*) are handled with a good deal of authority. One poem,
"Lied vom Meer," whose subtlety should warn off any translator
from an attempt upon it—a poem which rises and subsides like a
wordless cry—Mr. Leishman has attempted with unfortunate
results. And in the translations of the two tender and profound

poems that make up *Requiem* he again fails, because the looseness of the form demands a language more weighted, more resonant, than the English without effects into which it has been turned.

Die Sonette an Orpheus (eighteen of which in Mr. Leishman's earlier versions are included in the *Requiem* volume, and all of which, with the original German printed opposite the English versions, are included in the *Sonnets to Orpheus*) are part of the last work which Rilke accomplished. These poems, written in 1922 after ten years' silence, were "given" to Rilke when he was at last able to take up the task of completing his *Duineser Elegien*, begun in 1912 and interrupted by the First World War. "After months of solitary contemplation, utterance and release came to him in February, 1922, when, in a tempest of creative activity with which there is no parallel, except perhaps in the lives of some of the great musicians, the remaining eight elegies, the fifty-five *Sonnets to Orpheus*, and a number of poems he classified as *Fragmentarisches*, were written within three weeks."

These sonnets have been called, and are without doubt, among the profoundest poems of our time. In them Rilke expressed more deeply and, in spite of their difficult and compressed form, more fully and clearly than in any other work, his hard-won knowledge concerning love, existence, and death. Orpheus is taken as the symbol of the Mediator: the god with the lyre to whom both worlds are open, who not only knows the secret but works and expresses the secret in his song. Here Rilke made, instinctively and in his own medium, discoveries concerning the nature and workings of the unconscious, startling in their accuracy. For in his later maturity he was able to bring over into the modern world —when the "great traditional therapies" had broken down as guides to man's thoughts or answers to his suffering—the love which we can only call Christian, because of its profound pity and humility. Like Yeats, Rilke had spent his life creating a religion for himself. But beyond Yeats, who came to believe in man's pride and intellect as guides and symbols, Rilke, stubbornly confronting the real world with his sensibilities, continually testing one by the other, came at last to explain the one by the other, and made a connection between them. Unlike many converts to

Roman or Anglo-Catholicism in our day, he did not walk into a
ready-made spiritual system and close its door behind him. In the
self-imposed isolation of his later years he rediscovered the worth
of traditional and mythical residues, and drew from them insights of clinical worth and exactness. He belongs to the company
of those who, in our day, have uncovered forgotten truths concerning the human psyche and its relation to its world. His poetry
is great because of its spiritual validity, as well as for the validity
of its complicated and subtle art.

His belief that "one must praise, in spite of all"; that one must
renounce, let go, die and be reborn, endure; "that egoism and
childish revolt must be silenced"; that the things which rouse the
most terrible grief in us (such as the death of the young) must
hold for us the deepest meaning; that it is our force which must
use the mechanisms of a changing world for its own ends, not the
mechanisms which must weaken our force; that we exist (as the
rose, "that inexhaustible thing," exists), the fruit of powers beyond us, within us, which we must in some manner trust: such
belief, such openness, such adulthood give back to us the healing
of which cynicism, hatred, and an insistence on the complete
sufficiency of material systems deprive us.

> Sei—und wisse zugleich des Nicht-Seins Bedingung,
> den unendlichen Grund deiner innigen Schwingung,
> dass du sie völlig vollziehst dieses einzige Mal.

> Zu dem gebrauchten sowohl, wie zum dumpfen und stummen
> Vorrat der vollen Natur, den unsäglichen Summen,
> zähle dich jubelnd hinzu und vernichte die Zahl.

Although a cult of Rilke would be unfortunate (as modernly
all cults tend to become), it is important that his work be made
more accessible to students of modern poetry and modern thought.
For his work is one of the strongest antidotes to the powers of
darkness—hatred, split allegiance, guilt, and regression—that
our time has produced. And although the daring, yet accurate
imagery, the compressed thought, and the compressed texture of
this difficult poetry must come to us in a muffled and watered
form, whatever hand attempts its Englishing, we must be grateful for some means of approach to its music and its meaning.
With this Mr. Leishman's translations have provided us. Rilke
himself believed that translations were of some value; he trans-

lated certain works of Gide, Valéry, Mallarmé, Baudelaire, Louise Labbé, and Michelangelo.

Valéry wrote after Rilke's death:

> To have lost him means to have lost one who combined in himself not only the comprehension of all the beauty Europe has produced and a deepened recognition of the riches which spring from our complexity, but one who possessed an immediate and creative sensibility— the spirit of a coming age.

DUINO ELEGIES (1939)

Rainer Maria Rilke finished the *Duino Elegies,* now translated into English by J. B. Leishman and Stephen Spender, in 1922. Together with the fifty-five *Sonnets to Orpheus,* written in the same burst of creative energy, they mark the summit of his career.

The *Elegies* are extremely difficult in the original German for stylistic reasons alone. They are an amalgam of two tendencies: the German, wherein, with dangerous ease, abstractions can be personified and the concrete abstracted; and the Symbolist, which tends to throw up plastic and bizarre images in order to express subtle states and intuitions. Rilke's power over language was immense, and he could work in the most exigent forms. The *Elegies,* however, are written in what seems to be a relatively untrammeled manner. Actually, their style, based for the most part on the hexameter, is laborious and condensed. The language everywhere is welded and weighted, and nowhere blurred or diffuse. Rilke, in his struggle to indicate the mystery of man's destiny, to "open up a universe without barriers," pushed language to extraordinary limits, suiting the range of his insight. The translator's task is therefore one of almost insuperable difficulty. One badly chosen word will throw a whole passage out of tone, and one expanded phrase almost obliterate the meaning.

J. B. Leishman has spent years translating Rilke into English and in writing long, painstaking glosses on the meaning of his poetry. Because of his sincerity, patience, and love for Rilke's work, he has had some remarkable moments of success in his task. Stephen Spender, who is his collaborator here, has translated Rilke before this. He has, however, always brought Rilke over into Spender rather than the opposite. His choice as collaborator was not entirely wise, for whatever Spender's gifts may be, they are not exceptionally disciplined or austere; they often suffer from vagueness and a delight in throwing language around. His taste, moreover, is not sure. The one earlier translation of the *Elegies* into English, by E. and V. Sackville-West, erred by making the tone too literary in a traditional English way. The present translation often fails by coalescing with the German, by sliding over punctuation (and italics), by frequent awkward and even ridiculous use of words. It is true that efforts have been made to duplicate the interior assonances and the neologisms, and to indicate the fundamentally ungrandiose tone by means of elisions and ordinary speech. What has not been carried over in any way is the underlying emotional pulse of the poetry, so moving in the original.

Leishman has contributed an illuminating preface and many notes. The reader who wishes to pursue further studies will find an enormous amount of reference material here. It would be valuable, too, if Leishman's earlier translations were published in America.

Rilke, during the last ten years, has been treated to exegesis in four languages. His integrity will bother the new utilitarian school of criticism, certainly. He is a perfect target for its simplifications. He will be outlawed as a "dilettante," because he lived in castles (Duino was one) and actually, for a time, in a tower (Muzot). He dedicated the *Elegies* to a princess. He spent his life looking and feeling and contemplating; he loved solitude; he drew nourishment from works of art. In the *Elegies*, however, the ills of our time are traced back to their source, to the spiritual infection of a world without values. The cheapness of this world is delineated in the "Tenth Elegy" with tragic insight. And Rilke's suggested cure is of a clinical exactness.

WARTIME LETTERS (1940)

Rilke was thirty-eight years old in August, 1914, when this selection of his letters begins, and forty-six, in December, 1921, when it closes. The letters, therefore, are not exclusively "wartime." Their chief interest lies in the fact that they cover the most unproductive period of Rilke's life: the period when he was unable to write poetry and was forced, both by outer circumstances and his own spiritual state, to undergo the full experience of moral agony necessary before his final work could come into being. He had often spoken of the "heart-work" necessary before creation. In these years he was forced to experience that work anew; and it was, as is usual in great natures, great labor.

Rilke's spiritual health was precarious in 1914, as it had been for some years previously. Having accomplished an extraordinary amount of writing in the decade from 1904 to 1914, he now felt himself at a dead end: finished with one way of thinking and feeling, and not yet ready for a new phase. His nervous exhaustion was noted in 1913 by one of his close friends: "The impression he made on me was one of extreme anxiety; he talked excitedly . . . with extreme nervousness. . . . He had always given way to the feeling of other people, he said; now at last he himself was going to feel desire and love." The poet who in ten years had written down fully the account of his childhood and youthful neuroticism (in *The Notebooks of Malte Laurids Brigge*), and who in the 175 poems in the *Neue Gedichte* volumes had caught, in full complex beauty, his intuitions into nature, his own subtle mind, and the "things" created by man, might well be emptied of the impulse to create. Rilke had always known that his role was one of "openness." He was an instrument made to receive life, in all its manifestations, both monstrous and beautiful. But now, even before the outbreak of the war, he no longer functioned as this instrument; and his state of depression was so strong that he came to Munich to ask aid of a psychiatrist.

"The experience of the war was certainly the severest test of Rilke's conviction that whatever is, is right," one commentator has said. Rilke was on his way from Leipzig to Munich when war was declared. A note in the present volume suggests that what he saw on that journey across southern Germany—"the armed men, the singing, the farewells—must have swept him into the current of exalted excitement that caused him to write his only—and quickly deprecated—war poems." These poems ("Five Songs, August 1914") are truly hysterical productions. They show Rilke at his worst, and resurrect the sentimentality of the adolescent Rilke, before this for years outgrown. Their only value is that they prove no exalted poetry can ever again be written on the subject of modern war. It took Rilke only a week or so to discover their falsity; and from that time on, throughout the war, on the subject of war he was silent, except for the scathing analyses of "the whole sad man-made situation" frequently repeated in his letters.

The war, however, was not through with Rilke. Born in Prague, he had for years transferred his allegiance to Paris. Having lived in almost every country in Europe as a "guest friend," he was now forced to return to Germany in order not to be interned as an Austrian. Then, in 1915, after a military examination, he was found fit and promptly conscripted for service in the Austrian army. This conscription lasted for some months, and his service in Vienna was terminated only after the intervention of his publisher and other friends. These people have spoken of the experience, touching and terrible, of seeing Rilke in uniform.

He returned to Munich, to his own long struggle with his divided nature. The "cleft" in Rilke between "narcissism and objectivity" is nowhere clearer than in his correspondence at this time. "This cleft is common in most extreme artists, but Rilke was in danger of sheer disintegration through it." He now felt himself "a beginner," and saw the people about him in Munich as "finished" in the most invidious sense of the word. All talk of "evasion" and "escapism," applied often so glibly to Rilke in accordance with the dictates of modern jargon, seems particularly fatuous when the long slow process of his development during these years is examined. Rilke had written in 1906: "Those who live with courage . . . can never be deceived or disappointed in the essential realities of life. . . . When we accept the difficulties of life, it becomes easy (since we have enormous resources of strength within us). And we must adhere to difficulty, if we would make any claim to having a part in life. . . . What we are to understand by courage is a valiant attitude in facing the strangest and most inexplicable things that can happen to us." All this, which Rilke once knew, he had to relearn. In the most inauspicious circumstances he continued "to measure with the carat weight of the heart, in place of the false measure of suspicion, happiness, or luck."

These letters lead to the last poems—"because in them the development of these greater poems develops slowly, uninterruptedly, almost imperceptibly, through the whole course of the correspondence." At the end, the disoriented man has "suffered through" his problem and in 1921 is ready with a touching eagerness "to understand and adapt himself to the needs of others, especially of those younger and perplexed by life, as he himself had often been." The later letters are sometimes written to strangers who had written him for counsel. And they are a corrective to the tendency to make Rilke into a priest or prophet. His human defects show up clearly, especially his occasional tendency toward snobbery and dependence. He was above all things a poet, of a sensibility developed far beyond his time. He came to a reconciliation with himself, and to a triumph in his art, by using the most ancient wisdom combined with the most modern insights. He was opposed to modern brutality and, most of all, to the modern moral pretensions which cover it. He stands for the future, where "lamenting" need not cancel out "praise"; and to read him is an antidote against the fear, hatred, and revenge of the present. To read his poetry and his letters with understanding leads one toward a world where there are no victories, but only "assent."

FURTHER LETTERS (1945)

Rainer Maria Rilke considered his letters part of the body of his imaginative work. He stated this belief in his will (he died in 1926), no doubt remembering that he had often sent off to friends, in the freshness of recent experience, material that he later shaped into permanent form. Scholars have found omissions, confusions, and overlappings in the German editions of Rilke's letters, edited by his daughter, Ruth, and her husband, Dr. Carl Sieber. Any translation of these originals must repeat their faults in some degree. *Letters of Rainer Maria Rilke*, translated by Jane Bannard Greene and M. D. Herter Norton, is a selection from the correspondence between 1892, when Rilke was seventeen, and 1910, when he was thirty-five. It is a well-rounded collection, even though it leaves out too much of the shrewd and

practical Rilke. For example, the letters to his publisher, Kippen-
berg, beginning in 1906, are under-represented.

Those who are familiar with the entire correspondence in its
original form have pointed out the sameness of its tone, a sameness that at times seems to verge on obsession. It is true that a
surface monotony exists. Rilke never plays the fool, never hu-
morously belittles his work and aims, as less absorbed writers
allow themselves to do. If he seems continually to underline the
worth and dignity of his tasks, we must remember that certain
lightnesses may have been edited away, and we must remember
the peculiarities of his background and his time.

What is often called Rilke's "snobbery" is explained by the
correspondence. He often claimed aristocratic lineage, but he
never tried to hide the facts of his childhood—the cheap flat in
Prague, the neurotic mother, and the petty-official father. From
his background he acquired a horror of "the little official post" in
which, in the ordinary way of things, his life would probably
have been spent. He early discovered that when he asked anyone
for a job to carry him through difficult times, nothing whatever
happened, but when he asked anyone for money outright, or for
a pleasant place to write in, he almost invariably found immediate help. He was able, that is, to profit from the still-active
patron system, as it existed in pre-1914 Europe. He soon discovered in just what ways this system could save him from un-
creative routine and the pressure of poverty. His charm, his sensitiveness, and even the purity of his aims appealed to certain
men and women who were rich, appreciative, and often titled.
These people almost at once began to draw interest on their in-
vestment, in the form of exquisite works of literature composed
under their roofs or on their money. The picture of Rilke advocat-
ing the simple life and unremitting labor, in the letters he sent
out to his friends from a series of vast castles, great houses, and
Grand Hotels, has figured in the anecdotes of his detractors.
Another Rilke had to exist, and did exist. He could withdraw from
any situation with gentle stubbornness. He could live as a recluse
surrounded by Bohemian gaiety, as Cocteau and others have
testified. He loved solitude, even when it had to be accompanied
by squalor, and he was as good at getting out of castles, when
need be, as he was at getting into them.

These letters show Rilke growing from the indecisive, arty, and provincial young man into the severe, civilized, completely equipped artist. They provide a background for his first great works: *New Poems* (1907 and 1908) and the prose *Notebooks of Malte Laurids Brigge* (1910). Underneath the unvarying seriousness of surface, of which I have already spoken, an incomparable variety of observation, insights, and interests slowly gathers— "the bewildering richness of his mind." I know of no other correspondence that affords so much pleasure to the sympathetic reader. Little by little the panic and the complaints of the young poet subside, and we are listening to a man who has endured all the blows his civilization can deal and has profited spiritually by them all. The tendency to make a religion out of Rilke has been strong. Reading these letters, one can understand from what sources this tendency springs. For Rilke, far ahead of his time (see, for example, his analysis of Cézanne, written in 1907), recognized certain focal points of modern neurosis and unease. He understood disintegration because he himself had very nearly disintegrated. He sought unity, insight, composure, and patience because he had seen these qualities work cures. His search corresponds to our modern search, and contemporary poets who approach Rilke in seriousness and gifts unanimously agree that it was, and is, a kind of religious hunger that activated Rilke and at present makes modern man uneasy.

W. R. RODGERS
(1942)

Awake! and Other Wartime Poems, by W. R. Rodgers, is a first book by a young Ulsterman. It has been hailed by some as the first impressive book of contemporary war poetry to come out of England. The complete lack up to now of poetry in the manner of Rupert Brooke has bothered and annoyed a portion of the English and American public. It is this public's notion that such poems as Rupert Brooke's sonnet "If I should die, think only this of me" should appear, by some process of spontaneous generation, at the beginning of any war in which England is engaged. Perhaps it would be worth while to try to puzzle out why such poetry is modernly impossible and why the Rodgers book contains the kind of poetry we are going to get, in English, from those poets who manage to remain sincere through the present upheaval.

Classically, the two high types of war poem are the battle cry (or hymn), written in the definite iambics which presuppose the march's four-four time, and the elegy. The popular types of war song are quite different (although they are almost always marches or sentimental laments) and need not be dealt with here. But one likeness between formal verse and popular poetry must be recognized: at the beginning of a war both categories are gay; at the end of a war they are terrifying, coarse, satiric, and bitter. The post-Napoleonic ballad "Johnny, I hardly knew ye" is blood brother to the poems of Sassoon, written toward the end of the First World War. What formal "war poetry" cannot be is narcissistic, sentimental, or passive. The war sonnets of Rupert Brooke and the popular elegy "In Flanders Fields" are war poetry at its very worst. They were decadent and puerile twenty years ago; they are unthinkable now. What people who yearn back to them want is the stale and dowdy moral atmosphere of the early nineteen-hundreds. In spite of ourselves, we live in a more bracing air and are made of more sincere and sterner stuff.

The First World War impaired the notion that war poetry can be written by non-combatants. The only decent 1914–1918 verse was written by young men in their early twenties who were soldiers in the trenches—Wilfred Owen, Isaac Rosenberg, Charles Sorley, and Siegfried Sassoon. The hack writing of Kipling and Noyes made no impression, then or subsequently. One attempt at war poetry was made by both Rilke and Yeats. Rilke's hysterical "Five Songs, August 1914" were repudiated by him five days after they were written. Yeats wrote the superb "An Irish Airman Foresees His Death" and then announced his withdrawal into silence in "On Being Asked for a War Poem." The silence of these two men during those years is even now more impressive than volumes of exhortation and elegy would be. It was the soldiers who impressively spoke.

English writers and the more sensitive English citizen, through the worst days of the blitz, knew that hymns of hate could do no good. To their credit, be it said that they produced nothing smugly or romantically martial. They were working with bitter reality, from which there could be no sentimental, panicky, or nostalgic flights. It was borne in upon them that the citizenry could no longer gaily send off an army of dull-witted conscripts to the tune of, say, "*Malbrough s'en va t'en guerre!*" The day of what someone has called "baby wars" was over. The involvement was now total, and a tragic insight was the first need of a writer.

W. R. Rodgers, whether or not he is a soldier poet, is not a profound thinker, but a contemporaneous and candid spirit is in him. He has at his disposal a firm, rugged idiom, since Ulster still has here and there surviving pockets of primitive speech. He uses

the packed directness of the alliterative Anglo-Saxon of Hopkins'
and Auden's experiments and gives it surprising Celtic turns. His
unexpected and salty epithets pick out many unexpected details of
what he observes, from a fountain in a park to an airman in his
bomber. What is best about this poet is his glance into the future
and his realization that more than a casual peace must be demanded after the end of this war.

THEODORE ROETHKE
(1958)

Theodore Roethke, in his collected poems *Words for the Wind*, combines a close recording of the actual with a kind of lyrical incantation that Robert Lowell, more intent on the lyric as dramatic narrative, does not concern himself with. Roethke's childhood memories (he is now fifty-one) are as exact, in their way, as Lowell's, but Roethke often chooses to deal directly with subconscious images and to boldly penetrate the subliminal regions where the beginnings of instinct and impulse lie hidden. Terror and horror come through on both conscious and subconscious levels, and Roethke renders these with Jacobean forthrightness. At times, as in "The Sensualists," surely one of the most terrifying poems of our time, reality and dream coincide. Roethke, again like Lowell, can get full power out of language without slipping into rhetoric, and he can change from the strictest form to the freest without becoming trapped in the one or deliquescing in the other. And in his nonsense verse—a lesson to glum poets of every age—he laughs without bitterness.

CARL SANDBURG
(1936)

Flaubert kept a notebook record—a *sottisier*—of the stupidities of the French bourgeoisie, whom he despised. Carl Sandburg, over a long period of years, has filled what must have been many notebooks with memoranda of the speech and folklore of the American people, whom he loves. *The People, Yes*, his new book, is the latest collection of such data. His poetry from the beginning has included snatches of speech warm from the tongue of the American crowd. The earlier Sandburg (then, as now, a mystic realist in all the strength of his Scandinavian inheritance) bore marks of prettiness, vagueness, and sentiment—the weaknesses of this type of poetry. With time, a good deal of mist has blown away from Sandburg's thinking and style. *The People, Yes*, sturdily written and closely coordinated for all its seeming lack of form, is an attempt to give back to America its sense of myth and living folklore, without which, it is Sandburg's conviction, vision or no vision, a people dies.

America, Sandburg has found, renovates its folklore from day to day, without the slightest bit of trouble. The wisecrack keeps up the tradition of the saw and proverb, and the American people continue to clothe their superstitions, prejudices, fears, hatreds, hysteria, hope, and love with imaginative flights, reduced to a terse sentence, or with dry common sense, wrapped in wild humor. ("The farther up the street you go the tougher they get, and I live in the last house." "A fog so thick we shingled the barn and six feet out onto the fog." "The cauliflower is a cabbage with a college education.") Slogans, slang, popular songs keep coming on, and jokes still lay them in the aisles. Death and destiny, the bad break, disaster in general, can be defied if they can be laughed at. Sandburg, with loving care, has collected the things left out when masses of people have been reduced, by abstract thinkers, to black lines on a graph or white lines on a blueprint. There are few comments he has missed (by the people, for the people) concerning the journey that still begins with birth pangs and ends with the grave.

When Sandburg's mystic political vein begins to flow, the people become "the great pool wherein worn-out breeds and clans drop for restorative silence." They are at once the dupes of "the cockeyed liars and bigots" and the earth around the roots of a true leader—"the strong man, the priceless one, who wants nothing for himself." They give beautiful names to common flowers; are brave, uncomplaining, misled. Concerning them, nobody knows the answer; each man "must work out his guess for himself." Meanwhile, they do their chores, pay the installment on the bungalow, the radio, the car; wander through a frightening world of advertisements; live, die, laugh, and consume. And since generation after generation leaves as a heritage a sediment of superb wisecracks, Sandburg hopes. As long as the people continue to talk and laugh with style and humor, there is no need to despair.

KARL SHAPIRO

POEMS (1954)

To become the spokesman for one's generation is a difficult and often ultimately unrewarding role for a poet to take on. Karl Shapiro, after the publication of his first book in 1942, a year that found him, at the age of twenty-nine, a soldier in the South Pacific, was assigned this position by many of his contemporaries and elders. His recent *Poems 1940–1953* is a remarkably full chronicle of a troubled and tragic era. Shapiro grew up surrounded by the problems and confusions, both spiritual and material, of a crucial period of transition in America and the world at large. To the young writers of the early thirties, the poetry of the British Auden–Spender–Day Lewis group made a particular appeal. Shapiro learned the possibilities of poetry based on concrete situations from which large conclusions could be drawn, and a satiric sense showed up in his poetry from the first. He revealed, moreover, a skill in form from the beginning. The young American was therefore well prepared to chronicle the disturbing features of his time and place, including his experiences as a soldier. As a participant and survivor, he not only put down in detail the facts of a soldier's life but he mourned and celebrated, in elegies distinguished for their rightness of tone, the death of comrades-in-arms. War poems fade quickly, but two of Shapiro's—"Troop Train" and "Elegy for a Dead Soldier"—will certainly long engage interest and admiration. The poems in the present volume are not arranged chronologically, so lines of development and growth are difficult to trace. Shapiro has written several excellent poems since the war, but his latest work seems to have become rather embittered. A predilection for the nightmare concept appears in several later pieces; "The Phenomenon" and "In the Waxworks" have the quality of dark and entrapping dreams. Shapiro's best writing —so rational, so filled with a high sense of idealism—stands in direct contrast to these, and one can only hope that some freeing upward curve of the imagination will give him, in his maturity, access to new subjects to which his gifts may be fruitfully applied. Targets for the satirist surely exist at present, although in a more complacent decade it is difficult to find them, and courage is required to name and make them known.

THE BOURGEOIS POET (1964)

It is not unusual for a poet who has begun his career by writing in form to abandon formal practices, permanently or temporarily. For him to abandon them with vindictive cries and pronouncements is rare. Shapiro, once considered by many to be the poet-spokesman for his war generation, and who was the bearer of early fame and the author of a book on prosody, has for some time been carrying on a brisk and bitter campaign against metre, rhyme, and all stanzaic patterns. In *The Bourgeois Poet* (a title figure with whom he partly identifies himself but toward whom he shows a definite ambivalence), he has widened his attack to include all European art before the Renaissance (especially Gothic cathedrals, which he finds particularly sinister), all myth, metaphysics, and religion, much general "culture," and Charles Baudelaire, whom he considers a pretentious dandy.

The writing of the "confessional" poem (a popular genre at the moment) is bound to pull the poet out of strict form. The classic confessors, from St. Augustine to Rousseau, were not poets; in reading them, it is possible for one to see that the kind of confession that is good for the soul requires not the condensation of poetry but the discursiveness of prose. The Romantics were able to link up personal revelations with the sublime, and it could be argued that a negative attitude toward the sublime brings on a negative attitude toward form. It was Whitman who began singing intimate songs of the self that were independent of metre and rhyme, but in our own day we find both Yeats and Rilke writing autobiographies in prose while continuing to write lyric poetry of striking formal beauty. It is perhaps his younger contemporary Robert Lowell that Shapiro is emulating in these poems, written in what appear to be blocks of prose. Shapiro, of course, even as he inveighs against the pretensions and falseness of form and celebrates poetry as pure play, is skillfully manipulating a set of binding and intensifying devices that keep on adding unity to his composition—simile and metaphor, image and symbol, repetition and parallelism, exhortation and peroration.

It is difficult for a man to continue to make concessions to the status quo when very nearly all his impulses are for freedom and a clean sweep of the board. Such a man may well feel baffled and confined; to balance matters, he can only outline unconventional programs of action that it is unlikely he will be able to put through. Shapiro's ultimate ambition, he has recently stated elsewhere, is to write poetry that is "illimitable, irrational, and irresponsible." He has written no such poetry here. Frequently, when things get too difficult, he falls back on a most effective masking trick—on the use of a Surrealist random vocabulary and Surrealist *non sequiturs*. He is thus able to avoid—or to distort, blot, blur, and disguise—much plain statement. And the semi-rebellious poet makes certain concessions to the reader. He does not actually tamper with syntax and language, and his method is nicely balanced, with just enough anecdotage to keep up interest, just enough comic relief to provide amusement, and just enough shock and nonsense to insure attention. Shapiro's taste is oddly Philistine, and his opinions are rather weatherworn; Kropotkin, Thoreau, and Henry Miller are involved, along with that perennial and rather moth-eaten old anarch, the Marquis de Sade.

Shapiro, again elsewhere, has said that he looks forward to the day when his poems will be written "with a formlessness which should make you dizzy, nauseated, and give you vertigo." The prose poems in *The Bourgeois Poet* still stand far from that goal, too.

EDITH SITWELL

LAUGHTER IN A SWITCHBACK WORLD
(1925)

Miss Sitwell has for a long time rendered her vision of the world
through the baroque tradition, that stiffens the cloud into plaster
and sunlight into metal rays. It is a vision, one would suppose,
rigidly encased from reality's accidents and consequences. The
eye that has seen too much has built up a panorama wherein
the sea and clouds move, but as by a set of levers, and soft living
things become wood, gold, and lacquer—a switchback world,
peopled by personages called up from a mechanical *Commedia dell' arte*, devoid of mewing human sounds, with three gestures for love, and a raucous cry to signify despair. As though
something in her heart or mind coveted the unreality of a
child's fantasy, it is a fairy tale she tells and retells, however
full of hard surfaces and sophisticated implications. Her technique is beaten out in nursery rhythms, and the meaning swings
brazenly upon the rhyme. As in children's jingles, the rhymes
clap to, like hands beating, and up springs the image, like a bird.

Bucolic Comedies, although sprinkled through and prefaced
by paragraphs from Miss Sitwell's essays perfectly black with
disillusion, sustained unbroken these myths and distortions of
childhood. In *The Sleeping Beauty* the despairing voice sprang at
last openly out of her song, and in *Troy Park* the same voice,

unmistakably Miss Sitwell's own, speaks again. She at once stands within the clever clockwork kingdom she has made, and contemplates her own dead childhood.

Laforgue's shadow rests lightly upon Miss Sitwell. She sees men and women as the "terrible approximations" outlined by a caricaturist. The apish creatures scuttling upon adult business jig to a harried ragtime: the country gentleman skillfully shoots birds, the Countess airs her curled dogs, the red-faced man stumbles through a wet kitchen garden. Behind them rise lodging houses, "tall and lean," hotels, the *Metropole* and *Grand*—all the clutter of grownup existence. From these the hidden and resentful child grown old escapes into long poems mixed as dreams, full of lime-blossoms, honeycomb, amber, cherries, nutmegs, and waterfalls.

> The child went through this cold bucolic world;
> The mirage dew upon the ragged flowers
> And ass-voice, pig-voice, hen-voice without end
> Took on the tones she trusted. Oh, false friend
> And our own false heart, falsely crying . . .

Miss Sitwell's epithets, at times deft inventions forced into life by the exigencies of her technique, have often a fortuitous brilliance of their own which justifies them. Again she can look at leaves and shadow with the profundity of true emotional vision. It is only occasionally that her sincerity is to be doubted, and then, perhaps, it is a note of that sharp laughter which she turns upon herself and upon her crowded images, that sounds. We may laugh completely, as children do, at the nonsense of:

> . . . the navy-blue ghost of Mr. Belaker
> The allegro negro cocktail shaker,

and, in "Country Cousin," at the free variation on a phrase of Gertrude Stein's:

> My coral neck
> And my little song
> Are very extra
> And very Susie . . .

but she has other and sadder laughter. Words can be heard with the long accent of memory upon them:

Alas my lovely one, in a remote
And still land of the spirit was my home
And this has faded like a song, and only
On the clear brink of sleep or in the heart
Of music can I find it and return
Through the long lands and be a child again.

With such simplicity Miss Sitwell has brought reality into her
scene, before so carefully unreal. The carrousel world has cracked
because a human voice has cried within it out of mature horror
and despair. It must enclose, hereafter—along with the Mar-
gravine, Queen Claud, and the Noctambulo—the "mad Cassandra
tongues of birds" that shout "Troy is burning," and some echoing
"cold laughter of the water."

A SONG OF THE COLD (1948)

We look back on the Russian Ballet, which burst upon English
eyes and ears just before the war of 1914, and see that much
of its color and design has become dowdy and frumpish. This
aging process does not apply, however, to one of the literary
phenomena of the period to which the Russian Ballet contributed
—the early poetry of Edith Sitwell. For Miss Sitwell, a true
modern, was not taken in by the even then slightly obsolete
luxury of something like Rimsky-Korsakov's *Scheherazade;* she
went straight to the puppet booth of Stravinsky's *Petrouchka,*
and took over the role of the master puppeteer. How crisp, how
inventive, and how tireless she was, rigging up her backgrounds
and clothing her wooden dolls, and how many bizarre and
satirical charades she devised for them! She had imitators (they
crowded into *Wheels,* which she edited from 1916 to 1921), but
she alone had the key to her artificial little universe. She alone
could present the opposition between the puppet booth and the
Fair outside. She had something to satirize—the padded upper-
class Victorian and Edwardian scene, through which she had
evidently been dragged as an unwilling child at the end of a

governess' arm. And she had a dramatic instinct concerning the difference between reality and artifice, so she could intensify this difference by bringing her reader, from time to time, up against the question: Are these indeed puppets, or is there human pathos and laughter in these wooden breasts?

Human pathos, as time went on, became more and more a part of Miss Sitwell's imaginary world. Emotion, of a backward-looking kind but nevertheless full-bodied and poignant, exists in *The Sleeping Beauty* and in the more satiric *Bucolic Comedies,* both published in the early twenties. Her fairy-tale invention never flagged, but her figures were now dimly illuminated, more by the shadow of memory than by the glaring limelight of her times. The scene had shifted to lost childhood, the tone had become nostalgic, and there was a premonition of the moment when the Fair, with its shocking sights and sounds, would break through the walls of her tiny stage, when all the half-human dolls would die, insofar as they were human, or be put out of commission, insofar as they were dolls. This moment came, and the carnage and wreckage are perceivable and understandable in *Gold Coast Customs* (1929) and such shorter ensuing poems as "The Hambone and the Heart."

"One canot think of her in any other age or country," Yeats said of Miss Sitwell, but he goes on to trace her later nightmare visions to Webster and to Swift. *Gold Coast Customs* is Swiftian in its absolute rejection of humankind. Her first full glance at the real world is distorted and warped by horror, and the symbols she improvised to express her anguish are materialist ones, at the very boundary of sanity—symbols of money and blood, gold and cannibalism. It is not only the Fair but the jungle that finally engulfs the puppet booth, and for the next ten years Miss Sitwell is almost wholly silent.

The latest poems, written during and since this last war, are, in the opinion of many critics, Miss Sitwell's finest. She has adopted an entirely new set of metaphors—metaphors that, as Yeats remarked, she raises to myth-making proportions by carrying them over from poem to poem. Her symbols are now large and rather Biblical, and her tone is prophetic. She expresses her faith in a revelation that mankind can help to bring about and share, and she speaks with a new largeness of rhythm. But she has lost, in her progress toward the sibylline, all her whipping satire and all her sense of humor. She is no longer receptive to those short but intense moments of vision usual in her early works. She is more of a Romantic; she is more ordinary in general, and she is far less painstaking in technique, for a sibyl does not need the help of formal poetic devices; the cryptic utterance is effective enough in itself. Her newest book, *A Song of the Cold*, exhibits the prophetess in full panoply, but since she is only sixty-one, she may develop, as time goes on, a less monumental attitude. She has cast a good deal of her poetic bread upon the waters, and it is possible that she will be rewarded for her courage and intransigence by its multiplied return.

GARDENERS AND ASTRONOMERS (1954)

Women poets, when they assume the role of sibyl, draw to themselves certain undeniable advantages. They immediately take on ancient authority; they are able to indulge at length in rather loosely written verbal incantation and they are not required to make much sense. It is interesting to note how the popularity of Edith Sitwell increases the more she goes in for an incantatory tone and gnomic meaning. Her new volume of fifteen poems, *Gardeners and Astronomers*, will surely continue to delight her admirers. Charmingly designed and illustrated with line drawings of fish, constellations, leaves, thorns, flowers, butterflies, and an armillary sphere, the book has a seventeenth-century flavor, magic and science operating side by side. This, certainly, is a learned sibyl, who can call upon philosophers, emperors, kings, and queens as well as upon the astronomers Hipparchus and Kepler. (Her gardeners seem to be anonymous.) Anyone who has heard Miss Sitwell read knows how effective her poems are delivered aloud. In cold print, however, they often sound as though they had been composed aloud; they remind one of improvised arias for a baroque opera. The trouble with the sibylline is that it has no staying qualities. We are left with the memory of this poet's predominant theme—her love of the sun and of proud, warm-blooded creatures, including Man, and her hatred of cold, darkness, cruelty, and the reptilian in general. Miss Sitwell is so skillful and so dazzling that she almost persuades us that spiritual intensity follows upon verbal intensity, which may or may not be true.

STEPHEN SPENDER

TRIAL OF A JUDGE (1938)

Stephen Spender's *Trial of a Judge* is described as a tragedy in five acts. Its action is, briefly, as follows: A liberal judge with ideas of abstract and absolute justice condemns a group of Fascists for the brutal murder of Petra, a half-Jewish intellectual. Soon after this he is faced with the problem of how to treat some Communists who have been unlawfully carrying revolvers and who have inadvertently shot a policeman in the arm. He condemns the Communists, too. His wife, who is a reactionary, and his friend, who is a member of the government, bring pressure to bear upon him. He reprieves the Fascists. He then listens to the Communists, sees a Communist killed, retracts the reprieve, and grants the Communists a new trial. The Fascists, now in power, arrest the judge and bring *him* to trial. He clings to the idea of humane values, and Petra's fiancée says a few words about the necessity of love, but this show of antique European idealism does not save him from a prison cell and death at the hands of a Fascist firing squad. A chorus of Red prisoners, in the last act, chants a hymn of hope for future freedom and peace. They sort of forgive the judge, too, for his liberalism, which made him see with a "hypocrite mind."

Mr. Spender makes no mystery of his Communist sympathies, so perhaps it is not too Red-baiting to say at once that *Trial of a*

Judge is straight post-1935 Party-line liberal-scaring. (The Red faction in the play is so up-to-date that it calls upon the laws of democracy and the police, at one point, to protect it.) Going one step further into hypocritical-liberal dissection, and considering the play as a piece of writing, the critic must say that it marks a new low in Mr. Spender's career, is frightful poetry, and, academically speaking, no tragedy at all.

For tragedy must have some root in human motives. The human motives in the first act of *Trial of a Judge* go completely off the rails. The mother of the murdered man, for example, appears, and in our old-fashioned way we feel sympathy for her bereavement. This is the wrong reaction, we soon perceive. She is really a maundering old fool and, it later turns out, a symbol for Established Religion. The fiancée pregnant with the murdered man's child again touches our hearts, but once more our sympathy is misplaced. She takes up at once with the brother of her lover, and we feel foolish and confused, although we realize that her action must Mean Something. Mr. Spender, with loud cries of "Death!" from Communists and Fascists, and of "Heads will roll!" from the Fascists, endeavors to waken us to the fact that our gentle reactions put us right before the Fascist firing squad with the judge. But by the time the last act came on, with its final volley, this reader, for one, no longer cared. If peace and freedom are to be ushered in with such a farrago of mixed metaphors, dictated thinking, Eliotonian tigers (there are three of these), and Salvation Army choruses, perhaps it is better for anyone who admires good writing and insists upon keeping intact a sense of humor to seek out a grave and curl up in it. Without giving a series of silly speeches first.

There is a beautiful image of an airman looking down on a town on page 56.

RUINS AND VISIONS (1942)

Stephen Spender's new book, *Ruins and Visions,* is his first collection of shorter poems to be published in America since 1934. Spender's work has been preferred by some to the more astringent writing of Auden, and for a discernible reason. At bottom, Spender is not really "modern" at all; he writes in a style clogged with rhetoric and adolescent emotion and has a strong strain of nineteenth-century hope and hero worship, but his gift is undeniably real, and that he is a perfectly sincere and touchingly idealistic character is apparent. His gentleness and idealism show up even in the most obvious of his propaganda verse.

Ruins and Visions cannot be said to show a startling degree of integration. Reality, however, has moved in on the poet and he is now less sure of the efficacy of the abstract will. "I have deliberately," he says in the preface, "turned back to a kind of writing which is more personal, and have included within my subjects weakness, fantasy, and illusion." As a matter of fact, the later poems are far less illusory and fantastic than many of his earlier ones. He has left behind those long, sagging colloquies with himself, so characteristic of the delayed adolescent; he no longer wants to be somewhere where he isn't or return to somewhere where he once was. He is less sentimental about the perfect quality of love presumably to be found in the proletarian inhabitants of a house "at the edge of the railway lines." Perhaps, these later poems say, courage and patience in bearing an actual situation are as worthy as the determined effort to keep outside "the grownup world of cheating compromises." The reader should watch for the real majesty and sensitiveness of phrase, which become more conscious and controlled as the book goes on, and not be too easily tripped up by the sentences which mean nothing and are put in here and there like gargoyles.

COLLECTED POEMS (1955)

Twenty years ago, the "romantic" in any art was more suspect than it is today, and Stephen Spender seemed all the more romantic in his early work because he had not learned how to gauge his effects. His *Collected Poems* contains examples from all stages of his lyric career, and it is plain that he has become, over the years, more technically proficient and more open to gradations of thought and feeling. His revisions of his early poems (despite the protests of those English readers who seem to consider them sacred and unalterable texts) are on the side of verbal clarity and syntactic order. The young Spender looked out on his world with a mixture of horror and compassion; he was as quick to denounce human injustice as to celebrate human courage, and he sensed the pathos in human inadequacies only too keenly. He had, moreover, an eye for the physically splendid wherever found, and he was able to find this splendor in machines as well as in nature. André Malraux, in *The Voices of Silence*, remarks on the modern attrition of form and feeling in the arts as a whole, which stands in direct contrast to the opulence of design and the soaring transcendence of Renaissance and Romantic imagination. But a need for richness and for largeness, Malraux goes on to say, remains constant and basic, even in our time. Nowadays, in poetry, it is almost impossible to satisfy this need without slipping over into rhetoric or theatricality, but the devoted publics of Dylan Thomas and Spender prove that the high line still has its appeal. It is a virtue in Spender that he has moved steadily toward a controlled expression of the Romantic spirit and has continued to find subjects (the late war gave him many) entirely suited to his gifts. His feelings of pity, excessively apparent in his early poems, has taken on balance and direction. He has persevered in becoming emotionally centered and artistically responsible.

WALLACE STEVENS

THE AURORAS OF AUTUMN (*1950*)

Wallace Stevens is the American poet who has based his work most firmly upon certain effects of nineteenth-century Symbolist poetry. The title of his latest volume, *The Auroras of Autumn*, indicates that his powers of language have not declined; here is one of those endlessly provocative, "inevitable" phrases that seem to have existed forever in some rubied darkness of the human imagination—that imagination with whose authority and importance Stevens has been continually occupied in his later period. This preoccupation was once implicit in what he wrote; his images performed their work by direct impact. Stevens' later explicit, logical, and rather word-spinning defense of the role of the imagination has weakened or destroyed a good deal of his original "magic." The whole texture and coloration of his later verse is more austere; his subjects are less eccentric; even his titles have quieted down. What has always been true of him is now more apparent: that no one can describe the simplicities of the natural world with more direct skill. It is a natural world strangely empty of human beings, however; Stevens' men and women are bloodless symbols. And there is something theatrical in much of his writing; his emotions seem to be transfixed, rather than released and projected, by his extraordinary verbal improvisations. Now that he is so widely imitated, it is important to remember that his method is a special one; that modern poetry has developed transparent, overflowing, and spontaneous qualities that Stevens ignores. It is also useful to remember (as Apollinaire knew) that since the imagination is part of life, it must have its moments of awkwardness and naïveté, and must seek out forms in which it may move and breathe easily, in order that it may escape both strain and artificiality.

COLLECTED POEMS (1954)

The Collected Poems of Wallace Stevens was published this October, on the occasion of Mr. Stevens' seventy-fifth birthday; and E. E. Cummings' publishers remind us, on the jacket of his recent *Poems 1923–1954*, that this year Mr. Cummings has reached the age of sixty. Both these volumes are large; the Stevens runs to 534 pages and the Cummings to 468. One avant-garde tradition —sparseness of production—is thus broken, perhaps permanently. For these two veterans of little magazines and small or privately printed editions have been able to build up, over the years, a bulk of work without for a moment departing from their respective idiosyncratic methods. Neither poet has felt himself compelled to waste time in padding out his *œuvre* with forms antipathetic to his gifts, in order to attract a wider audience or to prove his skill in manipulating what the French call "big machines." The continuing creative energy of both and the constancy of their aim are apparent, but the impressive quality of their production testifies, as well, to a shift in the American literary situation. The fact that Stevens and Cummings now have fairly large and appreciative audiences proves how firmly, at mid-century, modern poetry has established itself, to the point that it now quite naturally circulates around recognized masters.

The dissimilarity between the personalities and methods of Cummings and Stevens shows up dramatically when their entire lyric output lies before us. A revolution in the arts, we again realize, takes on power when it attracts a variety of temperaments into its field of operations. The revolt against nineteenth-century standards and practices gained impetus when poets, like other artists, began to lay bare their inalienable, and often opposite, gifts in a perfectly frank and direct way. Tensions were thus set up, and modern sensibilities began to function from more than one angle and over a range of subjects. Cummings, whose relation to the 1914–1918 war was close and cruel, brought into American postwar poetry a bittersweet mixture of satire and sentiment. His typographical experiments, which gave him an early notoriety, today seem less important than his persistent attempts to break taboos—to bring back into formal verse vital material that Victorian taste had outlawed. Today, as we read Cummings' lyric output from beginning to end, we are struck by the directness with which he has presented himself—his adolescent daydreams as well as his more mature desires; his small jealousies and prejudices, along with his big hatreds; his negative malice and his fears, beside his positive hopes. His awareness of tradition, too, comes out plainly; he has reworked traditional forms as often as he has invented new ones, turning not only the sonnet to his own purposes but also the ballad, the nursery rhyme, the epigrammatic quatrain, and the incantatory rune. His habit of projecting a continuing present, avoiding any expression of remorse or regret, gave a glitter to his middle period; nothing in it casts a shadow. The pathos of his later elegies is all the more remarkable because no one could foresee its occurrence. But it is his satire that remains focal and sharp as his main contribution to the reinvigoration of modern verse. His targets have been, for the most part, well chosen, and he has made his stand clear—for the rights and value of the individual as opposed to the demands of the crowd and the standards of the machine. He scornfully stuck to his guns in times of crisis, when many of his contemporaries were deserting theirs. It is this underlying passion for simple justice that has given Cummings the power to uncover, point to, and stigmatize those dead areas of custom as only a satirist can effectively do it.

Stevens has never applied himself to the tasks of the satirist; he is by nature the contemplative poet *pur sang*, who distills symbols, meaning, and what he calls "ideas of order" from the crudity and the confusion of the actual. His ability to link the outer world of reality closely to the inner world of vision has been astonishing from the first. He never breaks into explosions of form or fusillades of feeling, but he is often lively and always in search of the ironic paradox. His poetry is securely based on reality; he was the first modern American, for example, to deal with the American scene in imaginative rather than purely topical or regional terms. Beginning with *Harmonium* (1923), Stevens used American place names with a sense of their awkward charm, and he has extracted the essence of American climate and atmosphere—of the American "spirit of place"— from Florida's subtropical abundance to New England's stern extremes of climate and contour. Stevens' later work (to the delight of the professors) contains elements of philosophical thought, but continually, as it were, in solution, for it is the full evocation of thought and emotion that he is after, not the cold, isolated, abstract idea. Taken together in these two formidable volumes, Cummings' and Stevens' talents, it is quite evident, complement and reinforce each other, and each poet in his way has indicated the imaginative direction, as well as outlined the complicated moral and spiritual exigencies, of our time. We must be grateful for Stevens' subtle discipline no less than for Cummings' boldness and verve, and be thankful that a native tenacity has allowed both poets to develop and endure.

ALLEN TATE

(1936)

It is interesting to note the amount of romantic wishful thinking
and bitterness in Allen Tate (the Southern classicist, of the aristocratic tradition compact). Tate is a pupil of Pound, Eliot, and
Valéry, a believer in the classic will, the champion of a special
cause. To him the modern world is a damned world, since a set
of special values has disappeared from it. For him the voices
of Senators Calhoun and Mason still resound, the "irrepressible
conflict" between the agrarian and industrial systems still goes
on. But all has been translated, in Tate's style and thinking, into
something rich and strange. The good old days when Representative Brooks thwacked Sumner on the floor of the Senate, when
Mason's home was burned by Sheridan, are not wholly over for
Tate, and it is romantic, though disguised, reverberations that
Tate hears from that past time. Tate's non-political poems—or,
rather, his least political poems—are his best. The title poem of
The Mediterranean and Other Poems is a beautiful lyric, and
there is much mature writing in the collection. I make one humble
wish: that Villon's line, beginning *"En l'an trentiesme de mon
âge,"* be overlooked for the next twenty years or so, as a title, a
part, or an introduction to English poems. Since Pound embedded
it in "Mauberley," it has gone the rounds and is by now, to put it
mildly, a modern poetic chestnut.

CAITLIN THOMAS
(1957)

Those who are shocked not only by Caitlin Thomas' disclosures in *Leftover Life to Kill* but by her temper and style as a whole should try to imagine how tiresome and truly shocking it would have been if she had written out of a cold, not a warm and generous, nature, if a trace of apology or calculation or concealment had been involved. In this book, at once a memoir of her dead poet husband and an account of her desperate attempts to face up to the prospect of life without him, Caitlin Thomas puts herself down without extenuation as a childish woman and as a bearer of the terrifying Irish qualities of violence and rakishness. But she is neither a slut nor a fool; there is a conflict here that could not exist except in a woman who is conscious of her immaturity —who longs to grow up, be sensible to some degree, and find her place in the world. The basic good sense and the ability to discriminate are there, although often almost savagely repressed.

Innocence and violence are terrible things. The severe rituals imposed on adolescents in practically every tribe known to anthropology insist on two basic dicta: *Grow up* and *Calm down*. In maturity, it is necessary, mankind has discovered, to suppress outbursts of strong emotion—joy, rage, grief—that may, in their

irrationality, disturb the general peace. The Greeks came to fear
those who threw themselves against the will of the gods. The
grave choruses of the tragedies continually warn, caution, and seek
to make reasonable the man or woman in the throes of whatever
overweening passion; the gods are sure to punish such pride.
Yet it is true, and always has been, that innocence of heart and
violence of feeling are necessary in any kind of superior achievement; the arts cannot exist without them. Caitlin Thomas here
proves herself to be one of those rare individuals who have been
able to keep hold of these dangerous qualities, in a pure state and
to a highly operative degree, into the years when most people
have lost them for good. This fact strikes the reader on the first
page of her book. She immediately leaps into a state of "pure
uncompromising abandon," and we are swept into it with her.
And we at once believe what she says and keep on believing in
spite of every obstacle she puts in our way. It takes foresight to
lie, and Mrs. Thomas seems never to have heard of foresight.

She has at moments the aplomb and daring, the almost insolence in dealing with atmosphere and facts, of the born writer.
She is always sentient, wound up, nervously attentive; she is
sometimes sharply witty and broadly humorous. Her epithets
crackle and sparkle; she moves into the most forbidding territory
with ease; she jumps barriers and tears down walls. With a child's
heedlessness and headstrong courage, although she may know
herself to be in the wrong, she sticks to her guns. Her despair
rarely degenerates into self-pity. She is able to put first things first,
and to mix successfully time present and time past, in what
finally turns out to be a well-constructed book.

She calls it a confession, but is it one? Confession implies a
sense of guilt, and to Mrs. Thomas it is God and life who are
guilty, not harassed human beings. It is, rather, a headlong descriptive analysis of herself and other people. Dylan Thomas,
man and poet, is here for the first time seen very nearly complete
—his dour origins, his deadly faults, his nearly as deadly virtues,
his poet's compulsions, his hidden yearning for respectability, his
household rules of behavior (no children at meals; the family
endimanché whenever possible), his consistent flight from reality,
his ungovernable plunge toward death. The relationship between
this man and wife, whose tutelary goddesses were certainly the

Furies, falls into place in a line or a phrase: "He said he loved me. . . . I believed him, and still do . . . my all-in-Dylan world. . . . He would flood me with a contempt of words; there is no fury like the weak, against the weak." Then there is America and the Americans, treated with alternate appreciation (for hospitality and generosity) and dislike ("the indistinguishable waves of gush"). Here is "the Killer, poetry reading" —the murderous (for him) money-maker into which role Thomas finally threw himself with frenzy, thereby arousing his wife's latent desire to be appreciated in her own right. After Dylan's death, the inhabitants of Wales and the natives of the island of Elba come into view (with few exceptions, totally repellent). Caitlin Thomas—brought up in Ireland as a "guerrilla lady," improvident but not completely impractical; the wife of an extraordinary man whose excesses and even triumphs filled her with presentiments of disaster; a grief-stricken widow; a passionate mother; and, finally, a woman newly in love—appears throughout, combining all these roles with many characteristics of an outrageous and exhibitionist child. We are not spared one detail of the background or foreground, and we are treated to insights of the most cruel and penetrating kind. Everything is presented raw and quivering. All this took some doing. It is remarkable, under the circumstances, that it was done at all, and with so little querulousness and contempt.

For the child, a fairy tale goes forward from darkness to light. The deformed stranger becomes the radiant prince, and the ugly duckling turns into a swan. For the grownup *manqué,* the story always unrolls in reverse. The kind, reliable, masculinely protective friend becomes a rogue; the happily remembered place, freedom's own, becomes a prison; and the hero or heroine is forced step by step from a position of some dignity and worth toward the status of the victim or the culprit. Caitlin Thomas' experiences on the island of Elba—a place so weighted, to begin with, with associations of detention and exile—bear many signs of a paranoiac nightmare come true. She returned to a scene where she and Dylan had once spent an "unspoiled" holiday. Time had passed; things had changed. She found ugliness and restriction where she had hoped for beauty and peace. The hotelkeeper, once her friend, becomes a tyrant; the lovely young boy to whom she loses her heart remains a playmate more than a lover. She is frozen by the winter climate; the sea rejects her; the very ground of the town and its environs becomes a difficult terrain, like the impeding surfaces we walk over in bad dreams; the mines in the district become "the cemetery of the earth"; and, worst of all, the endlessly attentive, endlessly suspicious natives become an audience of adversaries. The story that works itself out of this has little true drama in it, since it could be controlled only by attempts either to rebel against it or to wipe it out of consciousness. Situations keep lapsing into travesty and the grotesque, and the heroine finally flees the sought haven that had consistently rejected her. At the end of Mrs. Thomas' recital, it is hard not to feel that a little good sense or a drop of loving-kindness might have changed the outcome. But events seem to order themselves in this nightmare fashion for anyone who tries to face down life in general or his own destiny in particular. It would be a fine thing if Mrs. Thomas should go on to write another book, in which she tries not to kill life but to resurrect it.

DYLAN THOMAS
(1952)

Dylan Thomas' attraction for contemporary readers, and particularly for the younger generation, is partly based on poetic procedures that are more traditional than one might at first suppose, and these procedures are becoming more marked as time goes on. He has moved beyond his earlier Surrealist phase, so he now not only makes more sense but is able to project a variety of emotions, including tenderness and pity, instead of keeping up the steady stream of rhetoric that often resembled the rantings of a Welsh revivalist rather than the song of a Welsh bard. Another part of his appeal, it is true, still lies in his positive emotional orientation. In a period when emotional blankness and inertia pervade poetry in general, Thomas' power to feel joy and express exuberance sets him apart and makes his work interesting and valuable.

Thomas' bardic side is strongly evident in his new collection of six poems, *In Country Sleep*. In spite of his off rhymes and his devious syntax, and his habit of paradoxical epithet ("The mustardseed sun"), a holdover from Surrealism, the techniques of ancient balladry shine through. For he is as clever with full rhyme as he is with assonance; he is a master of effective alliteration, and he can manipulate refrain to underline and clinch his mean-

ing or to produce that incantatory quality on which all balladry
thrives. He is as close to living nature, moreover, as any Romantic. He names bird, fish, animal, plant, and flower, and he has
a sharp eye for the weather and times of day. A living world of
Celtic myth surrounds him. He contrasts, in the book's title poem,
a world of fairy tale and pagan folklore with a world of Christian
ritual and belief. But he is not content with mere contrast. He
contrives a connection between the two realms because he is
aware of the buried instinctive life they share. His shift into litur-
gical diction in the poem's second part is in itself a brilliant feat,
but he also manages a more subtle shift in key, modulating from
the minor of fear and terror into the major of calm and peace.
Joy in life as mystery runs through both.

Thomas breaks another modern poetic block in his direct celebration of sexual themes. The poem "In the White Giant's Thigh"
derives its title from one of those immense prehistoric designs
cut through the turf on the chalk hills of England and Wales.
Lying at night in one of these haunted places, the poet hymns
sexual feeling on a primitive level and in the most extravagant
terms, working in echoes of ancient vegetative myth. The same
sexual extravagance turns up in "Lament," but here the ballad
structure and the theme (an old man's concupiscence) are reminiscent of Yeats in his last period. Yet Thomas has his own
material, and has learned to use it with maximum effect, and
thus much modern poetry, written mechanically according to rule
of fashion, sounds weak, cold, and insipid beside his. He has
moved toward the heart of his original inheritance and by so
doing has been forced to incorporate into his work the formal
techniques of the folk ballad—techniques that suit his thought
and feeling and his clear perception of nature better than any
looser form possibly could.

NOTES ON TRANSLATION
AND TRANSLATORS

FROM THE GREEK, THE JAPANESE, AND THE CHINESE (1956, 1957)

Translators have so immensely enlarged the field of poetry in English since the early days of the modern movement that their tasks have come to be considered very nearly creative ones. They have opened up neglected areas, restoring importance to literatures either passed over as unimportant or avoided as repellent by nineteenth-century taste, and they have experimented endlessly with technical ways and means by which poetry ranging from medieval Provence to the modern Orient might be brought over into English in a striking and vivacious fashion. They have discovered, it is true, that certain close approximations to originals were no go; they have left behind for good certain experiments in classic quantity—Longfellow's attempt to transport classic dactylic hexameter into English more or less intact (*Evangeline*), as well as other efforts in this direction by Bridges and Gilbert Murray. Ezra Pound, in spite of his manifest idiosyncrasies, remains an example to a younger generation. He has taught it, for example, to maintain a scrupulous balance between formal and colloquial language and to adhere to a basic Imagist principle—the natural words in the natural order. Inflation of language and emotion, as far as modern translation is concerned, is a danger that no longer threatens to overwhelm the reader.

Richmond Lattimore, who in recent years has produced memorable English versions of the *Oresteia* of Aeschylus, the Odes of Pindar, and *The Iliad*, has turned his attention, in *Greek Lyrics*, to the independent short poem, which, he remarks in his preface, was the dominant form in Greece from the middle of the seventh century B.C. to the end of the sixth. These lyrics, coming after the age of the epic and preceding "the perfection of drama and the development of prose," were, he goes on to say, of the most varied kind. Written in various dialects, they were "secular or sacred; provincial or cosmopolitan; personal or objectively public; mere sequences of lines or couplets or elaborate stanzas and strophes." Hardly any original manuscripts now exist; the majority of the verses are fragments quoted by later authors, but a few "scraps of papyrus from Alexandrian Egypt" have been preserved. The fact that many of the poems are thus anonymous and incomplete gives an added pathos of time and loss to this material. Professor Lattimore, holding closely to the original metres, has produced renderings of great power and beauty. His feeling for the telling noun and verb, the simple yet poignant epithet, and the dramatic turn of syntax is marked. He has completely freed the poems from sentimentality, and the thrilling ancient names—Anacreon, Alcaeus, Simonides, Sappho—acquire fresh brilliance and vitality under his hand.

Kenneth Rexroth, in his preface to his translation of *One Hundred Poems from the Japanese*, speaks of likenesses between the poems in the *Greek Anthology* and Japanese poetry as a whole. The Japanese haiku (limited to seventeen syllables without stress accent) is, like the Greek epigram, short, concentrated, and often filled with a sensibility so delicate as to be almost indiscernible when scrutinized by untrained Western eyes. It is apparent that Rexroth has reproduced both the simplicity and the subtlety of his texts. The original lyrics are given, transliterated; the names of the poets are reproduced in calligraphy; and there are generous notes and a full bibliography. The volume, finely printed in Italy, carries its scholarship lightly, however, and is as elegant as it is informative.

In *One Hundred Poems from the Chinese*, Rexroth has examined the Chinese originals as well as various renderings in several languages with a scholarly and a literary interest. As a result, his own versions are simple, direct, and moving, with emphasis upon a colloquial turn of phrase. He has studied Tu Fu (T'ang dynasty) for many years; the poets of the Sung dynasty, also included, have occupied his attention for a shorter time. The volume has the same handsome format as his translations from the Japanese; notes, biographical and explanatory; and a valuable selective bibliography of earlier translations from the wide field of Chinese poetry into English, French, Italian, and German.

GUILLAUME APOLLINAIRE (1964)

Apollinaire's posthumous reputation (he died at the age of thirty-eight, in 1918, two days before the armistice, partly because of a shrapnel wound) has steadily grown, particularly since 1945, when a new generation of readers and scholars discovered what many of his contemporaries had overlooked—the pure and traditional quality of his basic lyric gift. Before 1914, he had proved himself the liveliest and most inventive of those poets who were experimenting with design in language in the same way, they thought, that the Cubist painters were dealing with line and color. Apollinaire's eccentricities could never quite conceal the true freshness of his style or the originality of his attitude toward the everyday occurrences of his time and place. In *Alcools: Poems 1898–1913*, William Meredith, himself a poet, has treated Apollinaire's most important collection (first published in 1913) to versions, literal at times and free at others, that bring the French poet's subtleties over into English with admirable effect, and the French originals appear on facing pages.

RENE CHAR (1956)

In René Char, a selection of whose poetry and prose has, with the collaboration of Richard Wilbur, W. C. Williams, and others,

been recently translated by Jackson Mathews and collected in a
bilingual edition—*Hypnos Waking*—we find a poet whose faith
is strongly attached to nature and to man. Beyond nature and the
heroism of the poet and the fighter (Char was a Resistance
leader) lies a void—*"le vide auquel je crois."* This negativeness
attaches Char more to the tradition of the French Symbolists,
whom the idea of *"le Néant"* both attracted and repelled, than to
the tradition of Blake, although Char's brief lyrics and aphorisms
have a distinct Blakean quality. Char's *"humanisme viril"* is
French to the core, and his superb and subtle language, even
though not in conventional form, is ultimately untranslatable.
He is the dreamer who has wakened from sleep but in the midst
of reality still remembers and praises his dream.

H.D.'S EURIPIDES (*1937*)

The "classics," as the whirligig of taste turns, generation after
generation, come in for some rather odd transformations. Homer's Homer becomes Pope's Homer; Ezra Pound rewrites Callimachus; and the *Ion* of Euripides, in the eighteenth century,
becomes *Creusa, Queen of Athens*, with all "the supernatural
element" left out. Gilbert Murray, in his translations, did his best
to completely muffle the original Greek with bad Tennyson and
worse Swinburne. Modern poets are now endeavoring to disinter
Greek drama from nineteenth-century gilt and ruffles. H. D., in
her current translation of the *Ion*, makes Euripides into an
Imagist, and that is a queer effect, too. She admits what she is
doing. She is out after "the core of Greek beauty," so she shears,
compresses, and prunes the varied and sinuous texture of the
Greek into brief cries and bright, detached images. She is out for
pure symbols of the Greek intellect, so everything is made static,
reduced to marmoreal form. She concedes the fact that "so-called
rationalists" have found in Euripides "irony lurking at every
corner." But she prefers to think, and write, in terms of "miracle."
This attitude produces some perfectly beautiful poetry, but reduces the play as a whole, in her version, to nonsense.

For if the *Ion* is not an ironic presentation of a God wreaking himself villainously on mortals, so that his blind victims—mother and son—very nearly murder each other as a result, it is difficult to make out what it is. Jean Cocteau, in his *La Machine infernale*, has underlined and expanded the fearful irony in Sophocles' *Oedipus Rex*. To excise the bitter criticism, which endears him to us as a fighter and a modern, from a play by Euripides leaves us nothing but the shell of his work. H. D. has given us a shell, and an exquisite one. But even pure and burning "miracles" pall, whereas irony and gumption live forever.

ROBERT LOWELL'S "IMITATIONS" (*1962*)

Far from being pale replicas, these "versions and free translations" often seem more highly colored than their originals. Lowell is primarily concerned with reproducing the concentrated energy of such poets as Villon, Heine, Baudelaire, and Rimbaud, and in his preface he frankly acknowledges his cuts and rearrangements. On the whole, he is precise as well as bold. Certain poets—Rilke, for example—come through with a new, attractively bitter flavor, and Pasternak, who has undergone a good deal of debilitating translation by others, here finally leaps from the page.

EZRA POUND'S VERSION OF SOPHOCLES' WOMEN OF TRACHIS (*1959*)

Pound's effort to bring over into a kind of American vernacular what has been described as the most intimate and touching of Sophocles' plays fails on every point, with the possible exception of the choruses, which are finely rendered on a "literary" level. Pound fails because of his ignorance of the contemporary American idiom; his slang is often obsolete, and in general substitutes coarseness for pathos. The noble Daianeira, along with certain

other characters, often sounds as though she had staggered on-
stage from the doors of an early-twentieth-century saloon. This
version, produced by the B.B.C. Third Programme in 1954, now
stands in print surrounded by four serious essays.

RICHARD WILBUR'S MOLIERE (1956)

Richard Wilbur's translation of Molière's *The Misanthrope*, which
recently appeared in a limited signed edition, is a further example
of how sensibility, aided by technical skill, can bridge the difference between another time, place, and literary circumstance and
today's. The bittersweetness of Molière's style and even the conventions of his theatre suddenly become, under Wilbur's discern-
ing treatment, modern and our own. The characters reveal themselves in words that seem effortless, and Wilbur's rhymed couplets
keep the stresses of natural speech, never slipping over into the
deadness of the threadbare phrase or the dullness of monotonous
rhythm; an impeccable ear is functioning throughout. Here is a
new master of translation's difficult art.

FROM THE GREEK AND THE FRENCH: CAVAFY, SEFERIS, ST.-JOHN PERSE, RACINE (1961)

It is difficult to discover modern poetry in English (or in any
European language, for that matter) uninfluenced, unfertilized,
and unadorned by modern translations. Serious and sustained
efforts have been expended in this century by translators—more
often than not poets themselves—to bring over into current
diction and acceptable contemporary form poetry of the far and
near past, as well as of the present. The accomplishment of these
tasks was long overdue. The nineteenth century in England and
America, in spite of crucial breakthroughs into new territory
(Edward FitzGerald into the Persian, and Douglas Hyde and

others into the ancient Gaelic), had attacked the problems of translation in a scattered way. A good deal of rather dilettante translating took place in genteel book-lined studies, including that of Henry Wadsworth Longfellow, in Cambridge, Massachusetts, where the then professor of modern languages at Harvard ranged over a remarkably wide field, from the Finnish *Kalevala* to Dante's *Divine Comedy*. Later, in Oxford, Professor Gilbert Murray, who was to be described by the young T. S. Eliot as a fine Hellenist but a very indifferent poet, rewrote Euripides. Meanwhile, Homer, Vergil, and classical literature in general either remained fixed in the language and form of Chapman, Pope, and Dryden or suffered under the hands of the most literal of scholars.

The bold forays of Pound into Provençal, Chinese, Greek, Latin, and Tuscan began in 1910, and during the last fifty years currents and crosscurrents have multiplied, so that at present little poetry, ancient or modern, in whatever tongue, has been passed over as being completely uninteresting or completely recalcitrant. And translators have left the hampering notion of word-for-word and line-for-line literalness far behind. They agree on certain points: that although the final "essence" of the poem cannot be transferred, it can be suggested, by fidelity to the emotional tone, by the exact carrying over of images, and by the application of an attentive ear to what Pound has called "the dance of intellect among words"; that unworkable metres must be eliminated; that the translator, moreover, can (and perhaps should) be more skilled in the language he is putting the poem into than in the language he is taking it out of; that he must never, as Rossetti warned, turn a good poem into a bad one. But he can loosen and interpret, and in some cases even condense and rearrange. "The best translation is to write in verse which is of our time," Richmond Lattimore has said. "We want a re-creation, not a reproduction. Contemporary verse offers a variety of variable forms unmatched, I think, in the history of our language; certainly it offers the chance of success in media far more variable than those which were thought available to Pope, or to Dryden either, or even to the Elizabethans."

Acting according to these principles, Lattimore himself, along with Robert Fitzgerald, Rolfe Humphries, Dudley Fitts, and C. Day Lewis, has given us new and striking versions of Greek and

Latin epic and lyric poetry, while Arthur Waley has found means
of making great quantities of Chinese poetry lucidly available
in English. Frank O'Connor has retraced centuries of Gaelic song.
J. B. Leishman has spent a lifetime in bringing Rilke to us from
the German practically intact. French poetry, from Baudelaire on,
has been translated endlessly. And since the early thirties the
poetry of French Surrealism, in translation, has become widely
international, sweeping into Wales (Dylan Thomas), Spain
(Lorca), and South America (Neruda). During the same period,
translations of the poetry of Eliot and Pound have strongly affected European and even Asiatic literature.

New areas of interest are now becoming rare, but one almost
untouched national group has recently attracted the attention of
translators in England and America. Modern Greek poetry has
concerned the British since the war years. *The Complete Poems
of Cavafy,* translated by Rae Dalven, with an introduction by
W. H. Auden; *Poems,* by George Seferis, translated by Rex War-
ner; as well as an anthology, *Six Poets of Modern Greece,* chosen,
translated, and introduced by Edmund Keeley and Philip Sher-
rard, have recently appeared. Constantine P. Cavafy (1863–
1933) became a friend of E. M. Forster during Forster's stay in
Alexandria during the 1914–1918 war, and through Forster his
poetry was brought to the attention of Eliot and Lawrence. Auden,
in his introduction, acknowledges his own debt to Cavafy, whose
work he has known for thirty years. He goes on to point out
Cavafy's remarkable power of projecting emotion and dramatic
idea without the aid of simile or metaphor ("Every line of his is
plain factual description without any ornamentation whatever")
and his exceptional honesty as a witness in the three fields of his
interest—"love, art and politics in the original Greek sense."
Cavafy, born out of his time, made for himself a myth of a Pan-
hellenic world bound together by loyalty to the Greek language,
and many of his subjects cast back to the ages of Constantine
and of the Byzantine Empire. These historical vignettes, organized
with the strictest economy and ironically projected, are a pleasure
to read. But Cavafy's erotic poems are often filled with attitudes
and directions of feeling that do not carry over from one culture
to another—not, at least, from his to ours. There seems to be a
definite Anglo-Saxon resistance to poems that express, on the

one hand, casual love affairs and, on the other, the longing and melancholy of a lover grown old.

The poetry of George Seferis—born in 1900, brought up in Smyrna, educated in Paris, and long a member of his country's diplomatic service—though much less original than Cavafy's, combines traditional vigor with modern subtlety. Where Cavafy is neat, hard, and unembellished, Seferis is rich in content and design—restless and openly emotional. His poetry, shifting between the ancient and the modern worlds, reflecting color from both, has not escaped a touch of the prevalent international style. This style, with its roots in Symbolism and Surrealism, is overtly manipulated in the work of the younger poets represented in the Keeley-Sherrard collection, which presents Odysseus Elytis (born in 1911) and Nikos Gatsos (born in 1912) as well as Cavafy, Seferis, and others.

Side by side with this little constellation of modern Greeks, two interesting versions of French originals have recently been published. St.-John Perse, whose work has been put into many languages, has been fortunate in his British and American translators ever since Eliot produced his exquisite version of *Anabase* in 1930. Perse's latest long poem, *Chronique,* has now been translated by Robert Fitzgerald. Perse has raised modern poetic procedures to a high pitch of effectiveness. *Chronique,* described by the Swedish Academy, on the occasion of Perse's receiving the Nobel Prize for Literature for 1960, as "a prophetic appeal to Europe to consider the fatal moment, the turning point in the course of historical events," has here been brought over into English in full rhetorical splendor.

"Racine's plays are generally and correctly thought to be untranslatable," Robert Lowell writes in an introductory note to his rendering of *Phèdre,* published in a volume with Jacques Barzun's translation of Beaumarchais' *Mariage de Figaro.* Lowell understands that the classicism of France's greatest poet is not only a matter of form but a matter of civilization—of highly organized rituals of manner, custom, and belief. He also understands that passion and truthtelling are bound into Racine's style, which consists, as a French critic recently remarked, "of a small number of extremely ordinary words that compose into a music." Lowell has faced his task with courage and resource. To manage five-

beat rhymed couplets (his substitute for the French rhymed
alexandrines) without stiffness, in straightforward idiomatic
English, is in itself a feat. In addition, the play, under his hands,
is filled with those happy discoveries of phrase that the French
call *trouvailles*, which arise less from pure luck than from intense
application to the work in hand, combined with intelligence and
a kind of creative grace.

PAUL VALÉRY
(1939)

American readers eager for acquaintance with Valéry's work have been meagerly served. Just after Valéry's reception into the French Academy in 1927, Malcolm Cowley translated *Variété I*, the collection of essays by which Valéry tried—not entirely successfully—to explain the researches into pure thought and "pure poetry" that had occupied him during twenty years of silence. Now, after a long lapse of time, and after Valéry has published many volumes in France, a new translation of miscellaneous essays appears, made up of pieces chosen from three books, *Variété II* (1930), *Pièces sur l'art* (1934), and *Variété III* (1936), together with an essay on Villon and Verlaine, published in France as a finely produced separate volume in 1937.

Faced with the last-named essay, the reader familiar only with the first, ten-years-old translation may well be puzzled about Valéry's development. For the essay on Villon and Verlaine is, obviously, a well-made piece of hack writing. It is not profound or even subtle; it might have been turned out by a journalist in the ordinary run of his work. Where are the evidences of labor and strain which Valéry once insisted must go into the act of writing? Where are the results of his belief in literature's difficult function? This essay, taken by itself, is proof of the change which has come over the man who once disdained to utter any thoughts at all; who admired, in literature, not so much works themselves as the "genesis" of works, and the spiritual elements which, in fusion, bring about the initial impetus in the artistic process. We see here a result of the circumstances which have transformed Valéry from a poet and thinker who, as he has said of Poe, "tried to unite a sort of mathematics with a sort of mysticism" into Valéry the academician, expected to have ideas on all sorts of artistic manifestations, have them often, and have them publicly.

Valéry's general ideas were never particularly varied, and they tended, as he has lately himself admitted, to harden into *idées fixes*. His sensibilities, on the other hand, have always been fine and complex. But he has spent many years in crying down his major gifts. His early strong admiration for Mallarmé, his acquaintance with Mallarmé's arduous poetic practice, and his youth spent in the anti-romantic atmosphere of the Symbolist movement gave him not only a dislike but also a positive feeling of guilt concerning literature sensuously or intuitively expressed. His poetry, he has said, has for him been a set of "exercises." He disparages the element of chance, "inspiration," and insists on the function of the will in art. He has swallowed without a tremor Poe's rationalizations of instinctive creative workings. He has peppered his writings with italics, as though he were constantly bearing down on their essential "thought." Beneath all this underscoring his style flows on fluidly, often with rhetorical magnificence. He is a writer, all his protestations to the contrary, endowed with a natural feeling for sonorous language, operating under the force of a highly refined and subtle intuition. Gifts of this kind cannot be concealed and cannot be forged. The fact that Valéry continually denies them lends to his work as a whole a faint, continual tone of sophistry. We believe in him only partially, and most completely when he has for a moment let down his guard.

One fortunate result of the demands made upon Valéry by his official position is the diminution of his habit of endowing certain artists with his favorite virtues. Although still extolling Protagorean man, "the measure of all things," he can now look more objectively on individual personalities. The essays in the present volume devoted to Stendhal and Baudelaire are truly distinguished pieces of analytical appreciation. The Stendhal essay throws light not only upon Stendhal but upon the complexities of his time. Stendhal, detached and ironic observer of the follies attendant, in the post-Napoleonic era, upon the beginnings of big business, bureaucracy, and middle-class decorum, who insisted upon following his own tastes in art and amusement while his contemporaries "ended by no longer believing in anything but money," Valéry appreciates as an example of free spirit. Again, in the Baudelaire essay, he places the poet in his rightful place as the man who broke through romantic extravagance into modern cleanness of expression and inexorable realism.

In contrast to these solid and illuminating pieces of criticism, Valéry's sad views of the breakdown of the human spirit in the modern world—he has been writing and rewriting these views for twenty years—sound feeble and complaining. Defining "the spirit" almost out of existence, he neglects to mention the sources, in ordinary human vitality, from which it continues even now to draw refreshment. How would an illustrious figure from the past view our civilization? he asks. Would not such a one be terrified of it, or disgusted with it? Since no vital response is struck out of himself, Valéry donates to men who might well be delighted with some manifestations of modern vigor his own elegant despair. Valéry is weakest when he allows his sensitiveness, lately absorbed into the chilly conservatism of the public man, to underestimate "the spirit's" essential toughness. Man may bomb himself off the earth, but it is unlikely that human attributes will recede back into the prehuman. And Valéry's illustrious ghost would recognize holdovers from the past in the present: crime, poverty, and riches. The reasons for these holdovers Valéry never allows himself to go into.

The present translation is uninspired. The translator, William Aspenwall Bradley, has edited the French: the essay "Mediterranean Inspiration," for example, has been cut in half, and the section containing some of Valéry's most fruitful writing, dropped. It would be a good thing if a more representative collection of Valéry's prose were published. His dialogues, considered by some critics to be his most valuable writing, his reminiscences of Mallarmé and Degas, a selection from his aphorisms and *aperçus*, the essays which establish his connoisseurship in the minor arts, together with many passages which succeed in drawing with great delicacy lines connecting man with the beauty and mystery of nature—such pieces of writing would give readers of translations a better view of the man than has been afforded them up to now. Such a book would be an antidote to the unhealthy tendency toward formula rather than feeling, in literature at large and in Valéry himself. It would present Valéry the poet *malgré lui*—his most valuable role. True poets are rare. There are always plently of real and disguised academicians.

ROBERT PENN WARREN
(1944)

After more than a quarter-century of "experiment," a new formal English poetic style seems finally to have emerged. What Browning, Swinburne, Tennyson, and Matthew Arnold would think of it is anybody's guess, even though all these formidable Victorians contribute to its present form. The contributions of Eliot and Pound derive from various neglected English poetic sources, as well as many non-English ones (French Symbolism and translations from the Gaelic and Chinese). The insistence made by the English poets of the thirties upon satire and the sharpness of ordinary speech are factors, but not to an overwhelming degree. This style is now a supple instrument. It has lost its early stiffness, inherited from the Imagists, and it is no longer heavily weighted with the learned tags dear to bright young people, or encumbered with certain affected theatrics carried over from the late nineties.

It is a formal style, and therefore difficult to apprehend at first glance. Critics have spluttered and fumed over its "obscurity" and Marxists have labeled it with their limited and old-fashioned reproach "ivory tower." Whether this style, having tentatively formed, is capable of endurance and growth, it is too early to say. What it needs at the moment is practitioners and an attentive, disintcrested audience. The folk line and the line of bourgeois literature can be counted on to keep flourishing; it is formal poetry that now needs critics and friends.

Two new books by American poets highly skilled in this new formal technique, who have highly complex mental and spiritual equipment to express by means of it, have recently appeared. Robert Penn Warren, a native of Kentucky, a Rhodes scholar, and a member of the Nashville "Fugitive" group, which, in the twenties, applied itself to a Southern renaissance of literature, philosophy, and classical learning, brings together work that dates from his student days on in *Selected Poems, 1923–1943.* His book is divided into two sections, in which the later poems come first. It is not easy, therefore, at once to trace the line of his growth, but the line is there, and, because it follows to some extent the emerging formal style, it is interesting to begin with his early poems and read backward toward his later ones. The "Fugitive" group was concerning itself with "regional" material long before the "regional" became a fashion. Mr. Warren's early treatment of his Kentucky background coincides with the "literary" stiffness which afflicted poetry at the time. Many of the poems show clear outlines of influence. Three very fine ones— "Pacific Gazer," "Calendar," and "The Garden"—are such close approximations of originals that the first two might be included in the canon of Hardy and the last in the canon of Marvell. But little by little the influences fuse. Mr. Warren ends by being able to write with great freedom. He can combine a clever approximation of "folk" with running comment in the manner of the late Eliot ("The Ballad of Billie Potts"). Consider "Mexico Is a Foreign Country: Five Studies in Naturalism" as proof of how Mr. Warren can at the moment absorb all sorts of material with the readiness of maturity. Language is beautifully handled throughout, and the poet has a point of view and the courage of his convictions. The two poems "Original Sin" and "Crime" show his complex perceptions and the modern poetic style working brilliantly together on subjects which perceptive modern poets keep coming back to: obscure psychological guilt and corruption, sadism, obsession—dissimulated under the fixed pattern of modern life and everyday conformity.

Robert Fitzgerald is some years younger than Warren. He is a graduate of Harvard, a classical scholar, and a translator, with a collaborator, of plays by Sophocles and Euripides. His expression, by the evidence of the poems in *A Wreath for the Sea*, is natively nimbler than Warren's. His observation is delicate but precise. He has a lyric gift which might easily have been diverted to petty uses. But the drawing back from tough reality, characteristic of the "aesthetic" period of modern poetry, has been overcome. Baudelaire's lesson on how the modern world can be incorporated into verse has been relearned. Fitzgerald's grasp of classic resonance and balance brings him out always on the side of simplicity; he is incapable of either rhetoric or bombast. His effects are sometimes rather muffled, but soon the expected translucence returns, and we are back in that humane region where the gravity of learning and the seriousness of art function, never out of touch with life.

It is in writers such as these that a style which avoids the confusion of Surrealism and the bigotries of polemics, which has no place for the accepted idea in the slick rhythm, for the academic-maudlin, for the fake man-in-the-street-tough, for the high-minded, simple-minded conventions, begins to come into its own.

EUDORA WELTY

(1941)

The definite Gothic quality which characterizes so much of the work of writers from the American South has puzzled critics. Is it the leftover atmosphere of the *roman noir,* so skillfully transferred to America by Poe? Or is it a true and indigenous atmosphere of decaying feudalism? Faulkner treats the horrifying and ambiguous situations thrown up by a background which has much in common with nineteenth-century Russia in a style darkened and convoluted by, it would seem, the very character of his material. Eudora Welty, who is a native and resident of Mississippi, in the stories of this volume, *A Curtain of Green,* has instinctively chosen another method which opens and widens the field and makes it more amenable to detached observation. She proceeds with the utmost simplicity and observes with the most delicate terseness. She does not try mystically to transform or anonymously to interpret. The parallel forced upon us, particularly by those of Miss Welty's stories which are based on an oblique humor, is her likeness to Gogol.

The tramp musicians, the inhabitants of a big house (either mad, drunk, or senile), the idiots and ageless peasant women, the eccentric families tyrannized over by an arch-eccentric, the pathetic and ridiculous livers of double lives, even the Negro band leader with his sadism and delusion of grandeur—all these could come out of some broken-down medieval scene, and all could have been treated completely successfully—with humorous detachment, combined with moments of tenderness and roaring farce—by the author of *The Inspector General* and *Dead Souls.* Like Gogol, Miss Welty opens the doors and describes the setting, almost inch by inch. She adds small detail to small detail: the fillings in people's teeth, the bright mail-order shirts of little boys, the bottles of Ne-Hi, the pictures of Nelson Eddy hung up like icons. We see what happens to representatives of an alien commercial world—here, traveling salesmen: how they become entangled against their will in this scene which goes on under its own obscure decomposing laws; or dissolve back into it, symbolically enough, in delirium and death. Even the women in the beauty parlor have a basic place in the composition; they are not so much modernly vulgar as timelessly female—calculating, shrewd, and sharp. Miss Welty's method can get everything in; nothing need be scamped, because of romantic exigencies, or passed over, because of rules of taste. Temperamentally and by training she has become mistress of her material by her choice of one exactly suitable kind of treatment, and—a final test of a writer's power—as we read her, we are made to believe that she has hit upon the only possible kind. But it is a method, in Miss Welty's hands, only suitable for her Southern characters on their own ground. The one story dealing with the North, "Flowers for Marjorie," goes completely askew.

Katherine Anne Porter, in her preface, surveys with much insight the nature and scope of, as well as the dangers attendant upon, the specialized talent of the writer of short stories. She warns against "the novel," a form held up to the short-story writer as a baited trap. She does not warn against the other trap, the commercial short story, and the other tempter, "the agent." It seems impossible that Miss Welty, equipped as she is, should fall into line and produce the bloated characters and smoothed-out situations demanded by "commercial" publications. But other finely equipped persons have given in. As for the novel, she needs to introduce only the slenderest unifying device, something analogous to "a smart britchka, a light spring-carriage of the sort affected by bachelors, retired lieutenant colonels, staff captains, landowners possessed of about a hundred souls," to write one whenever she wishes.

EDITH WHARTON

(1938)

Edith Wharton has told how she was haunted, before the books in which they ultimately appeared were written, by her characters, or, even, by their disembodied names. In her autobiography, *A Backward Glance*, she mentioned a name then in her mind: Laura Testvalley. *The Buccaneers*, Mrs. Wharton's last and unfinished novel, gives Laura Testvalley her scene and character. She is a governess, granddaughter of a hero of the Risorgimento (Gennaro Testvaglia), cousin to Dante Gabriel Rossetti, once employed by a duchess, and later governess in an "old" New York family. She goes on to the higher wages offered by a "new" family (whose money is based on "deals" and financial manipulation), takes the fortunes of the younger daughter in hand and pilots her, over the heads of the disapproving Newport and New York sets, to London, and into a titled marriage. The manuscript breaks off before the novel's dénouement: Laura's sacrifice of personal happiness in order that her former pupil, now the ranking duchess of England, may escape from her duties and her dull duke into "deep and abiding love" with a lover. The outline left by Mrs. Wharton describes the entire plot very clearly.

It is interesting to see how Henry James's insistence on "form"

in the novel was simplified by his friend and follower, Mrs.
Wharton, into mere adherence to plot. The plot must proceed,
through all its ramifications, even though characters be wrenched
out of shape to serve it. Minor figures, put in purely to prop up the
plan, soon are shuffled away, and are featureless from the beginning. The long arm of coincidence snaps up the roving actors
and places them down neatly in surroundings cleverly arranged
to suit their situation. The background is filled in with great
color and accuracy; there is continual movement; the details of
life in drawing room, ducal seat, and dower-house, on Saratoga
verandas, in a ruined Cornish castle, on American railway platforms, all suitably lighted by the atmosphere of the seventies,
are written down by a mistress of genre. But *The Buccaneers*,
for all Mrs. Wharton's cleverness and skill, is dead at the heart.
The book brings out, however, the way in which Mrs. Wharton's
work formed a bridge from the nineteenth-century novel to the
magazine fiction of the present where, in a superficially arranged
scene, manners, clothes, food, and interior decorations are described carefully and at length; how she contained in herself,
as it were, the whole transitional period of American fiction,
beginning in the bibelot and imported-European-culture era of the
late nineties, and ending in the woman's-magazine dream of
suburban smartness.

The essential numbness in her novels—with the exception of
Ethan Frome, where her talent for local color and her insight
into the simpler ingredients of human character succeeded, because she did not attempt too much—goes back to the fact that
she based her values not upon a free and rich feeling for life
but on a feeling for decorum and pre-Wall Street merchant respectability. James praised early in her career "her diabolical
little cleverness, the quality of intention and intelligence in her
style, and her sharp eye for an interesting kind of subject." Added
to these gifts was a highly trained taste, a thorough acquaintance
with the "great world" of her time, and a passion for artistic
people, provided, of course, that their background and manners
conformed to the rather stuffy standards of the late nineteenth-
century upper bourgeoisie. She admired, it should be remembered, not only Henry James but also Paul Bourget. An example
of her fundamental bias against the disordered life of the artist

is her astonishment when she discovered that George Sand's home, Nohant, showed no sign of the wild life which had streamed through it; it did not look *déclassé*, but on the contrary traditional and respectable. (The sympathetic attitude expressed in James's two essays on Sand is in strong contrast to Mrs. Wharton's surprise.) And Mrs. Wharton's mildly ironic description of life in great English houses should be put against the true dissection apparent in James's approach to the same subject. For the difference between a subject treated with ingenuity and one treated with imagination, Nan St. George, the "new rich" girl in *The Buccaneers,* and her family can be set beside Daisy Miller and hers. We love the living people and merely watch the puppets.

WALT WHITMAN
(1955)

Two books appearing early in this centenary year of the publication of *Leaves of Grass* cut close to the main facts of Whitman's life and legend and add lustre to the somewhat faded reputation of one of the most remarkable poets of the nineteenth century. Professor Gay Wilson Allen's *The Solitary Singer: A Critical Biography of Walt Whitman* is a workmanlike piece of documentation that scans all the sources, while the series of essays that make up *Leaves of Grass: One Hundred Years After,* edited, with an introduction, by Milton Hindus, subjects Whitman the man and poet to the most searching kind of criticism, "new" and otherwise. Taken together, the two books not only place Whitman in relation to his own time but make him fully relevant to ours, without omitting any puzzling and contradictory facts. Professor Allen's straightforward account does not stress Whitman's enigmatic character, but in the Hindus collection Whitman's masks are lifted by several hands. Leslie A. Fiedler, Richard Chase, David Daiches, Middleton Murry, and a number of others show what manner of man it was who, unknown in 1855, at the age of thirty-six, described himself in his first book as both "a kosmos" and "one of the roughs."

Fiedler discusses the shifts in Whitman's reputation since the poet's death. The old man who died in Camden in 1892 became for a time, particularly in the eyes of the young, a tribal bard. After 1918, however, his influence declined; postwar poetry began to move toward technical and emotional restraint at the same time that postwar thought began to take a dim view of man's relation to the universe. To that generation, Whitman's poetry seemed tiresomely exuberant and naïvely full of hope; even D. H. Lawrence, in acknowledging Whitman as one of his masters, accused him of "merging" instead of standing alone; and both Pound and Eliot gave Whitman little credit and no allegiance. (It is ironic to remember that Laforgue, to whom postwar poets *did* render allegiance, had tied Whitman to the beginnings of poetic modernism by his Whitman translations in the 1880s.) Meanwhile, research was bringing to light Whitman's more paradoxical side—his fibs and his "furtiveness," and evidence, in spite of the poet's repeated avowals of strong masculinity, of his "diffused" and largely feminine sexual nature. The reasons for Whitman's ruses and disguises were not then taken into account, so the American poet whose influence had been so vigorous and so powerful not only in America but in Europe was reduced very nearly to an old crank and an old fraud.

In 1955, the wheel of taste and of opinion has turned to the point where no critic, however academic or "new," can treat Whitman with complete harshness or indifference. These recent essays, including the editor's introduction, analyze, for the most part sympathetically, when they do not praise, the poet whose public life, it is now clear, according to Richard Chase, was "an evasion according to plan." Whitman's egotism troubles more than one contributor, but Fiedler is alone in being bothered by the poet's "third-rate mind, sentimental, obtuse, and indolent." Chase, on the other hand, points out Whitman's constant closeness to "unconscious depths," and presents him "brooding with the same sense of mystery on the most sublime and the most vulgar and sordid aspects of life." "The culture of his time," Chase goes on to say, "admired (much more so than our culture does today) the prophet, the orator, the sententious democratic reformer [as well as] rough plebeian masculinity. It would condone oddity of behavior (more so than now) so long as the main requirements

were met. Whitman met them. . . . [His poses] and his democratic program (valuable as these are in themselves) were the
massive irrelevance and waste required for the indulgence of
the essential Whitman—the young comic god and profound
elegist."

It is the young Whitman—in shirt-sleeves and a rakish felt
hat, handsome, dark-bearded, and relaxed—that looks out at us
from the engraved frontispiece of the original edition of *Leaves
of Grass,* printed in Brooklyn in the early summer of 1855. This
man of thirty-six had given up the role of journalist-dandy: he
had been a carpenter, a printer, an editor; he was now launching
himself as a poet. He had helped design, setting some of the type
himself, this "small quarto," clearly with the book's effective presentation of the poetry well in mind. The paper is large, to accommodate the length of the lines, and there are few runovers. The title
page, set in large lower-case letters, is well balanced, although
the type is hideous. The book's format shows, in every particular,
evidence of a firm and even knowledgeable taste doing its best
with inferior material, of originality and vigor extending into
the book's physical makeup.

The combination in Whitman of sure calculation with a radiant
innocence, of complication with simplicity, of self-protective
shrewdness with shocking frankness, nowadays links him in the
modern reader's mind with Blake, another artisan-artist who went
his own way. Whitman enlarged his lyricism, as Leslie Fiedler
remarks, into epic proportions; he reported accurately and interpreted fearlessly in a period when it was hard to do either.
Throughout his life, he kept to a humble social status in a society
where all the temptations were toward rise and respectability;
he remained loyal to his difficult family, and died, an old man,
"as clean as a scrubbed deal table"—indomitable, "disreputable,"
and enigmatic to the end. The secret of his poetry, in spite of his
army of imitators, died with him. Its pulse and "verve" are inimitable, for it is the first and last American poetry with all the
American swagger left in, besides being an example of the enduring kind of art that is based on perfect sincerity, that sup-
presses nothing, and that means everything it says.

RICHARD WILBUR

THE BEAUTIFUL CHANGES (1947)

What is now called the war generation continues to turn out poetry, and although some of its productions, taken singly, are rather inconsiderable, the over-all effect is interesting. This new and crucial age group is again appearing in numbers; we now have a larger basis for comparing these poets with their elders, and with each other.

The youngest, Richard Wilbur, is twenty-six. His publishers have felt impelled to use the words "romantic" and "emotional" in describing his volume of verse, *The Beautiful Changes,* and they are quite right; in the best senses of these words, it is both. Wilbur is still quite plainly entangled with the technical equipment of his favorite poetic forerunners, specifically Marianne Moore, Eliot, Rilke, and Hopkins, from whose work he has pretty well absorbed certain lessons. He has had the wit, however, to point up these influences from time to time with the invisible quotation marks of near-parody. Wilbur surpasses the majority of his contemporaries in range of imagination and depth of feeling. He has a remarkable variety of interest and mood, and he can contemplate his subjects without nervousness, explore them with care, and then let them drop at the exact moment that the organization of a poem is complete. This ease of pace, this seemingly effortless advance to a resolute conclusion, is rare

at his age; the young usually yield to tempting inflation and
elaboration. Wilbur's gift of fitting the poetic pattern to the
material involves all sorts of delicate adjustments of the outward
senses to the inner ear. Fidelity to Nature (that old-fashioned
virtue) underlies every word, and this fidelity is directed by intelligence and taste. Wilbur's is a talent so sure of its bases that
using the despised word "beautiful" (which he employs not
as an adjective but as a noun in his title) does not harm it in the
least. Let us watch Richard Wilbur. He is composed of valid ingredients.

THINGS OF THIS WORLD (1956)

In his third volume, *Things of This World*, Richard Wilbur makes
his involvement with the actual, as well as the spiritual, quite
clear. Things exist for him in full density and circumstance,
and he sees, hears, smells, tastes, and touches them with complete freedom. Wilbur has none of that monotonous pessimism
that afflicts so many of his contemporaries. Free (it would seem
by temperament) from the persistent presence of anguish and
anxiety, he can allow himself answers to some of his questions
and indulge in imaginative suppositions and explanations. Such
liberty is, of course, only comparative; Wilbur recognizes the
terrible shadows in the human situation. But his poetry deals
with the mystics' open mystery rather than the positivists' closed
fact. His earlier work announced a lyric talent of the first order;
in the last few years he has added new dimensions—humor and
deep discernment—to his original endowment. One of his latest
poems, "A Baroque Wall-Fountain in the Villa Sciarra," published
last year and included in this volume, is more than a technical
triumph; it is a poem of tender humor unexpectedly linked with
penetrating vision.

YVOR WINTERS
(1944)

Yvor Winters, whose selected poems, *The Giant Weapon,* have
recently appeared in the New Directions series "The Poets of the
Year," has held to unpopular modes of expression in poetry and
criticism for a long time. He has clung to what often seemed
crotchets, in a time particularly unfriendly, really, to displays
of determined individuality. His poetry, which at the start adhered to the severest tenets of Imagism, refused to break up and
deliquesce when Imagism went into a decline. It turned back,
instead, to the stylistic severities of the seventeenth century.
There it settled and there it developed, slowly and very nearly
without listeners, let alone friends and admirers. The fashion for
what Winters himself has called "chaotic reverie" spread on all
sides, but Winters went on writing and translating, and in 1940
he printed, on his own press, all of his work he had decided he
wished to keep, some hundred poems in all. The new volume
is much smaller; it contains thirty-three poems, written in the
past fifteen years. "It clearly shows Winters to be one of the
really significant poets of conservative tendency now writing in
America," his publisher says. That this conservative tendency
has become so rare that it is now almost *avant garde* is an interesting fact in itself.

How stern and dry, how sharp and narrow these poems look on the page. Some readers, to whom the looseness of modern verse has become a norm, will be ready and waiting to pin the word "neo-classic" to Winters' style and attitude. But when we examine this close-grained, coolly detached writing, we come upon many delicate yet firm effects which elude this small classification. Winters' general form and tone lend themselves to the didactic, and elegiac poems are here, but with a difference. This poetry's light, undercutting observation, its tenderness, which keeps it on the side of life and joy even when it seems most grave, its total avoidance of cliché, its lack of sentimentality, its deep interest in themes of truth and justice—these elements separate it completely from dead formality and generalized emptiness. Gradually we realize that Winters is revealing to us imaginative flashes into the relationship between man, nature, and man's artifacts (between, for example, the airplane and the night sky and the human watcher who experiences them both)—flashes so unexpected that we understand rather tardily that what we are reading gives us more of the future than of the past.

Several poems have a power of evoking atmosphere and tension that more "romantic" poets might well envy. "By the Road to the Air-Base" is one of these, and "Before Disaster, 1932-3" is another. Winters teaches English at Stanford, and his subjects are often drawn from his professional life. The limp and leaden academic tone has not touched these subjects, however. His passion for integrity comes to have a searchlight intensity. He loves the classic bases of life; he suffers when he finds these bases absent or broken. His interests appear to be limited only because he has made choices; his treatment of his material makes up in height and depth for what it has abandoned in breadth. But are his subjects actually so limited? We examine them a second time and find them surprisingly numerous. And the problems he deals with, whether abstract, as his insistence upon the worth of learning and discipline, or concrete, as his defense of a friend on trial for murder, are real problems. Winters has that rare sense: the cool power to appraise evil. He does not reject evil, or try to laugh it off, or attempt to streamline it into acceptable form. He looks it in the eye and brings a sober sense of compassionate justice to bear upon it.

His poem "To a Military Rifle, 1942," I feel, turns out to be one of the fine poems produced by the war. It is as far removed from ordinary war verse as a poem can possibly be and still deal with its subject. That Winters should have written this poem, which is a poem of the future, that he should continue to exist at all, that he should have persisted in his way of writing until the turn of the wheel brought him back as "modern"—these facts should delight us. They are proof that as a people we can produce untouchable probity and distilled power in the most unlikely times.

WOMEN

THE HEART AND THE LYRE (*1947*)

The record of the verse written by women in the United States is remarkably full, for a variety of reasons. In the first place, the country became an independent republic, well equipped with printing presses and paper, during the period when American women began to write in earnest. Then, a new and eager periodical and newspaper audience, with the sort of pioneering background which holds women in high esteem, awaited bits of feminine sentiment and moralizing dressed up in metre and rhyme. Finally, the critical standard of the country remained for a long time rather lax and easygoing. A great mass of verse, good, bad, and indifferent, therefore managed to get published. Through this prolific feminine production we can trace, with much accuracy, every slight shift in American literary fashion, as well as the larger changes of an emotional and moral kind. An examination of the rise and development of female poetic talent over a period of more than one hundred and fifty years in a society which, on the whole, encouraged that talent to function freely and in the open, brings to light various truths concerning the worth and scope of women's poetic gifts.

Before we survey the interesting, colorful, and frequently comic array of American women "poetesses" from Lydia Huntley Sigourney (1791–1865) through the youngest feminine contemporaries, let us look at some of the assumptions and prejudices that have long lodged in people's minds on the subject of women as poets. One rather hoary idea is that women put emotion before form and are likely to be indifferent technicians. Do they not usually, as well, imitate closely the poetic productions of men? A third dark suspicion concerning women's poetic powers troubled even the highly intelligent and ardently feminist mind of Virginia Woolf. Mrs. Woolf, in her delightful series of lectures published in 1929 under the title *A Room of One's Own*, is continually bothered by the thought that in spite of material and moral emancipations women may never write a work of wide and compelling force comparable, for example, to Shakespeare's plays. To exorcise this spectral doubt, Mrs. Woolf canvasses fully the history of woman's difficulties in the role of artist.

Women have always been busy and poor, Mrs. Woolf's argument runs; busy, because they are physically responsible for the production and early care of specimens of the human race; and poor because it seems that men's laws are often framed to keep them in that condition. Lack of education, the tyranny of families, the ridicule of society, as well as lack of independent means, have been factors which, perhaps, kept women from writing epic poems or long poetic plays. Mrs. Woolf gives every credit to the anonymous women who had a hand in composing folk tales, folk songs, adages, proverbs, and nursery rhymes (for it is, after all, Mother Goose, and *Ma Mère l'Oie*). And she is happy to note that, when new freedoms arrived in Europe and England at the end of the eighteenth century, women novelists, at least, appeared in numbers and with brilliance. But what of Shakespeare's supposititious sister—ignorant, penniless, and fearful of masculine jeers, had she tried to carve out a career for herself in the sixteenth century? It is at this point in her argument that Mrs. Woolf begins to stumble against the doubt that any woman is ever going to write a great poetic tragedy in five acts. Perhaps after a hundred years or so this goal will be realized, if the creative woman is given five hundred pounds per annum and, behind a door with a lock on it, a room of her own.

It was a little old-fashioned even in 1929 for Mrs. Woolf to choose a five-act poetic play as the final test of a woman poet's powers. Her vision was somewhat clouded by an Anglo-Saxon

literary point of view. Why should women, past, present, or
future, remain fixed in the determination to out-Shakespeare
Shakespeare? Can it be that there is no basic reason for women
to excel in the art of poetry by producing the same sort of poetic
structures as men? Men, as a matter of fact, stayed with the
five-act poetic tragedy far too long. Perhaps women have more
sense than to linger over an obsessing form of this kind.

We turn to the full and complete annals of American women
poets hoping that we may discover facts that will lead to a new
estimate of the poetic gift in women, as well as hints about its
present and future direction. The first women versifiers who appear on the American scene were, it must be confessed, unen-
dowed, grim, pious, and lachrymose. Mrs. Sigourney was provincial and naïve enough to glory in two titles: the "American
Hemans" and the "Sweet Singer of Hartford." She reigned, moreover, for a long period as the head of American female letters—
from shortly after Washington's second term as president until
just after the death of Lincoln, to be exact. She was fluent, industrious, and rather pushing; but she managed to put feminine
verse-writing on a paying basis, and give it prestige; even Poe did
not quite dare to handle her work too roughly. She gave simple
men and women along the Eastern seaboard and in the backwoods of the West something to be proud of; it is pleasant for a
young nation to have a vocal tutelary goddess.

During Mrs. Sigourney's lifetime the choir of female singers
enlarged. Soon a series of anthologies began to appear, exclusively
devoted to "songstresses." *The Ladies' Wreath* (1837), edited by
Mrs. Sarah Josepha Hale, who also edited *Godey's Lady's Book*,
was the first of these. Others followed; and by 1849 Rufus Griswold was able to make good profits with his collection entitled
The Female Poets of America. This collection went through several
editions and, after Griswold's death, turned up in the seventies
with a new editor. We are now in a new world. The more de-
pressing ante-bellum aspects of female piety and melancholy
have worn off, and we are presented with the spectacle of
women becoming ever more ardent and airy. The ardors of Poe's
women friends, Fanny Osgood and Mrs. Whitman, are now
surpassed by their successors. When we come to Edmund
Clarence Stedman's *An American Anthology* (1900), an often

unbroken phalanx of women with three (and sometimes four) invincibly Yankee names advances down the table of contents, and their work is now startlingly filled with evidence of culture, with whimsicality, self-preening, and affectation.

But although women's literary manners and, it would seem, their affections became ever more wayward and free, their grasp upon basic conventions remained firm. Even the Wisconsin farm girl, Ella Wheeler, who spiced her stanzas with hints of sin in *Poems of Passion* (1883) soon quiets down into marriage and respectability with a Mr. Wilcox. The list of these late-nineteenth-century women in Stedman, with their multiple names printed in chaste Gothic type, tends to become a blur. But if we search carefully for even the smallest sincerity and talent, personalities begin to emerge. Alice and Phoebe Cary; Celia Thaxter; the mill girl, Lucy Larcom, protégée of Whittier; Julia Ward Howe; Emma Lazarus, who was Jewish, and Louise Imogen Guiney, who was an "Irish Catholic"; Lizette Woodworth Reese of Baltimore and Harriet Monroe of Chicago; and, further back, crowded in with Mrs. Spofford, Mrs. Moulton, Thomas Bailey Aldrich, Joaquin Miller, and Edward Rowland Sill, we come upon an unpretentious name, easily overlooked, of a woman born in 1830 and dead in 1886: Emily Dickinson. Emily Dickinson represents the final flowering of a long Puritan tradition. Her genius has a hard, bitter, but real kind of civilization behind it; women poets share with men the need for some sort of civilized ground from which to draw sustenance. But it is apparently more difficult for women to throw off the more superficial fashions of any society in which they find themselves. The earlier history of women poets in America should stand as a warning to modern young women of talent. The special virtues of women are clear, in the same record. Women are forced to become adult. They must soon abandon sustained play, in art or life. They are not good at abstractions and their sense of structure is not large; but they often have the direct courage to be themselves. They are practical, intense, and (usually) both generous and magnanimous. They often have a true contemplative gift; and they are natural singers. They are capable of originality and breadth of emotional and intellectual reference as soon as their background opens to any breadth and variety. They are often forced to waste their powers

in an inadequate milieu, in social improvisation; to tack back and
forth between revolt and conservatism. Far from imitating men
to an untoward degree, they often experiment boldly with form
and language. Early in the twentieth century, Gertrude Stein,
working indefatigably and alone, begins to examine words with
the detached interest of the scientist and arrange them in abstract
patterns. A little later H. D. gives back to Greek themes some
of the pure severity of Greek poetry in the original. Marianne
Moore applies a naturalist's eye to objects of art and of nature,
describing "with an extraordinary magnificence of phraseology"
unlooked-for combinations and harmonies between matter and
the spirit. These women have had their male, as well as their
female, followers.

   Young women writing poetry at present are likely to consider
the figure of the woman poet as romantic rebel rather ridiculous
and outmoded. The youngest generation of women poets is, in
fact, moving toward an imitation of certain masculine "trends"
in contemporary poetry. They are imitating, moreover, the work
of male verbalizers and poetic logicians, rather than the work
of men who have carried through, out of a profound urgency,
major poetic investigations; there are few feminine disciples
of either Eliot or Auden, in these poets' later phases. Even the
greatly gifted Elizabeth Bishop, whose first book recently appeared, places emphasis more upon anecdote than upon ardor.
The fear of some regression into typical romantic attitudes is,
at present, operating from feminine talent; and this is not a
wholly healthy impulse, for it negates too strongly a living and
valuable side of woman's character. In women, more than in
men, the intensity of their emotions is the key to the treasures
of their spirit. The cluster of women lyric poets that appeared
on the American scene just before and after 1918 restored genuine and frank feeling to a literary situation which had become
genteel, artificial, and dry. Sara Teasdale's later verse; the best
of Edna Millay's early rebellious songs and meditations; Elinor
Wylie's ability to fuse thought and passion into the most admirable and complex forms; the sensitive, intellectual poetry of
Léonie Adams—all these poetic productions helped to resolve
hampering attitudes of the period.

   The great importance of keeping the emotional channels of

a literature open has frequently been overlooked. The need of the refreshment and the restitution of feeling, in all its warmth and depth, has never been more apparent than it is today, when cruelty and fright often seem about to overwhelm man and his world. For women to abandon their contact with, and their expression of, deep and powerful emotional streams, because of contemporary pressures or mistaken self-consciousness, would result in an impoverishment not only of their own inner resources but of mankind's at large. Certainly it is not a regression to romanticism to remember that women are capable of perfect and poignant song; and that when this song comes through in its high and rare form, the result has always been regarded not only with delight but with a kind of awe. It is a good thing for young women to bring to mind the fact that lost fragments of the work of certain women poets—of Emily Dickinson no less than of the Sappho quoted by Longinus as an example of "the sublime"—are searched for less with the care and eagerness of the scholar looking for bits of shattered human art, than with the hungry eyes of the treasure hunter, looking for some last grain of a destroyed jewel. Though she may never compose an epic or a tragic drama in five acts, the woman poet has her singular role and precious destiny. And, at the moment, in a time lacking in truth and certainty and filled with anguish and despair, no woman should be shamefaced in attempting to give back to the world, through her work, a portion of its lost heart.

IN BALANCE: BABETTE DEUTSCH, KATHERINE HOSKINS, RUTH STONE, BARBARA HOWES, MARIANNE MOORE
(1959)

Is it possible, at the moment, to separate poetry written by women from poetry written by men, or has women's poetry been so thoroughly absorbed into the poetic situation at large that to set it apart must seem nearsighted and time-wasting? Certainly, at their best, women poets writing in English have for a long time left sentimentality and an addiction to the cozier aspects of

existence far behind them and have proved themselves capable
of experiment. Recently, when masculine poetic talent has either
tended to flatten into formalism or come to depend upon shock
tactics of one kind or another, poetry written by women has gone
its own way and produced its own distinct lines of development.
In the last few publishing seasons a contrast between kinds of
feminine talent has become increasingly clear. We see on the one
hand an adherence to convention, in both material and method,
and on the other a pronounced liking, on the part of some women
writers, for extreme elaboration and ambiguity—toward a kind of
writing that might be called mannerist or even *précieuse.*

Recent volumes show women's talent, as it were, in balance.
Babette Deutsch's *Coming of Age* sums up a career. Miss
Deutsch's lyrics are dramatically pictorial; she presents moments
of everyday reality that turn out to be mirrors of her informed
convictions. She is an expert translator—of Rilke, Pushkin,
Baudelaire, Mayakovsky, and Pasternak—and some of her translations, which keep close to the form of the originals, are included.
Whether Miss Deutsch gives us a moment of urban life, a
vignette of nature, or an experience related to painting or music,
she operates at a high point of professional skill, out of a framework of civilized belief. The poet and the disciplined woman of
letters exist side by side and set each other off.

To move to Katherine Hoskins (whose third book, *Out in the
Open,* has recently been published) requires that the reader
pass through a wide arc of literary custom, practice, intention,
and style. We have become accustomed to metaphysical poetry
"wherein," to quote a scholar, "the poet achieves the reconciliation of clashing opposites." Miss Hoskins goes beyond this. The
term "baroque," which in our day has crept over from critical
discussions of art and architecture into discussions of music and
literature, surely applies to Miss Hoskins' verse. If "baroque
metaphors"—and I quote again—"distort and upset reality," Miss
Hoskins' metaphors certainly fall into this classification. As for
style, she dispenses at will with that accepted rule of modern
prosody—the natural words in the natural order. Syntactical in-
versions abound; impenetrable and peculiar modifiers accompany
equally odd nouns and verbs. And strain is present in experience
as well as in description: people walk through black marble, and

one senses the ocean in the rufflings of a cat's fur. Is this the poetic future, we ask ourselves as our eyes traverse these strange and overtaxed pages, in whose turgidity, it is true, an occasional moment of insight succeeds in holding our exasperated attention? We receive no reassuring answer from Miss Hoskins.

In an Iridescent Time, the first book by Ruth Stone, is a more direct expression of temperament than *Out in the Open,* although strangeness of diction and of angle of vision is frequent. Mrs. Stone seems to take delight in wrenching words out of progression and juxtaposing incongruous facts; she can be extremely artificial. But a dark melancholy, a sense of horror, despair, and foreboding, a bitter aftertaste of experience often come through; a truly macabre imagination is at work. And the poems are firmly based on reality; their titles make sense, often of a witty kind. It is recognizably a woman's nature that is expressed throughout. There is more than mannerism here.

Happily, it is possible to conclude on a rising note, with the mention of two recent books by women—one from a younger and one from an older generation—that can be read with complete pleasure. The first of these, *Light and Dark,* by Barbara Howes, confirms Miss Howes' early promise, with poems drawn from the heart of maturity in richness and variety. The second, Miss Marianne Moore's *O to Be a Dragon,* brings together fifteen new poems of Miss Moore's inimitable kind. Do not wish to be a dragon, Miss Moore. Stay as you are and refresh us with further praises of life and art, as you refresh us here.

NO POETESSES MAUDITES: MAY SWENSON, ANNE SEXTON (1963)

Now that the work of male poets writing in English seems to have settled down into a few standard categories of material (bland, horrific) and of treatment (formal, loose), it is interesting to notice that poetry written by women (once thought to be limited to a rather narrow vein of personal lyricism) has also sorted itself out into a few basic kinds. To separate the work of women writers from the work of men is, naturally, a highly unfeminist action. But beneath surface likenesses, women's poetry continues to be unlike men's, all feminist statements to the contrary notwithstanding. Women function differently, in art as in life, and it should be an enlivening rather than a dismal fact that there are some things they either cannot or are unwilling to do, and others that they do very badly.

The old untruth that female writers imitate male masters has been pretty well demolished. Since the early nineteenth century, women writers, in English as in other tongues, have freed themselves for good from damning and debasing eighteenth-century labels. Miss Austen, in Regency times, managed to put together one perfect kind of novel from the bits and pieces—journals and letters—scattered through earlier centuries by literate Englishwomen. Later, women began to appear in every true literary vanguard, often so far in front that the rank and file did not know of their existence. In this way, Emily Brontë and Emily Dickinson broke out of the binding confines of the personal over into broad regions of human complexity, and, more recently, Marianne Moore, Gertrude Stein (at her least compulsive), and the late Hilda Doolittle extended poetry's limits while reforming poetry's means.

But along with new freedoms and renewed skill, new limitations and few old ones in disguise began to appear. In life or in letters, a woman cannot successfully imitate a man's rougher conduct (George Sand's cigar and male travesty went out very early, even in the case of George Sand). She cannot seem to be totally abandoned or directly destructive. And it is difficult for her to throw reason to the winds; to a woman, pure illogicality seems not only silly but potentially dangerous. There are no *poétesses maudites* and there are no authentic women Surrealists. Surrealism, with its frequent harsh eroticism, its shock tactics, and its coarse way with language, comes hard to women writers, whose basic creative impulses usually involve tenderness and affection.

At the same time, some younger women, following in the footsteps of Marianne Moore, have become close but detached observers of the facts of nature and—sometimes—of art. Keeping themselves out of it, they display a woman's talent for dealing intensely and imaginatively with the concrete. May Swenson is perhaps the most skillful and devoted of this group. She applies a naturalist's care to her descriptions of animals, plants, flowers, landscapes, and seascapes, and a warm interest underlies this examination of her surroundings. She can, moreover, move through city streets without being chilled by their buildings and machines. *To Mix with Time*, which contains new and old poems, is a volume full of color and variety, and of high technical skill.

Anne Sexton, in her second book, *All My Pretty Ones*, as in her first, *To Bedlam and Part Way Back*, does take risks. She assumes the difficult and dangerous task of putting down the primary horrors of life, along with a good many of those secondary horrors which the imagination is able and willing to conjure up. Her realism deals with so many shocking secrets that her moderate use of Surrealistic language and method hardly counts; and these are almost always women's secrets that do not, in the ordinary way of things, get told. To outline personal relationships (and Mrs. Sexton's poems, unlike Miss Swenson's, are full of people) always at a high pitch of emotion requires courage; to describe fully the dark conflicts of the self without slipping over into the shrill voice of confession or the sobbing note of self-pity requires high control at every conscious and unconscious level. Mrs. Sexton sometimes crosses a boundary retrogressively— from large grief into small grievance, from natural fears to contrived ones. But she usually writes from the center of feminine experience, with the direct and open feeling that women, always vulnerable, have been shy of expressing in recent years.

VIRGINIA WOOLF

THREE GUINEAS (1938)

Virginia Woolf's aims, in *Three Guineas,* are incontestably noble ones. But her style is so elegant, so circuitous, and so soothing that the reader is halfway through the book before he realizes what is going on. So that it is just as well if the critic state at the outset that one should substitute "upper-class Englishwoman," or even "lady," for Mrs. Woolf's term "educated man's daughter."

Ten years ago Mrs. Woolf, in *A Room of One's Own,* turned the English patriarchal system inside out. In the present book the exposé of upper-class Englishman's tyranny over upper-class Englishwoman is continued. These women were considered, by their brothers, fathers, and husbands, about on a par with these gentlemen's dogs or horses, which must be well taken care of, make a fine display, and, if sold, fetch a good price. One sex, the masculine, had all the material power, all of the "higher education," and most of the expensive fun. Fathers prevented their daughters from earning a living, and husbands kept their wives from nearly everything except childbearing.

The First World War broke up the hard grip of such feudal holdovers. Women, in the national emergency, went into hospitals and munitions factories—the ladies, as Mrs. Woolf points out, sometimes still attended by their maids. After the war women won the right to vote and admission into many of the professions.

Time passed, and a new war became probable. But now conditions had changed so that it was possible for an "educated man" to write to an "educated man's daughter," asking her advice on how war could be avoided.

Three Guineas is Mrs. Woolf's answer to such a request. The question of male privilege, it is clear, has never ceased to agitate her. She brings up a whole new set of horrid facts proving the continued strength of male domination. From history, biography, and the newspaper, she wheels up evidence that woman's battle, in the upper income brackets, is not yet fully won. Women in the professions are still mistrusted, badly paid, and kept under. And what are these professions? How good are the assumptions on which they are based?

> We, the daughters of professional men, are between the devil and the deep sea. Behind us lies the patriarchal system, with its nullity, its immorality, its hypocrisy, and its servility. Before us lies the public world, the professional system, with its possessiveness, its jealousy, its pugnacity, its greed. It is a choice of evils. Each is bad.

Are women of Mrs. Woolf's class, then, to walk into man-made and time-hardened employments, without lifting a finger to change them? At this point Mrs. Woolf exposes her scheme for depositing some female goodness and sensitiveness in the social setup. Let "educated men's daughters," she says, exercise disinterestedness to the point of fanaticism. Let them "cultivate the virtues which have taught the daughters of educated men before this—Florence Nightingale, Emily Brontë, Christina Rossetti— i.e., poverty, chastity, and freedom from unreal loyalties." Let them refuse to sell their brains for money; hold that obscurity and censure are preferable to fame and praise; fling back badges, orders, and degrees in the giver's face; rid themselves of the pride of nationality, religious pride, school pride, college pride, family pride, and sex pride. Cleave to the example of Antigone, says Mrs. Woolf. Remember Antigone's profound statement concerning the duties of the individual to society: "It is not my nature to join in hating, but in loving."

The Outsider's Society, then, would consist of educated men's daughters "working in their own class—how indeed could they work in any other?" A long, tart note is here inserted which states that, since the middle class is much in need of improve-

ment, and since the lower class probably resent upper-class interference with their problems, the line had better be drawn definitely and finally. Upper-middle-class Englishwomen, thus fenced
off, are to erect, upon the class-consciousness and class education
dinned into them from the first moment they were dandled before
the nursery fire, a moral pattern so severe that it has never been
adhered to by anyone who was not by nature an artist or a saint.
That this Outsider's Society will ever materialize, under these
conditions, is unlikely.

So that, while *Three Guineas* can be read for its flashes of
that psychological insight and witty realism for which women
are so famed, one must check Mrs. Woolf continually in her
conclusions. Her style itself is a danger. At its worst, it curves
into the suavity of well-managed rhetoric under which all kinds
of beating about the bush may go on unnoticed. With it she can
deflect points on which she has no opinion or merely a class
opinion. What about these male regalias, for example? Are they,
as she says, the paraphernalia of a sex, or the awesome decorations of a class?

Mrs. Woolf has looked at women of the lower classes. She has
even written and published an introduction to a collection of
their life stories (*Life as We Have Known It*, 1931). She looked
at them, she admits, "with bewilderment and curiosity." She found
them "magnificent." But she decided, upon thinking the matter
over, that "it is better to be a lady," since ladies "desire ends, not
means." In *Three Guineas* Mrs. Woolf has had to venture a little
outside of a lady's prerogatives. Perhaps because she is not used
to considering means, she has not considered them very thoroughly. Forgetting that she is "an educated man's daughter," Mrs.
Woolf should go on being an artist. Patently, being a lady is
difficult, but artists have managed to make something of even
worse situations and inheritances.

THE CAPTAIN'S DEATH BED (1950)

The publication of the last posthumous collection of Virginia
Woolf's critical and biographical essays brings to a close that
phase of her career which began ten years after her novelist

phase. Her first novel was published in 1915; her first book of prose sketches came out in 1921; and *The Common Reader,* her first book of essays, was published in 1925. The present volume, *The Captain's Death Bed,* contains material from all periods; and its variety reminds us that Mrs. Woolf spent part of her time as a working journalist; that during the years she was endeavoring to expand, through various experiments, the English novel form, she was also quite capable of writing to order book reviews, pamphlets, and lectures.

One could just barely prophesy a critical future for the author of the earliest piece of critical writing here included: an "interior monologue" called "Reading," written in 1919. The stream-of-consciousnes style was not Mrs. Woolf's invention; both Dorothy Richardson (since 1915) and Joyce (since 1916) had worked out the method fully; and by 1919 the earlier chapters of *Ulysses* were in print. Also in the background were E. M. Forster and Lytton Strachey. "Reading" is centered in an old library, in an old house, on an old estate; it is romantically conceived and romantically projected; quaint and highly colored side glimpses of history, nature, and this-and-that keep breaking into the stream of meditation, and there is no literary analysis as such. But it is possible to detect in this piece very nearly all the elements of Mrs. Woolf's later critical manner. It is quite clear that she is not blindly following anyone as a literary guide; in fact, she often seems to be dramatizing her material according to the methods of painting rather than those of literature; and we remember how closely she had followed, through the career of her painter sister, Vanessa Bell, and the enthusiasm of her friend, Roger Fry, the art of the Post-Impressionists, from the time of their first London exhibition in 1910. Like these painters, she chooses her angle with care, she colors with brilliance, and she establishes a pattern with shrewdness. And in a few years she has acquired tremendous competence; the review of Cobden-Sanderson's *Journals,* written in 1926 and here included, goes like the wind. For now she can control her speed as well as her lighting and her design. Everything is particularized; and the sheer pleasure given to the writer by the act of writing is apparent at every point.

"She liked writing with an intensity which few writers have attained," Forster says of Mrs. Woolf in his memorial essay; but

she was at her best when she managed in some way to write at
one remove from life. Even in her novels she was forced to get
at life, for all her implicit insistence to the contrary, in some
oblique or indirect fashion: through some perspective of time or
some distortion of space. But when her material was the recorded facts of history and literature, she was able to function
with a good deal of freedom; always in the past, it is true. She
could not deal with her contemporaries; when she mentions them
at all her remarks are either ordinary or catty: *Ulysses* is "ob-
scene"; *Prufrock* is "obscure"; *Lady Chatterley's Lover* comes in
for ridicule in *Orlando;* and both Lawrence and Forster (Forster,
from whom she learned so much) have "failed," according to her,
in their early books. It was often her feminist-reformist side that
blocked her view; and her critical insight went down before her
frequent indulgence in that "poetization" of fact which consists
of "making things out more interesting than they really are—
the imposition of the writer's personality for which there is no
exact critical term," an indulgence against which Fry had warned
her.

   Once she had perfected her critical approach, however, she began to manufacture the most consistently acceptable version of
"impressionist criticism" to be found in her time. It is of the
highest interest to the student of this period to examine how she
clung to the classical virtues of lucidity and balance; in spite of
all her surface "originality," she never let go of the ancient
classical rhetorical devices. And she never became the indolent
"prose-charmer"—breaths of the vernacular float in from time
to time, and the effects of these gusts are always finely judged.
Writing thus by rule and by ear, Mrs. Woolf never allowed
herself to become awkward, rough, truly baffling, or bizarre, as
many of her more original contemporaries dared to be. She
never makes a fool of herself in any manner of which she is
conscious and can avoid. Before the unknowable, the ungraspable, her competence failed; but even here she was partial
mistress of the situation: she stopped the investigation at the
exact moment that it got out of hand. Time and again we come
upon the little flourish of style as she avoids the abyss.

   It is this skirting of evil, this inability to penetrate into the
heights and depths that finally makes her critical work rather

irritating. She claimed all the virtues and insights of the intuitive mind; but with true mystics, as with true poets, evil is never by-passed; a struggle is in order. One must talk back to God or Devil, so that the terror and horror of the facts can thereafter be absorbed into some acceptance of their mystery. With Mrs. Woolf the intellect continually intervenes. Her flights toward some "heightened state of being" are always coming up short against the sudden opacity of her spiritual nihilism: the underlying pessimism of the "enlightened" woman. Several of her female contemporaries who made no claim to any inordinate equipment of "brains" accomplished these flights quite easily; one has only to think of Isak Dinesen, of Colette, of the early Elizabeth Bowen—even of Katherine Mansfield and of Dorothy Richardson —to see that Mrs. Woolf is frequently intellectually pretentious and always emotionally immature.

On the other hand, how remarkable it is that this "lady" who, to quote Forster again, "had not much sympathy," had enough to write the sympathetic and penetrating "Memoirs of a Working Woman's Guild" (1930)—the essay which is the high point of the present book, if not of her critical work as a whole, wherein we can watch Mrs. Woolf transcending her prejudices even as she states them. How remarkable it is that this woman novelist who was incapable of creating the shimmer and tension of emotional relationships between men and women, except rather synthetically and in fragments, could see straight into the heart of Turgenev's success with the delineation of such relationships. Her intelligence and taste set her firmly against intellectual sham, which she could instantly detect. And if she sometimes yielded to the demand which she herself had created in a body of readers, for her special "little sensation"—her small but brilliant effect obtained by focusing on a man, woman, or career at a striking but not representative moment ("The Captain's Death Bed" here is a perfect example of this)—she was also able to appreciate, humbly and sincerely, the qualities of men and women who had made contact with that fact, process, and mystery which she never completely yielded to or understood, but which she speaks of again and again in the simple words: "life itself."

THE YALE SERIES OF
YOUNGER POETS

W. S. MERWIN (1953)

Young poets at present are more interested in the texture of their
poems—that is, the effects they can produce with vowels and
consonants, regardless of rhyme and rhythm—than in other
technical matters. Very few trouble themselves with severe and
complicated rhyme schemes or take any pleasure in ringing the
changes on verse forms that have long proved successful. Having
ruled out many possible shifts in emphasis, shape, and speed,
they end up by writing a sort of squarish or rectangular poem that
presents no challenge to the eye and little to the ear. Any young
poet who breaks away from this formula, therefore, makes a
special claim on our attention.

    W. S. Merwin, whose first volume, *A Mask for Janus*, won
last year's Yale Series of Younger Poets' Award, is twenty-five,
a graduate of Princeton, and already a highly proficient poetic
technician. He has gone back to certain French, Spanish, and
English verse patterns not merely in order to repeat them but to
freshen and revive those that still have charm and power. We
remember how Theodore de Banville, during the French Second

Empire, managed to revive the fifteenth-century rondel of Charles d'Orléans, making it a delightful carrier of the sentiment of his own time. Mr. Merwin, a far more contemplative and inner poet than Banville, has concentrated on rendering the weight and color of contemporary thought and feeling rather than on bringing to life items from the contemporary scene. He has, it is apparent, allowed each poem its freedom, within well-defined limits but without other restriction. So we get two sestinas, ballads (with and without a refrain and sometimes in more than one voice), a rondel and a "half-rondel" (original and very pleasant), a piece of blank verse, two long sets of quatrains, and an extremely skillful colloquy in six voices, with a refrain rhyming on two "o" sounds throughout. Not one of these poems shows the slightest sign of strain, and all point to a warm affection for the infinitely various possibilities of English rhyme and metre. This is a young man, obviously mad about writing the hard way, who has struck a balance between formal exigency and imaginative force that is rare at any time and almost nonexistent at the moment. The foreword by W. H. Auden emphasizes Merwin's instinctively dramatic use of mythical material—another aspect of his work that makes a promise for the future.

JOHN ASHBERY (1956)

Young people today show little or no interest in Pound's more erratic and more irritating mannerisms. But certain Poundian flexibilities and freedoms—of both style and approach—are now basic. A slight and on the whole healthy tendency toward difficult and peculiar verse forms still prevails. John Ashbery, in his first book, *Some Trees*, chosen by W. H. Auden as this year's award winner in the Yale Series of Younger Poets, comes up with a *canzone*, a pantoum, a sestina, and an eccentric sonnet. But Mr. Ashbery is far more interested in Surrealist manner and material than in Pound's eclecticism. Mr. Auden, in a preface, speaks of Ashbery's success in bringing over into verse the dreams and daydreams of childhood. Ashbery also exhibits, when he wishes, powers of straight observation, as in "The Instruction Manual."

On the whole, though, the poems seem a little contrived in both form and feeling, and are therefore somewhat boring.

JOHN HOLLANDER (1958)

At the moment, after a resetting of poetic conventions that has taken twenty years, gifted young poets, almost without exception, write in form. It is a pity that most of them turn out to be dull. Somewhere along the line of this revival of tradition, certain main facts seem to have been overlooked. The young formalist has every device of prosody to hand; he should be able to condense, mold, heighten, bind together, and project his material with ease, and produce, if not absolute pleasure, at least a poem that excites our curiosity and holds our interest. *"En art il s'agit d'être intéressant,"* Jules Laforgue wrote in the eighties, and Eliot, in recent years, has restated this principle: "The worst fault of a writer is to be uninteresting." What Eliot and Laforgue are saying is that no mastery of technique can make up for triviality and emptiness of subject, for the absence of those swift connections made by imagination and intuition between outer experience and inner meaning, or (most important) for a total lack of emotion.

A few recently published books have the power of drawing the reader on from page to page, in spite of irritating moments when the central impulse wavers and breaks off while the well-made stanzas march boringly on. *A Crackling of Thorns*, by John Hollander, chosen for publication in the Yale Series, carries one's attention again and again up to the verge of interest, only to disappoint it, very often, in a greater or less degree. Hollander has brought together a good many poems that must originally have been answers to technical problems: W. H. Auden, in his preface to the book, states that here is a "literary" poet, but asks "Why not?" There is no harm, for example, in writing a completely unemotional set of sapphics, or skillful imitations of Marvell and the madrigalists. Hollander has also written villanelles (now an utter technical cliché), a sestina (that dullest of forms when not written with wit and dramatized up to the hilt), and a *canzone*, which goes Eliot (in "The Dry Salvages") one better by having seven difficult rhymes in seven stanzas instead of six in six. He has parodied Shakespeare's "The Phoenix and the Turtle" (this took courage). His songs, with a light-verse touch, might easily be singable. But dullness keeps creeping in because the form and the language, with only the slightest emotional ballast, tend to float in and out of the reader's ear or to dissolve before his eyes. Hollander's poetry, in spite of his talent, just now is the poetry of the library and the seminar room. Of course, it may not stay there.

GEORGE STARBUCK (*1960*)

George Starbuck's *Bone Thoughts*, the newest volume in the Yale Series, shows virtuosity directed toward different ends and deriving from different sources. Starbuck, at twenty-nine, deals almost exclusively with the modern world, in a skeptical and corrosive style whose derivations are so apparent that he sometimes slips over from imitation into parody. Dudley Fitts's foreword mentions Starbuck's "technical bravura" and his occasional "jukebox rancor." He goes on to praise Starbuck's sense of structure, his "brutally specific wit," and his striking powers of perception. Starbuck is not only perceptive but satiric, and his satire is always directed toward a particular occasion, as satire should be. This lively, irreverent daring, backed up by an accomplished vocabulary and a fine ear, sets Starbuck off from the poets of generalized rebellion and announces the kind of talent that any younger generation is always in need of and is fortunate if it gets—bold, highly charged, and with a cutting edge.

ALAN DUGAN (*1962*)

A season that brings into one kind of versification or another not only a description of the depression induced by the eating of five buttons of peyote but also a pretty little masque, presenting

real people and private jokes, and designed to be given in the
garden of a Venetian palazzo, can hardly be called dull in choice
of material. But because the expert techniques that might have
brought this diversity to life have not been applied at necessary
points, and because touches of satire are generally absent, dullness has crept in.

To write even the mildest satire, the poet must feel himself
enough involved with human issues to be able to make distinctions and indicate opposites. Negative attitudes are ruled out;
the satirist cares. He may not care in any constructive way—he
may not even recommend change—but he is disturbed by what
he himself experiences and what he observes to be the experience
of others. For one reason or another, down the ages, there have
been no humorless satires and no formless ones. That the satiric
impulse, although currently feeble, is not entirely dead is proved
by the choice, in 1961, of Alan Dugan's *Poems* to be the year's
volume selected for the Yale Series of Younger Poets. And now
Poems has been given a National Book Award. Dudley Fitts, who
in 1960 took over the editorship of the Yale Series from W. H.
Auden, writes in his introduction that Dugan's "cast of mind
is hard, yet the detail is often wonderfully ingenuous and tender,
[and] there is a ferocious comic sense." Dugan can, in fact, throw
off a major piece of wit in a phrase, and he is not afraid of rough
talk. He can describe his own bafflements with a certain detachment, while showing himself vulnerable to the betrayals and
damages inherent in the human condition in general. He is,
in fact, at moments closely related to those satirists, from Martial
to Swift, who have released, in balanced language, their un-
equivocal utterances of shock and rage. But Dugan's sensibility
is not limited to the caustic insight and the dour conclusion; it
can play, with sympathy, over the tragic and the inexplicable,
the fantastic and enigmatic, in nature and man. This is not
young poetry, as Fitts points out. Nor—if the empty and ragged
fragments of "self-expression" that compose the bulk of contemporary verse are to hold as examples of modernity—is it modern.
It belongs to a timeless vein that comes to the surface of literature
unexpectedly and in unlikely places—a vein of powerful feeling
joined to energetic talent.

SANDRA HOCHMAN (*1963*)

A rather denatured kind of feminine Surrealism seems to be floating about at the moment. Dudley Fitts, in his introduction to *Manhattan Pastures,* by Sandra Hochman, his this year's choice in the Yale Series of Younger Poets, speaks of her "willingness to take risks" and of her "power to invest the ordinary with the strange." But Miss Hochman's risk-taking turns out to be comparatively mild; her assumed aggressive attitudes do not work out; the hallucinations and the tough words fail; and we are soon being treated to the wild image and to free-running verbalism alone. Male Surrealists, particularly of the original French, or André Breton, variety, are made of much sterner stuff.

WILLIAM BUTLER YEATS

THE GREATEST POET WRITING IN ENGLISH TODAY (1938)

William Butler Yeats, at the age of seventy-three, stands well within the company of the great poets. He is still writing, and the poems which now appear, usually embedded in short plays or set into the commentary and prefaces which have been another preoccupation of his later years, are, in many instances, as vigorous and subtle as the poems written by him during the years ordinarily considered to be the period of a poet's maturity. Yeats has advanced into age with his art strengthened by a long battle which had as its object a literature written by Irishmen fit to take its place among the noble literatures of the world. The spectacle of a poet's work invigorated by his lifelong struggle against the artistic inertia of his nation is one that would shed strong light into any era.

The phenomenon of a poet who enjoys continued development into the beginning of old age is in itself rare. Goethe, Sophocles, and, in a lesser degree, Milton come to mind as men whose last works burned with the gathered fuel of their lives. More often development, in a poet, comes to a full stop; and it is frequently a negation of the ideals of his youth, as well as a declination of his powers, that throws a shadow across his final pages.

Yeats in his middle years began to concern himself with the

problem of the poet in age. He wrote in 1917, when he was fifty-two:

A poet when he is growing old, will ask himself if he cannot keep his mask and his vision, without new bitterness, new disappointment. . . . Could he if he would, copy Landor who lived loving and hating, ridiculous and unconquered, into extreme old age, all lost but the favor of his muses. . . . Surely, he may think, now that I have found vision and mask I need not suffer any longer. Then he will remember Wordsworth, withering into eighty years, honoured and empty-witted, and climb to some waste room, and find, forgotten there by youth, some bitter crust.

We can trace, in Yeats, the continually enriched and un-deviating course of an inspired man, from earliest youth to age. We can trace the rectitude of the spiritual line in his prose and poetry alike. And there is not a great deal of difference between the "lank, long-coated figure . . . who came and went as he pleased," dramatizing himself and his dreams in the streets of Dublin (the youth who had known William Morris and was to know Dowson and Wilde), and the man who, full of honors in our day, impresses us with his detachment and subtle modernity. Yeats, the fiery young Nationalist, rolling up with his own hands the red carpet spread on a Dublin sidewalk "by some elderly Nationalist softened or weakened by time, to welcome Vice-royalty," is recognizable in the poet of advanced years who does not hesitate to satirize certain leaders of the new Ireland.

Yeats's faith in the development of his own powers never failed. He wrote, in 1923, after receiving from the King of Sweden the medal symbolizing the Nobel Prize:

It shows a young man listening to a Muse, who stands young and beautiful with a great lyre in her hand, and I think as I examine it, "I was good-looking once like that young man, but my unpractised verse was full of infirmity, my Muse old as it were, and now I am old and rheumatic and nothing to look at, but my Muse is young." I am even persuaded that she is like those Angels in Swedenborg's vision, and moves perpetually "towards the dayspring of her youth."

2

The Irish literary and dramatic movement, in general belief, rose, late in the nineteenth century, in some vague manner from the temperament of the Irish people. As a matter of fact, Ireland in Yeats's young manhood was as ungrateful a soil for art as any that could be found, in a particularly materialistic time. The native Celtic genius that Arnold had felt to be so open to the influence of a "natural magic" had been, for over a century, drawn off into politics. The Anglo-Irish tradition, having produced in the eighteenth century Swift, Congreve, Edgeworth, Goldsmith, Berkeley, and Burke, flowered no longer.

The Land Agitation (the struggle of the peasantry against their landlords) and the Young Ireland and Fenian Movements (the struggle of the Irish people against English rule) from the forties on had absorbed the energies and the eloquence of talented young Irishmen. Irish writers, as Stephen Gwynn has said, having been taught by Swift that written English could be used as a weapon against their oppressors, never forgot their lesson. The Catholic Emancipation Bill, by the efforts of Daniel O'Connell, was passed in 1829. In 1842 the Young Ireland Movement was given a newspaper by Thomas Davis: the *Nation,* whose motto was "to create and foster public opinion in Ireland and make it racy of the soil." The *Nation* also fostered a school of Irish poets. Their audience was eager for stirring and heartening words; the verse which spoke to it most clearly was the rhetorical and sentimental ballad, celebrating the Irish race and inciting it to action and solidarity. This verse, when it was not written in the sentimental and insipid vein made famous by Tom Moore, was filled, as has been pointed out, with the hortatory gusto of Lord Macaulay. Versifiers used its forms with skill, and one or two—Clarence Mangan and Sir Samuel Ferguson—touched them with real color and depth of feeling. But there is no doubt that Irish literature, in the years between 1848 and 1891, had fallen upon barren times.

The year 1891 brought Parnell's death. The tragic end of a leader intensely hated and loved, and the loss of much political hope thereby, threw the national consciousness violently back on itself. Yeats has described the situation (he was twenty-six at the time). "Nationalist Ireland was torn with every kind of passion and prejudice, wanting, so far as it wanted any literature at all, Nationalist propaganda disguised as literature. All the past had been turned into a melodrama with Ireland the blameless hero, and poet, novelist, and historian had but one object, to hiss the villain, and only the minority doubted the greater the talent the greater the hiss. It was all the harder to substitute for that melodrama a nobler form of art, because there had been, however different in their form, villain and victim."

At the breakup of the Catholic State in the wars of the seventeenth century, "Irish laws and customs, the whole framework of the Gaelic civilization, had been annihilated." Music, literature, and classical learning, loved by even the poorest of the Irish, had been driven into hiding, with only "hedge-schoolmasters" and wandering bards to keep them from oblivion. During the years when the *Nation* was coming to be the literary force behind Irish Nationalism, traditional Gaelic survived in the minds of Gaelic-speaking peasants. Elsewhere it had disappeared, and from these minds and memories it was rapidly fading. After generations of poverty and oppression, the orally transmitted songs and histories had become fragmentary. Few educated Irishmen knew them, since no educated Irishman knew Gaelic. The Irish language was forbidden in the national schools, and the sons of Anglo-Irish landlords and rectors who passed through Trinity College in Dublin learned English culture and English literature. Standish James O'Grady had published his *Bardic History* in 1880, but, since O'Grady was a champion of the aristocracy, the book made little impression on the partisan-minded country as a whole. When, in 1894, an Irish landlord with some literary ambitions, Edward Martyn, said to another of the same class, George Moore, "I wish I knew enough Irish to write my plays in Irish," Moore replied, "I thought nobody did anything in Irish but bring turf from the bog and say prayers." And Yeats has testified in an essay on the Irish Dramatic Movement: "When we began our work we tried to get a play in Gaelic. We could not even get a condensed version of the dialogue of Oisin and St. Patrick."

3

Where so much of the spirit of art had to be revivified, so many of its forms repaired, and so tight a mold of fanaticism broken, a man was needed who had in himself some of the qualities of

the fanatic—a man who was, above all else, an artist, capable
of making an occasional compromise with a human being, but
incapable of making one with the informing essence of his art.
New light and air had to be let into the closed minds and imagina-
tions of a people made suspicious and hysterically provincial
through persecution and disaster. It was impossible to weld the
opinions of factions, but all could be drawn into "one net of
feeling." A man of sensibility, however, was not enough. Not
only insight and imagination, but ruthlessness, fervor, disinterestedness, and a capacity for decision and action, were required.

William Butler Yeats first appears, in the memories of his
contemporaries, as a rarefied human being: a tall, dark-visaged
young man who walked the streets of Dublin and London in a
poetic hat, cloak, and flowing tie, intoning verses. The young
man's more solid qualities were not then apparent to the casual
observer. But it was during these early years that Yeats was
building himself, step by step, into a person who could not only
cope with reality but bend it to his will. He tells, in one of his
autobiographies, of his determination to overcome his young
diffidence. Realizing that he was "only self-possessed with people
he knew intimately," he would go to a strange house "for a
wretched hour for schooling's sake." And because he wished
"to be able to play with hostile minds" he trained out of himself,
in the midst of harsh discussion, the sensitive tendency "to become silent at rudeness."

The result of this training began to be apparent before Yeats
was thirty. George Moore has recorded how, on meeting him
in London (having been badly impressed by his "excessive" getup
at a casual meeting some years before), he thought to worst
Yeats easily in argument. The real mettle of his opponent soon
came into view. "Yeats parried a blow on which I had counted,
and he did this so quickly and with so much ease that he threw
me on the defensive in a moment. 'A dialectician,' I muttered,
'of the very first order'; one of a different kind from any I had
met before."

This intellectual energy, this "whirling" yet deeply intuitive and
ordered mind, with its balancing streak of common sense, had
come to Yeats through a mixed inheritance. The Yeats blood,

perhaps Norman, had been Anglo-Irish for centuries, and it is notorious that English families transplanted to Ireland often become more Irish than the native stock. Yeats's paternal grandfather and great-grandfather had been Protestant rectors, in County Down and County Sligo respectively, and there had been eighteenth-century soldiers and government officials on this side of the family. Yeats's mother was a Pollexfen; her stock was Cornish—that is to say, English-Celtic. Her father, William Pollexfen, a lonely strong man whom Yeats as a child loved and feared ("I wonder if the delight in passionate men in my plays and poetry is more than his memory"), had settled in Sligo as a shipowner, after a career as master of ships. Yeats spent several of his childhood years and many of his adolescent summers near the town of Sligo, and from that Western countryside, so full of the beauties of lake, mountain, and sea, and from its people, who still had Gaelic in their speech and legends in their memory, he drew the material of his early poetry.

Yeats has told of the deep emotional reserves in his Sligo-born mother, "whose actions were unreasoning and habitual like the seasons." From his father, John Butler Yeats, a man of original mind who had been trained in the law but turned to painting and to the pre-Raphaelite enthusiasms current in the seventies and eighties, Yeats early heard that "intensity was important above all things." The father's passion for Blake, Morris, and Rossetti soon was shared by the son. Yeats had some English schooling; he later was an art student in Dublin. During this period he became a Nationalist. The elder Yeats had friends among Unionists and Nationalists alike, and, well acquainted with the liberal English thought of his time, enthusiastically espoused the cause of Home Rule. His son's Nationalism was both intellectual and emotional. He became the friend of John O'Leary, an old Fenian who had returned to Dublin after imprisonment and exile for youthful conspiracies; and Maude Gonne, a great beauty and successful agitator, was also an influence helping to channel his youthful ardor toward the more heroic and mystic side of the Nationalist movement. In both of these people Yeats felt imaginative and courageous character which transcended political bigotry and dogma. At no time, from the beginning of his career onward, did he for a moment yield to the hard letter of Irish politics. It was the spirit in those politics he wished to strengthen and make serviceable. His ends, and the means to bring about his ends, were always clear in his mind. "We cannot move the peasants and the educated classes in Ireland by writing about politics or about Gaelic, but we may move them by becoming men of letters and expressing primary truths in ways appropriate to this country."

His art was poetry, and, almost from the first, he used that art as a tool, his avowed purpose being to rid the literature of his country from the insincere, provincial, and hampering forms of "the election rhyme and the pamphlet."

4

The music of Yeats's early poetic efforts was in part derived from Morris and Shelley. The earliest poems, published in the *Dublin University Review* in 1886, paid youth's tribute to romantic subjects and foreign landscape: Spain, India, Arcadia. The poems in *The Wanderings of Oisin*, published in 1889, celebrated Irish landscape as well. Actual Sligo place names appeared in them, and, along with imaginary words put into mouths of legendary Irish figures, Yeats had built poems on the single line of a song, or around a few words heard from peasants. Sligo continued to be the home of his imagination during the next ten years, when he was much away from Ireland, working as a journalist in London. His best-known early poem, "The Lake Isle of Innisfree," came to his mind in a London street, and expressed his homesick memory of an islet in Lough Gill, a lake near the town of Sligo.

In England he not only was drawn into the end-of-the-century literary movement, but played an active part in shaping it. With Ernest Rhys he founded, in London, the Rhymers Club, to which Lionel Johnson, Ernest Dowson, and Arthur Symons belonged. He knew Wilde and was published by W. E. Henley in the *National Observer*. Yeats went to Paris in 1894, at a time when Villiers de l'Isle-Adam's *Axël* was exerting its power over the young for the first time. This poem, "the swan song of romanticism," a mixture of Gothic gloom, Rosicrucian occultism, and Symbolist poetry, was to influence more than one generation of young writers. "*Axël* or its theme," Yeats wrote thirty years later, "filled the minds of my Paris friends. I was in the midst of one of those artistic movements that have the intensity of religious revivals in Wales and are such a temptation to the artist in his solitude. I have in front of me an article which I wrote at that time, and I find sentence after sentence of revivalist thoughts that leave me a little ashamed." Contact with such enthusiasm, however, did much to confirm Yeats's own belief in the importance of standing out for *l'art pour l'art*. He had been exposed, at exactly the proper moment in his young career, to literary excitement heightened into a kind of religious fervor. He brought back seeds of this stimulation to Ireland: to a soil which had lain fallow for a long time.

Meanwhile, in Ireland, an interest in Gaelic was growing. Douglas Hyde, a brilliant student at Trinity in Dublin, had learned Gaelic and had begun to translate Gaelic songs and legendary material into the beautiful Tudor English still spoken in the West. Gaelic idiom had been brought over into this speech, and Yeats immmediately recognized the language, English yet un-English, in which he wished to write. His poetry soon took to itself not only Gaelic effects of alliteration and assonance, but Gaelic effects of rhythm: that "gapped music" so delicate that it seems to come from the rise and fall of intonation in the Irish voice.

Many Irish people, particularly the young (as Joyce has testified), were haunted by the harplike fluidity of these songs, and imaginatively stirred by the traditional symbols, the heroic Druid figures Yeats revived. But political societies and the press turned against his aesthetic purposes. The poems in *The Wind Among the Reeds* (1899) were termed "affected," "un-Irish," "esoteric," "pagan," and "heretical." Yeats in later years was to admit a "facile charm, a too soft simplicity," in his early work. He soon began to clear his style of its symbolic trappings, to make it austere, flexible, resonant—an instrument of great lyric and dramatic range. Had he clung to the early style, with its long swing, almost like incantation, its heavy imagery, he would have limited himself unduly. Coming when they did, however, these evocations of Celtic beauty, heroism, and strangeness wakened, as more severe music could not then waken, Ireland's ears to the sound of its own voice speaking its own music.

5

Yeats had the good fortune to form, in the late nineties, one of the most important friendships of his life. He met Lady Gregory when his need for a staying influence was crucial. He had not entirely escaped the results of the romantic violence let loose (more into their personal lives than into their poetry) by the poets of the decade, in their revolt against respectable bourgeois strictures. He has indicated the nature of his own crisis in *Dramatis Personae*. "When I went to Coole [Lady Gregory's estate in Galway] the curtain had fallen upon the first act of my drama. . . . I must have spent the summer of 1897 at Coole. I was involved in a miserable love-affair. . . . Romantic doctrine had reached its extreme development. . . . My nerves had been wrecked."

Lady Gregory, whom Yeats met through Arthur Symons and Edward Martyn (Martyn's demesne, Tillyra, adjoined Coole), was a woman of much cultivation and generosity of spirit. Yeats had lost the power to impose upon himself regular habits of work. Lady Gregory, who was later to write out the Irish legends in the simple speech of the peasants of her countryside, took him from cottage to cottage collecting folklore. Coole and its environs were to give the mature Yeats a background for his later work, as Sligo had given him a scene for his earlier. With his technical apprenticeship and his most excessive enthusiasms behind him, Yeats turned away from the middle-class culture of Dublin to the people of Galway farms and villages. "Folk is our refuge from vulgarity." Once he had regained "a tolerable industry," his grasp on reality was further strengthened by the struggle to found what was to become the Abbey Theatre. To this task he and Lady Gregory, with the help of Edward Martyn and George Moore, now applied themselves.

Yeats knew that nothing was read in Ireland but "prayer books, newspapers, and popular novels." He also knew that the Irish had been trained, by politics and the Church, to listen. They were a potential audience, in the primary sense of that word. He had already formed in Dublin the National Literary Society, with the intention of giving "opportunity to a new generation of critics and writers to denounce the propagandist verse and prose that had gone by the name of Irish literature." He now wanted a literary theatre. He had written plays, but had no stage, unless it were the stage of small halls, where they could be presented.

Against him were ranged the entrenched powers of the commercial theatre, the Church, and the press, the last two informed with the special Irish fear of "humiliation" and misinterpretation, bred from Ireland's peculiar political situation. "But fight that rancor I must." He fought it for more than ten years, not only for the sake of his own plays, but for the plays of other Irish dramatists, particularly Synge. His own plays caused mild trouble. Synge's *Playboy*, presented in 1904, brought on a week of riots and emptied the Abbey Theatre for months. But Yeats held out, against an enraged Dublin and an intimidated company. By 1912 the public had learned how to listen to imaginative drama with appreciation, to satiric plays without resentment. The Irish Dramatic Movement had come through, at the cost of great energy and courage expended by its founders. Yeats then turned away from the "popular" theatre, and began to write plays which could be presented in a room by a few amateurs and musicians, plays which could carry his special music and dramatic formality with the least theatrical machinery.

6

"We should write out our thoughts," Yeats has said, "in as nearly as possible the language we thought them in, as though in a letter to an intimate friend." And again: "If I can be sincere and make my language natural, and without becoming discursive, like a novelist, and so indiscreet and prosaic, I shall, if good or bad luck make my life interesting, be a great poet; for it will no longer be a question of literature at all."

If we grant naturalness, sincerity, and vigor to Yeats's late style, we still have not approached its secret. Technical simplicity may produce, instead of effects of tension and power, effects of bleakness and poorness. What impresses us most strongly in Yeats's late work is that here a whole personality is involved. A complex temperament (capable of anger and harshness, as well as of tenderness), and a powerful intellect, come through; and every part of the nature is released, developed, and rounded in the later books. The early Yeats was, in many ways, a youth of his time: a romantic exile seeking, away from reality, the landscape of his dreams. By degrees—for the development took place over a long period of years—this partial personality was absorbed into a man whose power to act in the real world and endure the results of action (responsibility the romantic hesitates to assume) was immense. Yeats advanced into the world he once shunned, but in dealing with it he did not yield to its standards. That difficult balance, almost impossible to strike, between the artist's austerity and "the reveries of the common heart"— between the proud passions, the proud intellect, and consuming action—Yeats finally attained and held to. It is this balance which gives the poems written from (roughly) 1914 on (from *Responsibilities*, published in that year, to poems published at present) their noble resonance. "I have had to learn how hard is that purification from insincerity, vanity, malignance, arrogance, which is the discovery of style."

Technically, the later style is almost lacking in adverbs—built on the noun, verb, and adjective. Its structure is kept clear and level, so that emotionally weighted words, when they appear, stand out with poignant emphasis. "The Wild Swans at Coole" (1919) opens:

> The trees are in their autumn beauty,
> The woodland paths are dry,
> Under the October twilight the water
> Mirrors a still sky;
> Upon the brimming water among the stones
> Are nine-and-fifty swans.

Equipped with this instrument, Yeats could put down, with full scorn, his irritation with the middle-class ideals he had hated from youth:

> What need you, being come to sense,
> But fumble in a greasy till
> And add the halfpence to the pence
> And prayer to shivering prayer, until
> You have dried the marrow from the bone;

> For men were born to pray and save:
> Romantic Ireland's dead and gone,
> It's with O'Leary in the grave.
>
>   .   .   .   .
>
> Was it for this the wild geese spread
> The grey wing upon every tide;
> For this that all that blood was shed,
> For this that Edward Fitzgerald died,
> And Robert Emmet and Wolfe Tone,
> All that delirium of the brave?
> Romantic Ireland's dead and gone,
> It's with O'Leary in the grave.

On the other hand he could celebrate Irish *salus, virtus*, as in the poem "An Irish Airman Foresees His Death," and in the fine elegies on the leaders of the 1916 Easter Rebellion.

And Yeats came to be expert at the dramatic presentation of thoughts concerning love, death, the transience and hidden meaning of all things, not only in the form of a philosopher's speculation, a mystic's speech, or a scholar's lonely brooding, but also (and this has come to be a major Yeatsian effect) in the cracked and rowdy measures of a fool's, an old man's, an old woman's song. *The Tower* (1928) and *The Winding Stair* (1929) contain long meditations—some "in time of civil war"—upon his life, his times, his ancestors, his descendants; upon the friends and enemies of his youth.

The short plays, composed on the pattern of the Japanese Noh drama, which Ezra Pound had brought to Yeats's attention—*Four Plays for Dancers* (1921), *Wheels and Butterflies* (1934), *The King of the Great Clock Tower* (1935)—Yeats made the vehicle for the loveliest of his later songs, for all his later development of pure music:

> Come to me, human faces,
> Familiar memories;
> I have found hateful eyes
> Among the desolate places,
> Unfaltering, unmoistened eyes.
>
> Folly alone I cherish
> I choose it for my share,
> Being but a mouthful of air

I am content to perish.
I am but a mouthful of sweet air.

The opening song in the play *The Only Jealousy of Emer*
illustrates the variety of stress, the subtlety of meaning, of which
Yeats became a master:

A woman's beauty is like a white
Frail bird, like a sea-bird alone
At day-break after a stormy night
Between two furrows of the ploughed land;
A sudden storm and it was thrown
Between dark furrows of the ploughed land.
How many centuries spent
The sedentary soul
In toil of measurement
Beyond eagle and mole,
Beyond hearing or seeing,
Or Archimedes' guess,
To raise into being
That loveliness?

A strange unserviceable thing,
A fragile, exquisite pale shell,
That the vast troubled waters bring
To the loud sands before day has broken.
The storm arose and suddenly fell
Amid the dark before day has broken.
What death? what discipline?
What bonds no man could unbind,
Being imagined within
The labyrinth of the mind,
What pursuing or fleeing
What wounds, what bloody press
Dragged into being
This loveliness?

7

From youth on, Yeats has thought to build a religion for himself.
Early "bored with an Irish Protestant point of view that suggested, by its blank abstraction, chlorate of lime," he eagerly
welcomed any teaching which attested supersensual experience,

or gave him a background for those thoughts which came to him "from beyond the mind." "Yeats likes parlor magic," George Moore maliciously remarked, in the nineties. At that time, when religious belief and man's awe before natural mysteries were rapidly breaking up, the wreckage of the supernatural had been swept into mediums' shabby parlors and into the hands of quacks of all kinds. Many men of Yeats's generation took refuge in the Catholic Church. But Yeats kept to his own researches. He had experimented, when an adolescent, with telepathy and clairvoyance, in the company of his uncle, George Pollexfen, a student of the occult. He later studied the Christian Cabala and gradually built up, from his own findings and from the works of Blake, Swedenborg, and Boehme, his theories of visionary and spiritual truth. But he was never, as Edmund Wilson has pointed out, a gullible pupil. He invariably tried to verify phenomena. And today, when we know more than we once knew concerning the meaning of man-made symbols, the needs of the psyche, and the workings of the subconscious, Yeats's theories sound remarkably instructed and modernly relevant. His *Anima Mundi* closely resembles Jung's universal or racial unconscious, and even his conceptions of Image and Anti-Image, the Mask and its opposite, are closely related to psychological truth.

Of late years, after a lifetime spent in efforts to break up the deadening surface of middle-class complacency, Yeats has drawn nourishment from the thought of the relation of eighteenth-century Anglo-Irish writers to their society. These men—Swift, Berkeley, Grattan—had behind them, he believes, a social structure capable of being an aid to works of imagination and intellect. The ideal of the artist built into his background, sustaining it and sustained by it, Yeats has termed "Unity of Being." He has striven all his life to give Ireland a sense of what such a society can be, and to make himself an artist worthy of the energy which built "the beautiful humane cities."

In age, he shows no impoverishment of spirit or weakening of intention. He answers current dogmatists with words edged with the same contempt for "the rigid world" of materialism that he used in youth. He is now content to throw out suggestions that are not, perhaps, for our age to complete, as it is not for our age fully to appreciate a man who reiterates: "If we have not the desire of artistic perfection for an art, the deluge of incoherence, vulgarity, and triviality will pass over our heads." But adherence to that creed, and that creed alone, has given us the greatest poet writing in English today, and Ireland the greatest it has ever known.

> Move upon Newton's town,
> The town of Hobbes and of Locke,
> Pine, spruce, come down
> Cliff, ravine, rock:
> What can disturb the corn?
> What makes it shudder and bend?
> The rose brings her thorn,
> The Absolute walks behind.

THE OXFORD BOOK OF MODERN VERSE
(1936)

It is no small task to gather into one anthology, and to reconcile critically, the schools of English poetry which have flourished since the death of Tennyson. William Butler Yeats, the editor of *The Oxford Book of Modern Verse* (1892–1935), has attempted it. The book opens with Pater's lines on the "Mona Lisa," printed as *vers libre*, because Pater, according to Yeats, was the one writer who had the entire uncritical admiration of the post-Victorian generation. It proceeds through Victorian holdovers (Bridges, Blunt), through the smoky lyrical flames at the end of the nineteenth century (Wilde, Dowson), into the comparatively airy and open years at the beginning of the twentieth. The Georgians take up the tune on their oaten pipes; the Imperialists, the seafarers, the Imagists arrive along with a few Hindus and Irish; Pound brings in echoes from Provence, Alexandria, and China; Eliot (the other American included) changes and distills. Sitwellian fireworks begin to fizz and whir, and war breaks up the game. Twenty years after the war a new school appears; young men who were children in 1914 begin to write at white heat, disabused with a wrecked and disordered world.

Yeats, who all his life has suspected politics, will not admit that it is political passion alone which now moves the young.

"Suffering has compelled them to seek beyond the flux. . . . Here stands not this or that man but man's naked mind." His preface closes on a note of belief in the sincerity and intellectual passion of these young men. He does not assign the influence of his own sincerity and intellectual passion to them, although there is more Yeats in all of them than many of them would care to admit.

Yeats's preface is simple in tone, catholic in appreciation, profound in judgment. Hurrahs for his side and contempt for the side of others do not occur in it. Some poetry, because he cannot read it without pain, he omits. (Wilfred Owen's work, which Yeats rejects because "passive suffering is not a theme for poetry," is the one real omission from the book.) Some poetry (Hopkins') he reads with great difficulty, but includes at length. He has several rather peculiar enthusiasms (for W. J. Turner, Herbert Read, Dorothy Wellesley, and C. Day Lewis). On the other hand, he singles out poets whose gifts have been somewhat overlooked: Sturge Moore and Oliver Gogarty. He includes one discovery, Margot Ruddock, whose poems remind him of Emily Brontë's. And he appreciates Tagore along with Auden and Mac-Neice, Edith Sitwell at her emotional best, Pound at the high point of his style, D. H. Lawrence at the most intense of his sensibilities. He neither overemphasizes nor underestimates the stream of Irish song let into the stream of English by Synge and by the later translations of Lady Gregory and Frank O'Connor. His selection from his own work is superb.

"I think England had more good poets from 1900 to the present day than during any period of the same length since the early seventeenth century," Yeats says, in closing his argument and findings. A clear, heartening statement to hear after the many hollow groans often emitted concerning our time. On the evidence here presented, the reader is inclined to agree with one of the good poets of all time.

ON THE DEATH OF YEATS (1939)

I have been busy with a single art, that of . . . a small unpopular theater; and this art may well seem to practical men, busy with some program of industrial or political regeneration, of no more account than the shaping of an agate; and yet in the shaping of an agate, whether in the cutting or the making of the design, one discovers, if one have a speculative mind, thoughts that seem important and principles that may be applied to life itself, and certainly if one does not believe so, one is but a poor cutter of so hard a stone.

August, 1912

Yeats's break with his early style and subject matter—though the break never was, and never needed to be, complete—dates from 1909 or a year or two earlier. It has been said that this break was the result of his entrance into practical affairs. This statement is only partially true. Yeats's youthful ambition was to be a man of action, and he was more active in organization—in the Nationalist movement and literary societies—in his twenties than at any later time. It was only when he broke with the popular theatre, which had interested him for ten years, and refused to make any further attempt to satisfy middle-class ideals of art that the resonant tone characteristic of the later poems sounded for the first time.

Synge died in 1909. Two years earlier the *Playboy* riots had occurred. And it was in this same period that Yeats witnessed the scandal raised by popular opinion and the Irish newspapers over the question of whether the city of Dublin should build a gallery to house Sir Hugh Lane's gift of Impressionist paintings. He witnessed, that is, in an acute form, the hostility of the middle class toward disinterested artistic expression, as it had been witnessed a generation earlier in France. The bourgeois mind demanded that art be moral or useful, and not only discredited the artist's function but outlawed the artist. Flaubert and Baudelaire were summoned before courts of law, and in Ireland the citizens of Dublin attacked Synge with outright violence.

Ireland, because of its ambiguous political status, threw up bourgeois culture late. And it was there produced in such a clear form that the transformation of the countryman's economy into that of the town dweller is an easily visible process. Yeats wished to give his country not only a sense of its former greatness but also a feeling for the nobility of the arts in general. After the bigotry aroused by *The Playboy,* he began to see that his ideal was antipathetic to his audience.

> I believed . . . that a new intellectual life would begin, like that of young Ireland, but more profound and personal . . . I could not foresee that a new class . . . would change the nature of the Irish movement. . . . Power passed to small shopkeepers, to men who had risen above the traditions of the countryman without learning those of cultivated life . . . and who, because of their poverty, ignorance, and superstitious piety, are much subject to all kinds of fear. Immediate victory, immediate utility, became everything, and we artists, who are servants not of any cause but of mere naked life . . . became as elsewhere in Europe protesting individual voices.

This was written in 1907. In 1909 Yeats begins to speak of "the mask," and to write those direct poems filled with scorn for "Paudeen" and Paudeen's wealthy "betters." *Responsibilities* (1914) developed this phase fully. The role of action was finally refused, and the artist's role finally accepted.

The common admonition administered to a writer when he refuses to express the opinions and ideals current in his lifetime, choosing instead his own subjects and symbols, is that he thus risks preciosity and final sterility. Yeats, in refusing to cater to the middle, had two fields open to him—"aristocratic" and "vulgar" expression. These ends of the scale are equally rejected by the bourgeoisie: subtlety puzzles and coarseness shocks them. Yeats wrote his new plays in a form derived from the aristocratic Noh drama of Japan. He interested himself in the most "unserviceable" subjects—the Cabala, spiritualism, Hindu philosophy, Byzantine civilization. In *A Vision* he built up a whole mystical system and applied it to historic facts. The later plays are so wrapped in symbol that they approach sheer incantation, and Yeats steadily refused to make their intention clear. He said to a musician who was to write music for these plays: "Lose my words in patterns of sound as the name of God is lost in Arabian arabesques. They are a secret between the singers, myself, and yourself."

The revolt against the idea of art's usefulness could hardly be pushed farther than Yeats in this manner extended it. Did the poems, then, written in this vein, in the last thirty years of his life, from the age of forty-four to the time of his death at nearly seventy-three, suffer?

On the contrary, they went on to ever greater degrees of power and suggestiveness; they touched the borders where poetry becomes ultimate evocation, and the regions where religion rises from universal mystery.

> These lovers, purified by tragedy,
> Hurry into each other's arms; those eyes
> By water, herb, and solitary prayer
> Made aquiline, are open to that light.
> Though somewhat broken by the leaves, that light
> Lies in a circle on the grass; therein
> I turn the pages of my holy book.

For two years, between the ages of sixty-seven and sixty-nine, Yeats wrote no poetry. "I had never been so long barren." Then began a new period of creation, to which we owe the great poems which have been appearing in English and American magazines during the last few years. In these poems "aristocratic" and "vulgar" forms unite. The songs and meditations are often "coarse" and written in as simple a form as street ballads or broadsheets. Yeats never abandoned the ballad forms first learned from Sligo peasants in his childhood: one or two appear in every volume, and the "Crazy Jane" songs in *The Winding Stair* (1933) are late and intense examples of the type. The last ballads go beyond even these; there is nothing quite like them in literature. The last lyrics of Goethe, written in age, seem literary in comparison. These poems are unstained by any breath of false resignation or "ennobling" feeling. They express the sane bawdiness of healthy old age, in phrases written, nonetheless, with every distinction, every knowledge of effect, every delicate sympathy native to a sensitive nature. Meditation and speculation are there, but behind them, to the last, still exist "naked life" and the vivid sensual world.

Any artist old or young can take courage from these poems. And he can discover in Yeats's prose writing—which developed, like the poetry, from elaboration into simplicity, and documents fully the struggle of a long life—old evils again to be combatted, however new and disguised their modern forms. A battle has been fought against them up to the very last days of a man recently dead, who emerged the victor.

LAST POEMS AND PLAYS (1940)

Old men mad about painting are more fortunate than old poets. With a brush strapped to their wrist, if necessary, old painters can go on with their work. But poets use words, and with words, thoughts and opinions are apt to leak in. And if they are childish opinions, or if the thoughts have stiffened, are mawkish or reactionary, the last poems become ridiculous and unreadable in a later period. Aging Wordsworth and Browning did not do the concept of the old poet as sage any good turn, but Hardy and Yeats have again proved that the old poet need not be the old-fogey or the old fool.

The poems in Yeats's *Last Poems and Plays* have no "noble" or "wise" (in the Victorian sense) wrappings upon them. They are, on the contrary, the most naked and terrible he ever wrote. They call up terror; they do not soothe; they shed cold and ruthless light on man, his motives, and his works; and they keep repeating the unpalatable truth that life is horror and failure as well as joy and accomplishment, that patterns superimposed on man cannot reach his devious and cruel heart. They are concerned with lust, betrayal, wildness, and rage, and they are written in the randy measures of street ballads as often as in the purer metres of literature. At the same time, they are concerned with "beautiful lofty things"—with all that mankind knows of love, courage, and the gall that fights against stupidity, half-truths, and injustice. Sometimes, even, they are the love poems of an old poet still capable of love, as witness one of the tenderest poems in English, "John Kinsella's Lament for Mrs. Mary Moore."

Yeats, as an old man, came to reject with complete scorn all middle grounds. It was to the simplest or to the most complex he turned: to peasant songs, or to the most disinterested, useless, and gallant of man's actions and art. He has been accused of writing Fascist marching songs; it is impossible to read this last book of poems and not know that to be a slander, even if Yeats's own

answer to this lie did not already exist in print. Yeats's frequent
bitterness on the subject of politics is based on the political history
of Ireland since the death of Parnell. It is necessary to know
that history in order to understand Yeats's anger against the
present situation in his native land. It is necessary only to have
an ear, a heart, and some experience of living, however, in order
to appreciate the power and beauty of the poems in general.
The Irish poets whom Yeats exhorts to "learn their trade" have
here an example of what kind of spirit poetry demands. And
future generations, of whatever nationality or belief, are not
likely to be stirred to pity or contempt by Yeats's stoic epitaph:

> Cast a cold eye
> On life, on death.
> Horseman, pass by!

COLLECTED POEMS (1951)

The first edition of the *Collected Poems* (1933) broke off with
the volume *The Winding Stair,* published in the same year. The
final collected edition adds to the earlier work the poetry written
by Yeats from about 1935 to 1939, the year of his death. This
additional material embodies, therefore, the last preoccupations,
as well as the last stylistic development, of the great Anglo-Irish-
man, born in 1865, whose first book appeared in 1889. The record
is thus closed of a long career spent almost exclusively in further-
ing the ideals of disinterested art in a period marked by triumphs
of rationalism and of the machine; the cause of the individual
in a time of human depersonalization; and the cause of a small
nation in a period given over to various forms of imperialism.
The means that Yeats chose to achieve his ends have often been
derided; and it is true that his "magician" side often brought
about curious shifts in his conduct and thinking. His life,
moreover, does not follow any conventional pattern of peace
found after conflict, of humility following after pride, of spiritual
reconciliation in age. But if the last poems often present the picture of a pride-ridden old man who clings to his crankiness with

an almost insane zeal, they also present an old poet continuing to explore his complicated nature and his complicated times up to the last—while extending the limits of his art with unflagging ingenuity, subtlety, and daring.

Yeats never "adjusted" to the conditions of his age or of his society. He not only constructed a religion for himself, but he spent many years "docketing the universe": building a picture of time, space, and causality which fitted the needs (and no doubt quieted the fears) of his own peculiar temperament. His ideals were both spiritual and aristocratic; he gave his allegiance to peasant and aristocrat; and he wasted neither time nor sympathy on "passive suffering" or ideas of human progress. In his universe, built in the form of a Great Wheel, man's soul went through successive incarnations—bound to an impersonal fate, but rescued by the possibility of a personal destiny. This destiny left man freedom to act and to create—to oppose the work of the spirit to the mechanisms of nature.

It was the failure of mankind in general—and of Irishmen in particular—to grasp and forward this destiny that provoked in Yeats, as time passed, an increasing bitterness and irritability. He himself had taken on discipline early; he had put off his youthful indolence and had spent years working in the more practical side of the drama, at the Abbey Theatre. But in the field of art an Irish middle class, newly come into power, let him down; and Irish politics took a turn of which he did not approve. Because of these struggles against opposition, Yeats's wit, shrewdness, and powers of intellect began, in his middle years, to develop and come into view. He began to write with ease concerning the contemporary scene, and to display his prejudices without fear. His mind became infinitely restless and ceaselessly inquisitive. He also developed, along with growing powers of invective, a kind of magnanimity—a magnanimity, it is true, which worked best in retrospect. In the poems written many years after the Easter Rebellion of 1916, he was able to celebrate the heroism of his enemies as well as of his friends; and his later work is filled with praise of human nobility, wherever found.

Around 1935, after a period spent in efforts to compromise with the Irish Free State government, under which he had served as a Senator, he came perilously near adopting ideas of un-

democratic coercion and force. He quickly withdrew from this
position; and the only trace of his passing belief in "marching
men" comes through in the extravagant marching songs. In the
years from 1936 to 1939 he experienced a tremendous renewal
of power. This renewal expressed itself in two definite, and
opposed, poetic manners. On the one hand, he began to elaborate
poems of the "Crazy Jane" variety, in which, to old broadsheet
rhythms, unstinted praise of coarse human vitality is set against
the powers of church, state and, indeed, every ordinary form of
orderly life. At the same time he continued to produce, in his
more "lofty" style, celebrations of human greatness, usually in
the form of elegies to the past glories of his own generation. He
flaunted "an old man's frenzy" and an old man's pride; but if
he often pushed intensity toward harshness, he instinctively kept
to intensity, knowing that without passion no art can live. Even
in the midst of his die-hard show—which at moments verged
on the theatrical—he slipped in passages of self-mockery bred
of self-knowledge; and beneath his praise of crude human vitality
a new note of pathos can be detected. Something stiff, divided,
and hieratic drops away from the personality. The wiles of the
old magician are transcended; and the final impression is one of
a self-fulfilled artist using, up to the end, for selfless purposes, the
unbroken spirit of an indomitable man.

INDEX